CHRISTIAN BAPTISM

CHRISTIAN BAPTISM

A Fresh Attempt to Understand the Rite
in terms of Scripture, History, and Theology

Edited by
A. GILMORE

with an Introductory Chapter by
E. A. PAYNE

THE JUDSON PRESS

CHICAGO   PHILADELPHIA   LOS ANGELES

Printed in Great Britain by
The Camelot Press Ltd., London and Southampton

CONTENTS

PREFACE

THE WORK WHICH FOLLOWS WAS BEGUN IN THE SUMMER OF 1955 by four Baptist ministers in Britain. They were influenced by several factors. Whilst realizing that the subject of baptism was rapidly becoming of increasing importance in the ecumenical world, they were conscious also of the paucity of recent Baptist writing on the subject. The time seemed ripe, therefore, for someone to reconsider the principles of believers' baptism in the light of recent scholarship. In view of the commitments of many Baptist scholars, however, it seemed unlikely that any one man would be able to produce a major work, dealing with all aspects of the subject, in the near future. Consequently it seemed desirable to bring together a group of men, of similar age and background, though of different schools of thought, in order to consider the production of a composite volume. Accordingly, inquiries were set in motion, and the group which is responsible for this work was formed.

Our aim throughout has been to re-examine the doctrine of baptism from Biblical, historical, and theological points of view, so as to make it clear to members of other denominations how Baptists view these matters, though we are aware that what we have written carries certain far-reaching implications for our own churches.

Our method has been such as to produce the fruits of group thinking rather than a simple collection of essays. Each contributor was asked to examine a certain field and to submit a draft manuscript to each member of the group. Several meetings of the group have been held, at which these draft manuscripts have been discussed and criticized. We have tried in these discussions to secure as wide a measure of agreement as possible. Each writer was then asked to revise his work. Ultimately each one must be held responsible for the contribution that appears under his name, but each has tried, as far as his conscience will allow, to ensure that his article embodies the opinions of the group.

We are conscious of certain omissions, for we have tried to

focus attention on the main issues in the present debate. We have also tried to apportion the space for each section according to its importance in baptismal discussions as a whole.

From the very beginning of the project we have conferred regularly with Dr. E. A. Payne, M.A., the General Secretary of the Baptist Union of Great Britain and Ireland, and wish to express our appreciation to him for all the counsel and guidance which he has given us at every stage. It is a particular pleasure to us that he was able to write the Introduction.

Our thanks are also due to the Principal and Staff of Regent's Park College, Oxford, for their hospitable accommodation, to the Rev. Professor H. H. Rowley, D.D., F.B.A., of Manchester, for reading through the manuscript of Chapter 3 and making many helpful suggestions, to the Rev. J. R. C. Perkin, M.A., D.Phil., of Altrincham, for help in the writing of Chapter 7, and to the Rev. G. A. Griffith, of Northampton, for typing the final manuscript and for many other similar services.

A. G.

Northampton,
England.

CONTRIBUTORS

THE REV. A. W. ARGYLE, M.A., B.D., *Tutor, Regent's Park College, Oxford.*

THE REV. G. R. BEASLEY-MURRAY, M.A., M.TH., PH.D., *Principal, Spurgeon's College, London.*

THE REV. S. I. BUSE, M.A., B.D., *Lecturer in New Testament Studies, University College of North Wales.*

THE REV. NEVILLE CLARK, M.A., S.T.M., *Baptist Minister, Rochester.*

THE REV. A. GILMORE, M.A., B.D., *Baptist Minister, Northampton.*

THE REV. D. R. GRIFFITHS, M.A., M.TH., *Lecturer in Biblical Studies, University College, Cardiff.*

THE REV. D. M. HIMBURY, B.A., B.D., B.LITT., *Principal, The Baptist College of Victoria, Melbourne.*

THE REV. W. M. S. WEST, M.A., D.THEOL., *Tutor, Regent's Park College, Oxford.*

THE REV. R. E. O. WHITE, M.A., B.D., *Baptist Minister, Birkenhead.*

THE REV. S. F. WINWARD, M.A., B.D., *Baptist Minister, London.*

ACKNOWLEDGMENTS

The cost of producing manuscripts, and of our frequent meetings, has been borne partly by the members of the group, and partly by generous gifts from certain members of Baptist churches who were interested in our work. We wish to record our thanks to the following for gifts of cash:

ALDERMAN A. L. CHOWN, of Northampton.

ALDERMAN C. A. CHOWN, of Northampton.

MR. H. W. CHOWN, of Northampton.

MR. C. A. CROSS, M.A., LL.B., of Prestwich.

MR. E. R. GRIEF, J.P., of Long Sutton.

SIR HERBERT JANES, of Luton.

MR. W. PARKER-GRAY, of Northampton.

MISS E. PARRY, of Meols, Cheshire.

MISS N. PARRY, of Meols, Cheshire.

MR. W. G. SARGEANT, of Newhaven.

MR. A. L. SIMPKIN, M.C., of Sheffield.

Also Friends from the Baptist Churches of Wales, through MR. T. J. EVANS, M.B.E., of Carmarthen.

ABBREVIATIONS

A.J.S.L.	*American Journal of Semitic Languages.*
A.J.Th.	*American Journal of Theology.*
A.R.G.	*Archiv für Reformationsgeschichte.*
B.Q.	*Baptist Quarterly.*
C.R.	Corpus Reformatorum.
C.T.S.	J. A. Robinson (ed.); *Cambridge Texts and Studies.*
E.G.T.	Expositor's Greek Testament.
E.R.E.	J. Hastings (ed.), *Encyclopaedia of Religion and Ethics.*
E.T.	*Expository Times.*
E.Tr.	English Translation.
H.D.B.	J. Hastings (ed.), *Dictionary of the Bible.*
H.D.C.G.	J. Hastings (ed.), *Dictionary of Christ and the Gospels.*
H.T.R.	*Harvard Theological Review.*
H.U.C.A.	*Hebrew Union College Annual.*
I.C.C.	International Critical Commentary.
J.B.L.	*Journal of Biblical Literature.*
J.E.H.	*Journal of Ecclesiastical History.*
J.Q.R.	*Jewish Quarterly Review.*
J.T.S.	*Journal of Theological Studies.*
M.Q.R.	*Mennonite Quarterly Review.*
M.T.Z.	*Münschner Theologische Zeitschrift.*
N.C.T.	English Non-Conformist Texts.
N.T.S.	*New Testament Studies.*
R.H.P.R.	*Revue d'Histoire et de Philosophie religieuses.*
R.S.V.	Revised Standard Version.
R.T.K.	*Realencyclopädie für protestantische Theologie und Kirche.*
S.J.Th.	*Scottish Journal of Theology.*
S.N.T.S.	Studiorum Novi Testamenti Societas.
T.B.	*Theologische Blätter.*
T.B.H.S.	Transactions of the Baptist Historical Society.

T.L.Z.	*Theologische Literaturzeitung.*
T.R.	Textus Receptus.
T.R.	*Theologische Rundschau.*
T.S.K.	*Theologische Studien und Kritiken.*
T.W.N.T.	G. Kittel and G. Friedrich (eds.), *Theologisches Wörterbuch zum Neuen Testament.*
T.Z.	*Theologische Zeitschrift.*
V.C.	*Verbum Caro.*
Z.A.W.	*Zeitschrift für die alttestamentliche Wissenschaft.*
Z.N.W.	*Zeitschrift für die neutestamentliche Wissenschaft.*

EDITOR'S NOTE. Titles of books and articles are given fully the first time they are referred to in each chapter or section of chapter. After that, they are referred to under the author's name. Where more than one work by the same author is referred to within any one section, then the full reference is given each time. All Biblical quotations are from the Revised Standard Version.

Introductory Chapter

1

BAPTISM IN RECENT DISCUSSION

by E. A. Payne

ONE of the notable features of the theological discussions of the past thirty years has been the increasing attention given to baptism.

When the representatives of the churches met in Lausanne in 1927, at the first World Conference on Faith and Order, they agreed that the observance of the generally acknowledged sacraments of baptism and the Lord's Supper is one of the "characteristics" whereby the church can be "known of men". Of baptism it was said:

> We believe that in Baptism administered with water in the name of the Father, the Son, and the Holy Spirit, for the remission of sins, we are baptized by one Spirit into one body. By this statement it is not meant to ignore the difference in conception, interpretation, and mode which exist among us.

In the early exploratory stages of the Faith and Order Movement, the first task was the mapping out of the field and the marking of the chief points of tension. It was sometimes necessary to remind even theologians that they were—in the words of Bishop Palmer, of Bombay—"not plenipotentiaries negotiating a treaty, but responsible students of the truth of God". Churches which had had relatively little contact with one another or whose relationships were strained had first to set out their own doctrine and practice and then to find a common language for the purposes of discussion. After Lausanne, it was decided to concentrate attention on the doctrine of Grace and on the problems connected with the ministry and sacraments.

When the second World Conference on Faith and Order

met in Edinburgh in 1937, it proved possible to make more elaborate agreed statements regarding the sacraments. But the report indicates that questions of validity and valid order were uppermost in the minds of many of the delegates, and it proved necessary to add a number of footnotes and qualifications to what was said. The main statement regarding baptism was as follows:

> Baptism is a gift of God's redeeming love to the Church; and, administered with water in the name of the Father, the Son, and the Holy Spirit, is a sign and seal of Christian discipleship in obedience to our Lord's command. It is generally agreed that the united Church will observe the rule that all members of the visible Church are admitted by Baptism.
>
> In the course of discussion it appeared that there were further elements of faith and practice in relation to Baptism about which disagreement existed. Since the time available precluded the extended discussion of such points as baptismal regeneration, the admission of unbaptized persons to Holy Communion, and the relation of Confirmation to Baptism, we are unable to express an opinion how far they would constitute obstacles to proposals for a united Church.

To the first sentence of this statement the Baptist delegates felt it necessary to add a footnote making clear that they could apply it only to those "capable of making a personal confession of faith".

Baptism seemed still to stand on the periphery of the main themes engaging the theologians. The position taken by Baptists and the Disciples of Christ was regarded as no more than their denominational characteristic or eccentricity.

The ecumenical scene was transformed during the next decade. Inter-confessional discussion was interrupted by the war, though the plans for a World Council of Churches, which would draw together the Faith and Order and Life and Work Movements and associate them with the International Missionary Council, went slowly forward. Somewhat unexpectedly, during the war, the meaning and practice of baptism became the subject of acute controversy in several different countries and in more than one Christian tradition.

So far as the theologians were concerned, the issue was

first provocatively raised by Emil Brunner. In his Olaus Petri lectures in Uppsala, published in 1938 under the title *Wahrheit als Begegnung*, Brunner declared his view that "Baptism is not only an act of grace, but just as much an act of confession stemming from the act of grace". Neither the Lutheran nor the Reformed attempts to relate New Testament theology to the baptism of infants appeared to him satisfactory. "The contemporary practice of infant baptism can hardly be regarded as being anything short of scandalous," he said.

Brunner's lectures had to wait five or six years before they were available in an English translation (*The Divine-Human Encounter*). By then the tempo of the debate, to which they had given rise on the Continent, had been greatly increased by a lecture by Karl Barth. Delivered in May, 1943, and published immediately thereafter with the title *Die kirchliche Lehre von der Taufe*, this lecture condemned as fundamentally unsatisfactory any baptism of children, even those of Christian parents. "Neither by exegesis nor from the nature of the case can it be established that the baptized person can be merely a passive instrument or recipient. . . . In the sphere of the New Testament one is not brought to baptism; one comes to baptism." This attack upon infant baptism by so formidable and influential a Biblical theologian had widespread repercussions throughout the Reformed and Lutheran Churches. (Barth's attack has since been carried a good deal further by his son, Markus Barth, in *Die Taufe—Ein Sakrament?*) In several countries some of the younger pastors sought to change their practice "without tarrying for any" and found themselves in difficulties with their ecclesiastical authorities. Barth's lecture was translated into English (*The Teaching of the Church Regarding Baptism*, 1948), French and Swedish, and excited widespread interest. F.-J. Leenhardt, of the University of Geneva, in *Le Baptême chrétien* (1944), abandoned the attempt to find evidence for infant baptism in the Scriptures, though he was prepared to argue that the rite could be observed in a way that did not entirely abandon the basic Scriptural implications of baptism. Many defenders of infant baptism had been content with the view that "the argument *a praxi ecclesiae* is the only, but also a sufficient

B

ground for affirming the legitimacy and laudability of Paedo-baptism"—to quote the late Dr. N. P. Williams. It was now clear that there must be a re-examination of the New Testament evidence, if the views of Brunner and Barth were to be refuted. O. Cullmann in *Die Tauflehre des Neuen Testaments* (1948, E.Tr. *Baptism in the New Testament*, 1950) and J. Jeremias in *Hat die Urkirche die Kindertaufe geübt?* (1949), have been among the scholars who have essayed the task of defending the current practice of the main Christian traditions on Biblical grounds.

While this debate was developing, there were parallel but independent discussions within the Anglican Church. In 1942 the Convocations of Canterbury and York set up joint committees to investigate the grave disparity between the numbers of children presented for baptism and those brought to confirmation and communion. A first interim report, under the title *Confirmation Today*, appeared in 1944. It revealed considerable differences of opinion within the committees, but declared that "the Church is not pre-cluded from the consideration of some alternative to the existing sequence, Baptism, Confirmation, Holy Com-munion". "It has been said with some force", the report admitted, "that it is infant Baptism rather than adult Confirmation which needs justification." As a contribution to the ensuing debate, Dom Gregory Dix, early in 1946, delivered a lecture on *The Theology of Confirmation in Relation to Baptism*, in which he argued that infant baptism should be regarded "always as an abnormality, wholly incomplete by itself and absolutely needing completion by the gift of the Spirit and the conscious response of faith". Baptism without confirmation was, in his view, only half a sacrament. At the same time, the Bishop of Oxford (Dr. K. E. Kirk) advocated what he called a return to "primitive precedents", the conjoining of baptism and confirmation once more, the administration of both when "years of discretion" are reached, and the reintroduction of admission to the catechu-menate to take the place of infant baptism. The Archbishops thereupon appointed a Theological Commission to advise on the relations between baptism, confirmation, and holy communion. Its report, which appeared in 1948, was entitled *The Theology of Christian Initiation*. The view was accepted that "the present-day counterpart to the primitive initiation is not Baptism alone, but Baptism together with Confirmation, followed by First Communion".

The Anglican discussions were more conditioned by practical considerations than were those on the Continent. This may be seen in the second interim report of the Joint Committees, *Baptism Today* (1949) and the final report *Baptism and Confirmation Today*, which did not appear until 1954. In the latter it was stated that:

Infant Baptism is only in line with the full teaching of the Church if:
(i) it is accepted that it points forward to Confirmation and Holy Communion;
(ii) there is reasonable chance of the child being taught to "improve his Baptism";
(iii) the instruction of baptized children in the Christian Faith and life be regarded as a matter of the utmost importance.

An important Anglican contribution to the exegetical and theological discussions appeared, however, in 1951—*The Seal of the Spirit*, by G. W. H. Lampe, a study in the doctrine of baptism and confirmation in the New Testament and the Fathers. "Spirit-baptism" and "water-baptism" were, in Lampe's view, inseparably linked in the apostolic church. "The indwelling presence of the Spirit, a Person and not a *donum gratiae*, is mediated to the believer through Baptism as the sacrament of conversion; but that personal presence comes to be apprehended more fully, and more deeply experienced, as the Christian proceeds on the course of his life in the Spirit." The special linking of the gift of the Spirit with confirmation and the laying-on of hands, suggested by some Anglican theologians, seems to Lampe unjustified.

In the 1930s, the Congregational Union of England and Wales set up a commission "to investigate the mind of Congregationalists concerning the two sacraments—the Lord's Supper and Baptism". Its report made clear that a number of Congregationalists had ceased to be satisfied with the view propounded by R. W. Dale that baptism is purely a declaratory act and need not therefore be restricted to the children of believers; nor could they be content to regard it as an act of dedication by parents. Many favoured a return to the classic Calvinist view that baptism is "the initiatory sign by which we are admitted into the fellowship of the Church", though uncertain how to apply this to infants. "They are within the Church", it was said, "but on a provisional basis."

The report was a revealing but unsatisfactory one. Nathaniel Micklem and J. S. Whale began to press for a greater insistence on the sacraments as "effectual signs of grace". "The Sacrament of Baptism", declared Whale in his widely read *Christian Doctrine* (1941), "administered almost exclusively to infants, and unrepeatable, obviously emphasizes the objective givenness of the Gospel of Redemption." No serious attempt was made to relate such a view to the New Testament. It was Methodist scholars who entered this field. H. G. Marsh, in *The Origin and Significance of New Testament Baptism* (1941), and W. F. Flemington, in *The New Testament Doctrine of Baptism* (1948), offered careful studies of New Testament teaching and practice. Both admit that the typical New Testament baptism was that of an adult believer, and that the New Testament statements cannot all be used in reference to infant baptism without modification. Flemington took no cognizance of the criticisms of Brunner and Barth, but he rejected Dix's view that confirmation rather than baptism was the predominant element in Christian initiation.

The third World Conference on Faith and Order was not able to meet until 1952 in Lund. The churches had by then been drawn much closer together as a result of the formation of the World Council of Churches and the theological climate had changed greatly since Edinburgh 1937. The delegates were under much less temptation to regard themselves as "plenipotentiaries", far more ready to co-operate together as "responsible students of the truth of God". Three preparatory Commissions had been at work, one on the Nature of the Church, one on Ways of Worship and one on Intercommunion. The first laid before the Lund conference an important series of statements by the main Christian communions, each of which included brief reference to baptism. The second Commission noted the current discussions on baptism, but its concern was with liturgical worship in general. It was the third Commission

—that on Intercommunion—which opened up a new line of discussion on baptism.

The Commission's preparatory volume contained a paper by T. F. Torrance on "Eschatology and the Eucharist".

> The New Testament [he said] regards Baptism and Eucharist as two aspects of the same event and . . . it is Baptism rather than the Eucharist which is all-inclusive. Both have to do with incorporation into Christ, but whereas Baptism is all-inclusive and final, the Eucharist is the continual renewal of that incorporation in time (p. 305). . . . To refuse the Eucharist to those baptized into Christ Jesus and incorporated into His resurrection-body (i.e. the Church) amounts either to a denial of the transcendent reality of holy Baptism or to attempted schism within the Body of Christ (p. 339).

In its report to the churches, the Lund conference drew attention to the last of these sentences with the remark: "We believe that this challenging statement might provide the starting point for further fruitful ecumenical discussion." When the second Assembly of the World Council of Churches met in Evanston two years later, it carried this somewhat further with the declaration: "We must learn afresh the implications of the one Baptism for our sharing in the one Eucharist."

It was agreed after Lund to set up a new Theological Commission to study "the nature of the Church in close relation both to the doctrine of the person and work of Christ and to the doctrine of the Holy Spirit". This Commission has begun its work and laid before a meeting of the full Faith and Order Commission of the World Council of Churches in New Haven in 1957, a paper on baptism as the basis for a full day's discussion.

Two further developments must be recorded. In 1953 the General Assembly of the Church of Scotland set up an influential commission on baptism with T. F. Torrance as convener. A first interim report was issued in 1955, a second in 1956, and a third in 1957. It is already clear that the commission is engaged upon a full-scale defence of infant baptism on exegetical, theological, and historical grounds. With the help of Cullmann's interpretation of the New Testament evidence and Pierre Marcel's exposition of Covenant theology (cf. *Le Baptême*, 1950; E.Tr. *The Biblical*

Doctrine of Infant Baptism, 1953), it is contended that "Baptism belongs to almost every page of the New Testament". "In the Christian practice the Sacrament of Baptism came to take the place of circumcision which was the sign and seal of the Old Covenant. It is to be understood accordingly." "The idea of 'believers' baptism' exclusive of infants is entirely modern." In flat contradiction of Karl Barth, it is stated that "we are passive subjects in Baptism". "The infant is inserted into the sphere where the Word increases and multiplies, where the Word judges and slays and makes alive—the Church."

The second recent development has been in the field of church union negotiations. The schemes now before the churches of Ceylon and of North India and Pakistan both provide for the recognition of alternative forms of baptism. Each of the two forms—described in the Ceylon scheme as "sponsored baptism in infancy" and "believers' baptism"—is to be interpreted in the light of the following statements, which should be compared with the declarations of the Lausanne and Edinburgh Conferences, and in the light of the theological discussions of recent decades:

1. Baptism is a sign and seal of engrafting into Christ and entrance into the covenant of grace. In Him we receive the new birth, the forgiveness of sins and the gift of the Holy Spirit. Those who are baptized are by this sacrament solemnly admitted into the fellowship of the Church and engaged to be the Lord's.
2. The grace of Christ conferred in Baptism is appropriated unto salvation by repentance and faith. . . .
3. Full Christian initiation is a process which is concluded only when the initiate participates for the first time in Holy Communion. [*Scheme of Church Union in Ceylon*, Third Revised Edition, 1955, 12; Cp. *Plan of Church Union in North India and Pakistan*, Third Revised Edition, 1957, where somewhat different language is used.]

A person who has received sponsored baptism in infancy is to be admitted to communicant membership of the church only after a service of confirmation, which includes the personal acceptance of the vows made on his behalf when he was baptized. It is too early to say whether or not the Ceylon and North India schemes will prove acceptable to the negotiating churches and those in other parts of the world with which they are at present in communion.

Baptists have taken strangely little part in the theological controversies of the past two decades. In the early stages they watched, perhaps with mixed feelings, the scholars in communities, which had often condemned Baptist idiosyn-crasies, attacking Paedo-Baptism on theological and practical grounds. For a generation or more their own interpretation of the rite of believers' baptism had been influenced by an essay by the late H. Wheeler Robinson, *Baptist Principles*, which first appeared in 1911 and has since been many times reprinted. Administered to believers, in accordance with what Wheeler Robinson believed to be the indubitable evidence of the New Testament, baptism implied a cleansing from sin, the gift of the Holy Spirit and an experiential union with Christ. It involved the view that "the Church is a spiritual society composed of converted men who acknow-ledge the supreme Lordship of Christ". By 1950, however, it was apparent that neither Brunner and Barth and their sympathizers in the Reformed and Lutheran Churches, nor those Anglicans who were uneasy about their current practice, were about to become "Baptists". In preparation for the eighth Baptist World Congress a Commission on the Doctrine of Baptism was set up. It was soon clear that there were wide differences of viewpoint and practice among Baptists, and that with all other Christians they must give themselves to a renewed study of the New Testament. After the Congress, therefore, a statement and a questionnaire— *The Doctrine of Baptism* (1951)—were issued by the Baptist World Alliance and the pamphlet has helped to stimulate thought and discussion in many different countries.

Baptist scholars have not been entirely silent. As early as 1944 Johannes Norgaard, of Denmark, showed in *Den Kristne Daab* an awareness of some of the emerging issues in Biblical theology. In 1952 Johannes Schneider, of the University of Berlin, published *Die Taufe im Neuen Testament*, an important contribution to the discussions on the Con-tinent. This he has since supplemented with a lecture, *Taufe und Gemeinde im Neuen Testament* (1956; E.Tr. *Baptism and Church in the New Testament*, 1957), which summarizes his view and makes reference to some of the material found

in the Dead Sea Scrolls. H. H. Rowley has dealt trenchantly
with the use made by some scholars of analogies from
circumcision and proselyte baptism (cf. *The Unity of the Bible*,
1953, Ch. VI). In *An Approach to the Theology of the Sacraments*
(1956), Neville Clark has given a careful review of the New
Testament evidence in order to show that no satisfactory
theology of baptism can be arrived at except in conjunction
with a reconsideration of eucharistic doctrine. More recently
three young Scandinavian scholars have issued three essays
under the title, *Dopet-Daaben-Daapen* (1957), while to the
third edition (1958) of his *What Baptists Stand For*, Henry
Cook has added an appendix on "Infant Baptism in Recent
Debate".

It remains true, however, that both within their own
communion and outside it there is a growing feeling that
Baptists should share in the present discussion, in the light
of the latest Biblical and historical scholarship, the renewed
interest in Biblical theology, and the ecclesiastical developments in Asia and elsewhere. The essays that follow are
offered as a contribution thereto.

2

SCRIPTURE, TRADITION, AND BAPTISM

by S. F. Winward

"BY what authority are you doing these things, or who gave you this authority to do them?" (Mark 11: 28). This challenge of the Jewish hierarchy to our Lord serves to remind us at the outset of the basic importance of the problem of authority. What is the nature of authority? If we are all agreed, as may be assumed, about the ultimate source of all authority, then what are the channels through which it is mediated? By what authority do we teach and act? Any useful discussion of the theology and practice of baptism must face this question at the outset. It is important that we should not embark on such a discussion with the unexamined assumption that all Christians or churches accept one and the same authority for their theology and practice of baptism. This assumption is frequently made and tends to render any such discussion unfruitful. In this chapter, therefore, we intend to discuss the question of authority, with special reference to the bearing of this problem on the theology and practice of baptism.

From the very beginning the Baptists have appealed to the Holy Scriptures in general, and to the New Testament in particular, for their theology and practice of baptism. Baptists throughout the world would unanimously agree with the opening "declaration of principle" of the Baptist Union of Great Britain and Ireland: "That our Lord and Saviour Jesus Christ, God manifest in the flesh, is the sole and absolute authority in all matters pertaining to faith and practice, *as revealed in the Holy Scriptures.*" This is a statement both about the source and the medium of authority. With these two statements all other Christian churches would, without exception, agree. God manifest in Jesus Christ the Living Word is the sole source of all authority, and this authority is mediated through the Holy Scriptures. But, while accepting the statement *so far as it goes*, some other Christian communions would maintain that it does not go far enough. They would disagree, not with what is stated, but with the assumption that everything necessary has been stated about the mediation of the Lord's sole authority. Granted that the Lord's authority is uniquely mediated through Holy Scripture, is that the sole channel of His authority? Should not the statement have ended "as revealed in the Holy Scriptures and in the Holy Tradition"?

This same question is raised in a rather different form if we inquire who is to interpret the Holy Scriptures which all Christians recognize and accept as the unique medium of the Lord's authority. The "declaration of principle" cited above does not ignore this fact, that any authority must needs be interpreted. The sentence "as revealed in the Holy Scriptures" is followed by "and that each church has liberty, under the guidance of the Holy Spirit, to interpret and administer His laws". Here the local church, the local fellowship of believers, is regarded as the organ of interpretation, under the guidance of the Holy Spirit. But should not this statement read "and that the whole church, the church catholic, has liberty, under the guidance of the Holy Spirit, to interpret and administer His laws"? And is not the interpretation of the whole church identical with the living tradition—or at least an important part of the tradition? Furthermore, may there not be within the whole body of the church, set there originally by the Lord Himself, or raised up subsequently by the Holy Spirit, certain special organs of interpretation—such as the sacred ministry, or the succession of gifted teachers and doctors of the church, or general councils representing the whole body? It is at least clear that the nature of the authority to which appeal must be made is not obvious, and must not be taken for granted in any useful discussion.

The practice of the Baptists in appealing to the Holy Scriptures in general and to the New Testament in particular as the *sole* authority for the theology and practice of baptism is open to serious objection and criticism on several different grounds. In the first place—and this has special relevance for the *practice* of baptism—it may be said to overlook *the special missionary situation of the primitive church*. Even if it is granted that there are no explicit references to infant baptism in the New Testament, nothing at all may be inferred from this. It could hardly be otherwise in the young church, in a missionary situation, in which the gospel message was being preached for the first time to adults. Naturally in such a situation, the conversions made and the baptisms recorded will be of adults turning from Judaism or paganism to Christ. The church continued to be in such a missionary situation throughout the whole period when the New Testament documents were being written, and it therefore reflects this special and temporary situation. Special and temporary, because a new situation was bound to arise with the second and third generation of Christians, and with the gradual spread and triumph of the faith in society. A practice which was inevitable and appropriate in one situation cannot be regarded as obligatory in all situations, although it may again become appropriate in a similar situation—as on the mission field.

> The Church of the New Testament in a missionary situation, a tiny body in a sea of paganism, is significantly different from the church of the fourth century. . . . What of the Middle Ages when nearly all Europe was baptized and the distinction, characteristic of the New Testament, between the church and the world disappeared? Is that just "sin"? Is not church history bound up inextricably with world history?—so much so that it becomes impossible to take the doctrine of the New Testament and apply it *simpliciter* after nearly 2,000 years of history have passed over the church's life.[1]

According to Cullmann, it is this special missionary situation which accounts for the nexus to be observed in the New Testament between baptism and faith. "The declaration of faith is a sign of the divine will that baptism take place, demanded from *adults* who individually came over from Judaism or heathenism, but in other cases lacking."[2] Faith will inevitably precede and accompany baptism, and should

[1] D. E. W. Harrison, "Scripture and Tradition: the situation to-day", in F. W. Dillistone (ed.), *Scripture and Tradition*, 143.

[2] *Baptism in the New Testament*, 55.

be required as a necessary sign from God that baptism may be administered, in the case of an adult coming over from unbelief or heathenism. Thus there will always be a close relationship between faith and baptism in a missionary situation, but outside that situation it is maintained that baptism may legitimately precede the faith of the one baptized.

There is a second weighty objection to appealing to the New Testament as our *sole* authority for faith and practice. For why should it be assumed that the extant *writings* of the apostles or of their companions enshrine and embody the whole of the apostolic tradition? Not all the writings of the apostles have come down to us. We are without Paul's letter to the Corinthians written prior to our Biblical 1 Corinthians (1 Cor. 5: 9), and we are unable to read his letter to the Laodiceans (Col. 4: 16, unless this be identified with "Ephesians"). We lack the epistle Jude was "very eager to write" about "our common salvation" (v. 3). It is possible, and in the case of personal letters, probable, that the apostles and their disciples wrote many other letters not preserved for us. Furthermore, the apostolic letters we have are occasional, accidental in character, elicited in response to the problems of local churches. The excitement about the advent at Thessalonica, the work of the Judaizers in Galatia, the disturbances at Corinth, the heresy at Colossae—but for the occurrence of such local and temporary problems, many of them would not have been written at all. Is it not then arbitrary to appeal *exclusively* to this small corpus of writings as containing the whole of the apostolic tradition? This question is accentuated by a study of the formation of the New Testament canon. No doubt the apostolic writings as a whole, the epistles, and the gospels, are clearly distinguishable from other early Christian writings. The line of demarcation is, however, not always clear or easy to defend. Why should 2 Peter be included and *The Didache* excluded? Or why should we accept The Apocalypse and exclude *The Letter of Clement to the Corinthians*? The paramount importance of the New Testament writings is not disputed by any body of Christians. But can an *exclusive* appeal to them be really justified? Is it legitimate to affirm that they—and their interpretation of the

Old Testament—are our sole authority for faith and practice?

The most serious objection, however, is that such an exclusive attention to the New Testament writings is a denial of the doctrine of the person and work of the Holy Spirit. For does not such a view presuppose that the work of the Holy Spirit, in revealing the truth as it is in Christ, is confined to a strictly limited period of time? But did the Holy Spirit cease to reveal the things of Christ to us in A.D. 100 or in A.D. 115 or whatever is the exact date of the latest New Testament writing? Does He not rather continue to work, and continue to reveal the truth to and within the church until the end of time? It is not suggested that the Holy Spirit reveals to us new truth, entirely unrelated to the original deposit. He is Christ's exegete and interpreter, making explicit what was implicit and given from the beginning. The Lord Himself is recorded as saying "I have yet many things to say to you, but you cannot bear them now. When the Spirit of truth comes, he will guide you into all the truth; for he will not speak on his own authority, but whatever he hears he will speak, and he will declare to you the things that are to come. He will glorify me, for he will take what is mine and declare it to you" (John 16: 12ff.).

Now, granted that this promise finds its fulfilment in the writings of the apostles, is it legitimate to confine its application to them? Do not the teachers and doctors of the church, guided by the Holy Spirit, continue to make explicit what was implicit in the original deposit? For example, a developed and explicit doctrine of the Holy Trinity is not to be found in the New Testament. But almost all Christians would agree that the Fathers at Nicea and Constantinople were but stating explicitly, if imperfectly, what is implicit in the New Testament itself. Now if it is conceded that the work of the Holy Spirit as Christ's exegete continues within the church, then why draw an arbitrary line somewhere about A.D. 100 and affirm that only Christian writings prior to that date may be regarded as authoritative for faith?

There are then several weighty objections to regarding the Scriptures as our *sole* authority. And all these objections gain strength when due weight is given to another truth, the "great mystery", the relationship between Christ and the church. For the church herself was prior to the *written* word, and originally transmitted the Gospel and the tradition of the Lord's words and deeds within her own life. Did she cease to do this because part of that tradition, roughly between the years A.D. 50 and 100, was committed to writing? Did she not rather continue within her own life, and alongside of Scripture, to transmit the tradition received from the apostles? And if so, must there not be, alongside of Scripture, a second source of doctrine and practice—the Holy Tradition? This is the doctrine of the Roman Catholic Church as defined at the Council of Trent. The truth and discipline of the Gospel is contained

> in written books and in unwritten traditions which were received by the apostles from the lips of Christ Himself, or by the same apostles at the dictation of the Holy Spirit, and were handed on and have come down to us transmitted as it were from hand to hand. Following the example of the orthodox fathers the synod receives and venerates, with equal pious affection and reverence, all the books both of the Old and New Testament . . . as also the said traditions as well those appertaining to faith as to morals . . . as having been dictated either by Christ's own word of mouth or by the Holy Ghost and preserved in the Catholic Church by a continuous succession.[1]

These words say, and are expounded by Roman teachers to mean, that tradition is equal in importance to Scripture as a source of faith.

This is, of course, not the only view of the relationship between Scripture and tradition. Indeed, the word "tradition" itself has many different meanings, and it will be necessary to distinguish these later on, and to determine in what sense we are using the word. Only then shall we be in a position to discuss its relationship to Scripture. But it is at least clear that this appeal to Scripture *and* tradition as sources for our faith and discipline has an important bearing on the subject of baptism. We can no longer appeal to Scripture and ignore tradition—or at least if we do ignore tradition, we must be able to advance adequate and convincing reasons for such a procedure. For the practice of infant baptism, while it may according to its exponents be justified from Scripture, will always derive strong support from the long tradition of the church. Indeed there are those

---

[1] J. Waterworth, *Canons and Decrees of the Council of Trent*, 18.

who would justify it on that ground alone. Dr. N. P.
Williams, for example, has already been quoted in this
respect.[1]

What then is tradition? Is it legitimate to appeal to it as a
source for doctrine and practice? What is the true relationship between Scripture and tradition?

In attempting to answer these questions we shall first of
all examine the teaching of the New Testament itself on
the subject of tradition. This will be followed by an examination of the various meanings given to the word "tradition"
in the history of the church. Finally, the relationship between
the Scriptural tradition and ecclesiastical tradition will be
discussed in the light of this examination.

A. *"Paradosis" in the New Testament*

1. In the Gospel of Mark (7: 1-23) we are able to study the
attitude of the Lord Himself to "the tradition of the elders".
The scribes had built a "hedge" round the written Torah in
order to protect it and ensure its faithful observance. As
Josephus explains:

> the Pharisees have delivered to the people a great many
> observances by succession from their fathers, which are not
> written in the law of Moses; and for that reason it is that the
> Sadducees reject them, and say that we are to esteem those
> observances to be obligatory which are in the written word,
> but are not to observe what are derived from the traditions of
> our forefathers.[2]

The scribes, however, did not themselves regard this oral
tradition as an addition to the written word, but rather as a
legitimate and necessary interpretation of what it contained.
This huge mass of interpretation, which eventually cul-
minated in the written Mishnah and the two Talmuds, was
the burden grievous to be borne, the heavy yoke, in exchange for which Christ offered His comparatively easy
yoke and light burden (Matt. 11: 28-30). He had no
sympathy with these elaborate rules and rigid regulations
which made life unnecessarily hard and complicated for the
common people, and He offered to them instead a simple
following of the Old Testament law interpreted in a prophetic
spirit. Jesus therefore rejected the tradition of the elders

[1] See Chapter 1, pages 17f.   [2] *Antiquities*, XIII, 10, 6.

which made "void the word of God" or turned it into a grievous burden, and over against this tradition affirmed the authority of the Old Testament Scriptures.

It would, however, be a misleading over-simplification simply to assert that Jesus rejected tradition and accepted Scripture. On the one hand He may have accepted traditions which were good and useful in themselves, although non-Scriptural (e.g. Luke 16: 19-31). On the other hand, He appears to regard parts of the Torah itself as no longer binding. It is difficult to say from Mark 7: 1-23 whether, after rejecting the tradition of the elders, Jesus went the full length of rejecting also all the Scriptural Levitical regulations governing ritual purity. The gospel tradition may here be coloured by the attitude of the early church towards the Jewish law. But even if so, the church was simply making explicit what was implicit in Christ's attitude to the ceremonial law.

It must be admitted that our Lord's attitude to the scribal tradition has had a profound influence on the attitude of many Christians to tradition in general. Failing to distinguish between things that differ, the Lord's rejection of the scribal tradition has made them suspicious of, if not hostile to, all tradition. While avoiding such an uncritical attitude, it is relevant to our purpose to note that our Lord did not accept beliefs or practices just because they were a part of "the main stream of tradition". Like the ancient scribes, Christians too must avoid the sin of "making void the word of God through your tradition which you hand on" (Mark 7: 13).

2. Luke begins his gospel by referring to "the things which have been accomplished among us" as having been "delivered (παρέδοσαν) to us by those who from the beginning were eyewitnesses and ministers of the word". Elsewhere, Luke quotes Peter's description of these eyewitnesses as "the men who have accompanied us during all the time that the Lord Jesus went in and out among us, beginning from the baptism of John until the day when he was taken up from us—one of these men must become with us a witness to his resurrection" (Acts 1: 21, 22). Christ called and trained the apostles, that He might send them forth as eyewitnesses of His ministry, death, and resurrection.

"That gospel-message was not left by our Lord to be sown broadcast by whoever should choose to take it up, but was committed by Him to twelve men whom He chose and trained for the purpose, and who are described as 'witnesses chosen before of God'."[1] This task of "traditioning" the Gospel, "of passing on the essential facts of the Christian revelation in such a way as to ensure that their real nature is grasped"[2] was not, however, confined to the Twelve as A. G. Hebert suggests. In fact the apostle Peter in the passage just quoted, in which the special position of the Twelve is acknowledged, refers to a wider circle of eye-witnesses of the ministry and resurrection, from which a choice can be made to replace Judas. If, as is probable, Luke 24: 33-43 is the same event as John 20: 19-23, then it was to "the eleven gathered together *and those who were with them*" that Jesus said, "as the Father has sent me, even so send I you". That which was transmitted by the apostles and eye-witnesses—the *Paradosis*—has several aspects which may be distinguished.

3. The ministers of the Word were heralds making public proclamation "of the essential facts of the Christian revelation" to the non-Christian world. The *Paradosis* is primarily this proclamation; it is the essential gospel message, the *kerygma*.

It is in this primary sense that the apostle Paul refers to the act of "traditioning" in 1 Corinthians 15: 1-4. "Now I would remind you, brethren, in what terms I preached to you the gospel, which you received, in which you stand, by which you are saved, if you hold it fast—unless you believed in vain. For I delivered (παρέδωκα) to you as of first importance what I also received, that Christ died for our sins in accordance with the Scriptures, that he was buried, that he was raised on the third day in accordance with the Scriptures." The repetition of the phrase "in accordance with the Scriptures" is significant. The apostles do not proclaim bare facts, mere historical events, but events interpreted in the light of the Old Testament Scriptures "in such a way as to ensure that their real nature is grasped". The content of the *kerygma* has been admirably

---

[1] A. G. Hebert, *The Form of the Church*, 34.
[2] D. Jenkins, *Tradition and the Spirit*, 28.

analysed and expounded by C. H. Dodd[1] and need not here be repeated. It must now suffice to make the point that the *Paradosis* is the Gospel.

4. When Luke refers to "the things which have been accomplished among us", he is referring to a body of tradition much more extensive than the *kerygma*. He has in mind *the whole tradition of the Lord's words and deeds*, together with stories about Him. Existing originally in the first decades following the resurrection as oral tradition, it has already been in part committed to writing in the many narratives to which he refers. At an earlier stage, the apostles in their letters made frequent use, directly and indirectly, of this oral tradition, which they are transmitting together with other preachers and teachers within the Christian communities. If the disciples and converts were to "learn Christ", and if the churches were to be guided aright when confronted with difficulties of belief and conduct, it was essential that they should know "all that Jesus began to do and teach, until the day when he was taken up". The *Paradosis* then consists of the transmitted words and deeds of Jesus. That which is transmitted may be just a saying of the Lord, as in 1 Thessalonians 4: 15, or 1 Corinthians 7: 10. It may, however, be a larger body of material combining both the words and the deeds of the Lord. Thus in 1 Corinthians 11: 23-26 we have saying and event combined in the account of the Last Supper, introduced by the words "for I received from the Lord what I also delivered ($\pi\alpha\rho\acute{\epsilon}\delta\omega\kappa\alpha$) to you". In the gospels we have this tradition in its final written form. And so we must now add to our first statement —the *Paradosis* is the Gospel—the further assertion, the *Paradosis* is (for us) the gospels.

5. The transmission of the Lord's words and deeds is the "traditioning" of a pattern of life and conduct. And so by a natural extension of the above meaning, *Paradosis* comes to mean "the way", the Christian pattern of living. Paul can write to the Thessalonians, "So then, brethren, stand firm and hold to the traditions ($\pi\alpha\rho\alpha\delta\acute{o}\sigma\epsilon\iota\varsigma$) which you were taught by us, either by word of mouth or by letter" (2 Thess. 2: 15). From the context it may be inferred that by "traditions" the apostle means the whole body of teaching, both

---

[1] *The Apostolic Preaching and its Developments*, 38-45.

doctrinal and practical, which he had transmitted to them either verbally during the mission or subsequently by letter. But later in the same letter he writes, "now we command you, brethren, in the name of our Lord Jesus Christ, that you keep away from any brother who is living in idleness and not in accord with the tradition (παράδοσιν) that you received from us" (3: 6). Here the reference is specifically to moral conduct—the disciples must follow the transmitted pattern of life, revealed in the words and deeds of the apostles (Phil. 4: 9). This pattern of life is corporate as well as individual. There is, for example, a tradition of worship and of conduct at worship which is followed "in all the churches of the saints". A local church, such as that at Corinth, is not at liberty to depart from it.[1] "What! Did the word of God originate with you, or are you the only ones it has reached?" (1 Cor. 14: 33, 36). Clement of Rome, writing later to that same turbulent church at Corinth, recalls them from strife and jealousy to the "canon of our *paradosis*" (7: 2), i.e. to the whole Christian way of life. He is calling upon them to act according to the transmitted pattern of conduct—the way Christians should do things. The *Paradosis* is "the Way".

6. Since the rise of "form criticism" intensive study has been given to the oral tradition, and in particular to the manner in which it was preserved and shaped by the vital needs and problems of the Christian community. Professor Cullmann has, however, now drawn attention to another and neglected aspect of this process of transmission.[2] For we are not to conceive of it as being a merely human activity, as if it were "traditioned" simply by the apostles and those closely associated with them. The living Lord, the Head of the church Himself, presides over and guides this process of transmission. We are not to think of Him as being present only at the source or start of the process, as if the tradition with the passage of time went further and further away from Him. The living Lord is present in the church, and is acting through the action of the apostolate. Professor Cullmann draws attention to the false antithesis often presented to us in

---

[1] Cf. the statement on page 26 "that *each* church has liberty to interpret and administer His laws"!

[2] *The Early Church*, 66-69.

discussion of the meaning of 1 Corinthians 11: 23—"For
I received from the Lord what I also delivered to you".
This must mean, we are told, either that the apostle received
the Gospel by direct and unmediated revelation from the
risen Lord, or that he received it indirectly through the
original eyewitnesses, the Lord being the ultimate source of
the process. The fact is that he received it *directly* from the
Lord *through* the other apostles, because the Lord is immediately and directly involved all along in the transmission.
In this connection attention is drawn to the significance of
the *present* tense of the verb in 1 Corinthians 7: 10. "To the
married I give charge, not I but the Lord."[1] Although
the apostle is here drawing from the oral tradition—the
Lord's saying on divorce—he uses the present tense because
the Lord is at present speaking through the tradition He
has transmitted. The *Paradosis* is living, because the living
Lord is transmitting it. It is the whole on-going life of the
church, which is one with the life of her Lord.

7. From this brief study of the word *paradosis* in the New
Testament, it will be seen that any antithesis or contrast
between tradition (in the sense it has *in* Scripture) and
Scripture is completely false. For Scripture is the tradition
as committed to writing by the apostles or those closely
associated with them. It is true, of course, that we cannot
simply identify the apostolic tradition with Scripture, for
the former may have been, so to speak, a much larger circle
within which the smaller circle of Scripture falls. It can be
reasonably maintained that aspects of the apostolic tradition
have been transmitted to us quite apart from the Scriptures.
But at least we may not contrast Scripture and tradition.
The primary tradition is Scripture and Scripture is the
primary tradition. The two are one.

B. *"Paradosis" in Church History*

One of the greatest difficulties in discussing the relationship between Scripture and tradition arises from the fact
that only one of the two terms has a defined meaning. There
is now general agreement as to what is meant by "Scripture".
On the other hand, many different meanings or at least
subtle shades of meaning have been ascribed to the word

[1] *The Early Church*, 68.

"tradition" in the history of the church. To use this term as if one and the same meaning had been given to it by all, in all periods of church history, is a common cause of confusion. Furthermore, the term "tradition" has no fixed or agreed meaning in contemporary discussion, and it often requires careful study to discover the precise sense in which any given writer is using it.

1. For the Fathers of the early church the *Paradosis* is Scripture. The church is built upon the foundation of the apostles and prophets, and appeal is constantly made to the writings of the apostles and the Scriptures of the Old Testament. At first very little use is made of the actual word *paradosis*, but constant appeal is made to the apostolic writings. It is, however, recognized that the genuine apostolic tradition may be transmitted orally as well as in the apostolic books. Papias believes that it is still accessible to him in the personal reminiscences of old men, "for I did not suppose I could get such profit from the contents of books as from the words of a living and abiding voice". This oral tradition, however, is preferred not to the recognized apostolic writings, but to the writings of "those who record strange precepts".[1] With the passage of time, and owing to the conflict with Gnosticism and other heresies, the tendency became more marked to appeal exclusively to the apostolic writings as embodying the genuine apostolic tradition. For the Gnostics claimed to be the recipients of an esoteric tradition imparted by the apostles to a select few, and delivered orally.

> In Gnosticism, therefore, we encounter for the first time the idea of unwritten tradition as an authority for doctrine. Unlike orthodox tradition, it is neither the raw material, as it were, of what is to become Scripture, nor the explication of what is contained in Scripture. It is wholly independent of Scripture and is even superior to it, since only in the light of the tradition can Scripture be understood. Doctrine and practice alike are founded upon it.[2]

In controversy with the Gnostics, the Fathers appeal to the apostolic writings as transmitting the true and genuine

[1] Eusebius, *E.H.*, 3, 39.
[2] G. W. H. Lampe, "Scripture and Tradition in the Early Church", in F. W. Dillistone (ed.), *Scripture and Tradition*, 41.

apostolic tradition. The Scriptures are thus regarded as the canon or rule by means of which all other traditions may be checked and proved to be false or acceptable. Not that the Fathers themselves received only such traditions as were explicitly attested in Scripture. Irenaeus, for example, "appeals to tradition in support of facts which are now universally rejected, and of stories which contain very dubious elements".[1] He often approaches both the methods and assumptions of the Gnostics by an uncritical acceptance of untrustworthy traditions. But he stands out over against them in his appeal to Scripture as the primary and author-itative tradition. "All that is true in his teaching rests on the sure foundation of the direct words of Christ and the recorded testimony of His apostles. It is based on that rock of truth, not on the sandy and crumbling foundations of oral tradition."[2] While, therefore, the early Fathers do recognize other traditions as apostolic, yet their general teaching and attitude is to regard Scripture as the primary tradition at the bar of which all other tradition—even when it claims to be apostolic—must be tested.

2. During the period from the middle of the second century to the end of the fourth century, the connotation of the category "tradition" was altered and greatly extended. The process was of course gradual and not at all uniform. This extension of the meaning of "tradition" took place in several different directions. The most important of these was the increasing tendency to appeal to the teachings and writings of the early Fathers of the church. The patristic tradition was added to the apostolic tradition. Not that the former was regarded as a new addition to the latter—rather it was the true and valid interpretation of it. Furthermore, and especially after Nicea, the tradition of credal forms was accepted as an essential part of the whole tradition. But this too was regarded not as an addition to, but rather as a brief summary of, Scriptural doctrine. Athanasius affirms "the holy and inspired Scriptures are self-sufficient for the proclamation of the truth",[3] and justifies the non-Scriptural word *homoousion* because it interprets the true sense of Scripture. But the fact remains that a growing body of interpretation was slowly being added to the apostolic

---

[1] F. W. Farrer, *Lives of the Fathers*, i, 102.   [2] *Ibid.*, 104.   [3] Gent. 1.

Scriptural tradition. This tendency to regard earlier credal and conciliar pronouncements as part of the authoritative tradition, can be seen clearly in "The Chalcedonian Definition" which begins by renewing "the undeviating creed of the One Hundred and Fifty who subsequently met together in Great Constantinople". At the time of St. Augustine, the tradition includes not only Scripture, the patristic teaching, credal and conciliar authority, but also "the immemorial custom of the universal Church, which, if no later origin can be properly assigned to it, must be counted as apostolic".[1]

There is thus a gradual expansion of the meaning and content of "tradition" during the first few centuries. Although regarded mainly as an interpretation and explication of what is given in Scripture, yet, even if this assumption is granted, the *corpus* of tradition has grown enormously.

3. The tendency we have just noted, to interpret Scripture by an authoritative corpus of tradition, moves almost imperceptibly to the stage at which Scripture and tradition are regarded as the dual authority for the church's faith and practice. This tendency may be seen in Vincent of Lerins. He does still indeed regard the canon of Scripture as all-sufficient, and yet it is not sufficient because it can be interpreted in so many ways "that almost as many opinions seem capable of being drawn out of it as there are individuals". It is therefore necessary "that the line of prophetic and apostolic interpretation should be guided according to the norm of the sense of the universal church", and this norm is *quod ubique, quod semper, quod ab omnibus*.[2] But although Vincent appeals to the double authority of Scripture and tradition, we still detect the habit of subordinating tradition to Scripture, since the former is still regarded as the necessary interpretation of the latter. In the relevant decree of the Council of Trent, however, we have the logical conclusion of the tendency to appeal to the double authority of Scripture and tradition. The counter-reformation, in reaction against the Reformers' doctrine of the supremacy of Scripture, affirmed the dual authority of Scripture and tradition.

> Following the example of the orthodox Fathers, the synod receives and venerates, with *equal* pious affection and reverence, all the books both of the Old and New Testaments . . .

[1] G. W. H. Lampe, *loc. cit.*, 48.   [2] *Ibid.*, 50.

as also the said traditions as well those pertaining to faith as to morals . . . as having been dictated either by Christ's own word of mouth or by the Holy Ghost and preserved in the Catholic Church by a continuous succession.

These words have a twofold implication. First, there are some doctrines and practices ordained by Christ or the apostles, not found in Scripture, which have been faithfully "traditioned" in the church. Secondly, that tradition is an *independent* and authoritative source of faith or morals, alongside of Scripture, although never in disagreement with it.

4. The Edinburgh Conference on Faith and Order of 1937 defined tradition as "the living stream of the Church's life". This full and rich conception owes much to the renewed contact of the western churches with the churches of the Orthodox east. Here, as in the New Testament, the living Lord transmits the tradition, which is a manifestation of His life and presence within the church.

> To accept and understand tradition we must live within the church, we must be conscious of the grace-giving presence of the Lord in it. We must feel the breath of the Holy Ghost in it. We may truly say that when we accept tradition we accept, through faith, our Lord, who abides in the midst of the faithful; for the church is His Body, which cannot be separated from Him. That is why loyalty to tradition means not only *concord* with the past, but, in a certain sense, *freedom from* the past, as from some outward formal criterion. Tradition is not only a protective, conservative principle; it is, primarily, the principle of growth and regeneration.[1]

In this conception the familiar, if misleading, antithesis between the conservative and progressive principles, between "hide-bound tradition" and the Holy Spirit, is transcended. The tradition is the on-going life of Christ within His church.

These four examples will serve to show the different meanings which have been or are attached to the word "tradition". Of the present situation and discussion Daniel Jenkins says "the connotation which these terms—Scripture and tradition—bear is subtly changing, with the result that it is difficult to know the precise sense in which they are

[1] G. V. Florovsky, "Sobornost: the Catholicity of the Church", in E. L. Mascall (ed.), *The Church of God: an Anglo-Russian Symposium*.

being used without a great deal of further inquiry".[1] We must not, then, in studying the relationship between Scripture and tradition, assume that the latter has a fixed or universally accepted meaning. Not only is it possible to accept some traditions and reject others, it is also possible to reject a whole conception of tradition and to accept another. Tradition itself is a fact of vital importance—not only apostolic or Scriptural, but also ecclesiastical tradition. By what criterion is the latter to be judged, and what is the right relationship between the two? To these questions we now turn.

C. *The Relationship between Scriptural and Ecclesiastical Tradition*

Holy Scripture containeth all things necessary to salvation, so that whatsoever is not read therein, nor may be proved thereby, is not to be required of any man, that it should be believed as an article of Faith, or be thought requisite or necessary to salvation.[2]

This statement about the supremacy and self-sufficiency of the Scriptures may be taken as the characteristic protestant attitude to the problem of Scripture and tradition. It is not denied that ecclesiastical tradition has value, but it may not be regarded as an authoritative source for doctrine, unless such doctrines are found within or may be proved from Scripture. But this appeal to the supremacy of the Scriptures made by the Reformers and their successors, cannot be made in the *same* way or on the *same* grounds to-day. As a general result of Biblical and historical criticism, our attitude to the Bible itself has undergone little less than a revolution. We cannot now go back on these insights, and in particular, we must take seriously the truth that the Bible itself is the tradition of the people of God, whether of the Old or the New Israel. Is it not then arbitrary and unjustified, since we can no longer fall back upon theories of verbal inspiration, to contrast the two kinds of tradition? On what grounds can it be maintained that the tradition of the people of God in its literary form is authoritative from one historical period, but that the tradition of the people of God ceases to be authoritative, although it may have value, after a certain period? The contemporary protestant answer to this question

[1] *Op. cit.*, 13.   [2] *The Book of Common Prayer*, Article VI.

is best studied by an examination of the thesis of Professor Cullmann.[1]

> The time within which the history of salvation is unfolded includes the past, the present, and the future. But it has a centre which serves as a vantage-point or norm for the whole extent of this history, and this centre is constituted by what we call the period of direct revelation, or the period of the incarnation. It comprises the years from the birth of Christ to the death of the last apostle, that is, of the last eyewitness who saw the risen Jesus and who received either from the incarnate Jesus or the risen Christ the direct and unique command to testify to what he had seen and heard. This testimony can be oral or written.[2]

The mighty acts of our redemption, the incarnation of Christ, His life and ministry, His passion and death, His resurrection and exaltation, the outpouring of the Holy Spirit and the establishment of the church, are "once for all" unique events, and constitute the "central" period of the history of salvation.

> If we consider the Christian faith from the point of view of time we should say that the scandal of the Christian faith is to believe that these few years, which for secular history have no more and no less significance than other periods, are the centre and norm of the totality of time.[3]

Taking this "central period" as our starting point we can see the history of salvation unfolding in two directions—backwards in the history of Israel which moves to its fulfilment in the incarnation of Christ, and forwards in the history of the church. "The problem of Scripture and tradition concerns the place we give to the period of the church with reference to the period of the incarnation."[4] This period of the church is itself a continuation of the history of salvation, but it is not "the period of the incarnate Christ and of his apostolic eyewitnesses".[5] As the chosen eyewitnesses of the incarnate and risen Christ, the testimony and office of the apostles were unique and incapable of transmission.

> The function of the bishop, which is transmitted, is essentially different from that of the apostle, which cannot be transmitted. The apostles appoint bishops, but they cannot delegate to

---

[1] *The Early Church*, 59ff.   [2] *Ibid.*, 76.   [3] *Ibid.*   [4] *Ibid.*, 77.   [5] *Ibid.*

them their function, which cannot be renewed . . . this means that the apostolate does not belong to the period of the church, but to that of the incarnation.[1]

Now *the testimony of the eyewitnesses of unique and final events must itself be a unique testimony.* They alone can say "that which was from the beginning, which we have heard, which we have seen with our eyes, which we have looked upon and touched with our hands, concerning the word of life—that which we have seen and heard we proclaim also to you" (1 John 1: 1, 3). The apostle Peter was an eyewitness of the word made flesh, and therefore his testimony in gospel and epistle differs not only, so to say, in degree of inspiration, but uniquely from the letters of Ignatius of Antioch. Paul was an eyewitness of the risen Lord, and therefore his writings are in a quite different category from those of Augustine, even although the latter may have been as great a theologian. In other words, "the scandal of particularity", the ascription of unique and final significance to an event or series of closely related events within history, carries with it the scandal of ascribing a unique significance and authority to the testimony, whether oral or written, of those who witnessed these unique events. Furthermore, the apostolic period was necessarily of strictly limited duration, coming to an end with the death of the last of the eyewitnesses of the incarnation and the resurrection. For whatever elements in the apostolate were capable of transmission to successors, that of having been an eyewitness could not in the nature of the case be so transmitted. The corpus of unique writings was therefore necessarily produced within a limited time.

Now the early church itself recognized this unique character of the apostolic testimony by establishing the canon.

The fixing of the Christian canon of Scripture means that *the church itself*, at a given time, traced a clear and definite line of demarcation between the period of the apostles and that of the church, between the time of foundation and that of construction, between the apostolic community and the church of the bishops, in other words, between apostolic tradition and ecclesiastical tradition. Otherwise, the formation of the canon would be meaningless.[2]

[1] *The Early Church*, 78.　　[2] *Ibid.*, 89.

By establishing the principle of a canon the Church recognized that *from that time* the tradition was no longer a criterion of truth. It drew a line under the apostolic tradition. It declared implicitly that from that time every subsequent tradition must be submitted to the control of the apostolic tradition.[1]

One serious criticism may be advanced against Professor Cullmann's thesis. Modern historical criticism of the New Testament writings no longer permits us to ascribe them all to the apostles or eyewitnesses of the Word made flesh. It may be questioned whether any of our four gospels is *directly* apostolic. Even if we accept the gospel of Mark as Peter's testimony and ascribe the gospel of John to the son of Zebedee, yet certainly Luke the physician and the compiler of our first gospel were not eyewitnesses. And in what sense can we ascribe the Pastoral Epistles or 2 Peter to the apostles, if they were not written until perhaps the second decade of the second century? No doubt the New Testament comes either directly from the apostles or from men closely associated with them. But the addition of the last few words blurs the distinction made by Cullmann between apostolic and ecclesiastical testimony. He has in fact over-stated his case, and made too sharp a demarcation. And we are faced with this problem, not only as between one book and another (e.g. 1 Thessalonians and the Apocalypse), but also in judging of the value of a unit of material within any given book. Can it be seriously maintained that the tradition preserved in Matthew 17: 24-27 (the coin in the fish's mouth) is of equal value to that preserved in chapter 19: 13-15 (the blessing of the children)? If, as the form critics have shown, the gospel tradition was not only preserved but also shaped and modified by the early Christian communities, how then is it possible to draw a hard and fast line between apostolic and church tradition?

This criticism, however, does not invalidate Professor Cullmann's main thesis. It does mean that the New Testament itself is no exception to the apostolic precept "Test everything; hold fast what is good." It also means that we must not *overdraw* the distinction between apostolic and ecclesiastical tradition. But the main point stands. The

[1] *The Early Church*, 90.

incarnation is a unique eschatological event. A limited
number of chosen eyewitnesses, "the glorious company of
the apostles", witnessed that event. Their testimony and
that of men closely associated with them was committed to
writing. These writings therefore are unique, authoritative,
and normative. *The Scripture is the primary tradition, and by
this "canon", this norm, all other tradition must be judged.*

> The Biblical books *are* placed by Christians in a class apart
> from all other writings and are treated as Holy Scripture,
> given by divine inspiration and profitable for doctrine. This
> is . . . because they are primary witnesses to and interpreters
> of the sequence of historical events, culminating in the coming
> of Jesus and His Church, in which Christians believe that God
> was working His purpose out and achieving the Salvation of
> mankind.[1]

D. *Some Conclusions*

From this brief survey of the relationship between
Scripture and tradition, some conclusions may be drawn
which have an important bearing upon the theology and
practice of baptism.

1. It is of vital importance that we should see the Scriptures, both of the Old and New Testaments, as themselves a
deposit of the developing tradition of the people of God.
There is something behind the writings themselves, and that
not just the oral tradition, but the whole on-going life of the
people of God. That "living stream of the church's life"—
whether it is the church of the old covenant or the new—
must be studied as such, with due regard to the fact that it is
a living, moving, developing, on-going tradition.

But in spite of a knowledge of this fact, many scholars
continue to appeal to the Bible as if it were a fixed, static
tradition, every part of which has equal value. It is possible,
for example, to construct a theology of baptism by treating
the whole Bible as a kind of elevated but flat plateau,
separated from all other traditions, but itself a uniform
tradition. The valuable stress now being placed upon the
unity of the Bible and "the reinterpretation of the New
Testament in terms of its setting in the Hebraic mind", may
actually accentuate this wrong attitude. It may lead, for

---

[1] A. Richardson, *Christian Apologetics*, 202ff.

example, to the interpretation of baptism in terms of circumcision and the old covenant, almost with the assumption
that the teaching of the Hebrew prophets and the incarnation and work of Christ made no essential difference.
But

> for the Church the Old Testament is canonical only in so far
> as it is explicitly orientated towards the New; in other words,
> because the time of the incarnation is regarded as normative
> for the time which preceded it, and as the criterion by which
> it is to be understood. Thus the apostolic writings are the
> norm not only of the post-apostolic, but of the pre-apostolic
> period.[1]

It is not suggested that there is a uniform development from
"lower" to "higher" in the Biblical tradition.

> The earlier is therefore not necessarily on a lower level than
> the later: there is retrogression as well as progression; and the
> task of discrimination can never be simply a matter of estab-
> lishing, if we can, a chronological sequence.

But all the same

> we have not merely the right but the duty to discriminate
> within the Scripture records between different levels in the
> apprehension of God's nature and purpose and to reject the
> lower levels once and for all in favour of the higher. For only
> by so doing can we once again be loyal to the notion of a
> revelation which God has given through the medium of
> historical events, and to the faith that Christ Himself is the
> final source and norm of all truth in this sphere.[2]

When we claim, therefore, that the Bible is "the primary
tradition", we need to stress the word "tradition" as well as
the adjective "primary". We must no longer treat it as a
quarry, from any part of which we may find stones to build
up our doctrines. We must rather study it as the literary
record of a living, on-going tradition, attempting to evaluate
all the parts of that tradition by reference to the Living
Word, who is "the Lord and King of Scripture".

2. It is also of importance that all Christians should appreciate the positive value of ecclesiastical tradition, and enter

---

[1] O. Cullmann, *The Early Church*, 94.

[2] H. H. Farmer, "The Bible: its Significance and Authority", in G. A
Buttrick and N. B. Harman (eds.), *The Interpreter's Bible*, i, 27.

into it as fully as possible. For the assertion that the Scriptures are the prime tradition does *not* carry the implication that they are the only genuine embodiment of the apostolic tradition. The apostolic tradition was much wider than the New Testament writings which now embody it, and as there was an unbroken continuity in the life and development of the church, it is only reasonable to assume that it was faithfully transmitted in other ways also. Dom Gregory Dix has rightly drawn attention to the importance in this connection of the liturgical practice of the primitive churches. Before any part of the New Testament was written, the worship of the church patterned on the synagogue and "the Upper Room" was already taking shape. And in particular the sacraments of baptism and the eucharist were an embodiment of the Gospel, the *kerygma* in action.

> We know now too, that the apostolic *paradosis* of practice, like the apostolic *paradosis* of doctrine, is something which actually ante-dates the writing of the New Testament documents themselves by some two or three decades. . . . I am not for a moment seeking to question the authoritative weight of the New Testament Scriptures *for us* as a written doctrinal standard. I am only trying to point out that there is available another source of information on the original and authentic apostolic interpretation of Christianity, which the Scriptures pre-suppose and which must be used in the interpretation of the Scriptures. I do not deny that in time the recognition of this fact will be bound to lead to some considerable readjustments of ideas for more than one set of people.[1]

We may well agree that the study of early liturgical practice would lead to "considerable readjustments of ideas", especially in relation to baptism, particularly when full weight is given to the development of credal confessions in close association with the baptismal rite.

Worship and liturgy, however, are not the only way, other than Scripture,[2] in which the original apostolic tradition may have been transmitted. "What you have heard from me before many witnesses entrust to faithful men who will be able to teach others also" (2 Tim. 2: 2). "The pattern of the

[1] *The Theology of Confirmation in Relation to Baptism.*

[2] The liturgy, of course, is partly embodied in Scripture, e.g. the fragments of hymns in the epistles.

sound words" was "traditioned" by the local elders and by the itinerant ministry of the church. At baptism the candidates are said to "have become obedient from the heart to the *standard* of teaching to which you were committed" (Rom. 6: 17). Indeed, the apostolic doctrine and practice, faith and morals, worship and custom, were transmitted in and through the whole body of the church, whose life is one with the life of Christ. Far too many protestants adopt a wholly negative attitude to ecclesiastical tradition. They jump from the Scriptures to the present day, as if nothing of value had been preserved or transmitted in the intervening centuries. It is a necessary part of our Christian discipline to become aware of, and to enter appreciatively into, the tradition of the whole church, for both truth and freedom are to be found by those who are rooted and grounded in the whole tradition, and not by those who discard it.

In this connection it must be frankly admitted that the statement with which we began "that each local church has liberty, under the guidance of the Holy Spirit, to interpret and administer His laws" is open to easy and serious misunderstanding. As an affirmation of the responsibility of the local congregation of believers it is wholly admirable. But it can easily be misinterpreted to mean that the individual church, like the individual Christian, is at liberty to discard or ignore, not only the tradition of its own communion, but of the whole church universal, and go straight to the Bible. Since no community can in fact go straight to the Bible free from any sort of prejudice or principles of interpretation, such an attitude results in bondage to a very narrow tradition with inadequate rootage in the past. We must learn to comprehend the truth "with *all* the Saints", paying special attention to those with whom we most disagree. To do this involves a positive and appreciative attitude to the tradition of the whole church.

3. But a "positive and appreciative attitude" to tradition does not mean, or should not mean, an uncritical acceptance of all tradition. Still less should it mean being bound by outmoded traditions like Lazarus in his grave clothes. For the Christ who is "Lord and King of Scripture" is also Lord and King of tradition, and He not only conserves all that is good and true in it, He also judges it. He may also

stir up His people to discard it either because it is untrue or because "time makes ancient good uncouth". Here it is important to recall what was said earlier about the attitude of our Lord to tradition. His was a twofold attitude of both acceptance and rejection. His general attitude to the past, to the Scriptures and the history and tradition of His people, was that of reverence and acceptance. But not of uncritical acceptance, for not only did He reject "the tradition of the Elders", but also His antithesis "it was said . . . but I say" implies a positive criticism of Scripture itself. We can never afford to forget that it was in the defence of age-long tradition that the Jewish hierarchy sent Jesus to the cross.

From the early centuries the church has suffered because of this marked tendency to accept tradition without positive criticism. With a commendable eagerness to "hold fast what is good", she has often forgotten the first part of that apostolic precept—"test everything". Even the early Fathers of the church, while loyal to the Scriptures, are prone to accept traditions which we to-day can only regard as worthless.[1] It is therefore the height of folly to assume that because this or that is a part of ecclesiastical tradition, it ought therefore *on that ground alone* to be accepted. Such an attitude is as misguided as the opposite tendency of others to reject all church tradition just because it is church tradition. The right attitude is to test all ecclesiastical tradition, and hold fast to what is good. But by what standard is this test to be made and who is to make it? The answer is that all ecclesiastical tradition must be tested by the apostolic tradition as embodied in Scripture—and this test must continue in all ages to be made by the whole body of the church. All Christians, all churches, all communions have the responsibility and the right to make this test. They have also the responsibility to listen to one another, since the Holy Spirit is given to the whole church and He is not the monopoly of any one part of it.

4. It has just been asserted that the criterion by which ecclesiastical tradition must be evaluated, is the apostolic tradition embodied in Scripture. It is important to realize,

---

[1] Some of the traditions accepted by Papias as early as A.D. 150 would now be regarded as legends.

D

however, that the latter is not simply a *paradosis of doctrine*, but is also a *paradosis of practice*.

In Section A above an analysis was made of the conception of *paradosis* in the New Testament itself. It was found to be a rich and complex conception, having reference not only to the *kerygma* or proclamation of the essential gospel message, but also to the whole tradition of the Lord's words and deeds, to the pattern of Christian life and conduct, to worship and custom. Indeed it was probably the case that the apostolic *paradosis* of practice preceded the *paradosis* of doctrine, in the sense of *developed* doctrine. It follows therefore that an appeal to apostolic tradition is also an appeal to apostolic practice. Baptists, for example, have always defended the practice of believers' baptism on the ground that it was the practice of the apostles and of the church in the apostolic age. But it must be frankly admitted that the appeal to apostolic practice is beset with a grave difficulty. How can we distinguish between what is essential and what is merely accidental in apostolic practice? We do not regard ourselves as under an obligation to wear flowing robes and beards, to speak in Greek or Aramaic, to impart the kiss of peace at the eucharist, to assemble for church worship in our homes—although these and many other such-like things were customs of the apostles. On what grounds do we accept the apostolic tradition for worship preserved in 1 Corinthians 11: 17-34, and reject the apostolic tradition for worship preserved in 1 Corinthians 11: 2-16? It may be said in reply that the pattern for the observance of the Lord's Supper is an *essential* part of the tradition, whereas the instructions for the veiling of women at worship, while applicable to pagan Corinth in A.D. 54, are not essential but merely *temporary*, valid only in those circumstances. But if the need to make such a distinction is granted (and all Christians do in fact make it), on what grounds do we make it?

The answer to this question has a direct bearing on the practice of believers' baptism. Reference has already been made to the argument of Professor Cullmann that *believers'* baptism belongs to the special missionary situation of the primitive church. It is not an *essential* part of the apostolic tradition. It was appropriate and indeed inevitable in that *temporary* situation, but it cannot be regarded as obligatory in all situations. In others words, this part of apostolic practice belongs to special circumstances (like the veiling of women at Corinth), and is not essential. The argument rests, of course, upon the unexamined assumption that the missionary situation of the early church was temporary. It is certainly useful to draw a distinction between the church at work in a pagan society, and the church at work in a society deeply influenced in some respects by the Christian faith and ethic. But the contrast between "missionary situation" and "church situation" is altogether misleading. The church is in fact always in a missionary situation. This is not only because the Christians in any given society are always a minority, but also because the church is always in a missionary situation with reference to each rising generation. The children, even of Christian parents, are not born "in Christ", and need to be won through the preaching of the Gospel and their response to it in repentance and faith.

The point must be conceded, however, that we cannot necessarily justify a church practice to-day, simply by appealing to the practice of the apostles. Baptists have been slow to acknowledge this, and have tended to assume that because believers' baptism was the practice of the apostolic age, it must be obligatory in all ages. The rite can only be shown to be obligatory if it is an *essential* part of the apostolic *paradosis* of practice, and not just due to the temporary circumstances. How then may we distinguish between the essential and the incidental in apostolic practice? It may be said in reply that *essential practice arises out of the very nature of the Gospel itself*, and is the inevitable outward expression of the Gospel. Essential apostolic practice is the *kerygma* in action, whether in personal or corporate conduct, in worship or in the sacraments.

5. Finally, we must make full allowance for the fact of growth and development in the church under the inspiration and guidance of the Holy Spirit. Such a growth is discernible within the pages of the New Testament itself, and it is quite arbitrary and unreasonable to demand that no further development be allowed after the end of the first century. The New Testament is not a "blue-print"; it does not provide us with an explicit system of doctrine or ethics, or a pattern of worship or church order, which may be slavishly

copied and reproduced by the churches of all subsequent ages. This assumption is frequently made by those who raise the cry "back to the New Testament". In this sense we cannot go back. We must move on with the Lord the Spirit, who makes explicit that which from the beginning was implicit in Christ, and evermore causes new light and truth to break forth from God's word.

But of course all development may be of two main kinds; and that is why our attitude to all development, as to church tradition, must always be one of positive criticism. A development may be a legitimate growth, as when the acorn grows into the oak, the potential becomes actual, the implicit fully explicit. In this sense most Christians would accept "Nicea" and "Chalcedon" as necessary and legitimate (although still imperfect) attempts to make explicit, under the pressure of false teaching, what is implied in the New Testament. But unfortunately not all growth and development is according to the norm; it may also be a distortion or perversion of the original. The Christian ministry as seen in the New Testament developed into the sacerdotal priesthood, and the fellowship of believers into an hierarchical organization under a supreme dictator. And of course in history itself we do not find this simple "either . . . or"; legitimate development and subtle distortion and perversion go on side by side, and like the wheat and the tares cannot easily be separated. This is but to say again, that all development must be tested at the bar of the apostolic tradition in Scripture. If it is condemned, it is not on the ground that it is a development—but on the ground that it is not a legitimate development of the original deposit. If it is accepted, it is not necessarily on the ground that it is there, explicit in Scripture—but on the ground that it is a legitimate development of that which is implicit in Scripture, or can be proved to be in harmony with "the faith which was once for all delivered to the saints".

These, then, will be the two characteristics of the living church—growth and development under the guidance of the Holy Spirit, and the perpetual reformation of its life by reference to the Word of God. Tradition, the living stream of the church's life, will always be subject to Scripture, the apostolic testimony to Christ, just because the Christ of to-day is the same as the Christ of yesterday, and will abide the same for ever.

In order to guide our subsequent discussion, therefore, we may summarize these conclusions as follows:

1. God manifest in Jesus Christ the Living Word is the sole source of all authority, and this authority is mediated through the Holy Scriptures. We must not, however, appeal to the Bible as if it were a fixed static tradition, every part of which has equal value. Since it is the literary record of a developing tradition, all its parts must be examined and evaluated by reference to the Living Word, who is the "Lord and King of Scripture".

2. The apostolic tradition has also been transmitted in unbroken continuity in the life and history of the church. We must not therefore attempt to jump from Scripture to to-day as if nothing of value had been preserved in between. It is a necessary discipline to study, appreciate and evaluate the tradition of the whole church.

3. Our Lord both accepted and rejected ecclesiastical tradition, and for us also there must be no uncritical acceptance of it, since error as well as truth has been transmitted. We must test everything in ecclesiastical tradition by the apostolic tradition as embodied in Scripture—and this test must be made in all ages by the whole body of the church.

4. There is an apostolic tradition of practice as well as of doctrine. But we cannot necessarily justify church practice by appealing to the practice of the apostles, which may be due to the temporary circumstances. A practice can only be regarded as essential if it arises out of the very nature of the Gospel itself.

5. We must accept the fact of growth and development within the church under the inspiration and guidance of the Holy Spirit. A development must not be rejected simply because it is a development, but only on the ground that it is not a legitimate development of the original deposit. If it is accepted, it is not necessarily on the ground that it is explicit in Scripture, but because it can be shown to be a legitimate development of what is in Scripture.

3

JEWISH ANTECEDENTS

by A. Gilmore

JUST as the nature of authority cannot be settled by reference only to one specific period of the church's history, no more can the doctrine of baptism be evolved by looking simply at the New Testament and the apostolic age. It is rather that from those focal points we must look backward, in order that we might see the background to baptism, and forward, in order that we might its subsequent development. It is the purpose of this chapter to look backward and survey the landscape against which Christian baptism came to birth in order that later contributors may then assess its meaning and value.

It is not our intention, however, to view every possible Jewish antecedent, or to consider every possible reference to baptism which has been unearthed from the Old Testament.[1] To do that would require a volume and, even if it were possible, would tend here to cloud the main issues. It so happens that in the course of discussions on baptism during the last two decades, attention has been focused on certain factors which are generally thought to lie behind the New Testament doctrine of baptism, and therefore to have influenced its development. They are the rite of circumcision, the fact of ritual cleansings and Jewish proselyte baptism, and the ancient symbolism of the Old Testament prophets brought before us by recent Old Testament scholarship. We intend to take each of these points in turn, first to discover their real significance, then to point out what is their

---

[1] For the Jewish antecedents, see F. Gavin, *The Jewish Antecedents of the Christian Sacraments*, W. Brandt, *Die jüdischen Baptismen*, J. Thomas, *Le Mouvement Baptiste en Palestine et Syrie*, and for Old Testament types and analogies and the way in which they were used by the Reformers, see G. W. Bromiley, *Baptism and the Anglican Reformers*, 33f.

relationship with baptism, and finally to suggest certain lines of thought which ought to guide and stimulate baptismal discussions. Before we proceed further, it should be clearly understood that we are not attempting to draw final conclusions regarding baptism on the basis of those antecedents; we are trying rather to assess their relevance to the subject under discussion.

A. *Circumcision*

Broadly speaking,[1] the argument from circumcision is that just as circumcision marked the entry of an individual into the privileges of the old covenant, so baptism naturally marked the entry of an individual into the privileges of the new covenant,[2] and that therefore the details of the two rites should approximate as closely as possible. It is argued that as the old covenant included Abraham's offspring along with Abraham, and as the offsprings, too, received the richest blessing which the covenant disclosed, we cannot therefore believe that infants to-day are excluded from what the Abrahamic covenant provided.[3]

Karl Barth[4] has criticized the assumption that because there is a certain parallel between the two rites, it is therefore legitimate to argue that baptism, like circumcision, must be performed on infants, regardless of other factors. H. H. Rowley,[5] similarly, refers to the "usual confusion" on this matter when it is argued that, for the church, baptism has taken the place of circumcision as the sacrament of admission into the immutable covenant of God, which is essentially the same in all dispensations, after which it is assumed that the subjects of the two rites should be the same.

---

[1] Dom Gregory Dix, "Confirmation or the Laying on of Hands?" in *Theology*, Occasional Papers, No. 5 (1936), 1, is one exception to this because he regards confirmation as the central rite and therefore the Christian equivalent of circumcision. Cf. L. S. Thornton, *Confirmation Today*, 9. G. W. H. Lampe (*The Seal of the Spirit*, 87), however, does not believe that this approach has succeeded.

[2] O. Cullmann, *Baptism in the New Testament*, 57.

[3] J. Murray, *Christian Baptism*, 48ff. O. Cullmann (*op. cit.*, 57) bolsters the same argument on the terminological grounds that σφραγίς in the Old Testament means circumcision, and σφραγίζεσθαι is used in the New Testament of baptism.

[4] *The Teaching of the Church regarding Baptism*, 43.

[5] "Marcel on Infant Baptism", in *E.T.*, lxiv (1952-53), 362.

With these considerations in mind, we shall examine (1) the origin and significance of circumcision, (2) the nature of its connection with baptism, and (3) the relevance of this relationship to the present discussion.

1. The origin of circumcision lies buried in obscurity. We know that it was practised by other nations as well as by the Hebrews,[1] though there is some doubt as to whether it was originally a physiological or a religious ceremony.[2] It is possible that from a very early time it was both, being a consecration of one's sexual life, and belonging to the time when a man was instructed into the existence of a good God, who was a defender of morals and condemned adultery.[3]

We are on firmer ground, however, when we come to the Hebrews, for there its significance was wholly religious. It was the outward symbol of a covenant with God, and was performed in infancy.[4] There are two accounts of its institution, the older one in Exodus 4: 24ff. (J), and the fuller one in Genesis 17: 1-13 (P). It was the rite whereby a child was received into the fellowship of the pure God-consecrated people, and it included the obligation to conform to all the divine ordinances that were binding on that body.[5] Where it was not carried out on a male, then that man would nullify the covenant.[6]

What were the elements, therefore, which made this rite so distinctive? There were three.

(a) *It was an act of initiation into the people of God.* F. W.

[1] M.-J. Lagrange (*Études sur les Religions Sémitiques*, 244ff.) suggests that it is a practice which grew up in a relatively little developed social community, and that it then relied on the great nations for its continuation. According to the ancients, circumcision came from Egypt and spread all over the world, but Lagrange holds to the view that it originated with the Ethiopians, who passed it on to the Egyptians when they (i.e. the Ethiopians) began to go down the Nile Valley. There is also evidence that it was found among the Arab tribes, and to some extent among the Phoenicians.

[2] E. Renan (*Histoire du Peuple Israël*, 123) maintains that it had a purely physiological cause and that this accounts for the fact that it is so widespread, whereas E. Kautzsch ("The Religion of Israel", in *H.D.B.* (Extra Volume), 622), whilst admitting that among many tribes it is connected with puberty and is a sign of maturity, goes on to add that it has also a religious meaning and is best viewed as an act of consecration.

[3] M.-J. Lagrange, *op. cit.*, 243.

[4] In other races it usually coincided with arrival at puberty.

[5] E. Kautzsch, *loc. cit.*, 716.

[6] G. F. Moore (*Judaism*, II, 17f.) says the link is so strong between circumcision and the covenant, that it is possible for circumcision itself to be called the covenant.

Dillistone[1] has shown how circumcision seems to have attained a position of special importance at critical times in Israel's history, such as at the Exodus (Exod. 12), at the entry into Canaan (Josh. 5), and at the time of the return from exile (Gen. 17),[2] and from this he concludes that circumcision was regarded as most important when Israel's separation from other nations needed to be emphasized, and when her relationship with her own God needed to be reinforced. But because the nation was a religious community, bound by covenant to Yahweh, circumcision was reinterpreted also as a sign of that covenant. It therefore marked a man's separation from heathenism, and his acceptance by the God of Israel.

This carries two implications. First, circumcision belonged to the time when a man made his original act of separation from heathenism in favour of the God of Israel;[3] it was initiation into the old covenant. Secondly, every male Jew must have undergone the rite as soon as was possible, or the idea of separation could never have been retained; once the ceremony was complete the recipient entered into membership of the covenant people.

But who were the covenant people? In the case of the old covenant, they were the members of the nation which God had chosen, plus their proselytes and their proselytes' descendants. Circumcision, therefore, was an initiation ceremony into the people of God in the sense that it was an initiation into the particular nation which God had chosen. Moreover, it was a ceremony for males only,[4] and in some cases was practised side by side with baptism.[5]

[1] *Christianity and Symbolism*, 199ff. A. Lods (*Israël*, 198ff.) says that for the Hebrews circumcision was nothing more than a social rite until the exile. Then, when the Jews came into contact with the Babylonians and the Persians who did not practise it, it became a symbol of nationality and religion. Cf. F. Sierksma, "Quelques remarques sur la circoncision en Israël", in *Oudtestamentische Studien*, ix (1951), 136-69.

[2] We might also add to this list the Maccabaean age, when parents were crucified because they circumcised their children, with their babes hung around their necks.

[3] It was one of three acts at this time, but of the three it was the most vitally important ceremony of entry into the covenant. (G. W. H. Lampe, *op. cit.*, 83.)

[4] See H. H. Rowley's reply to P. Ch. Marcel on this point, in "Marcel on Infant Baptism", in *E.T.*, lxiv (1952-53), 362.

[5] We shall see later how all converts to Judaism underwent circumcision and proselyte baptism. Some Hellenistic Jews later tried to argue that circumcision had been replaced by baptism and was no longer necessary, but they were firmly opposed by the Palestinian Jews who insisted on both and won the day. (W. O. E. Oesterley, "Circumcision", in *H.D.C.G.*, I, 331.)

(*b*) *It was an act of consecration to the nation's God.* Circumcision, besides initiating its recipient into the people of God, also entitled the recipient to the privileges and responsibilities which God had made with His people;[1] it was the "seal" of God's ownership. It is important to remember, however, that circumcision was essentially the sign that a man belonged to the people whom God had chosen, rather than the sign that a man had a claim upon the mercies of God. It was the sign that divine favour *had been* shown to him, but not the claim that divine favour *must be* shown to him.[2] Consequently, more attention should be paid to circumcision as the sign of responsibility than to circumcision as the sign of privilege, and this was in fact the way in which it was normally understood among the prophets of the Old Testament, who tended to see it as a spiritual conception.[3]

(*c*) *It was an act which required faith for its fulfilment.* If this should seem to be a strange claim to make for a ceremony which was normally performed on eight-day-old infants, let it be remembered that as a general rule the Bible leaves no room for meaningless ritual, and declares that ceremonies derive their value and effectiveness solely from the fact that they are the vehicle of the Spirit.[4] This is true of circumcision. Even P. Ch. Marcel[5] has been at pains to point out that faith is a condition of entry into the covenant, and that the beneficiaries of the covenant must answer God's promise, "I am your God and your Saviour", with the reply by faith, "I am Thy child". There is evidence, too, that this is the way in which the Fathers[6] interpreted circumcision, for they saw it as a ratification of a convert's justification,

---

[1] E. Kautzsch (*loc cit.*, 716) says that because circumcision was an act of purifying, it must therefore be followed by an act of consecration, and because it is the rite whereby a child is received into the fellowship of the God-consecrated people, it includes the obligation to conform to all the divine ordinances that are binding on this Body. Cf. I. Broydé, "Circumcision", in *Jewish Encyclopedia*, IV, 92.

[2] For a fuller discussion of this point see N. H. Snaith, *Hymns of the Temple*, 56ff.

[3] E. Kautzsch (*loc. cit.*, 686) quotes Jer. 4: 4 as an example of this. Cf. W. O. E. Oesterley and G. H. Box, *The Religion and Worship of the Synagogue*, 258, and F. Sierksma, *loc. cit.*, 166.

[4] This is particularly true of the prophetic teaching in later Judaism; that is, in the period with which we are most concerned. Cf. H. H. Rowley, *The Unity of the Bible*, 166.

[5] *The Biblical Doctrine of Infant Baptism*, 99ff.

[6] G. W. H. Lampe, *op. cit.*, 91.

and H. H. Rowley[1] argues that it is the failure to appreciate this point which has led the church to dispense with faith for what has become the normal Christian baptism.

Unfortunately for the Baptist apologist, it is not possible successfully to argue, as some have tried,[2] that because faith preceded circumcision in the case of Abraham, therefore faith must precede baptism in the case of Christians; for, as has been pointed out,[3] the case of Abraham is unique since he is "the father of the faithful". We are not concerned, however, to draw attention to the order of faith and circumcision or of faith and baptism; what is really important is that faith and circumcision were associated together, and that circumcision derived its meaning only from its connection with the faith of the person circumcised.

It is against this interpretation of circumcision that we may now proceed to the possibility of a connection with circumcision under the old covenant and baptism under the new.

2. Once circumcision and baptism are associated together, and once attention is drawn to their similarities, there is a great temptation to press the analogy too far and to draw false conclusions. It may be claimed for instance that because they are both acts of initiation, and because circumcision was normally performed on infants, therefore baptism must similarly be offered to infants. Again, because failure to circumcise a child deprives that child of the benefits of the old covenant, it may be claimed that failure to baptize a child deprives him of the benefits of the new covenant. Or again, because circumcision is valid only when associated with faith, it may therefore be claimed that baptism is valid only when accompanied by faith, and since there is a division of opinion as to whether faith under the old covenant precedes or follows the ceremony, so there is justifiable doubt as to the chronology of faith and baptism. But all these "claims" suffer from the same defect; they assume that the link between baptism and circumcision is sufficiently close for these conclusions to be valid. That link must therefore be examined.

---

[1] *The Unity of the Bible*, 157, n. 4.

[2] H. Martin, "Baptism and Circumcision", in *B.Q.*, xiv (1951-52), 219.

[3] O. Cullmann, *op. cit.*, 66, and P. Ch. Marcel, *op. cit.*, 101ff.

First, there is little evidence that the Jews themselves affirmed this link and then drew conclusions from it. For many Jews, as we have already observed, circumcision and baptism were practised side by side, and I. Abrahams[1] holds to the view that in the Christian era it is mostly assumed that those baptized have been circumcised previously. Moreover, Christian Jews were encouraged to circumcise their children,[2] which hardly implies that they thought baptism had replaced circumcision, and the absence of any reference to baptism in the circumcision controversy at Jerusalem (Acts 15)[3] tends rather to confirm the view that so far as the Jews were concerned baptism and circumcision were two quite different ceremonies. Indeed, Acts represents baptism as having been practised from the start, but knows nothing of the idea that it is a substitute for circumcision.[4] The most that can be said is that so far as the Jews are concerned, circumcision and baptism are both rites of admission, but to quite different communities; Jewish Christians therefore were circumcised on entering the old Israel, and baptized on entering the new.[5] To assume that because they are both rites of admission they were both administered under precisely the same conditions is to be in grave error.[6]

Secondly, recent New Testament scholarship has cast doubts on the assumption that baptism is the New Testament equivalent of circumcision.[7] G. W. H. Lampe,[8] for instance, concludes that the New Testament writers contrast circumcision and baptism rather than compare them, and that

[1] *Studies in Pharisaism and the Gospels*, 37. It is wrong to maintain, as does W. O. E. Oesterley (*loc. cit.*, 331), that because the Hellenistic Jews (in controversy with the Palestinian Jews) held that baptism was adequate without circumcision, they regarded the two rites as analogous. It is much more probable that they realized that one had been completely superseded by the other, in which case it cannot be argued that the pattern of the new must be the same as the pattern of the old.

[2] H. Martin, *loc. cit.*, 218.

[3] L. Newbigin (*The Household of God*, 37) adds to the silence of Acts 15 the silences of Romans and Galatians.

[4] H. H. Rowley, "The Origin and Meaning of Baptism", in *B.Q.*, xi (1942-45), 313. Cf. *The Unity of the Bible*, 159.

[5] J. MacCormack, "Infant Baptism", in *E.T.*, lxv (1953-54), 125f.

[6] H. H. Rowley, "Infant Baptism", in *E.T.*, lxv (1953-54), 158.

[7] W. F. Flemington (*The New Testament Doctrine of Baptism*, 62, 70, and "An Approach to the Theology of Baptism", in *E.T.*, lxii (1950-51), 356-59) is one who makes this assumption.

[8] *Op. cit.*, 5, 56, 62, 85.

even in Col. 2: 11ff. and Eph. 2: 11 circumcision is contrasted with the spiritual circumcision in Christ effected through baptism. What is put in place of the old circumcision, therefore, is not simply baptism, but the inward and spiritual circumcision[1] which is consummated in baptism, so that according to Paul union with Christ does away with the need for physical circumcision.[2]

Thirdly, the evidence for this link is not very strong in the history of the church. Certainly the tendency among the early Fathers is more to contrast the circumcision of the flesh with the circumcision of the heart than to compare circumcision of the flesh with baptism.[3]

It may be argued, of course, that the present tendency with regard to baptism and circumcision is a valid tendency in spite of the fact that there is not much evidence for it in the three places just referred to. The most recent and thoroughgoing attempt to identify circumcision and baptism is that of P. Ch. Marcel,[4] who maintains that the Covenant of Grace "is essentially the same in all its dispensations, although its form of administration changes". So keen is Marcel, however, to see the similarities that he focuses almost all his attention on those considerations which demonstrate the unity of the covenant throughout its different dispensations, only alluding to the "changes" in form of administration. One wonders indeed whether a distinction between old and new was ever necessary.

Now every scholar will admit that there are similarities between the old and new covenants, and indeed between

---

[1] H. Martin, *loc. cit.*, 220. C. Masson (*L'Épître de Saint Paul aux Colossiens*, 125f.) says that circumcision when undergone by the believers was not to be compared to the poor human rite; it was the work of God, accomplishing once and for all that which the circumcision of men could only pre-figure. Now since flesh is, for Paul, the seat of sin, to strip a man of his flesh in this sense is to deliver him from the sin which brings death upon him. This Divine circumcision therefore takes away the very root of sin, and is called the circumcision of Christ because God has fulfilled it in the death of Christ. He then goes on to show them that they were united with Christ when they were buried with Him in baptism.

[2] H. H. Rowley, "The Origin and Meaning of Baptism", in *B.Q.*, xi (1942-45), 313, and *The Unity of the Bible*, 157f.

[3] The evidence for this view cannot all be listed here, but it has been carefully surveyed by H. H. Rowley ("The Origin and Meaning of Baptism", in *B.Q.*, xi (1942-45), 311f.) and G. W. H. Lampe (*op. cit.*, especially 169, 171ff., 239, 245f., 261f.).

[4] *Op. cit.*, passim, but especially 72ff.

circumcision and baptism, but writers like Marcel[1] who wish to press the comparison should not lose sight of certain basic differences between the covenants which must affect one's interpretation of their initiatory rites. We shall mention two.

(a) *Whereas the old covenant had a "sign", the new covenant had an "effective sign".* Circumcision, we have seen, was the mark of God's ownership, bringing a child into the responsibilities of the covenant. But the one thing it failed to do was to equip him for those responsibilities. It was a badge or outward sign, and did not partake of a sacramental character.[2] Though accompanied by faith, there is no evidence that it either awakened faith or strengthened it; it was simply a reminder to the circumcised that he belonged to God.

Baptism, on the other hand, has commonly been regarded as in some way effective. Paul acknowledges a link between faith and the way it is awakened or sustained,[3] and the Christian church has followed him in this approach. The Anglican,[4] for instance, believes that in Scripture baptism signifies the public acknowledgment of Jesus as Lord, and that the blessings of baptism flow from the union with Christ thus gained. The Free Churchman, similarly, would endorse the view of P. T. Forsyth[5] that baptism is the sacrament of the new birth, not in the sense that it produces the regeneration, but in the sense that it richly conveys it by our personal experience into its home. Outside this country, Karl Barth[6] has done as much as anyone in recent years to counteract extreme sacramentalism, but he too sees the special work of baptism to be that of sealing; it is the sealing of the letter which Jesus Christ has written in His Person and with His work. Thus understood, he goes on to argue that in the words of Scripture we must say of it that it saves, sanctifies, purifies, mediates, and gives the forgiveness of

---

[1] Cf. O. Cullmann, *op. cit.*, 45f.

[2] W. O. E. Oesterley and G. H. Box, *op. cit.*, 258; G. W. H. Lampe, *op. cit.*, 91.

[3] W. F. Flemington, *The New Testament Doctrine of Baptism*, 79-81.

[4] E. J. Bicknell, *A Theological Introduction to the Thirty-Nine Articles of the Church of England*, 466ff.

[5] *The Church and the Sacraments*, 209f. Baptists have often held to the merely symbolical view of baptism, though some of their leading thinkers have found room for a more sacramental interpretation. Cf. H. W. Robinson, *Baptist Principles*, 13; A. C. Underwood, *A History of the English Baptists*, 268f.

[6] *Op. cit.*, 29.

sins and the grace of the Holy Spirit: ". . . it effects the new birth, it is the admission of man into the covenant of grace and into the church".

Certainly this kind of language could never have been used of circumcision. Under the old covenant it was sufficient for men to know that they belonged to God, and must realize their responsibilities to Him; under the new covenant, men must know also that the Spirit of Jesus Christ was their Spirit. The death and resurrection of Jesus had made all the difference. The old covenant demanded service; the new covenant offered strength for service. Failure to appreciate this distinction does violence to the nature of God's offer in Christ.

(b) *Whereas the old covenant dealt with a race, the new covenant was personal.* We have already seen how circumcision marked a man's entry into the people which God had chosen for the fulfilment of His purposes, whereas in the New Testament baptism seems to mark a man's acknowledgment of the claims of God upon his life. This point is variously stated. It is sometimes said that circumcision marked initiation into a race, and baptism into a believing community.[1] By others it is seen as the difference between a national covenant and an individual covenant, or between a family covenant and an individual.[2] Such distinctions are all right, provided it is remembered that it is not just a distinction between corporate and individual, since the new covenant is also corporate. The difference, rather, is that between "impersonal-racial" and "personal-corporate".

The point which must not be overlooked, however, is that the fundamental principle on which the people of God is constituted is different in the case of the new covenant from what it is in the old. In the old covenant, birth and proselytization are the significant factors; in the new covenant, the significant factor is faith.[3] Only a limited number of those circumcised under the old covenant could claim to have realized their circumcision to the full in the circumcision of the heart;[4] yet the new covenant concerns only those who reach this stage of conviction. Circumcision

---

[1] H. Martin, *loc. cit.*, 214.
[2] This point was a favourite with the Anabaptists in controversy with the Reformers. (G. W. Bromiley, *op. cit.*, 99.)
[3] Cf. L. Newbigin, *op. cit.*, 36.   [4] Cf. Karl Barth, *op. cit.*, 43f.

was the mark of entry to Israel; baptism is the mark of entry to the "Israel within Israel". If it be objected that this is to make the new covenant more exclusive and particularist than the old, P. Ch. Marcel[1] unwittingly supplies the answer, for he argues that the covenant of the New Testament is "universal" in the sense that it is extended to all nations without limitation. That being the case, the covenant with the "inner" Israel is universal if it is remembered that the opportunity to believe is open to all. To disregard this essential difference in the terms of the two covenants is to beg a very important question indeed.

It is in the light of this understanding of circumcision, and its links with the old and new covenants, that we are now in a position to consider the relevance of this matter to the present baptismal discussion.

3. It should be noticed first how the tendency has changed. From the beginning there were those who saw a similarity between baptism and circumcision, but who left it at that. At the time of the Reformation there grew up the idea that they were identical ceremonies to be compared and contrasted one with another. To-day, it is being argued that baptism must be interpreted in a certain way because that is how circumcision is interpreted. The time has come when the development should be re-considered and its validity examined.

If these two initiatory rites are to be identified, and conclusions about one made on the basis of conclusions about the other, then it would appear that the normal pattern of initiation (whereby children born within the covenant are baptized at birth, and converts are baptized with their families on conversion), is approximately correct, for this is what happened in the case of circumcision.

But such an interpretation gives rise, as we have seen, to several other problems which have not been adequately settled. What, for instance, is the difference between circumcision "the sign" and baptism "the sacrament", and if the two rites are as identical as some would have us believe why do we trouble to distinguish between them at all? Furthermore, if circumcision requires faith, and has no value without faith, what is the place of faith in baptism

[1] Op. cit., 74.

and what is the position of the baptized unbeliever? Surely in this case it would be more logical to postpone baptism until there is at least some evidence that the faith is there, especially as this would seem to accord rather more with the terms on which the new community is constituted. And what is the position when baptism and circumcision are practised side by side, and even on the same person?

This identification raises also practical problems. For example, only the children of Jews received circumcision at birth; are therefore only the children of professing Christians eligible for baptism? If so, how do we define "professing Christians"? Again, on what grounds then do we baptize females? They were not circumcised. It is no answer here to switch over to matters of proselyte baptism;[1] on the analogy of baptism and circumcision they ought not to be baptized.

Our conclusion, therefore, is that although there is a similarity between baptism and circumcision, it is more in the nature of an afterthought,[2] and much too slender to support the structure it is to-day called upon to bear. To press such a similarity too far may be very dangerous, and the analogy is more wisely used in support of arguments already established on other grounds. Under the new covenant, union with Christ did away with the need for circumcision, and created the need for something to bring home to a man his union with Christ and the realization that he was possessed by Christ's spirit. It was this need which was filled by baptism.

B. *Ritual Cleansings and Proselyte Baptism*

1. In the Old Testament, "uncleanness" could be the result of a number of factors.[3] Originally it had no moral content. "Purification" was the removal of a ceremonial taint by ceremonial means, for which water was frequently used.[4]

---

[1] T. F. Torrance ("The Origin of Baptism", in *S.J.Th.*, 11 (1958), 158-71) has recently tried to overcome this problem by saying that circumcision is one aspect of proselyte baptism, but this is not very convincing and will surely raise more problems than it solves.

[2] H. Martin, *loc. cit.*, 217ff.; H. H. Rowley, "The Origin and Meaning of Baptism", in *B.Q.*, xi (1942-45), 309ff.

[3] For a survey of these factors, see A. W. F. Blunt, "Clean and Unclean", in *H.D.B.* (One Volume), 144ff.

[4] Exod. 30: 19ff., Lev. 15: 5, 8, 13, 16; 16: 4, 26, 28.

E

With the development of ethical religion there is evidence to suggest that these lustrations developed a moral content,[1] though we must beware of making a distinction, such as would be quite alien to Jewish modes of thought,[2] between the exclusively ceremonial and the exclusively moral. The Jew did not attempt to determine where the ceremonial ended and the moral began. "The result of the inclusion of the moral in the sphere of the religious", according to G. F. Moore,[3] "is that the physical means efficacious in removing uncleanness are employed to purify a man from moral defilement, or to protect him against the consequences of his wrong doing." N. A. Dahl[4] admits that the whole system of purifications tended to lose its inner meaning in later Judaism, but maintains that the inner connection between cultus, moral and religious ideology had not been completely lost. On the contrary, there is then a tendency to give the ritual performances a symbolic meaning.

Against such a background, proselyte baptism is to be examined. Oesterley and Box[5] maintain that lustrations in the Old Testament had two main ideas: (a) cleansing, (b) total immersion in the cleansing element; it is further argued that Jewish baptism must therefore imply total immersion, and that in both cases the washing was intended to take away something that was offensive to God.

But it must be remembered that proselyte baptism was more than "another" lustration. It was an initiation ceremony, performed once only; it differed from other lustrations in that whereas they were performed in private, baptism took place before witnesses, being accompanied by a catechism and a solemn exhortation; furthermore, lustrations were self-administered, and baptism was administered by others.[6] As with lustrations, however, it is a

---

[1] W. F. Flemington (*The New Testament Doctrine of Baptism*, 3) cites a few examples.

[2] F. Gavin (*op. cit.*, 5ff.) has stressed the points that Jewish thought was radically non-dualistic, and that the Jew did not consciously separate "inner" and "outer", "ceremonial" and "moral". Cf. H. W. Robinson, *Redemption and Revelation*, 140f.; G. F. Moore, *History of Religions*, II, 43: D. Daube, *The New Testament and Rabbinic Judaism*, 107.

[3] *Op cit.*, 43.

[4] "The Origin of Baptism", in *Interpretationes Sigmundo Mowinckel Missae*, 40.

[5] *Op. cit.*, 256f.

[6] H. H. Rowley, "Jewish Proselyte Baptism", in *H.U.C.A.*, xv (1940), 313-34. Cf. T. F. Torrance, "Proselyte Baptism", in *N.T.S.*, i (1954), 150ff.

mistake to see it as purificatory rather than moral or spiritual; to do that is to rely on secondary evidence and has little bearing on the Judaism of New Testament times.[1]

Proselyte baptism therefore may be described as one of a number of Jewish lustrations, but one which transcends all others in its interpretation. In this sense it is the most likely place to look for a possible antecedent to Christian baptism, but before we discuss its meaning we must clarify our minds on the date of its inception.

The difficulty arises from the fact that there is little or no evidence for the baptism of proselytes prior to A.D. 65, when the Jews pronounced all Gentiles unclean and baptism became essential for all Gentiles passing over to Judaism. It has been argued,[2] therefore, that this is the origin of proselyte baptism, in which case it can only be an antecedent of Christian baptism if the institution of the latter be put quite late. The argument, however, has not been easily accepted.[3] H. H. Rowley[4] has produced some evidence for proselyte baptism before the destruction of the Temple, and L. Finkelstein[5] has questioned whether indeed it was the Synod of A.D. 65 which declared pagans levitically impure, or whether it was just that that conclave re-enacted many laws and gave sanction to many customs which had been prevalent before it. It is an issue which cannot be decided for certain on the evidence in our possession, but the general trend among scholars to-day is to accept the view that proselyte baptism was commonly accepted before the Christian era,[6]

---

[1] D. Daube, *op. cit.*, 106f.

[2] S. Zeitlin, "Studies in the Beginning of Christianity", in *J.Q.R.*, xiv (1923-24), 131, and "The Halaka in the Gospels and its relation to the Jewish Law at the time of Jesus", in *H.U.C.A.*, i (1924), 359.

[3] An early opponent was J. Starr ("The Unjewish Character of the Markan account of John the Baptist", in *J.B.L.*, 51 (1932), 231n.), who accused Zeitlin of ignoring certain evidence. Cf. L. Finkelstein, "The Institution of Baptism for Proselytes", in *J.B.L.*, 52 (1933), 203ff.

[4] "Jewish Proselyte Baptism", in *H.U.C.A.*, xv (1940), 316. Cf. G. F. Moore, *Judaism*, III, 110.

[5] *Loc. cit.*, 203-11. Cf. H. H. Rowley, "Jewish Proselyte Baptism", in *H.U.C.A.*, xv (1940), 317ff.

[6] As early as 1887, this view was upheld by A. Edersheim (*The Life and Times of Jesus the Messiah*, II, Appendix xii, 747), who believed that, in spite of certain arguments to the contrary, this opinion was now established. The strength of Edersheim's position is seen from the fact that S. Schechter ("Some Rabbinic Parallels to the New Testament", in *J.Q.R.*, xii (1899-1900), 421) and M. Dods ("Baptism", in *H.D.C.G.*, I, 168b), do not even hint that the matter is in doubt. I. Abrahams (*Studies in Pharisaism and the Gospels*, 36) admits

and was in fact the antecedent of the baptism of John. It is indeed difficult to accept the only alternative, that the Jews took the ceremony over from the Christians and adapted it to suit their purposes.

Our intention therefore is to examine the nature and meaning of Jewish proselyte baptism, and then to consider its connection with, and possible influence on, Christian baptism. Jewish baptismal teaching may be conveniently summarized under five headings.

(a) *It was for convinced and instructed converts, and it was a witnessed ceremony.* It was one of three rites that admitted Gentiles to the "Covenant People",[1] all of which stress the element of conviction since it is impossible to imagine a Gentile undergoing them without knowing what he was doing, or entering into them without wishing to do so. This is not to say that children were not baptized, for the corporate nature of the family demanded that when a Gentile accepted baptism and became a Jew, all his family accepted baptism and became Jews also. There were, however, two important qualifications:

(i) children born subsequently were not baptized at all.

(ii) children baptized as members of a proselyte family, and not of their own volition, retained the right to renounce the engagement entered into on their behalf as soon as they reached years of maturity, and such a child was not regarded as properly an Israelite until he had attained his majority.[2]

Moreover, instruction and examination were both part

---

the point cannot be proved, but sees no reason to doubt it. Even when the debate between Zeitlin and his opponents was in progress, A. Büchler ("The Levitical Impurity of the Gentiles in Palestine before the year 70", in *J.Q.R.*, xvii (1926-27), 15n.) had no hesitation in suggesting that its origin dated from *c.* A.D. 17-18, and F. Gavin (*op. cit.*, 85) even suggested that the practice grew up earlier than, but certainly by, the second century B.C. In more recent days, a similar view has been held by W. F. Flemington (*The New Testament Doctrine of Baptism*, 4ff.), H. H. Rowley ("Jewish Proselyte Baptism", in *H.U.C.A.*, xv (1940), 320), H. G. Marsh (*The Origin and Significance of New Testament Baptism*, 7ff.), and T. F. Torrance ("Proselyte Baptism", in *N.T.S.*, i (1954), 154), and taken for granted by O. Cullmann (*op. cit.*, 9, 25, 56, 62f., 65), and T. W. Manson (*The Servant Messiah*, 42ff.). Suspicions are, however, cast on this view by W. Brandt (*op. cit.*, 59), J. Thomas *op. cit.*, 366), and T. M. Taylor ("The Beginnings of Jewish Proselyte Baptism", in *N.T.S.*, ii (1956), 193-98).

[1] Cf. H. G. Marsh, *op. cit.*, 7, J. Juster, *Les Juifs dans l'Empire Romain*, I, 255, n. 1., and W. O. E. Oesterley and G. H. Box, *op. cit.*, 255.

[2] For fuller details of these points, see H. H. Rowley, "Jewish Proselyte Baptism", in *H.U.C.A.*, xv (1940), 321, and "The Origin and Meaning of Baptism", in *B.Q.*, xi (1942-45), 310f.

of the baptismal act,[1] which must be performed in the presence of witnesses.

It is therefore obvious that the elements of conviction and understanding played a vital part in the ceremony.

(*b*) *It was an initiation ceremony, marking a break with the old life, and a joyful acceptance of the new.*[2] The evidence for the idea of initiation is threefold:

(i) it was demanded of all who entered upon the Jewish way of life, but not for those born into Jewish families.

(ii) unlike other Jewish lustrations it could not be repeated.

(iii) once a candidate had undergone the ceremony, he was regarded as "a new-born child",[3] and he acquired a new status before God and before Israel.[4]

(*c*) *It was an act of dedication.* For the Gentile convert, baptism was an act of total dedication to the God of Israel.[5] The totality of the dedication is revealed, to some extent, by the rules governing the amount of water to be used; it must be sufficient to admit of total immersion,[6] and it is equally essential that every part of the body shall reach the water.[7] Hence, just as nothing is kept back from the water, so nothing is kept back from God.

(*d*) *It carried with it the idea of cleansing.*[8] The purpose of Jewish lustrations, as we have seen, was to obliterate uncleanness, and Oesterley and Box[9] maintain that if such

[1] A full account of the pattern of instruction is found in D. Daube, *op. cit.*, Pt. II, ch. v, "A Baptismal Catechism". Cf. A. Seeberg, *Die Didache des Judentums und der Urchristenheit*, 1.

[2] In the east, water was traditionally a symbol of separation. Cf. F. W. Dillistone, *op. cit.*, 197ff.

[3] D. Daube, *op. cit.*, 112. Cf. F. W. Dillistone, *op. cit.*, 185.

[4] F. Gavin, *op. cit.*, 52.

[5] H. H. Rowley, "Jewish Proselyte Baptism", in *H.U.C.A.*, xv (1940), 327.

[6] W. O. E. Oesterley and G. H. Box (*op. cit.*, 256), and H. H. Rowley ("Jewish Proselyte Baptism", in *H.U.C.A.*, xv (1940), 323ff.), claim that Jewish baptism is always by total immersion. Cf. F. Gavin, *op. cit.*, 37. C. F. Rogers ("How did the Jews baptize?" in *J.T.S.*, 12 (1911), 437-45, and 13 (1912), 411-14, and in "Baptism and Christian Archaeology", in *Studia Biblica et Ecclesiastica*, v, 239-57) has challenged this view, but he has been adequately answered by I. Abrahams ("How did the Jews baptize?" in *J.T.S.*, 12 (1911), 609-12). For further evidence see D. Daube, *op. cit.*, 111f.

[7] H. H. Rowley, "Jewish Proselyte Baptism", in *H.U.C.A.*, xv (1940), 322; I. Abrahams, "How did the Jews baptize"? in *J.T.S.*, 12 (1911), 611; and F. Gavin, *op. cit.*, 46f.

[8] For the connection between water and cleansing, see F. W. Dillistone, *op. cit.*, 193.

[9] *Op. cit.*, 256.

washings were frequently necessary for Jews, then it would indeed be surprising if there were not some ceremony which was, among other things, an initial purificatory act for Gentiles becoming Jews. The dangers of interpreting baptism in terms of lustrations have been pointed out by H. H. Rowley[1] and must not be disregarded. It is indeed a mistake to see baptism as cleansing and nothing more, but that cleansing is included in it can scarcely be doubted.

(e) *It was more than a symbol or declaration; it was an effective sign.* Oesterley and Box[2] have carefully examined the sacramental nature of Jewish washings in relation to sin, and believe that since washing does, in a sense, effect a reconciliation, it is therefore a sacrament. Similarly they regard the baptism of John and of the Essenes as sacramental. Yet they do not believe that proselyte baptism was sacramental, though logically it ought to have been. The reason that it was not was that when the Jews learned more of God they saw that the sacramental idea was partly crass and they cast it away, losing the truth germ with it.

This attitude is very puzzling and raises certain problems,[3] but H. H. Rowley[4] suggests that what Oesterley and Box mean is that baptism for the Jew was not an *ex opere operato* rite, mediating grace automatically. In the case of the true proselyte, he believes there can be no doubt that the Jews saw the ceremony as mediating grace, in which case the act of baptism completed the work of faith and mediated admission into the elect community. Conversion was not reckoned as conversion until it was completed in baptism. Whether this *is* what Oesterley and Box mean may be questioned; that it accords more readily with such evidence as we possess is unquestionable.

Such are the salient features of Jewish proselyte baptism. We must now examine the baptism of John against this background.

2. Our two sources for the life and work of John the Baptist

---

[1] "Jewish Proselyte Baptism", in *H.U.C.A.*, xv (1940), 314ff., "The Origin and Meaning of Baptism", in *B.Q.*, xi (1942-45), 309f., and *The Unity of the Bible*, 151ff.

[2] *Op. cit.*, 257ff.

[3] For instance, was immersion therefore really important? Why did the sacramental element come to the fore again in John?

[4] "Jewish Proselyte Baptism", in *H.U.C.A.*, xv (1940), 327ff.

are the New Testament[1] and Josephus,[2] though new evidence is constantly coming to the fore from an examination of the Dead Sea Scrolls.[3] Apart from certain elements which Josephus omits, both main sources paint substantially the same picture. There is also good reason to believe that the Synoptists' accounts are the most reliable, so that the relatively minor differences need not deter us.[4]

There are certain obvious similarities between John's baptism and the baptism of proselytes.

(a) Both involved total immersion. It is generally agreed that John followed the most likely Jewish custom.[5]

(b) Both were administered, and not performed by the subject himself. This point has been queried by some[6] who have tried to maintain that proselyte baptism was self-administered, but such a claim is not proven. Moreover, this argument is only one of a number, and it would not be surprising that John should have a share in the administration since he was baptizing in his own right, regardless of what was the Jewish custom. I. Abrahams,[7] at any rate, is content to accept the similarity.

(c) *Neither ceremony could be repeated.*[8] In the light of these similarities, therefore, and bearing in mind that John was brought up to take the baptism of proselytes for granted, it is not difficult to believe that in a moment of inspiration he modelled his act of baptism on the mode of baptism that he knew, adapting it and adjusting it to meet his needs. Much has been lost, however, because such adaptation has been overlooked with the result that the uniqueness of

---

[1] Matt. 3: 1-12, Mark 1: 1-8, Luke 3: 1-17, John 1: 7, 15, 19-34.

[2] *Antiquities*, XVIII, 5, 2.

[3] This evidence has been presented, for example, by W. H. Brownlee ("John the Baptist in the New Light of Ancient Scrolls", in *Interpretation*, ix (1955), 71-90, and revised and reprinted in K. Stendahl (ed.), *The Scrolls and the New Testament*. 33-53), and the implications examined by J. A. T. Robinson ("The Baptism of John and the Qumran Community", in *H.T.R.*, 50 (1957), 175-91).

[4] T. W. Manson (*op. cit.*, 39), H. G. Marsh (*op. cit.*, 49), and W. F. Flemington (*The New Testament Doctrine of Baptism*, 23f.), all deal with these differences and their significance.

[5] I. Abrahams, *Studies in Pharisaism and the Gospels*, 38.

[6] W. F. Flemington, *The New Testament Doctrine of Baptism*, 16f., and Vincent Taylor, *The Gospel According to St. Mark*, 155.

[7] *Studies in Pharisaism and the Gospels*, 38.

[8] I. Abrahams, *ibid.*, 42; T. W. Manson, *op. cit.*, 43; H. G. Marsh, *op. cit.*, 45, 56; and Vincent Taylor, *The Life and Ministry of Jesus*, 47.

John's baptism has not been fully brought out.[1] Moreover, the evidence collected from Qumran helps to explain and interpret some of these changes and adaptations, if it can be assumed that John had had some connection with this community.[2] To such modifications we must now turn.

(a) *John's baptism was public, whereas proselyte baptism was private.* It is true that proselyte baptism had to be administered in the presence of witnesses, and that provisions were made against clandestiny, but the purpose of the witnesses was to be a guardian of correct procedure; it was their job to examine the candidate and satisfy themselves that he was sincere in what he was doing. John's baptism, on the other hand, was a public declaration of repentance in the presence of all the people. On examination, however, it will be seen that the modification is due to the emphasis in the message which John preached. In Jewish baptism people were passing from one creed to another and must therefore be examined; in John's baptism they were simply resolving to be better than they had been before, and of such there could be no examination; there would only be a profession. This difference, therefore, rather suggests that John took the familiar rite and made of it what his message required.[3]

(b) *John's baptism symbolized a change of heart, whereas proselyte baptism symbolized a change of creed.* This is more forcefully stated by those who say that John's baptism was moral, and proselyte baptism was ceremonial, but it has been shown[4] that the latter is not a fair description of Jewish baptism. What we have here is probably no more than a difference of emphasis. In the case of the proselyte the uppermost thought was his changed relationship to Judaism; for John, the uppermost thought was the candidate's changed relationship to God. The ceremonial has receded into the background, the moral has come to the fore.[5]

[1] This point is adequately examined and dealt with by J. Thomas, *op. cit.*, 85-88.

[2] This assumption is now made by a good many scholars: e.g. F. F. Bruce, *Second Thoughts on the Dead Sea Scrolls*, 128ff.

[3] This possibility is acknowledged by H. H. Rowley ("The Origin and Meaning of Baptism", in *B.Q.*, xi (1942-45), 309-10).

[4] I. Abrahams (*Studies in Pharisaism and the Gospels*, 39-41), and H. H. Rowley ("Jewish Proselyte Baptism", in *H.U.C.A.*, xv (1940), 332f.), who answers the arguments of J. Starr (*loc. cit.*, 232).

[5] This explanation is accepted by W. F. Flemington, *The New Testament Doctrine of Baptism*, 16f.

The bridge between these two viewpoints is perhaps provided by some evidence from the Dead Sea Scrolls,[1] where it is stated that "perverse men" shall not enter the water, since they will not be cleansed until they have turned from their wickedness. N. A. Dahl[2] takes this to mean that the ablutions will not profit a man as long as he has not really repented, and sees in it a parallel to the severe words of John the Baptist to the multitude (Luke 3: 7-9). Moreover, there is other evidence that Qumran saw baptism as representing a decisive break for the individual, who in the act repudiated his former association with a corrupt world and offered himself to a new purity.[3] So that if John, as is suspected, had had associations with the community of Qumran, this adaptation of proselyte baptism becomes meaningful and intelligible.

(c) *John's baptism has an eschatological association, marking initiation to a new age which John believed was on the point of being established.*[4] Proselyte baptism began and ended in time; John's baptism looked forward to the dawn of the Messianic age, and sought to prepare people for it.[5]

Certainly this is a new feature, but surely one which is quite understandable when we remember that John's whole purpose was to prepare people for the coming of the Messiah. Just as proselyte baptism initiated Gentiles to Judaism, so John wanted to initiate all who were repentant into the Messianic community. When the Messiah came He would gather together those initiates as the true sons of Abraham. But there is also here again a similarity between John's "new note" and the covenanters of Qumran and Damascus,[6] and if John had had contact with them his changed approach becomes all the more understandable, for they too saw baptism as a means of preparing

---

[1] *Manual of Discipline*, 5. 10ff.
[2] *Loc. cit.*, 43. Cf. R. E. Murphy, *The Dead Sea Scrolls and the Bible*, 61.
[3] J. A. T. Robinson, *loc. cit.*, 182f.
[4] H. H. Rowley, "Jewish Proselyte Baptism", in *H.U.C.A.*, xv (1940), 333f., *The Unity of the Bible*, 153f.; Vincent Taylor, *The Gospel According to St. Mark*, 155; H. G. Marsh, *op. cit.*, 23ff.; W. F. Flemington, *The New Testament Doctrine of Baptism*, 17.
[5] T. W. Manson, *op. cit.*, 45.
[6] Cf. N. A. Dahl, *loc. cit.*, 44, and R. E. Murphy, *op. cit.*, 61. J. A. T. Robinson (*loc. cit.*, 183-85) points out that this eschatological note is not found in proselyte baptism, or in any other of the baptist sects, but that it is found in Qumran whose members saw themselves as a community whose function was to lay a foundation of truth for Israel.

a nucleus in Israel for a baptism still to come. It was on these grounds that John applied his baptism to Jews as well as to Gentiles, thereby abandoning completely the racial qualification and substituting for it the requirement of repentance and faith. No longer was it sufficient to be a descendant of Abraham; to be a true offspring one must also have faith.

Our conclusion, therefore, is that of all possible antecedents to John's baptism, that of proselyte baptism is the most likely, for the essential ideas of the two are closely similar,[1] and where they differ it is clearly in order to clarify the essential message of John; but there is also a strong possibility that John's adaptations of the rite arose more or less directly from the teaching of the community in Qumran.

We must now consider the relevance of both these rites to Christian baptism.

3. Already it will have been obvious to the reader that there are certain points of resemblance between proselyte baptism and John's baptism on the one hand, and proselyte baptism and Christian baptism on the other. But it is just not possible to take out of these older rites what we would like to find there, or to wear such spectacles that we only see what we are looking for. For example, if we are going to argue that children of Christians should be baptized because children of proselytes were baptized, then we must also argue that Christian children born subsequent to their parents' conversion should not be baptized because the proselytes' children born subsequent to their parents' conversion were not baptized. This point cannot really be over-emphasized, for it is one of the chief points where the oft-drawn analogy between proselyte baptism and Christian baptism breaks down; yet although it has been frequently put forward, and by no less a person than H. H. Rowley,[2] it has never really been satisfactorily answered. Indeed, the way in which it is ignored rather suggests that a satisfactory answer is not to be found.

Christian baptism is not just a "child" of John's baptism, in the sense that once you can understand the parent you can also understand the offspring. What we have to face, rather, is the fact that here we have three ceremonies,

---

[1] N. A. Dahl, 43f. Cf. H. G. Marsh, *op. cit.*, 65.　　　[2] *The Unity of the Bible*, 160.

outwardly very similar, and all growing up probably in less than a hundred years' time. Since it is unlikely that these rites would be deliberately copied from one another, it is more reasonable to suppose that they grew up side by side, influencing one another almost unconsciously.

If, then, this was the milieu in which Christian baptism was nurtured, there are certain questions to do with Christian baptism about which we must make up our mind.

(*a*) How far does Christian baptism signify a change of heart and how far a change of creed? Proselyte baptism put the emphasis on the creed, and John's baptism put it on the heart. Is it possible to find a combination of both in Christian baptism, finding its *raison d'être* in a change of heart, and resulting in a change of creed? If it is, then the wheel has gone full circle.

(*b*) The only instances of the baptism of children from this early and formative period are the baptism of the children of proselytes; in all other cases, baptism was of responsible people. If this implies that Christian baptism is for believers only, then we must determine the place of children in the church, especially the children of Christian parentage.[1]

(*c*) We have shown how both proselyte baptism and John's baptism were by total immersion in order to symbolize total dedication. It is unlikely that the Christian would be any less diligent in expressing the totality of his dedication than was his Jewish counterpart. If therefore he retained the idea of dedication with its current expression, it is surely a matter of importance that this idea and expression should still be with us.

These are not questions which can be wholly settled by a study of Jewish antecedents. Many other influences combined with these to make Christian baptism what it is. But if we are to acknowledge that it grew up in this setting, then these are matters which no student of baptism can afford to ignore.

C. *Prophetic Symbolism*

1. No reader of the Old Testament can overlook the way in which the prophets were given to acts which in some way symbolized the message they had to proclaim. Some of the

---

[1] This point is taken up in Chapter 8. Cf. *infra*, 310ff., 321ff.

most obvious examples are to be found in the major prophets,[1] and if we begin by examining those we shall discover five principal characteristics.[2]

(*a*) Each act is the result of a direct command by Yahweh[3] and, when performed, is normally accompanied by a "Thus saith the Lord". This characteristic is important because it makes clear the distinction between prophetic symbolism and primitive magic. In the case of magic, the aim is to change the will of God; in the case of the symbolism of the prophets the aim is to reveal the will of God and to help it to become effective.[4]

(*b*) Each symbolic act performed bears a resemblance to the event symbolized.

(*c*) Each act is accompanied by a word of explanation, so that there is no danger of its being misunderstood.

(*d*) Once performed, the fulfilment of the prophecy contained in the symbolic act is inevitable.[5] This is not to say that the act brings about the fulfilment altogether, neither is it to suggest that the prophets had power over God Himself or over the natural forces of the world. The inevitable fulfilment is to be attributed rather to the fact that the prophet spoke and acted only when so commanded by Yahweh. Consequently, the event was certain when the prophet spoke: what he did was to reveal it as the will of God. Yet it was more than just *mere* revelation, for, as H. W. Robinson[6]

[1] Is. 20; Jer. 18-19, 28-29; Ezek. 4: 1-3, 4-8, 9-13; 5: 12, 24. Less obvious examples include the names which Isaiah gave to his children and the marriage of Hosea. Cf. W. F. Lofthouse, "Thus hath Yahweh said", in *A.J.S.L.*, 40 (1923-24), 231-51.

[2] Similar investigations with similar results have been made by F.-J. Leenhardt, *Le Baptême chrétien*, 12, and G. Fohrer, "Die Gattung der Berichte über symbolische Handlungen der Propheten", in *Z.A.W.*, 64 (1952), 101-20, and *Die Symbolische Handlungen der Propheten*.

[3] H. W. Robinson, "Hebrew Sacrifice and Prophetic Symbolism", in *J.T.S.*, 43 (1942), 136. Cf. F. W. Dillistone, *op. cit.*, 148.

[4] For fuller explanation concerning the distinction between prophetic symbolism and magic, see H. W. Robinson, "Hebrew Sacrifice and Prophetic Symbolism", in *J.T.S.*, 43 (1942), 132; "Prophetic Symbolism", in *Old Testament Essays* (1927), 15; *Redemption and Revelation*, 250; H. H. Rowley, "The Nature of Prophecy in the Light of Recent Study", in *H.T.R.*, xxxviii (1945), 29 (and reprinted in H. H. Rowley, *The Servant of the Lord*, 119); *The Faith of Israel*, 27f.; and F. Gavin, *op. cit.*, 19.

[5] L. H. Brockington, "'The Lord Shewed Me': the Correlation of Natural and Spiritual in Prophetic Experience", in E. A. Payne (ed.), *Studies in History and Religion*, 39.

[6] *Old Testament Essays* (1927), 15, "Hebrew Sacrifice and Prophetic Symbolism", in *J.T.S.*, 43 (1942), 129-39. For the same idea and its implications, see

has pointed out, the prophetic act is part of the will of Yahweh, to whose complete fulfilment it points. It brings that will nearer to its completion, not only by declaring it, but in some small degree by effecting it.

(*e*) These prophecies are invariably prophecies of doom, though provision is made for one event which can avert the fulfilment of the prophecy. That one event is a change of heart on the part of the people. If the prophecy were one of blessing, then nothing could avert its fulfilment.[1]

If we move outside the writings of the major prophets, we soon find further examples of this kind of prophetic activity. Broadly speaking, however, such cases fall into two main classes:

(*a*) *Those which closely approximate to the prophetic symbolism of the major prophets.* The incident of Elisha wounded (1 Kings 20: 35ff.), for instance, bears all the marks of later prophetic symbolism, except that the actual resemblance between the symbol and the thing symbolized is a little more remote. In other instances we find this kind of symbolism associated with good prophecies, as well as with prophecies of doom (e.g. 1 Kings 22: 11, 2 Kings 13: 16), or where the fulfilment is not strictly inevitable but depending on some future action (e.g. 1 Kings 22: 11), or where the command of Yahweh is not quite clear (e.g. 2 Kings 13: 16). Such instances, it will be noticed, are all prior to the major prophets, and may well be the work of the forerunners of the later and more established method.

(*b*) *Those which scarcely approximate to the prophetic symbolism of the major prophets at all, but which do approximate to the practice of mimetic magic.* Examples of this kind include Exod. 9: 8ff., Josh. 8: 18ff., 1 Kings 18: 42ff., 2 Kings 4: 4ff., but in every case several features of the symbolism of the later prophets are absent. Moreover, in these instances, the prophet was not so much concerned to proclaim to the people what Yahweh had declared, as he was to bring about what he believed Yahweh's purpose to be. The underlying principle

H. H. Rowley, "The Nature of Prophecy in the Light of Recent Study", in *H.T.R.*, xxxviii (1945), 28 (and reprinted in H. H. Rowley, *The Servant of the Lord*, 89-128); N. H. Snaith, *Mercy and Sacrifice*, 33; F. W. Dillistone, *op. cit.*, 275f.; W. M. Clow, *The Church and the Sacraments*, 69. The effectiveness of the act is actually illustrated by L. H. Brockington, *loc. cit.*, 40.

[1] F. W. Dillistone, *op. cit.*, 148.

here is that "like produces like", and we are therefore more in the realm of primitive magic than in the realm of prophetic symbolism.[1] Again, however, it will have been observed that in this group we have moved back in time one stage further still. Probably it was from these humble beginnings that the symbolism of the later prophets developed, but that being the case we must beware of judging the later development by the source from which it sprang. H. W. Robinson[2] admits that prophetic symbolism may have originated in magic, but he is quick to add that it was sublimated by the faith of the prophets.

Side by side with this development in symbolism there went on also a certain transformation in the Jewish attitude to sacramental teaching. According to Oesterley and Box[3] the Jews had no sacramental teaching. These authors agree, as we have seen, that God revealed Himself to all tribes in some measure, and that in consequence all tribes had their sacraments in primitive form; in some cases, so primitive that we call it magic. As man learned more of God, he realized that the sacraments were partly crass, though they contained some truth. In this situation, the Jew discarded the crass and lost the truth germ with it. Hence the absence of sacramental teaching among the Jews, and the reason why baptism for them was not a sacrament.

Yet it would seem that the truth germ was not entirely lost, and is to be found to some extent in the symbolism of the major prophets, which holds an intermediate place between the imitative magic of primitive peoples and the sacramentalism of the New Testament.[4]

This interpretation also fits in with that of F. Gavin,[5] who insists that the Jews did have some sacramental teaching though it was rudimentary and germinal. It was not set out openly because the Jew was not given to theological formulation, but it meant that the relation between God and

[1] W. O. E. Oesterley and T. H. Robinson (*Hebrew Religion*, 75ff.) cite several instances where mimetic magic is to be found in the Old Testament including Exod. 9: 8ff. and 1 Kings 18: 42ff.

[2] "Hebrew Sacrifice and Prophetic Symbolism", in *J.T.S.*, 43 (1942), 129-39.

[3] *Op. cit.*, 258ff.

[4] H. W. Robinson, "Prophetic Symbolism", in *Old Testament Essays* (1927), 2.

[5] *Op. cit.*, 3ff.

the Israelite could be changed by means of the proper performance of a rite, believed to be divinely ordained, utilizing material means. This must surely include the symbolism of the prophets and is in harmony with the general pattern of development we have made out.

We must now consider the connection of John the Baptist with the practice of prophetic symbolism.

2. According to the New Testament, John is regarded as the last and the greatest in the line of succession of the Old Testament prophets.[1] The description that is given of him suggests the Old Testament prophets,[2] and T. W. Manson[3] uses Luke 3: 2 to show that John received a prophetic "call". His message, moreover, is closely allied to theirs, partly in that it had about it the same sense of urgency and partly in that, like theirs, it was a call to action. This call to action was also preceded by a pronouncement of judgment which would most certainly overtake his hearers unless they changed their way of life and so averted the coming disaster.[4]

If, however, John is to be linked with the prophets of the Old Testament in this way there can be no doubt that he goes beyond them in that he brings together his call to moral renewal and his announcement of the coming of the Messiah, and then calls upon the people to express their repentance by taking part in the symbolic act of baptism by immersion. In this symbol, according to C. K. Barrett,[5] both notes of his preaching are brought together: the repentance was to be sealed in baptism, and the prophecy of the One who was to come was also conceived in terms of baptism. Such a view upset the current popular notion that the coming of the Messiah would herald the dawn of a new age for all who could claim their descent from Abraham, and substituted for it the promise of a bright future for all who could show the fruits of repentance.

[1] His greatness is recognized by the nation as a whole (Matt. 14: 5; 21: 26; Mark 11: 32; Luke 20: 6), and testimony to the extent of that greatness is borne by Jesus Himself (Matt. 11: 9ff.; Luke 7: 26ff.).

[2] Cf. 2 Kings 1: 8; Zech. 13: 4; Mal. 3: 1. These comparisons are brought out by A. W. F. Blunt, *St. Mark*, Clarendon Bible, 134; C. K. Barrett, *The Holy Spirit and the Gospel Tradition*, 28; and W. F. Flemington, *The New Testament Doctrine of Baptism*, 14.

[3] *Op. cit.*, 38.

[4] Cf. Vincent Taylor, *The Life and Ministry of Jesus*, 46, C. K. Barrett, *op. cit.*, 29.

[5] *Op. cit.*, 29f.

Because of John's connection with the prophets, however, and because he employs symbolic actions to reinforce his message, we are justified in asking how far his symbolism is in line with the symbolism of the major prophets. Remembering that prophetic symbolism itself developed in the Old Testament, and remembering how John's message goes further than that of the major prophets, it would not be surprising if we found also certain new developments in his symbols. But we must recall the main features and examine them.

Sufficient has been said to indicate John's oneness with the Old Testament prophets on the question of judgment and repentance, and although we have no actual evidence that he declared that his utterances were the direct oracles of God before he began to baptize, we have seen how, like his predecessors, he had a "call" to prophecy, and we may well regard our Lord's participation in his baptism as Divine confirmation of what he was doing. This covers features (*e*) and (*a*) respectively, and on them no more need be said.

But what are we to say of the resemblance between the symbolic act and the event symbolized? (Feature "b".) The note of urgency in John's message finds expression in the instant baptism of those who accept it: the picture we are given is that of a multitude, listening to this energetic and forceful preacher, and coming forward one by one as the veil falls from their eyes and they see the urgency of his word.

The most important element of John's message, however, and one of its two new aspects, is his call to moral renewal. No longer can salvation come through membership of a tribe or nation, but only through a change of heart.[1] The people who accept this aspect of John's teaching must cut adrift from the old by repentance, and take up the new, and such an acceptance must find its expression in a changed life. All this was adequately symbolized in baptism, partly because washing in water was an accepted means of signifying inner cleanliness among the Jews, and partly because it was associated in people's minds with a new beginning.

The other new note in John's teaching was his emphasis on the future and the One who should come after him. Here

[1] T. W. Manson, *op. cit.*, 44f.

again, the symbol, like the Word, points forward, and it was John's intention to bring together a group of people who had undergone an experience of repentance, and who had expressed that common experience in a common rite. Symbol and event were obviously very closely allied in John's mind.

There is, however, one vital difference between John's symbolism and the symbolism of the prophets, and it should be mentioned at this juncture. It is the fact that he invited others to join with him in performing the symbol; the success of what he did depended on the extent of the co-operation which he got from his hearers. At first sight, this appears to put John's symbolism in a quite different class, but on reflection it will be seen that this new element serves rather to enhance the significance of features (c) and (d).

Because John invites the co-operation of his hearers, the word of explanation which normally accompanied the prophet's symbol assumes a new importance. In the case of the prophet, the word of explanation was intended to help the hearers to understand what the prophet was saying, but in the case of John it was the *sine qua non* of the people's response. No one could intelligently partake of John's rite except he knew what John intended by it, and so it is accompanied by John's interpretation (Luke 3: 7-14), giving one or two examples of what he understands by moral renewal. If this is the kind of thing that went on on the banks of the Jordan then there can be no doubt that the people who co-operated with John understood what they were about.

Similarly, the fact of intelligent co-operation from the people leads to the increased efficacy of the rite. In the case of the prophets, the fulfilment of the act was inevitable because the act was part of the revealed will of God. In the case of John, the fulfilment of the act was inevitable because it was part of the revealed will of God *and men were seeking to co-operate with Him.*

Our conclusion, therefore, is that John the Baptist undoubtedly stands in the prophetic tradition and that his symbolism approximates in most respects to that practised by his predecessors, but that to their conception he adds the idea of a co-operative people. This new idea we believe to be

F

demanded by the new aspect of his message and it is not surprising that it requires him to make certain other deviations from what we have regarded as the norm of the major prophets.

We must proceed next to consider the implications of this for our understanding of Christian baptism.

3. Theological conclusions about Christian baptism must not be drawn simply on the basis of Old Testament prophetic symbolism and John's baptism, but certain issues are raised in this way, which subsequent contributors may deal with from their particular angle.

(a) Is the *raison d'être* of baptism a command from God? Doubts may be cast on the authenticity of Matt. 28: 19,[1] but its very existence does testify to the fact that the early apostles believed that they had the authority of God for what they did and no branch of the church believes that she has any less a mandate than had the apostles. At the same time, we must not take anything for granted. It was not enough that the prophet received a command; he must do just what he was commanded. So our first task must be to ensure that we have the authority of the Risen Lord for the baptism we perform.[2]

(b) If there is to be a connection between the symbolic act and the event symbolized, then it would appear that we have to determine the mode of baptism by its meaning. We must begin, therefore, by asking what we mean by baptism, and how far that meaning can be adequately symbolized. The answer to these questions may well lead to modifications in every branch of the church.

(c) Is the willing co-operation of the subject for baptism essential? The symbolism of the prophets became of non-effect if there were a change of attitude on the part of the people concerned as a result of which they repented and turned to the Lord. John's baptism was made of non-effect if those who were baptized went back on their baptism. We must make up our minds therefore what this means for Christians who are baptized. It implies that the rite can only

---

[1] Cf. H. H. Rowley, *The Unity of the Bible*, 167n. Kirsopp Lake, "Baptism (Early Christian)", in *E.R.E.*, II, 380-81, does not accept these as genuine words of Jesus, but P. W. Evans (*Sacraments in the New Testament*, 9ff.) defends them.

[2] Cf. W. F. Flemington, *The New Testament Doctrine of Baptism*, 30.

be performed satisfactorily where it is understood by the subject, and such an interpretation might well deliver us from an over-emphasis on *baptism* (by which it tends to be administered to all regardless of their ability to appreciate it), and also from an over-emphasis on *conversion* (by which baptism tends to become a mere declaration or ratification of something which has already happened).

(*d*) Do we believe that Christian baptism is a mere demonstration, simply declaring what God has done in Christ, or does it actually help the will of God towards its fulfilment? If it does, then we are bound to face up to the question of what happens when it is not performed.

(*e*) Is baptism an act of initiation, bringing together the disciples of Jesus, in the same way that John's disciples united in a common experience those who wished to prepare themselves for the coming of the Messiah?

(*f*) John gave some examples of the ethical implications of moral renewal and baptism; are there not, then, ethical implications for Christians as a result of their baptism, and, if there are, how are they to be defined?

If some of our conclusions appear to be in the form of a question, it must be remembered that our assignment was to consider these antecedents of Christian baptism to see what they meant and what their implications were. Besides raising these issues, the antecedents to which we have referred do inevitably suggest certain lines along which the answers are to be found, but the answers themselves must come from the New Testament and the early church. Our chief concern has been, as it were, to hang up a "back-cloth" against which Christian baptism may be seen. As we proceed it may be that we shall find certain features of that "back-cloth" merging imperceptibly into the general picture.

BAPTISM IN THE NEW TESTAMENT

A. THE BAPTISM OF JESUS

by R. E. O. White

IT is open to question whether, if Jesus Himself had not been baptized, baptism would ever have become a Christian sacrament; but it is certain that any form of the rite which did persist would have possessed a very different nature and import. The essential difference between John's version of proselyte baptism and Christian baptism as we meet it in Acts *is* the baptism of Jesus.

The Evangelists are as agreed about the main elements of the story as they are about its importance. Mark makes the simple statement of fact that Jesus came and was baptized; Matthew says this was the purpose for which Jesus journeyed "from Galilee to the Jordan to John" (3: 13); but Luke announces the event in a curiously incidental fashion: "Now when all the people were baptized, and when Jesus also had been baptized and was praying, the heaven was opened . . ." (3: 21). Much has been made of this odd mode of expression, to suggest that Luke desired to "slur over something inconsistent with his account of Jesus' birth"; or that Luke did not regard the baptism as the supreme experience which the theory of endowment would suggest; or, as O. Cullmann held, it is Luke's own way of emphasizing that the baptism of Jesus was vicarious. "It is clear . . . why Jesus must conduct himself like other people. He is distinguished from the mass of other baptized people, who are baptized for their own sins, as the One . . . who suffers *for all others*."[1] A.

---

[1] O. Cullmann, *Baptism in the New Testament*, 18; cf. J. Denney, "Holy Spirit", in *H.D.C.G.*, i, 732; H. G. Marsh, *The Origin and Significance of New Testament Baptism*, 103.

Plummer[1] thought that Luke meant to imply that Jesus was baptized alone, when the crowd had departed, but he adds, "It is as if the baptism of all the people were regarded as carrying with it the baptism of Jesus almost as a necessary complement." It will be contended below that Luke regarded Jesus' baptism as a perfectly natural and inevitable act which only the accompanying phenomena made in any way remarkable. Apart from the very debatable passage in Matthew 3: 14, 15 there is no attempt anywhere in Scripture to explain *why* Jesus was baptized; explanation was unnecessary.

Whether or not the actual immersion was self-administered, the presence of the Rabbi (in the case of proselyte baptism) and of the prophet (in the case of Johannine baptism) was necessary in order to give validity to the rite. The relation between baptized and baptizer (the "father of baptism") could be construed as that between lesser and greater, pupil and master, and it is probable that this conception governs the representation of Christ's baptism in the Fourth Gospel, where the whole story is reconstructed to emphasize John's subordination to Jesus as a mere witness of the glory of the Messiah. This is also the clue to Matthew's addition to the common material at this point, an addition which has given rise to considerable confusion. Matthew records a reluctance on the part of John to baptize Jesus— "I have need to be baptized by you, and do you come to me?" (3: 14). W. F. Flemington[2] thinks this unhistorical, since there is no other hint in the Synoptists that John was yet conscious that the "mightier One" was Jesus: "The verses read like an early attempt to meet the objections of those who claimed that our Lord's submission to 'the baptism of repentance unto remission of sins' involved a tacit acknowledgment of wrongdoing". With almost all commentators, W. F. Flemington then quotes the *Gospel According to the Hebrews*[3] for evidence that the early church was concerned by the contradiction between Christ's sinlessness

[1] *St. Luke* (I.C.C.), *ad loc.*
[2] *The New Testament Doctrine of Baptism*, 26.
[3] Jerome, *Contra Pelag.*, iii. 2: "Behold, the Lord's mother and brethren said to Him, John the Baptist is baptizing unto the remission of sins: let us go and be baptized by him. Then He said unto them, What sin have I done that I should go and be baptized by him?—unless perchance this very saying of mine is a sin of ignorance."

and His repentance-baptism. W. F. Flemington himself thinks there is no contradiction, inasmuch as the baptism represented for Jesus identification with the people He came to save, not confession of any sin of His own; but the interpretation of the colloquy with John in the light of the puzzle about a sinless One repenting has the support of the majority of scholars.[1] T. W. Manson[2] sees two purposes in these verses, which he thinks are unhistorical: they "emphasize the subordination of John to Jesus . . . and attempt an answer to the question why Jesus undergoes a repentance-baptism if He is without sin".

Despite this array of scholarship, the interpretation offered remains singularly unconvincing. It appears impossible to decide upon the *historicity* of the conversation with John. In view of Mark's account of the Messianic secret (supported by the Fourth Gospel's insistence that only *after* the baptism did John recognize Jesus as Messiah), it is difficult to believe that John objected to baptizing Jesus because He was the Christ, and even more because He was sinless. Yet the incident is too difficult, the saying of Jesus too striking and too ambiguous, to read like the deliberate invention of the later community. If the story is true, we have to assume that John knew enough about Jesus to feel that the message of repentance or judgment was not for Him.

But the *meaning* of the conversation, for Matthew and the church, is less uncertain. It is hard to see how the question of Christ's sinlessness came to be intruded into the matter at all: the quotation from the *Gospel According to the Hebrews* indicates nothing of Matthew's intention, and while its answer to the problem, however unsatisfactory, is at least relevant, the same cannot be said about the answer Matthew supplies. "Thus it is fitting for us to fulfil all righteousness" (3: 15) does not in the least answer the question about the incongruity of sinless repentance. The truth is that if the story were invented by the church or by Matthew to reply to *this* difficulty, then it has simply piled problem upon problem: the issue at stake is not mentioned, the answer

[1] M. Dods, "Baptism", in *H.D.C.G.*, i, 170a; J. Denney, *The Death of Christ*, 18; *Jesus and the Gospel*, 199; G. H. Box, *St. Matthew* (Century Bible), 95; H. G. Marsh, *op. cit.*, 102; A. Plummer, *op. cit.*, 100; A. E. Rawlinson, *St. Mark* (Westminster Commentary), 251; O. Cullmann, *op. cit.*, 16.
[2] *The Sayings of Jesus*, 149.

given is irrelevant and almost unintelligible, and it is impossible to see what practical use the tradition would be in meeting the cavils of outsiders.

But there was, as we know, another question agitating the early church, to which the baptism of Jesus was acutely relevant: the relation of Jesus to John. When Matthew's words are closely attended, it becomes plain that the antithesis posed is precisely that between the two persons involved: "*I* need to be baptized by *you*, and do *you* come to *me*?" (3: 14). The question represented as troubling John's mind is the question of status, authority, the personal equation. The same point underlies the emphasis Matthew lays upon the words about the prophet's unworthiness to bear the sandals of Him who was to come: if this task is too great for John, how unthinkable it is that he should baptize Messiah![1] If this be the question at issue—who baptizes whom?—the answer attributed to Jesus gains more point: "the act being right, we shall not stay upon personal questions as to who shall perform it". If this be the meaning, we may conclude that Matthew's way of robbing the baptism of any implication of Jesus' subordination to John is neater, and closer to the earliest tradition, than that of the Fourth Gospel.[2]

This view has been propounded by A. Fridrichsen,[3] who maintains that the scandal of the baptism of Jesus is not to be found in His sinless submission to a baptism of repentance, but rather in the fact of the baptism of the Messiah by his Precursor; "that", says A. Fridrichsen, "is why John, instead of insisting on the sinlessness of Jesus, humiliates himself before Him, and protests his inferiority." G. Bornkamm[4] goes somewhat further and suggests that this

[1] *The Gospel of the Ebionites* (Epiphan. xxx. 13) says "John fell down before Jesus, and said: I pray Thee, Lord, baptize Thou me. But Jesus prevented him . . ." Cf. T. H. Robinson, *St. Matthew* (Moffatt Commentary), 17: the purpose of the dialogue "is clearly to show that John recognized Jesus. . . . When He who baptizes with the Holy Spirit comes, John has need to get baptized by Him." Cf. E. F. Scott, *The Fourth Gospel*, 77ff.; Luke 16: 16.

[2] It is not denied that in the total context of theology Christ's baptism does raise the problem of sinless-repentance; and indeed the problem of the divine Sonship. It is contended merely that these problems are not present in this passage.

[3] "Accomplir toute justice", in Jubile Alfred Loisy, *Congrès d'Histoire du Christianisme*, i, 168.

[4] "Enderwartung und Kirche im Matthäusevangelium", in W. D. Davies and D. Daube (eds.), *The Background of the New Testament and its Eschatology*, 245. For these last two citations I am indebted to Dr. G. R. Beasley-Murray.

conversation puts the question concerning the relation of the Messianic baptism (with Spirit and fire) just preached by John, to the baptism now being carried out on Jesus by John, whilst at the same time it asks about the function of the Messiah that has now arrived, who appears not as a baptizer but as a candidate for baptism, and without the winnowing fan in His hand. "The saying of the Baptist . . . therefore means: 'My time and my baptism is past and the hour of your (Messianic) baptism has come. . . .' "

We must probably accept the tendency to objectify the rending of the heavens, the descent of the dove and the voice, as a watermark of the later tradition. All three belong to the language of symbolism, and are familiar to Jewish thought; the whole account is in the poetic imagery of Jewish Midrash. The opened heavens implies that the summons to Jesus originates in a theophany; the vision and the voice express the message of the unseen, conveying both revelation and equipment for the task appointed; and the voice is made to speak in Old Testament quotations. Mark's "He saw the heavens being cloven asunder" (1: 10) recalls the "rending of the heavens" associated with the descent of Yahweh in Isaiah 64: 1 (cf. Ps. 18: 9, 144: 5), and characterizes the manifestation as primarily one of *power*, but in Matthew and Luke the word is "opened", which (together with Luke's mention that this happened as Jesus prayed) suggests rather a *privilege* granted as a favour than a demonstration intended to impress. Matthew's "Behold, the heavens were opened" (3: 16) may suggest that others (or at least John) witnessed it, where Mark says merely that Jesus saw it, and Luke that it happened.

This raises at once the much-debated question of the nature of the experience—objective fact, inward vision, or subsequent symbolic description of a spiritual crisis in which a great decision was reached and a great assurance gained. The first of these possibilities is ruled out immediately we realize that it implies the "primitive notion of a solid firmament over our heads", a series of heavens one above the other.[1] The other two possibilities are not alternatives. "All the conditions for a vision significant of the divine call and

[1] Cf. 2 Cor. 12: 3, Eph. 1: 20, etc.; A. E. Rawlinson, *op. cit.*, 10; Vincent Taylor, *The Gospel According to St. Mark*, 166 and references there.

empowering must have been present"[1] and if the experiences accompanying the baptism were in fact a private crisis in the inner life of Jesus, only communicated to the disciples by the Lord Himself on some later occasion, this use of vivid symbolic imagery is exactly what we might expect. But this need not be all that is implied. Vincent Taylor poses the question whether Jesus was a "pneumatic person", and compares with the baptismal story Luke 10: 18 and Mark 9: 2-8 as evidence that there were times when Jesus in ecstasy saw truth in the form of vision. He thinks it best to explain the whole baptismal experience as inward and spiritual, but adds that "it is not excluded that for Jesus Himself the experience included auditory and visual elements". E. F. Scott[2] similarly thinks the experience was probably ecstatic in its nature and may well have been accompanied by a vision.

The same explanation must be offered to reconcile the varying statements of the Evangelists concerning the descent upon Jesus of the dove. Matthew and Mark refer to the Spirit "descending like a dove" (Matt. 3: 16; Mark 1: 10), Luke has "in bodily form, as a dove" (3: 22), and John certainly makes the dove objective by saying that John saw it; a dove-like manner of descent becomes a dove-like form and finally a dove. Again what was originally a private experience of Jesus, possibly with visual accompaniment, has been progressively externalized in the process of tradition. Scholars vie with each other in finding erudite meanings for the dove-symbol, but without denying its suggestion of purity and peaceableness we may accept the Jewish evidence which links it with Gen. 1: 2 and so with the Spirit of God.

The third phenomenon attending the baptism, the heavenly voice, is recorded in the same varied way and again has its analogue in Jewish thought, this time in the *Bath Qol*. Mark introduces the voice very abruptly: Jesus "saw the heavens opened . . . the Spirit descending . . . and a voice (nominative) . . . from heaven . . ." (1: 10f.); copyists sought to smooth the construction by supplying "came". This might imply that only Jesus heard it; but Matthew, by repeating his "Behold . . ." and putting the words into the third person, presupposes an audience (3: 16f.). Luke states

---

[1] Vincent Taylor, *op. cit.*, 617ff.   [2] *Kingdom and Messiah*, 157.

the fact simply, preserving the first person.[1] The Fourth
Gospel has no voice, but the divine attestation of Jesus as
Christ, the Son, baptized with the Spirit, is given previously
and privately to John. A similar attestation, though different
in content, occurs in John 12: 28, where what is thunder to
most, and an angel to some, is to Jesus the voice of God.

The successive heavens above the earth could, at appointed
times (so the Jews thought), be opened, and the "echo of
the voice of God" be heard on earth, the idea being that of
a decree promulgated in heaven but overheard on earth.
When an utterance of God in audible speech was to be
described the Rabbis shrank from saying "God said . . .",
using instead the convenient reverential periphrasis "a
Bath Qol came (was given)". A striking feature of the Bath
Qol is that its revelation is usually expressed in the words of
the Hebrew Old Testament or Apocrypha, though in the
New Testament this applies only to the baptismal address.
It can be no accident that the Scriptures with which the
mind of Jesus was filled should be the vehicle for the new
revelation which came to Him in the high hour of His
dedication and reception of the Spirit.

More important, however, than the accompanying
phenomena is the "content" of the experience, and this is
enshrined in the bestowal of the Spirit and in the words of
the address. That Jesus received the Spirit at His baptism is
emphasized by all the records, the Fourth Gospel making up
for its omission of the dove by stressing that the gift of the
Spirit to Jesus was permanent and measureless (1: 33, 3: 34).
There lies here a very real problem for Christology, but for
our purpose it is sufficient to interpret the fact in the light
of Messianic prophecy. Thus, in Isaiah and Joel it is the
anointing of the Spirit which equips Messiah, and the diffusion of the Spirit which marks the Messianic age. All the
Messiah shall require for rule—the Spirit of wisdom and

---

[1] In Luke, the Western Text has the reading, "Thou art my Son, the Beloved,
this day have I begotten Thee." Either the Western Text is original, and
reflects an early Adoptianist view, in which case T.R. has been assimilated to
Matt.-Mark (Moffatt); or T.R. is original, in which case it has been assimilated
in the Western Text to Ps. 2: 7 under the influence of second century Adoptian-
ism (H. G. Marsh, op. cit., 104, quoting Dibelius). O. Cullmann (op. cit., 16)
rejects the Western reading, noting that Ps. 2: 7 is quoted in Acts 13: 33, Heb.
1: 5 in relation to the resurrection, and may have been introduced into the
baptismal context therefrom.

understanding, the Spirit of counsel and might, the Spirit of knowledge and of the fear of the Lord; and all that the Servant shall require to save—the anointing to bring good tidings to the afflicted, to bind the broken hearted, proclaim liberty to the captives, the opening of the prison to them that are bound; and all that makes His character the perfect vehicle for divine salvation—"He shall not strive nor cry", meekness and gentleness shall mark His method, righteousness and truth shall be His girdle, peace and salvation His aim—all is ascribed to His endowment with the Spirit of the Lord. There can be no reasonable doubt that in early Christian thought Isa. 42: 1f., 53, and the anointing of the Messiah with the Spirit are fused in one composite conception of Jesus, and that this conception finds clear expression in the story of the baptism.

The descent of the Spirit in the baptism of Jesus marks a supreme turning-point in the development of the Christian rite. From this moment the negative, ritual, purificatory aspect of Jewish and Johannine baptism is overlaid with the positive and enriching character of Christian baptism; renunciation of the past is taken up into the reception of grace and power for the future; and the rite which had expressed mainly what man does to fulfil God's will becomes now also a rite expressing something God does to make man's obedience effective.

The precise meaning of the address to Jesus is much debated, discussion centring mainly upon the extent to which *Messianic* or *Christological* implications are to be discerned in the words "Thou art My Son, the Beloved (Only-begotten)". The solution probably lies, as so often in these New Testament ambiguities, in the rapidly changing connotation of words in that creative period when all terms and conceptions were being revalued and reinterpreted—not least by Jesus Himself. Thus we may say the title "Son" was Messianic, provided we add that Jesus did much more than fulfil the accepted Messianic role, and the title shared in the changing meaning of Messiahship. Or we may say that the basic fact is the filial consciousness of Jesus, so long as we add that the title Son must not be assumed to bear as yet the theological and metaphysical meaning it bore later for the church, but was for Jesus charged with ethical and

spiritual meanings and possessed still a Messianic background. It is probable that in the Temptation we see the
current Messianic conceptions in the process of reinterpretation by Jesus in the light of the filial relationship; and this
confirms the view that the revelation which came to Jesus
in His baptism was that of a clear and assured Sonship
which by its nature, as well as by the history of the title,
involved complete dedication to the Messianic work waiting
to be done, but which at the same time transfigured that
Messianic role almost beyond recognition.

It is true that the phrase "In whom I am well pleased"
might be regarded as a commendation of "the quiet thirty
years" and even as simply the meaning of "Thou art My
Son", but B. H. Branscomb[1] points out that "the two ideas
of divine love and divine choice for a task" are "close
together in Hebrew thought", and with Vincent Taylor and
W. C. Allen stresses the aorist tense as pointing to a definite
act of approval. Thus "in whom I am well pleased" recalls
"in whom my soul delighteth", as clearly as "the Beloved"
recalls "my chosen One". It is, however, Isaiah 42 and not
Isaiah 53 which is quoted, and the idea of suffering is not
explicitly present in the address. Perhaps we should be content to say that the Servant idea is present, with all its
potentiality for development along the line foreshadowed in
Isaiah 53, as Jesus Himself came to see. "Certainly there
could be no truer index to Jesus' life than a combination of
Psalm 2: 7 with Isaiah 42: 1f.—the Son of God as King and
the Servant of the Lord—and this combination, if we go on
the evidence, dates from the high hour in which Jesus
entered on His public work." It is certain that Jesus was
profoundly influenced by the Servant conception[2] and there
can be little doubt that it was He who first related the
Messiah-Son and the Servant of Yahweh, and so transformed the whole Messianic concept as to disappoint
fatally the popular expectations.

[1] *The Gospel of Mark* (Moffatt Commentary), 19; Cf. Vincent Taylor,
The Gospel According to St. Mark, 162, quoting W. C. Allen's suggestion that the
aorists are modelled on those in Isa. 42.

[2] Vincent Taylor, *Jesus and His Sacrifice*, on Luke 22: 37, Mark 8: 31; 11: 31;
10: 33; 9: 12*b*; 10: 45; 14: 21. "Behind the ambiguous passages in Acts there
lurks an original Aramaic tradition in which the Messiah was described unambiguously as the Servant of the Lord." Cf. Acts 3: 13, 26; 4: 27, 30; 8: 32,
Luke 24: 26, Matt. 8: 17; 12: 18, 1 Peter 2: 22, Heb. 9: 28, Rom. 4: 25,
1 Cor. 15: 3, Phil. 2: 5-8, John 1: 29-36; 12: 38, Rev. 5: 6; 13: 8; 14: 4.

It is abundantly clear from the foregoing brief reconstruction that His baptism was a crucial experience for Jesus; it hardly needs to be added that in such a story there was ample suggestion and warrant for a new and vastly enriched conception of what baptism could mean also for those who followed in His steps.

Much is made, in current baptismal controversy, of the so-called "explanation" of Christ's baptism. The "problem" is variously conceived and the solutions suggested are legion: but most of the difficulties arise from the paradox that the sinless Jesus underwent a baptism of "repentance". Reason has been given above for denying that Matthew alludes to this question, but something should be added concerning the question itself. A. M. Hunter[1] has well said that the problem "is surely academic, for we have no reason to suppose that the question of His sinlessness occupied His mind at this time." This point is crucial: for if we make our Lord's consciousness of sinlessness a difficulty for His baptism, then we reach the curious and intolerable position that any normal pious and devout expression such as He might learn at His mother's side—the penitential Psalms, the Passover confession, even the normal prayers of a Jewish home— were for Him inappropriate, and must have been studiously avoided. This is utterly artificial. We may be certain that the fact of His immaculate innocence emerged in the course of His development, and was in no sense so positively present to His mind before His baptism as to prevent His sharing in the normal piety of His family and nation. There was meaning in John's baptism into which Jesus could enter without first needing sins to confess; sinlessness was no barrier to baptism, even though for all but Him that baptism signified, along with other things, repentance for sins committed.

Seen in historical perspective, the baptism of Jesus needs no explanation other than that provided by His previous development, and His high estimate of John. Jesus being what He was, and holding the opinion of John which He held, the fact that He was baptized is not nearly so strange as His omission of baptism would have been. "The baptism of John is from heaven . . . that is sufficient for Jesus. The question is not whether Jesus has or has not sins to

---

[1] *The Work and Words of Jesus*, 36.

confess, but whether He is to obey the call of God which comes through the last and greatest of the prophets."[1] This is the true significance of the casual way in which Luke records the great event. To this extent, also, the motive of *obedience* is discernible in the "example" of our Lord's acceptance of this divinely authorized act of "righteousness".

It is obvious, however, that while such may be the historical, and sufficient, explanation of our Lord's coming to baptism, there are in the event numerous "growing points" of doctrinal development of which the most important for our purpose are the association of baptism in water with the gift of the Spirit, with sonship, and with the conception of the Servant. This last is especially significant because it is set forth repeatedly as the "explanation" of Jesus' baptism, and made to bear the main weight of argument for infant baptism. Such a process is naturally somewhat tortuous, and what has been already said suffices to show that as "explanation" it is irrelevant and unnecessary; nevertheless, even as a theological inference from Christ's baptism it demands careful examination. What is the relation between the Servant idea and Christ's baptism, and what bearing has it upon baptismal theology?

In Vincent Taylor's words, "It is not clear from the Markan account that at this point Jesus was conscious of being the *suffering* Servant, for the words quoted are from Isaiah 42 and not 53; but it is reasonable to infer that His sense of a suffering destiny is lineally connected with the initial experience of baptism."[2] Jesus did take up the Servant idea in relation to His death,[3] and the Servant-song quoted in the address does refer, though vaguely, to the possibility of the Servant's "failing or being discouraged". He was the Servant; the Servant was foreseen to suffer for the sins of others; the Temptation, with its rejection of easier paths to the Messianic throne, has within it the foreshadowing of the cross. Jesus' baptism illustrates, as does His working at the

---

[1] T. W. Manson, *op. cit.*, 149f. If we could be sure that Lk. 7: 29 is intended as a saying of Jesus, we should possess a final pronouncement upon the obligation of John's baptism upon all; it is probable, however, that the words contain Luke's comment (cf. Moffatt, R.S.V.), though doubtless they also rightly express the mind of Jesus.

[2] *The Gospel According to St. Mark*, 618f.; A. M. Hunter (*op. cit.*, 37) finds in the baptism of Jesus the ideas of Messiah, Servant, and Suffering Servant.

[3] Summary of opinions in H. H. Rowley, *The Unity of the Bible*, 132f.

carpenter's bench, His tiredness, hunger, temptation and sorrow, how completely He entered into the life of man; and He being what He was, the first step involved the last. In that sense plainly, the baptism, like the incarnation itself, already involved the cross—logically, and theologically, though not necessarily as something always consciously foreseen.

Very many commentators, however, go much further than this, and find in the concept of the Servant who is numbered with the transgressors and bears the sin of many, not only the main solution of the problem of Christ's repentance-baptism, but, in many cases, the basis for a theory of universal, *vicarious* baptism, which in turn becomes a major argument for infant baptism. This line of inter-pretation is not new, but has recently received a new prominence, especially in the work of Oscar Cullmann. The baptism of Jesus, so the argument runs, was "an initiation into His passion", an integral part of His self-identification with sinners, and a first step in vicarious sinbearing; it was thus vicarious in nature, a general baptism into which we are privileged to enter by individual baptism; and since it was accomplished before, and independently of, any faith or response of ours, it ought therefore to be applied antece-dently to personal faith and understanding: that is, to infants.

This thesis is defended by Cullmann with ingenious exegesis and subtle interpretation, especially of "My beloved Son", "fulfil all righteousness" (taken in a Pauline sense), Luke 12: 50, Mark 10: 38, and "Lamb of God"; and upon it some very far-reaching theological conclusions are based. One is often conscious of deep and grateful agreement with much of the underlying thought in these suggestions, combined with serious misgivings about the exegesis, and about the use being made of the insights gained. Anything like adequate discussion would demand far more space than is here available, and it can only be asserted, with an un-fortunate but inevitable impression of dogmatism, that the interpretation seems often forced, the logic unconvincing, the consequences sometimes disconcerting. The idea of Christ's vicarious baptism appears nowhere in the New Testament; His vicarious *death* is everywhere, but the con-sequence drawn from it is that they who truly believe *need not die*. The logic which builds upon vicarious baptism a demand that all be baptized is hard to follow. The theory is altogether precarious, brilliantly but unconvincingly supported, and historically unnecessary.

But if the significance of Christ's baptism for baptismal theology is not to be discovered in the conception of vicarious baptism, it remains true that Christian baptism, apart from the baptism of Jesus, would have been a very different rite. This is not to ignore the great differences between His baptism and ours—differences not always weighed by those who appeal, somewhat unthinkingly, to "Christ's example in baptism". His was not in any ordinary sense a baptism "unto remission of sins" as ours must be (Acts 2: 38), and whatever "vicarious repentance" might mean it is certain that if it applied to His act it does not apply to ours. Similarly, as W. F. Flemington[1] says, "Jesus was possessed by the Spirit and was the Son of God as one of His followers could never be", and only with corresponding reservations can it be said that His baptism constituted for Him an initiation, either into the kingdom or into new relationship with God. We must therefore speak of "following Jesus through the waters of baptism" only with great care. But while all this is admitted, the baptism of Jesus remains of crucial significance for Christian practice, and it is to that event, rather than to proselyte or Johannine baptism, that we must look for the determining factor in Christian baptism.

Briefly, the baptism of Jesus affects the meaning of the baptismal rite in at least five ways. First, it lends to the practice His personal authority, thus ensuring for all His followers that baptism may never be a "mere" rite, devoid of truth, value or importance. Secondly, it lends a note of positive enrichment, rather than of negative renunciation, to baptism; expectation of immediate and future blessing becomes as prominent in the mood of the baptized, as regret for the past—a change of emphasis which led directly to more sacramental interpretations, and which rests upon the experience that came to Jesus. Thirdly, our Lord's submission to the rite has added to the motives for its acceptance the powerful one of personal dedication and obedience—the emulation of the attitude in which He also

[1] *Op. cit.*, 121.

approached the decisive event; baptism thus is linked to one
of the most formative and fundamental of New Testament
conceptions, the *imitatio Christi*. Fourthly, our Lord's
experience at Jordan has added to baptism a "filial over-
tone"—an awareness, given and received, of filial relationship and privilege, which becomes a constitutive element in
the Christian doctrine of baptism (John 3, Gal. 3: 26, 27,
Rom. 8: 14-17, etc.).[1] And finally, our Lord's experience
in baptism transformed the rite by linking with it the
reception of the Holy Spirit; the prophets' association of water
and the Spirit is here translated into reality and becomes
normative for the Church[2]—baptism becomes the "sacrament for the transmission of the Spirit".

Taken together, these five new elements in the baptismal
conception, deriving almost wholly from the baptismal
experience of Jesus, abundantly justify the contention that
it is to His act we must look for the *main* origin of the Christian
rite. It remains only to add that not one of these new
dimensions of meaning, derived from the baptism of Christ,
can be predicated, except in the most faint and distorted
fashion, of the rite of infant baptism. Conscious obedience
or imitation of Jesus, positive dedication to new ideals,
acceptance of the new endowments of grace, the awareness
of belonging to the divine family, the moral and spiritual
regeneration consequent upon personal appropriation of
the gift of the Spirit—none of these can be affirmed to be the
experience of the baptized babe, except with all kinds of
reservations, qualifications and assumptions that modify
their meaning beyond recognition. All that happened in
baptism for Jesus, at about thirty years of age, as the crown
of one stage of development and the deliberate entrance
upon another, is beyond the understanding and experience
of the child, and it is no exaggeration to say that when
scholars pass from discussion of Christ's baptism to discussion of infant baptism they leap a gulf of meaning and
implication in which deep differences in connotation are
concealed by the simple device of using one word—baptism
—in two totally different meanings. Christ's baptism was *not*
merely something done to Him; the effect of His baptism was

---

[1] W. F. Flemington (*op. cit.*, 29, 121f.) well emphasizes this.
[2] O. Cullmann, *op. cit.*, 10-14; cf. also *Early Christian Worship*, 76.

not traceable to the objective act, the authority of the baptizer, prevenient grace working independently of human response, proleptic or vicarious faith, or any of the other theological devices invented to "explain" the efficacy of infant baptism. The relation of infant baptism to Christ's baptism is in fact neither one of theological consistency nor precise historical derivation, but is largely accidental, if not indeed a purely verbal coincidence.

B. BAPTISM IN THE SYNOPTIC GOSPELS

by R. E. O. White

Our Lord's submission to John's baptism, His recounting of the experience subsequently to the disciples, and His challenge to the Pharisees to acknowledge that John's baptism was "from heaven", constitute together, as we have seen, a solemn warning against the temptation to disparage baptism as a "mere rite, a form, or ceremony", from motives of either evangelical or ecumenical enthusiasm. At the same time, the absence from the detailed instructions given to the Twelve and to the Seventy for their Galilean missions of any command to baptize; the absence of baptism from the stories of converts like Levi, Zacchaeus or Mary Magdalene; and the absence of any exposition of the meaning and place of baptism in the life of the kingdom, all constitute an equally solemn warning against any attempt to make baptism *necessary* to salvation, or to make of it a supernatural rite conveying in itself the grace that saves.

This does not mean that Christian baptism has no place in the Gospel Jesus preached, or that it lacks His authority. These are precisely the questions we must investigate. But it does mean that any form of the rite which is claimed to bring men into saving relation with God, and to initiate them into the life of God's kingdom, must be scrupulously in harmony with His own terms and conditions of salvation, or stand condemned as an unwarranted and presumptuous addition to the Gospel of Christ.

When we seek the relation between the apostolic practice of baptism and the teaching of Jesus, two main questions arise: the conditions upon which Jesus offered salvation to men, and the extent to which the Lord's authority may be claimed for baptism. Each of these main questions has two relevant aspects; the former requires us first to define our Lord's terms for spiritual initiation *generally*, and then, in view of the form baptism assumed in the church, to inquire as to His attitude and teaching concerning the relation of the kingdom to children; the latter main question must seek its answer by inquiring whether Jesus practised baptism, in any form, and whether He commanded it for the church.

Jesus came to seek and to save that which was *lost*. Such is the natural state of man to which Jesus addressed Himself. All our sources are agreed that the terms upon which men may exchange this natural state of "lostness" for life under God's rule as Christian disciples, are two, however variously they may be described: repentance and faith. Repentance, as with John, is μετανοία, the total change of attitude, the re-orientation of life, the turning from what life has been to a new and holier ideal. The call to ethical redirection of life is not one whit less clear and uncompromising in Jesus' message than in John's. Neither evangelists nor sacramentalists have always been faithful to Jesus' insistence that repentance is a *sine qua non* of salvation.

The second condition, faith, is already implicit in the turning to God which constitutes, with turning from self, the meaning of repentance. Of such saving faith, knowledge of Christ and the inward witness of the truth are the sufficient foundations; the gospel message, or more accurately the Christ of whom it tells, is the object; prayer is its voice, and obedience its outcome. The familiar call, "Follow Me", implies beside the turning away from the self-directed life, a complete and implicit trust in Christ's worthiness to lead and authority to command.

In setting forth these terms of spiritual initiation and the qualities of the life to which He invited men, Jesus frequently made use of the two metaphors which become important growing-points of baptismal thought in later years: the metaphors of birth and death. "Whoever does not receive the kingdom of God like a child, shall not enter it. . . . Unless you turn and become like children you will never enter the kingdom of heaven. . . . Whoever humbles himself like this child, he is the greatest in the kingdom of heaven" (Mark 10:

15, Matt. 18: 3-4). The childlike spirit, everywhere insisted upon, is not easy to define, because things said about children and things said about disciples are sometimes confused: but as describing the state of heart which enters upon the blessings of God's reign it is usually understood as "receiving as a child receives"—"in humility and trust in the divine grace" without the desire to save face by asserting one's *right* to what is given, or by making adequate return which would leave giver and receiver equal again. So at least Luke understood the saying, linking it with the story of the Publican's prayer, "God, be merciful to me a sinner" (18: 13), interposing the saying "for everyone who exalts himself will be humbled, but he who humbles himself will be exalted" (18: 14), and addressing the whole to "some who trusted in themselves that they were righteous" (18: 9). So too Matthew understood it, relating the words "*humble himself like this child*" to the disciples' question about greatness in the kingdom. Only the child's unselfconscious acceptance of what is freely offered can bring a man into the kingdom, and only the same unselfregarding spirit can achieve the kingdom's quality of greatness.[1] It means "a man going back behind a good deal of his manhood and becoming like an unsophisticated child . . . it is just that 'wisdom' of the sophisticated man, making him suspicious, cautious, and unready to commit himself, which in many people inhibits the acceptance of Jesus Christ as Saviour and makes difficult the entrance into His kingdom".[2] The exchange of the normal self-confidence and self-assertiveness of adulthood for the childlike spirit is an essential element

[1] Cf. T. W. Manson, *The Sayings of Jesus*, 207. The reference to the "revelation to babes" is also relevant, but its bearing is different. In Matt. 11: 25 and Luke 10: 21f., the disciples return elated, from their mission; Jesus declares the thing to rejoice about is that their names are written in heaven—prophets and kings having desired to see what they see, but missing it; and even yet the "wise and prudent" leaders of religion are missing the greatest opportunity in Israel's history, while disciples, untaught and unspoiled by the traditions and prejudices of the schools, with the wit and spiritual intuition to discern the truth (cf. Luke 12: 57), are experiencing in their own lives the power of the kingdom. These "unsophisticated" folk are "babes". The Church of Scotland (*Interim Report of the Special Commission on Baptism*, Part I, 22) defies fact and logic by quoting Matt. 11: 25 alongside 21: 16—"babes and sucklings"—to support a conclusion about little children "who may not know what they are saying", silently suppressing the fact that Matt. 11: 25 is evoked by the return of campaigning disciples, and not by a visit to a Christian nursery.

[2] A. Dakin, "Baptism of Believers Only", in F. C. Bryan (ed.), *Concerning Believers' Baptism*, 48f.

in the total re-orientation of mind and will which is repentance, and the use of the child-simile to describe it provides
the starting point for the Johannine doctrine of the new
birth, and so for the later connection of baptism with
regeneration.

With equal emphasis our Lord insists that none can follow
Him or know the life of the kingdom who do not first
deny themselves and take up the cross after His example.[1]
In all three gospels the confession of Christ's Messiahship
is followed by the announcement that Christ must suffer and
the "revision" of the terms of discipleship to include this
factor: the acceptance of the cross, the denial of self, the
losing of one's own life ("soul") for Christ's sake and the
Gospel's becomes another variation of the demand for moral
and spiritual readjustment as the necessary step towards
attaining the kingdom. The spoken word received dramatic
reinforcement when those who had heard and wondered
at it saw Jesus die, and still further when His call to share
His death was continually repeated in the communion
service of the apostolic church.

The seed thoughts of both the doctrines later connected
with baptism—new birth and crucifixion with Christ—are
thus present in the teaching of Jesus, but it is essential to
note that they are present strictly and only as metaphors for
those moral and spiritual terms upon which entrance to the
kingdom, the Messianic salvation, and eternal life were
offered to men. It is especially at this point that upholders
of believers' baptism find the attitude of Paedo-Baptists
quite incomprehensible. It seems incredible that the church
should ever be found denying, or obscuring for a moment,
these conditions of repentance and faith so clearly enun-
ciated by Jesus—yet such denial is a commonplace of
Paedo-Baptist apologetic. If infant baptism is held to bring
the infant within the kingdom of God, to initiate him into
the sphere where grace operates, to impart spiritual life or
regenerate the soul, then plainly the whole of Christ's
teaching on the conditions of discipleship and the way into
life is rejected and denied; if it be held that this teaching
applies only to the unbaptized adult still needing to be
evangelized, then (apart from all other implications of this

[1] Matt. 16: 24, Mark 8: 34f., Luke 9: 23.

startling position) Christ's teaching is, for the vast majority of people in Christendom, simply irrelevant. To speak of the means of entering the kingdom in terms not of moral principles, spiritual ideals, and direction of the will, but of rites, institutions, "fellowships", ceremonies of initiation performed upon those incapable of apprehension or response, is to leave far behind us the whole message and challenge of Jesus. It is, in fact, to unmoralize the Gospel, and so to demoralize it, "as if baptism made a soul a Christian at some subliminal depth".[1] The contention for believers' baptism is in the end the contention for the moral and spiritual content of the original message of Jesus, the defence of a conception of the Gospel which shall preserve undimmed the ethical realism and vision of the sermon, the parables, the epigrams of the Master.

The question of the child's relation to the kingdom remains, however, and we turn to seek the teaching of Jesus upon it, fully realizing that we shall have space only to touch the fringe of a large issue whose discussion must presuppose a whole theological system and involve matters far removed from the practice of baptism. Baptist groups have not been very ready to define their own view on the place of the infant in the Gospel and the church, leaving it to be assumed that the infant, like the unevangelized, is "in the hands of God".[2] The reply of the Baptist Union of Great Britain and Ireland, (adopted by the Annual Assembly 1926) to the Lambeth Appeal on Church Unity (1920) includes the sentence: "We recognize that those concerning whom Jesus said 'Of such is the kingdom of heaven' belong to God, and believe that no rite is needed to bring them into relation with Him." This is hardly a theological statement until the word "belong" is clearly defined, and the problems raised for baptismal theology by any attempt to define it have rarely been considered.

That Jesus cared for the child in a manner totally new in religious thought is abundantly plain. Everywhere in the Synoptic story, from His own childhood to His commendation of the children's temple praise in the week of His passion, the fact is underlined that "hardly anything is

---

[1] P. T. Forsyth, *The Church and the Sacraments*, 198f.
[2] For a fuller exposition of this point, cf. *infra*, 310ff., 321ff.

more characteristic of Jesus than His attitude to children" and His sympathetic insight and valuation of childhood is regulative for the Christian's thought and responsibility towards the young. Yet in none of these utterances does the crucial question of the child's relation to the kingdom of God explicitly arise, and nowhere does our Lord suggest that in their case the basic requirements of repentance and faith are unnecessary, irrelevant, or superseded by "pious" birth, innocence, or helplessness. We may well feel that some adjustment of thought is essential when such questions are raised concerning infants: but so far as His recorded words take us, the question is left open. It is important to remember that Jesus was equally sympathetic towards, and equally quick to defend, the sick, the afflicted, the leper, the out-caste, the sinful—without in the least implying that sickness, affliction, leprosy, ostracism or sin, any more than infancy, constitute sufficient qualifications for entrance to the kingdom, or reception of Christian baptism. The place of the child, and of all who are helpless, ignored, despised, or in need of friendship, in the *love of Christ*, is indisputable; their reception into the church, entrance into the divine kingdom and initiation into spiritual life is a wholly different matter, and far from indisputable.

With all that Jesus said about the way men enter into life clearly in mind, we turn to the two passages in which, it has been affirmed, some kind of infant initiation is set forth. Devious indeed are the ways by which the Blessing of the Children is made to yield justification for infant baptism. Seeking to establish its original meaning and purpose, we note first that infants are brought[1] not for baptism but for "blessing" (Matthew says simply that Jesus was desired to "pray"). There is not the least indication that the "blessing" conferred was in any sense of the phrase "baptismal" or initiatory blessing, any more than His blessing on enemies, peacemakers, the poor in spirit, the pure in heart, on Peter, the faithful servant, the eyes that see, the eucharistic bread, or the assembled disciples at the

[1] Mark 10: 13f. and parallels; argument about the probable age of the children is pointless. The mention of those who brought them, the graphic words of Mark, "He folded His arms about them" (cf. 9: 36), and Luke's "babes", sufficiently prove at least the presence among others of children of very tender age.

ascension. Christ's "blessing" was doubtless "efficacious"[1] but its meaning in the gospels plainly varies between the pronouncement that certain are happy, the wish that others *be* happy, the invoking of divine favour, and the giving of thanks for favour received; all argument about His conferring on the children the capacity to receive Him, or the Holy Spirit, or to have fellowship with Him[2] is simply irrelevant. If infants *are* capable of these things, then obviously baptism is appropriate for them: but this is the point at issue and it must not be introduced into the passage in order to make the passage relevant to baptism.

The touching of the children with the hand recalls Jacob's blessing of the sons of Joseph (Gen. 48: 14), and is said to be still a natural gesture of the Rabbi in invoking divine favour upon the children of the synagogue. To allude here to the "healing" touch of Jesus is to suggest that His touch *conveyed* supernatural power, and must imply also that once at least the hem of His garment did the same: this brings us on to extremely dangerous ground, and it ignores the important cases where healing was achieved without His presence with the sufferer. The touching of the leper and the blind is nearer to a caress, a means of communication of His feeling and intention (as the anointing of eyes with clay, the placing of fingers in the ears of the deaf), than to the waving of a magician's wand. For Luke, of course, the laying on of hands implies something much more, being associated (in Acts) with the recognition of new converts by those in authority, and the gift of the Spirit; Luke therefore does not mention that Jesus "laid His hands upon them", though he says the children were brought that Jesus might "touch" them.

The pronouncement, for the sake of which doubtless the story was first preserved, is according to Mark and Luke twofold—

(*a*) "Let the children come to me, do not hinder them; for to such belongs the kingdom of God."

---

[1] The Church of Scotland (*Interim Report of the Special Commission on Baptism*, Part I, 25) says, "Was the blessing of the children by Jesus efficacious or not? To that we can only answer: It was without doubt efficacious. Christ's blessing of the infants makes them capable of receiving the Holy Spirit . . . He who made them creates in them the capacity for receiving Him . . .".

[2] *Loc. cit.*, and O. Cullmann, *Baptism in the New Testament*, 42.

> (*b*) "Truly I say to you, Whoever does not receive the kingdom of God like a child, shall not enter it."

Matthew has (*a*) only at this place, his version of (*b*) occurring at 18: 3: "Truly I say to you, unless you turn and become like children, you will never enter the kingdom of heaven." This version, and the context in which Matthew sets it, make unmistakably clear his understanding of the words as implying that the kingdom belongs to the *childlike*, and this will involve a "conversion" for all who would enter. Mark's and Luke's (*b*) shows equally plainly that this is how they understood (*a*) too. For "Receive the kingdom of God like a child" manifestly does not mean "*when* a little child" but "in a little child's way"—"simply and naturally, without making any claims",[1] "unselfconsciously receptive, and content to be dependent, such that the kingdom is received not as an achievement but as undeserved",[2] "the childlike disposition . . . its grateful acceptance of that which was offered".[3] The last-named expositor links the saying with Jesus' repeated criticism of much of the religion of His contemporaries as too often proud and self-righteous; Vincent Taylor, too, summarizes the meaning of the incident in the words: "It reveals how He transmuted eschatological conceptions of the kingdom and presented it as a gift of God and an experience into which, if they have the receptiveness of a child, men may enter here and now." In spite of this, Vincent Taylor can remark "the children are not treated as symbolic . . ." and paraphrase Christ's meaning as "the kingdom belongs to children". Unless all else that Jesus said about the kingdom is to be rejected, the kingdom of God is emphatically not a kingdom of children; and if the kingdom belongs to children because they are children, and so presumably, naturally receptive, then *age* is made the surest of all qualifications for membership—which is absurd. As we have seen, Jesus constantly addressed Himself to the reason and conscience of adults, and so sought His followers. All three Evangelists, on the evidence just given, plainly take the words to mean "Of such as children is the kingdom

[1] Vincent Taylor, *The Gospel According to St. Mark*, 423.
[2] A. E. J. Rawlinson, *The Gospel According to St. Mark* (Westminster Commentaries), 137.
[3] B. H. Branscomb, *The Gospel of Mark* (Moffatt Commentary), 180.

of heaven"—the kingdom belongs to the *childlike*. Nothing is said of the relation of the child himself to the kingdom and to eternal life; but the incident is another priceless illustration of Jesus' attitude of love and gentleness, goodwill and prayerfulness, towards the child.[1]

It is quite certain that, despite the use of this passage in the various baptismal Orders, infant baptism is not built hereon. "Had man appointed an ordinance of the imposition of hands from the authority of this passage it would not have been so strange, but to argue that children must be baptized because they may be blessed by Jesus has no colour of plausibility."[2] Yet Paedo-Baptists have not in fact followed the more obvious suggestion of the incident (if the question of infants' relation to the kingdom is to be read into it at all), but have reserved the laying on of hands for a later and more responsible occasion. To use the story to support a practice which emphatically Jesus did not follow on the occasion described, while denying its relevance to another practice which equally clearly Jesus did use on that occasion, is to leave no doubt that special pleading is misusing the narrative for illegitimate ends.

The remaining passage in the Synoptic gospels which has been made to carry Paedo-Baptist apologetic is Matt. 18: 5-6 (with Mark 9: 33-37, Luke 9: 46-48). All three gospels attach the saying about receiving a little one in Christ's name to the discussion as to who should be greatest in the kingdom, with the child set in the midst and the sharp lesson on childlikeness. Luke emphasizes that this (and *not* initiation into the kingdom), is the theme by adding, "he who is least among you all is the one who is great" (9: 48); Mark has the equivalent comment, "If anyone would be first, he must be last of all and servant of all" (9: 35). Luke's conjunction of thought seems to be: the receiving[3] of a little child is one example of the general principle of reverence for

---

[1] It is impossible to examine here the various arguments by which support for infant baptism has been prised out of this incident: for additional comment on the methods used, see the present writer's "Theology and Logic", in *B.Q.*, xvi (1956), 356f.

[2] A. Carson, *Baptism*, 202.

[3] "Whoever receives this child in my name receives me, and whoever receives me receives him who sent me; for he who is least among you all is the one who is great." "He who is least" must (if the sentence is to be intelligible) be "this little child" and those like him; whom to receive is to receive Christ. It is the equivalent of "despise not . . .".

the "least" among men—and reverence done for him is reverence done for Christ, the Friend of all whom men despise. Mark's arrangement suggests, somewhat similarly, that receiving one such little one is a typical example of that service of all which is the only way to greatness. Again, to make the sentence intelligible, "to be servant of all" must have some relevance to "receiving a little child"; and since such service of the child is accepted as service of Christ, the words provide another, and welcome, example of the principle of "Inasmuch . . .", to be added to those in Matthew 25: 31f.—and have nothing to do with initiation or baptism.

This exegesis should govern our understanding also of Matthew's version: but Matthew gives a different turn to the incident. Beginning with the question of greatness, the child set in the midst and the exaltation of childlikeness, Matthew passes to receiving one such child *"in My name"* (with no intervening link of reverence or service for the "least"); then comes (as in Mark) the solemn warning to those who, on the other hand, cause one of these little ones *"who believe in me"* to stumble; the thought passes to their occasions of stumbling (the foot, the hand, the eye), to "See that you do not despise one of these little ones", the lost sheep, and "So it is not the will of my Father who is in heaven that one of these little ones should perish", closing with instructions on how to deal with offences within the Christian fellowship, and how to regain the erring member. The loose connection of thought is essential evidence of the true meaning here; and it is necessary to examine this because, ignoring the Markan and Lukan understanding of the sayings, Paedo-Baptist exegetes have read baptismal meanings (*a*) into the phrase "little ones who believe in me", and (*b*) the reference to "receiving one such little one in my name". The former interpretation involves some extremely curious argumentation[1] and in the end presupposes an (admittedly incomprehensible) infant-faith. The latter method reads a perfectly arbitrary meaning into the words "receive in my name". It is easy to show that Jesus used similar language in other contexts to mean simply "receive, make welcome, take to one's heart, on my account",

[1] R. E. O. White, *loc. cit.*, 358f.

and that this is the more natural meaning here in respect of needy children. In any case, if "receive one such little one" means reception into Christ, into the kingdom and baptism, then plainly "receives me" *in the same sentence* must mean receiving Christ "into Christ, into the kingdom, and baptism"—which is absurd.

The shifts and distortions to which exegesis is put in seeking baptismal meanings in all these passages about children are indications that the meanings are being imported and not discovered, and that the original meanings are quite other, and much simpler, than Paedo-Baptist interpreters suggest. But this is not sufficient to answer our original question about the place of children in the kingdom and the Gospel, according to the teaching of Jesus. The truth is that there is little that can be said upon His authority. The duty of the disciple to be childlike, and to show care towards the child, is plain: the theological status of the child himself remains undefined. The one certain thing that can be said is that the child shares with all the needy, helpless, and (in that age) undervalued members of the human family in the special care, protection and defence of Jesus: that in the fullest, strongest sense of the word and with all its implications for time and for eternity, Jesus *loved* the child. It would seem to follow (though here we pass beyond Jesus' teaching and Synoptic evidence) that the universal redemption wrought by Christ at Calvary extends its "benefits" or efficacy to every child innocent of rejecting because innocent of understanding. Yet baptism is not the appropriate sign, any more than is communion, of the special situation involved in the child's innocence of moral responsibility. To say that baptism marks this special relation of the undeveloped soul to the divine purposes is to impart to baptism a novel, arbitrary and wholly un-supported meaning which New Testament baptism nowhere possesses. As well say that we shall agree to let communion mark this relation—or the laying on of hands, as Jesus did—or some special service of dedication and presentation, such as Mary and Joseph shared at the gift of Jesus. But baptism is in New Testament theology the mark and em-bodiment of a relation of obedient, believing, converted, surrendered, covenanting hearts with a God whose grace is apprehended in the death of Christ and confessed by deliberate acceptance of initiation. To adopt it to mark a wholly different situation in the case of infants is to prostitute its meaning and destroy its character.

It is against the background of Jesus' teaching upon how men enter into the kingdom of God, and what He thought of children, that we must now raise the question how far His authority can be claimed for Christian baptism, and for what form (if any) of that rite. The question of dominical authority for baptism is prior to all questions of its importance, sacramental efficacy or initiatory power, and as P. W. Evans[1] has shown, the "enduring emphasis" in theological pronouncements has always been "on the derivation of the Christian sacraments from the definite appointment of Christ Himself". Nevertheless this is now disputed, and though it is beyond question that the early church *believed* itself to have Christ's warrant for its baptismal practice the question cannot be evaded whether in this respect the apostles rightly interpreted the mind of Jesus or merely perpetuated a familiar religious rite for its own sake, as they continued to use synagogue and temple. The question of how men enter into salvation is far too important, and the difference between apostolic counsel (which may after all lose its relevance with change of place and time) and dominical command is too wide, to allow us to rest the baptismal imperative merely upon the custom or belief of the church—even the church of the first century.

Did Jesus so instruct the church?—leaving aside for the moment the much debated Great Commission (Matt. 28: 18f., Mark 16: 15f.), the gospels are strangely indecisive in their answer. It may be urged that Jesus, "with all His indifference to mere ceremonial" and His sharp criticism of ritual religion, was not likely to make obligatory any performance which could come so easily to be valued for its own sake, and obscure the spiritual challenge of His message; the absence of all reference to baptism from gospel stories of conversion, great faith, forgiveness of sinners, or the instructions to the campaigning disciples, is especially significant and seems to some fatal to any idea that Jesus approved baptism; the fact that the Spirit "was not yet given" during

[1] *Sacraments in the New Testament*, 6f.

Jesus' ministry might be said to make Christian baptism possible only after Pentecost; and the sixfold repetition of the saying about John baptizing with water but Jesus with the Spirit has been held to show that water-baptism was not expected of Messiah, and was not originally practised by the church.[1] This is a formidable array of arguments, and it suffices both to preclude dogmatism and to warn against making baptism necessary to salvation.

There is, however, much to be said on the other side. It must not be forgotten that Jesus was confronted with the rite from the beginning of His work. John had made baptism a feature of popular Messianic expectation, multitudes had submitted to it, arguments had arisen concerning it. For Jesus not to adopt or at least approve it necessarily involved at least a silent repudiation of it: and in the light of His own baptism, that of certain disciples, and His testimony that John's was "from heaven" such repudiation is surely out of the question. Nor could the church ever have adopted the ordinance had they known that Jesus was opposed, or indifferent, to it.[2] As to Jesus' general attitude, the use of dramatic gesture to convey spiritual meaning is wholly in line with Jesus' acceptance of the prophetic role[3] and with actions like the cleansing of the temple, the entry to Jerusalem, and the cursing of the fig tree. The argument that Jesus would not command baptism because He was not a ritualist begs the question twice in eleven words. Neither John's baptism nor Jesus' acceptance of it can be stigmatized as "mere ritualism", unless every action or posture which expresses as a psychological symbol an attitude of heart and mind is to be so stigmatized—in which case Jesus' approval not only of baptism but of synagogue attendance, standing to pray, the use of bread and wine in remembrance, must be so stigmatized.

Unquestionably Jesus opposed any reliance upon the

---

[1] B. H. Branscomb, *op. cit.*, 15. This argument holds only if the antithesis in the saying makes water-baptism and Spirit-baptism *alternative*, which is not the case. Cf. W. F. Flemington, *The New Testament Doctrine of Baptism*, 116, 124, and A. L. Humphries, *The Holy Spirit in Faith and Experience*, 158-60, on John 7: 37.

[2] H. G. Marsh, *The Origin and Significance of New Testament Baptism*, 121. Marsh's discussion of most of these points is very useful. Cf. W. F. Flemington, *op. cit.*, 25, 30, 31.

[3] Luke 4: 24; 13: 33, Mark 8: 28, Luke 24: 19; cf. W. F. Flemington, *op. cit.*, 118f.

performance of religious acts as efficacious in themselves apart from the state of heart which they express. He denied the value of fasting while the heart rejoices, and said hard things about Korban, ritual washings, and Sabbatarianism: but there is no evidence that He did not value acts and methods of devotion that effectively expressed the approach of the soul to God. It must not be forgotten that He sent the cleansed lepers to offer the appointed sacrifice "with no explanation that it was in the interests of conventional prudence, as one known to attack the cultus would have to have given"; He speaks of one reconciled to his brother coming and offering his gift at the altar; He defends the temple as the house of prayer and "God's dwelling-place"; He uses sacrificial language in metaphor and exposition without hinting disapproval of its basic assumptions; He instituted His own memorial meal in complete accord with His reverence for the festivals of His people, especially for the Passover. All this abundantly justifies Vincent Taylor's summary of Jesus' attitude to the cultus as "detached, without repudiating", occasionally commanding its observance, and "while alive to its limitations yet recognizing (its) place in the religious life of the nation".[1]

Nowhere does Jesus suggest that religion can consist in wholly inward states of soul that seek and find no expression in appropriate acts of devotion and commitment, such as baptism might provide. On the whole, using only the Synoptic story, it must be said that the balance of probability is on the side of Jesus' approval of baptism during His ministry, the silence concerning the rite being explained either by the assumption, in a baptizing church, that reference to it was unnecessary, or by the selective nature of our records, or by the unreadiness of many to accept it during His lifetime, or the unreadiness of the disciples, on their training missions, to perform it—none of which is satisfactory, but nevertheless may point towards the truth.[2] The record of the Fourth Gospel to the effect that Jesus baptized, or countenanced His disciples' doing so, at Jordan, and that

[1] *Jesus and His Sacrifice*, 49ff. Cf. H. G. Marsh, *op. cit.*, 122.
[2] W. F. Flemington (*op. cit.*, 128) well remarks on the similarity of the position concerning the Lord's Supper, if there had not arisen at Corinth the need for correcting misunderstandings. For both rites we have a recorded act of Jesus, a command in a disputed text, and apostolic practice assuming His authority.

this led to contention with certain followers of John, is highly
debatable but what weight it has[1] serves to strengthen the
probability that the early church had firm and unambiguous
memories behind its practice of baptism in Jesus' name.

Nevertheless, through the greater part of the church's
history almost the total weight of the church's conviction
that Jesus meant her to baptize has rested on the words of the
Great Commission of Matthew 28. The importance of this
passage cannot be exaggerated. According to its terms,
baptism stands related to the making of disciples on exactly
the same footing as "teaching them to observe all that I have
commanded you" (28: 20): that is, baptism is prescribed for
those receptive of the commissioned message. Further, the
passage adds one totally new note, perhaps unique in the New
Testament: that the *practice* of baptism by the church (as
distinct from its *acceptance* by the baptized) is an act of
obedience to divine command. The unique circumstances
of this great utterance, the association with the world-wide
commission, the link with the requirement of absolute
obedience, and the attachment of the unforgettable promise
of the Master's presence to the end of the age, all lend a
solemnity and power to the saying which reflect on to the
baptismal reference a significance even greater than the
simple command itself. We cannot forget that baptism is set
by this saying in the context of the ascension, the promise of
power, the vision of the world-church, and the assurance
of the unbroken fellowship of the risen Lord.

It is therefore with the greater reluctance that the difficulties and uncertainties surrounding the passage have to be
admitted. They are many and varied—so varied that they
lend no weight to each other and their force is not cumula-
tive,[2] nor sometimes even consistent. It must be borne in

[1] The increasing respect of modern scholars for the historical accuracy of the
Fourth Gospel (T. W. Manson, A. M. Hunter, W. F. Howard, R. H. Strachan,
A. H. McNeile and J. Moffatt quoting Jewish support for the discourses); the
general tendency of that gospel to play down the sacraments rather than invent
such a story; and the possibility that the baptizing was confined to the Judean
ministry of which the Synoptics say so little, leads the present writer to side
with those (M. Dods, C. A. Scott, H. Wheeler Robinson, J. H. Bernard, H. H.
Rowley) who in varying degrees incline towards accepting the Johannine
story of baptisms on Jesus' authority during His earthly ministry.

[2] Literary, historical, theological and textual arguments affect different
elements in the passage and either may be true or false without influencing
the others. On this, and for a thorough study of the whole question of
Matt. 28: 18f., see P. W. Evans, *op. cit.*

mind that objections raised against these verses tell equally
against dominical authority for *all* forms of baptism, not
simply against that one form which they so eloquently and
convincingly maintain—and indeed the doubts canvassed
must extend also to the whole Matthean record of ascension,
world-mission, and final promise, not merely to clauses oft-
quoted in baptismal controversy.

A meticulous examination of the various objections raised
against these verses, however, does not shake the conviction
that the words contain nothing that Jesus may not have
said, or that the church's later practice contradicts. The
embryonic Trinitarianism, baptismal usage, and missionary
zeal of the apostolic church require some such explanation
as Matthew's epilogue admirably supplies.[1] Dogmatism is
out of place, but there seems no convincing argument to
prevent our accepting the closing words of Matthew as
conveying the meaning of Jesus with no less confidence than
attaches to almost any other word or deed attributed to
Him; or to preclude our believing that the apostolic church
was fundamentally right in concluding that thus and thus the
risen Lord would have her do.

Such a conclusion is obviously of supreme importance for
the question of the dominical authority of baptism, and for
the meaning and application of the rite. The structure of the
Commissioning sentence (Matt. 28: 19, aorist imperative
with three dependent participles, one aorist—"having gone";

---

[1] J. Denney (*The Death of Christ*), on Matt. 28, writes, "There is a link wanted
to unite what we have seen in the gospels with what we find when we pass from
them to the other books of the New Testament, and that link is exactly supplied
by the charge of Jesus to make the forgiveness of sins the centre of their Gospel
and to attach it to the rite by which men were admitted to the Christian
society . . . it is quite impossible to believe that this representation of the gospels
has nothing in it." T. H. Robinson, *The Gospel of Matthew* (Moffatt Commentary), 237, says, "Very possibly the Trinitarian formula is a reflection back into
the narrative of the practice of the early Church, but there is no need to doubt
the essence of the command"; W. F. Flemington (*op. cit.*, 109, 129) thinks that the
authority of Jesus would be the most satisfactory explanation of the church's
practice of baptism, but goes on to suggest that Matthew's epilogue is not a
historical record but a poetic, dramatic, artistic representation of the Church's
conviction about it; P. W. Evans (*op. cit.*, 21) reached a similarly "indecisive"
conclusion about the exact wording, but thinks we may still have Jesus'
intention correctly reported. The Church of Scotland (*Interim Report of the
Special Commission on Baptism*, Part I) thinks few sayings better authenticated
than this, and this "the institution of baptism by the Risen Lord"; N. Clark
(*The Approach to the Theology of the Sacraments*, 16, 19, 29) thinks Matt. 28 on
many grounds suspect, so that little weight can be attached to its testimony;
the belief that here we have the institution of baptism is too simple and ultimately untenable.

H

two present—"baptizing . . . teaching . . .") makes it plain that the baptizing and teaching are coincident in time with the making of disciples, as component parts, or significant accompaniments, of that process. A change of gender in the *objects* of baptism brings out the suggestion that while the making of disciples is something to be applied (or attempted) in respect of "all nations" the baptizing and teaching will be applicable to those ($\mu\alpha\theta\eta\tau\alpha\acute{\iota}$, understood) who accept discipling—the Gospel is for all, baptism for disciples. In the Great Commission therefore baptism is set in closest relation to discipling (which, as Karl Barth said, is certainly no act that can be completed without the responsible decision of the one concerned), to teaching (which likewise presupposes a comprehending and responsive subject),[1] and to observance of commandments (again assuming moral response to an imposed and acknowledged obligation). It is related, that is to say, to personal commitment, intellectual apprehension and moral consecration, and this in closest accord with all the terms of initiation into the divine kingdom which we meet in the teaching of Jesus.

Part of the difficulty of conceiving our Lord's attitude to baptism is the persistent but erroneous assumption that baptism is essentially a ceremonial, ritual act, out of keeping with the depth and moral challenge of His teaching—in other words, that it is of the same *kind* as infant baptism. The difficulty is a very real one: we simply cannot conceive Jesus requiring such a form of initiation to spiritual life. The whole result of our study of the terms upon which men enter the divine kingdom and come to partake of eternal life precludes such a belief. Repentance and faith, a spiritual rebirth and a spiritual death, acceptance of the divine love and surrender to the divine rule—these are the gateways to blessedness, and apart from these none, whatever his racial or spiritual lineage, can know salvation. But if baptism be indeed the outward confession in symbolic and dramatic form of just these things, if the act of immersion be but the visible and irrevocable expression of such repentance and faith, acceptance and surrender, then it is in every way congruous with

---

[1] This remains true even if $\mu\alpha\theta\eta\tau\epsilon\acute{\upsilon}\omega$ be understood as "teaching children"; the capacity of the baptized to be taught is the crucial point at issue between believers' and infant baptism.

the whole message of the Master, and we need have no doubts that *such* baptism carries His authority and inherits His promise.

C. BAPTISM IN THE ACTS OF THE APOSTLES

by S. I. Buse

The Acts of the Apostles refers more frequently to baptism than does any other New Testament book. The Moulton-Geden concordance shows twenty-one occurrences of βαπτίζω in Acts over against fourteen in all the Pauline writings, ten in Mark and thirteen in John, and six occurrences of βάπτισμα as opposed to three in Paul and four in Mark. Since the majority of the cases in the gospels concern the rite of John the Baptist, the actual contrast, as far as Christian baptism is concerned, is even greater than appears at first sight. The references in Acts are in accounts of events rather than in doctrinal statements, but the outlook of a religious community, at least in its most primitive period, is shown most clearly by its rites and practices. In fact, many of our problems about baptism in New Testament times are posed by the narratives of Acts.

The Universality of Baptism

R. R. Williams[1] asserts that "it is very clear that baptism is the normal, indeed the invariable, gateway to membership in the Church" in the record of Acts. So dogmatic a statement is surprising in view of arguments that have often been put forward to support the opposite viewpoint. James Mackinnon,[2] for example, says that baptism may not have been "invariably required as a condition of salvation", on the ground of passages in the primitive preaching like Acts 3: 19 ("Repent therefore, and turn again, that your sins may be blotted out"), and 10: 43 ("Everyone who believes in him receives forgiveness of sins through his name"). While this argument can be countered by pointing to Acts 10: 48 ("And he commanded them to be baptized into the name of Jesus"), and stressing the fact that Peter saw the descent of the Holy

---

[1] "Baptism", in A. Richardson (ed.), *A Theological Word Book of the Bible*, 28.
[2] *The Gospel in the Early Church*, 15-16.

Spirit on Cornelius and his fellow Gentiles as divine permission to baptize rather than as a sign that baptism was unessential,[1] it is far from easy to meet an argument built on the absence of any reference to the baptism of the pre-Pentecost group. That the explanation is to be found in the possibility that the "hundred and twenty" may have been baptized by John the Baptist and that all that was then needed was the descent of the Holy Spirit is ruled out by the story of the disciples of John at Ephesus who had been baptized by John but had to be rebaptized into the name of Jesus. W. F. Flemington's suggestion[2] that "the original disciples" had less need of baptism because they had "seen Jesus" is cancelled out by his own remark that "the difficulty on this hypothesis would be the baptism of St. Paul himself. He claimed no less than the other apostles to have 'seen the Lord', yet he was admitted to the church by baptism." The possibility that the "hundred and twenty" might have submitted to baptism during the ministry of our Lord Himself is very remote: for the evidence for any practice of baptism by Jesus or His disciples is very slender and, even when it is admitted, refers only to the early part of His ministry: the complete silence of the Synoptic record is hardly countered by H. G. Marsh's supposition that it was due simply to a desire to stress the teaching and life of Jesus and does not necessarily mean that baptism was not practised.[3] Thus the conclusion is inescapable: *baptism may have been the normal rite of admission to the Christian community in the Acts of the Apostles, but it can hardly be described as either universal or necessary for salvation.*

The Relationship between Water-baptism and Spirit-baptism

Sometimes, in Acts, baptism is mentioned without any reference to the Spirit (16: 15, 33; 8: 38—unless we accept the variant reading); on at least one occasion baptism is the precondition of the gift of the Spirit (2: 38); on at least one the outpouring of the Spirit clearly precedes baptism (10: 44ff.); whereas another group of narratives implies that the gift of the Spirit is connected, not with baptism, but with the

---

[1] H. Schlier, "Zur kirchlichen Lehre von der Taufe", in *T.L.Z.*, 72 (1947), 327ff.
[2] *The New Testament Doctrine of Baptism*, 46f.
[3] *The Origin and Significance of New Testament Baptism*, 125.

laying on of hands. It is not surprising that widely differing views have emerged in the attempt to interpret such varied evidence.

1. Some[1] have understood Acts 1: 5 ("John baptized with water, but before many days you shall be baptized with the Holy Spirit"), as implying that at first Spirit-baptism superseded water-baptism. This would not have been surprising: water-baptism for John the Baptist was a pre-Messianic occurrence, which might have been considered no longer necessary after the eschatological gift of the Spirit had been received.[2] There is no real evidence, however, that this attitude was adopted. This text is surely an example of the kind of statement to which C. J. Cadoux[3] drew attention in which emphasis is gained by a rhetorical denial of another aspect, "without however seriously meaning that it ought not to be entertained". To rule out 2: 38 and 41 and the references to baptism in chs. 10 and 11 as redactorial is an arbitrary and unjustified procedure.

2. Others have insisted that baptism with water and the gift of the Spirit are bound together in Acts as in other parts of the New Testament, and that Peter's words on the day of Pentecost ("Be baptized every one of you in the name of Jesus Christ for the forgiveness of your sins; and you shall receive the gift of the Holy Spirit") show that baptism was normally accompanied by the gift of the Holy Spirit.[4] Such an assertion goes far beyond the evidence: for this is the only verse in Acts that explicitly links together baptism and the bestowal of the Spirit. Many scholars have denied the close connection even here.[5] They have insisted that the change of tense ($\beta \alpha \pi \tau \iota \sigma \theta \acute{\eta} \tau \omega$—$\lambda \acute{\eta} \mu \psi \epsilon \sigma \theta \epsilon$) and the manner in which the Spirit is mentioned, $\kappa \alpha \grave{\iota} \lambda \acute{\eta} \mu \psi \epsilon \sigma \theta \epsilon$ $\tau \acute{\eta} \nu \delta \omega \rho \epsilon \grave{\alpha} \nu \tau o \hat{\upsilon} \text{'} A \gamma \acute{\iota} o \upsilon \Pi \nu \epsilon \acute{\upsilon} \mu \alpha \tau o \varsigma$, after $\epsilon \grave{\iota} \varsigma \, \check{\alpha} \phi \epsilon \sigma \iota \nu \, \tau \hat{\omega} \nu$ $\acute{\alpha} \mu \alpha \rho \tau \iota \hat{\omega} \nu \, \acute{\upsilon} \mu \hat{\omega} \nu$, indicate that two distinct moments are envisaged, baptism with forgiveness of sins and the gift of the Holy Spirit. On this argument, $\kappa \alpha \acute{\iota}$, joining an imperative and a future form, has a consecutive sense. N. Adler

[1] F. J. Foakes Jackson and K. Lake (eds.), *The Beginnings of Christianity*, i, 337ff.
[2] J. Schneider, *Die Taufe im Neuen Testament*, 28.
[3] "The Use of Hyperbole in Scripture", in *E.T.*, lii (1940-41), 378ff.
[4] E.g. G. W. H. Lampe, *The Seal of the Spirit*, 33.
[5] E.g. N. Adler, *Taufe und Handauflegung*, 26ff.; M. Barth, *Die Taufe—Ein Sakrament?*, 142ff.

feels justified in saying that the reception of the Holy Spirit and baptism in Acts are quite separate the one from the other. It is difficult, however, to avoid feeling that such treatment of 2: 38 is to read into Luke's language a precision that is not there, especially when the somewhat parallel expression in 16: 31 is recalled: Πίστευσον ἐπὶ τὸν Κύριον Ἰησοῦν, καὶ σωθήσῃ σὺ καὶ ὁ οἶκός σου. Thus, 2: 38 should neither be explained away nor treated as determinative for the whole of the Acts of the Apostles.

3. Those who deny the connection between baptism and the bestowal of the Holy Spirit usually link the gift of the Spirit with the laying on of hands instead, claiming the support of a number of the narratives of Acts. The passages involved demand careful study.

(a) Of primary importance is the clear statement in Acts 8 and 9 that Philip's Samaritan converts were baptized by him but did not receive the Holy Spirit until the hands of the apostles were laid upon them some time afterwards. The attempts of a long line of interpreters to avoid the obvious significance of Luke's statement are far from convincing. Many have argued that πνεῦμα ἅγιον in this passage means gifts of the Spirit such as speaking with tongues or miracle-working and that such an interpretation fits in well with the Simon Magus episode. Among recent writers, Schlier[1] has adopted this viewpoint, saying that Luke found it unnecessary to mention that the Samaritans had received the Spirit at the moment of their incorporation into the body of Christ and that only the *charismata* were transmitted by the laying on of hands, a statement justifiably rejected with scorn by W. G. Kummel.[2] J. E. Oulton[3] tries to prove from the narrative of Acts that the Samaritans received the Spirit at the time of their baptism. He says that

the passage as a whole clearly suggests that, before the apostles came, the newly formed community of Samaritan Christians enjoyed the inner life that is the gift of the Spirit. There are in fact certain resemblances between the description of its life in 8: 5-13 and the description of the life of the new converts in Jerusalem after Pentecost in 2: 41-47. Simon and therefore

[1] *Loc. cit.*, 328f.
[2] "Das Urchristentum", in *T.R.*, xviii (1950), 35.
[3] "The Holy Spirit, Baptism and the Laying on of Hands in Acts", in *E.T.*, lxvi (1954-55), 236ff.

a fortiori the others "continued" with Philip, with which we may compare "they continued in the apostles' teaching". They give heed to Philip "with one accord". . . . Signs are done among them. There is much joy in their midst.

The argument is obviously strained: for the similarities to which attention is drawn are merely verbal. The joy of Acts 8 was prior to baptism and the result not of the coming of the Spirit but of seeing miraculous healings. πνεῦμα ἅγιον is never used of the gifts of the Holy Spirit rather than of the Spirit Himself in the New Testament.[1] A more reasonable, but still unsatisfying, attempt to explain away the connection of the bestowal of the Spirit here with the laying on of hands rather than with baptism is that of G. W. H. Lampe[2] who suggests, while half-committing himself to the charismatic view, that the case of the Samaritans was exceptional:

> The preaching of the Gospel in Samaria represented a crucial moment in the advance of Christianity. Hence, after the baptism of the first Samaritan converts, the leaders of the Church's mission come down from Jerusalem, and by the sign of fellowship and "contact" incorporate them into the apostolic (i.e. missionary) Church, with the result that there occurs a Samaritan "Pentecost", at least to the extent that visible signs are manifested of the outpouring of the Spirit.

(*b*) There may be more ground for questioning whether Paul received the Holy Spirit by the laying on of Ananias's hands before his baptism. The statement made by Ananias (9: 17) seems to involve both the restoration of Paul's sight and the imparting of the Holy Spirit. But D. Daube[3] has reminded us that we have to distinguish between the kinds of action indicated by the Hebrew words for the laying on of hands. *Samakh*, the word which would be used in connection with the gift of the Holy Spirit, involves leaning, indicating "the pouring of one's personality into another being". "One does not 'lean one's hands on a blind man's eyes', one only places them there." The word used for the restoration of Paul's sight would be *sim* or *shith*. This would lead to the conclusion that

> Ananias did not confer the Spirit on Paul in the way Peter and John conferred it on the Samaritans. What Ananias was

---

[1] N. Adler, *op. cit.*, 85f.   [2] *Op. cit.*, 66ff.
[3] *The New Testament and Rabbinic Judaism*, 224ff.

ordered to do, and did, was to restore Paul's sight. As this marked the last phase of a change of heart, he knew it would be followed by the gift of the Spirit. The Spirit was not, however, thought of as transferred by Ananias but as falling upon Paul direct from heaven.

(c) The third example is perhaps the most puzzling of all. The Spirit is given to the "disciples" at Ephesus after Paul has laid his hands on them. The unusual element in the incident is that, before the imparting of the Spirit, the disciples had to be rebaptized. It is difficult to find any reason for this. It is not enough to say that their previous baptism was not a Christian one.[1] The men concerned were not just followers of John the Baptist: for "disciple" is the designation of the Christian everywhere else in Acts[2] and Paul's question implies that the men were Christian believers: "Did you receive the Holy Spirit when you believed?" (19: 2). Yet Apollos was not rebaptized and, even if we argue with W. F. Flemington[3] that the fact that he was "fervent in Spirit" makes his case somewhat different, re-baptism rather than laying on of hands alone remains a problem. The most ingenious solution yet offered is that of Markus Barth.[4] He regards verse 5 as the end of Paul's speech rather than the resumption of Luke's narrative. Thus Paul is pictured as saying that John the Baptist, by linking with his baptism a demand for belief "in the one who was to come after him, that is, Jesus" (19: 4), had really baptized his hearers "in the name of the Lord Jesus" (19: 5). Markus Barth claims that, since all the gospels show that John the Baptist recognized Jesus as the "one who should come", Paul's description of John's baptism as really baptism into Christ would be in conformity with the tradition behind the gospels.

The thesis is very attractive. Its acceptance would reduce the complexity of our problem. There are, however, a number of considerations that throw doubt on its validity. Presumably a great number of the converts on the day of Pentecost had been baptized by John just three years

[1] Cf. H. Schlier, *loc. cit.*, 328.
[2] H. G. Marsh, *op. cit.*, 156; G. W. H. Lampe, *op. cit.*, 75; H. Lietzmann, *The Beginnings of the Christian Church*, 81.
[3] *Op. cit.*, 47.
[4] *Op. cit.*, 169ff.

previously—yet as far as they were concerned "the baptism of John" was not regarded as equivalent to baptism into the name of Jesus. Nor is this surprising. It is surely unthinkable that the baptism of all those who flocked to John during his great mission of repentance could have been considered as in a sense Christian. Moreover, as J. Hering[1] has pointed out, the hypothesis involves the absurdity that Jesus would have submitted to baptism into His own name.

How can evidence that appears to lead to such diverse viewpoints be co-ordinated? Some[2] have said that baptism and laying on of hands are parts of a "single complex of associated ideas" and that "baptism, when mentioned alone, stands for the whole baptismal mystery and includes the laying on of hands". The only possible passage that could be held to support such a position is the strange story of the "disciples" at Ephesus, and that is not enough to balance the occasions on which there is complete silence about the laying on of hands.[3] The only satisfactory solution must be one that takes full account of the differences within the narratives of Acts and suppresses none. That seems to involve an assumption either (i) that Luke was working with different sources which he failed to co-ordinate, or (ii) that he himself thought differently from one of his sources, or (iii) that the record has preserved for us hints of stages of development in baptismal doctrine and practice within the early church.[4] Whatever we choose among these, it is clear that there is a definite division in the Acts of the Apostles between the passages that connect the Spirit with the laying on of hands and those that say nothing about the latter rite. The division coincides with one that we might make on other grounds: for the former class is in the parts of Acts dealing with Philip and Paul and the second class in those sections of Acts in which Luke is dependent upon Semitic sources.

Another fact links up with this. The other distinctive element in Christian baptism was that it was in ($\dot{\epsilon}\nu$ or $\dot{\epsilon}\pi\iota$) or into ($\epsilon\dot{\iota}s$) the name of Jesus. Whether there is any

---

[1] "Le Baptême dans le Nouveau Testament", in *R.H.P.R.*, 33 (1953), 256.

[2] E.g. L. S. Thornton, *Confirmation, its Place in the Baptismal Mystery*, 73ff., with quotations from F. J. Foakes Jackson and K. Lake (eds.), *op. cit.*, 134-6.

[3] N. Adler, *op. cit.*, 98ff.

[4] B. S. Easton, *Early Christianity*, 100f.; F. J. Foakes Jackson and K. Lake (eds.), *op. cit.*, i, 238ff.; J. Weiss, *History of Primitive Christianity*, ii, 622ff.

difference in meaning between the use of the three preposi-
tions in the phrase has been a matter of dispute,[1] but manuscript variations give good reason for thinking that $ἐν$ and
$ἐπί$ were used interchangeably in this connection. What
demands explanation is that "into the name" is used in the
parts of Acts dealing with Philip and Paul and "in the
name" in the rest. Even if $ἐν$ and $εἰς$ were equivalent
terms, it can hardly be mere coincidence that one term is
used in one section and the other in the rest, particularly
when this division coincides with the one we have already
noticed between passages that connect the illapse of the
Spirit with the laying on of hands and those that contain
accounts of the bestowal of the Spirit without that rite.

We may summarize the salient points of our discussion of
the relationship of baptism and the Spirit in Acts, as follows:

  (i)   there is no indication that Spirit-baptism at any stage
        superseded water-baptism,
 (ii)   to assert that baptism and the gift of the Spirit
        always go together in Acts is to go beyond the
        evidence,
(iii)   in part of Acts there is a close connection between the
        gift of the Spirit and the laying-on of hands, but there
        are signs that this was a development later than the
        primitive Jerusalem church.

Infant Baptism

In the part of Acts that stresses the connection between
the laying-on of hands and the gift of the Spirit occur
passages that talk about the baptism of households. Many
have claimed that this proves administration of the sacrament to very young children within the New Testament
period. It would make a very neat hypothesis to see within
the Acts of the Apostles a development from an early stratum,
with baptism in the name of Jesus coinciding with the
reception of the Spirit, to a later stratum, in which you have
baptism even of infants followed by the laying-on of hands
with the bestowal of the Spirit. But such a view cannot be
justified. While H. G. Marsh[2] says confidently that "we

---

[1] F. J. Foakes Jackson and K. Lake (eds.), v, 123-24n.; H. G. Marsh, *op.
cit.*, 180f.; M. Goguel, *L'Église Primitive*, 311f.; H. Bietenhard, "Onoma", in
T.W.N.T., v, 274.
[2] *Op. cit.*, 176.

have definite statements regarding the baptism of households . . . and it is impossible to imagine that no children
were included in their numbers", that absence of children
is far from unimaginable is shown clearly by statements of
scholars of widely different standpoints.[1] Not only may
"households" mean slaves rather than children, but, for the
relevance of the argument for infant baptism, the children
involved would have to have been of so tender an age that
they could not express their own belief in baptism, which
is far too much to assume without proof. It is not surprising
that in recent studies attempts have been made to provide
further grounds for such an interpretation.

One has been sought in the religious environment of the
early Christian church. In the Gentile world children
as well as their parents were initiated into the mystery cults,
but the influence of the mystery religions on Christian
thought and practice would not be strong enough during the
period under discussion.[2] In Judaism the children of
proselytes were baptized when the parents entered the
Jewish community.[3] As Mr. Gilmore has pointed out above,
however, baptism was required of the children of proselytes
only at the time of their parents' admission, and children
born subsequently did not have to undergo the rite, so that
those who use this argument have therefore to add another
analogy, that of baptism and circumcision, in a rather
strained effort to make up for the obvious inadequacies of an
argument from proselyte baptism alone. E. Stauffer[4] contends that the word "house" bore ritual significance in the
Old Testament and that the formula "the whole house"
"demonstrably included the small children". Even if the
case were regarded as proven for the Old Testament, its
relevance for Luke's narratives in Acts would still remain
doubtful. It is significant that the mention of "households"
is in the more Hellenistic stratum of Acts and, as J. Schneider

---

[1] E.g. J. W. Hunkin, "The Organization and Worship of the Primitive
Church", in T. W. Manson (ed.), *A Companion to the Bible*, 476; T. Preiss, "Le
Baptême des Enfants et le Nouveau Testament", in *V.C.*, I, iii (1947), 120;
O. Cullmann, *Baptism in the New Testament*, 24.

[2] J. Leipoldt, *Die urchristliche Taufe im Lichte der Religionsgeschichte*, 73ff.; A.
Oepke, "Urchristentum und Kindertaufe", in *Z.N.W.*, xxix (1930), 81f.;
A. Benoit, "Le Problème du Pédobaptisme", in *R.H.P.R.*, 33 (1953), 134.

[3] See discussion in earlier chapter dealing with Proselyte Baptism, 65ff., together with O. Cullmann (*op. cit.*, 26), as example of the vast literature involved.

[4] *New Testament Theology*, 161, 298-99.

has pertinently remarked,[1] we may well doubt whether a Hellenist like Luke when he used the word "house" would have Old Testament ritual language in mind. Ignatius writes to Polycarp (viii. 2) about the bishop's wife "with the whole of her house *and her children*".

That these are efforts to prop up a tottering edifice is shown when we turn to the relevant passages in the Acts of the Apostles itself. The answer of Paul to the jailer should not be thought, as Cullmann has suggested,[2] "to impose the demand to believe upon the jailer alone, but to promise the salvation to him and his house": for verse 32 tells us that Paul and Silas preached the Gospel to the man and his household and verse 34 implies that they all believed. Acts 18: 8 tells us that "Crispus, the ruler of the synagogue, believed in the Lord, together with all his household; and many of the Corinthians hearing Paul believed and were baptized", the total effect of which is to stress the place of belief in baptism. The only case in which "house" could possibly be used as proof of the baptism of infants in Acts is that of Lydia, and, without indulging in fanciful speculation and suggesting that there is no indication that she was even married, we can say that there is no justification for taking "house" in this instance in a way different from that of Crispus.[3]

J. Jeremias[4] appeals also to Acts 2: 39, arguing that the τέκνα are not the coming generations, but the sons and daughters of those who are listening. He insists that the eschatological character of the passage supports his argument. But, over against this, we may place the constant use of the phrase in the Old Testament with reference to descendants and the declaration of Paul in 13: 32f.: "We bring you the good news that what God promised to the fathers, this he has fulfilled to us their children . . ." In any case, even if the children of the converts were in the mind of Peter when he spoke, there is no indication they were to be baptized or to receive the promise while they were still children. In fact, part of Jeremias's argument is based upon the parallelism

---

[1] *Die Taufe im Neuen Testament*, 37.
[2] *Op. cit.*, 53.
[3] On the whole paragraph see J. Schneider, *Taufe und Gemeinde im Neuen Testament*, 38f.
[4] *Hat die Urkirche die Kindertaufe geübt?*, 26.

to 2: 17 which shows that the child must be old enough to prophesy when he receives the promise.

Cullmann[1] has suggested that the use of κωλύειν in three passages in Acts is due to the fact that it comes out of an early baptismal liturgy, but it should be noted that each time the word is used in a baptismal context the phrasing is different. This is a strange phenomenon if liturgy is involved. Peter's questions in 10: 47 and 11: 17 are rhetorical—a stylistic device foreign to liturgical usage.[2] Markus Barth has effectively subjected the theory to ridicule, showing that it involves the ridiculous idea that God would stand as a suppliant before Peter asking that the Gentiles might be baptized, as if the power to grant or withhold permission for baptism was in the apostle's hands.[3] O. Heggelbacher[4] raises as an objection to Cullmann's thesis that there is no mention of a third person besides the candidate and the administrant in the *Didache*, nor, for that matter, in Acts 19: 5. We note that κωλύειν is used in relation to those who were casting out devils in the name of Jesus, while they were not His followers. Are we to draw the conclusion which Cullmann does with reference to children that there was discussion about baptizing such people in the early church? In fact the word seems one Luke or his sources likes: he uses it in the gospel at 6: 29 and 11: 52, where Matthew employs a different verb, and in 23: 2 which is peculiarly Lucan.[5]

A further, more general, argument in support of the infant baptism hypothesis is that the picture of baptism which is presented in the Acts of the Apostles is primarily one of divine activity. Cullmann talks in startling terms of the additions made to the church by baptism as "an absolutely free work of God independent of both our human state and our faith".[6]

As we have already indicated, there is overwhelming evidence of the close connection between believing and baptism in Acts. W. F. Flemington has produced a most impressive list of passages which link with the sacrament "hearing the Gospel", or "believing".[7] The people baptized on the day of Pentecost were "those who received his

---

[1] *Op. cit.*, 71ff.   [2] M. Barth, *op. cit.*, 156.   [3] *Op. cit.*, 156f.
[4] *Die christliche Taufe als Rechtsakt nach dem Zeugnis der Christenheit*, 50f.
[5] For a fuller discussion of this word in the Synoptic gospels see *supra*, 104ff.
[6] *Op. cit.*, 32.   [7] *Op. cit.*, 49.

(Peter's) word" (2: 41). The Samaritans were baptized
"when they believed Philip as he preached good news about
the kingdom of God and the name of Jesus Christ" (8: 12).
A similar remark is made about Simon specifically. It was on
hearing the Gospel or believing that Lydia, the Philippian
jailer, the Corinthians and the disciples at Ephesus are said
to have been baptized. Whatever may be said of the
"Western" reading of 8: 37, it is clear witness at the date of
the reading itself to the connection between baptism and
believing. To avoid the implications of these passages,
Cullmann goes to desperate lengths in an attempt to prove
that faith follows rather than precedes baptism.[1] It is true
that faith has to continue after baptism, but it must not be
forgotten that it is also the presupposition of it. Schlier,
himself an advocate of infant baptism, says uncompromisingly:

> According to Acts, faith preceded baptism. In it is manifest
> the first union with Christ through personal acceptance of the
> word. But faith precedes baptism in such a way that it prepares
> for it and leads to it. Belief precedes baptism as the condition
> without the fulfilment of which one could not have been
> baptized.[2]

It appears to have been customary, at the stage represented
by Acts, for baptism to follow repentance and faith without
any such intervening period of instruction as seems to have
been required later: the Philippian jailer and "all his" were
baptized immediately in the middle of the night.[3]

The necessity for repentance and belief shows that the
baptizand in Acts is regarded as far from passive. Indeed
on occasion Luke uses the middle voice for submission to
baptism. If the candidate plays no active part in his baptism,
how can Cullmann's "unambiguous passive" be put in the
form of a command, "Be baptized!" in answer to "What
shall we *do*?"[4]

In reaction to the position represented by Cullmann
other scholars tend to go to the other extreme and to make
baptism a more or less purely human action. Markus
Barth, for example, says that baptism in the Acts of the
Apostles cannot be regarded as an act of God, except in so

[1] *Op. cit.*, 50f.   [2] *Loc. cit.*, 331f.
[3] O. Heggelbacher, *op. cit.*, 57.   [4] M. Barth, *op. cit.*, 159.

far as any act of belief is divinely motivated: it is the response of the baptizand in repentance and belief.[1]

> One cannot regard baptism in Acts 2: 38 as a work of God or even as a form of the word of God. . . . When they are commanded to submit themselves to baptism, the carrying out of baptism is an act of their obedience, which follows God's miraculous act—and not itself a miraculous act of God. We should not profane God's wondrous act or mix it up with human or ecclesiastical activity. . . . The members of the community answer God's acts and words in and with the carrying out of baptism.

We have no right, however, to think of the human activity in baptism as the all-important factor. We must remember the significant fact that in Christian baptism the candidate does not baptize himself. It seems of little consequence who the actual ministrant was[2] during the period of Acts, but there are no cases of self-baptism.[3] The Christian convert was baptized by someone who was acting as the representative of his Lord. Only when the two sides of baptism, the human and the divine, are seen together is Luke's picture viewed whole.

It is clear, therefore, that, as far as the record of Acts is concerned, there is no evidence to support the view that children who were too young to confess their belief were baptized. This, however, in no way precluded a full emphasis on the activity of God in baptism, as some recent writers would assume. As Mr. Clark will show in Chapter 8, it is by no means necessary to practise the baptism of infants to give the working of God in the sacrament its full and proper place.

Our examination of the evidence of the Acts on baptism has presented us with a most varied picture, but some

---

[1] *Op. cit.*, 135f.   [2] R. Bultmann, *Theology of the New Testament*, i, 135.

[3] This has been disputed on the ground of the use of the middle voice in 20: 16, supported by an assertion that the Jews would not tolerate a change from auto- to hetero-baptism (Cf. H. G. Marsh, *op. cit.*, 75ff.; B. S. Easton, "Self-Baptism", in *A.J.Th.*, 24 (1920), 513ff.). But both contentions can be answered easily. The middle voice is "obviously due to its combination with the following words. . . . If the precise meaning of the Greek is to be pressed, it is surely to be interpreted, 'have yourself baptized', a sense in which the middle voice of βαπτίζειν is frequently used in the Fathers, who certainly do not understand it in the reflexive sense" (G. W. H. Lampe, *op. cit.*, 86). For John the Baptist to baptize others instead of witnessing their performance of a self-administered rite would be a minor innovation in comparison with his daring act of demanding that even Jews should be baptized.

features stand out clearly. Baptism is regarded as important, but not as absolutely essential. It is not necessarily bound up with the gift of the Holy Spirit. There is no evidence of its administration to any but those who were capable of repentance and confession. Nor can all this be dismissed as temporary and superficial practice, which, as Mr. Winward has shown,[1] would have no authority for us to-day. It has behind it a total view of the gospel and of the rite of baptism, which in its full implications expresses both the Gospel of God's grace and the human response to it, neither of which must be forgotten or under-emphasized.

D. BAPTISM IN THE EPISTLES OF PAUL

by G. R. Beasley-Murray

Paul provides more material for a doctrine of baptism than any other writer in the New Testament. It is not possible to deal here with every saying of his that includes, explicitly or otherwise, a mention of baptism. I shall adopt the procedure of discussing at length his cardinal utterances on it, dismissing more briefly the sayings of lesser import. By this means his peculiar contribution to the understanding of baptism should become clear. A few notes will be added by way of conclusion.

Rom. 10: 9-10. The significance of this saying, in which no mention of baptism occurs, lies in the virtually unanimous conviction of modern scholars that its summary of the Christian confession as "Jesus is Lord" is a citation of the primitive baptismal confession, made by a candidate about to be baptized.[2]

We have here intertwined a complex of associated concepts.

1. The Apostolic Gospel, "the word of faith which we preach" (verse 8). Its primary content is the resurrection of Jesus and His exaltation to Messianic lordship. This reproduces the primitive proclamation of the Palestinian church, whose testimony was summed up in "the resurrection of the Lord Jesus" (Acts 4: 33). But according to Luke,

[1] See *supra*, 51.
[2] See e.g. Joseph Crehan, *Early Christian Baptism and the Creed.*

Paul also was accustomed to preach "Jesus and the resurrection" (Acts 17: 18), and with his epistles before us we know that Paul proclaimed neither the resurrection without the cross nor the cross apart from the resurrection. Hence for the apostle faith in the risen Christ led to justification (verse 10, and see Rom. 4: 25—also a primitive formulation).

2. Faith's assent to the Gospel of the Resurrection. While the object of faith here is a proposition about Christ, its immediate juxtaposition with the acknowledgment of Christ as Lord shows it is not intended to be purely a credal affirmation. It proceeds "from the heart", hence "the intellectual faith in Jesus is also a disposition of the whole interior man".[1]

3. Confession that Jesus is Lord is made in baptism. Emphasis is thus laid on the part played by the one baptized: he both "calls on the name of the Lord" (cf. Acts 22: 16) and declares his faith in Christ as Lord (cf. Acts 8: 37, Western text). The candidate is then baptized "in the name of the Lord Jesus", as Acts repeatedly narrates. This element of baptismal liturgy was regarded as of great importance. It not only persisted through New Testament times into the later church but became elaborated into credal affirmations on the one hand and catechetical instruction on the other. I Peter illustrates both aspects of this development: in 3: 18-22 we see the beginnings of credal elaboration in the baptismal confession, and it is likely that the early chapters of the epistle formed a baptismal homily. Other hints of the baptismal confession may be seen in 1 Tim. 6: 12, Eph. 5: 26, and possibly Heb. 10: 23. For us the importance of the confession of the name by the baptized lies in its bringing to expression the candidate's faith in Christ. "The essential thing insisted on by the church was that the relation of the baptism to Christ should be unambiguously recognizable."[2]

4. Since faith in Jesus as the risen Lord brings justification, and confession of His name deliverance from this world and the life of the age to come (verse 10), the baptismal act in which both are expressed is the supreme moment in the believer's experience of salvation. The enigma of the relation

---

[1] M.-J. Lagrange, *Épitre aux Romains*, 258.
[2] A. Schlatter, *Theologie des Neuen Testaments*, ii, 492. See also P. Feine, "Taufe I, Schriftlehre", in *R.T.K.*, xix, 401, H. G. Marsh, *The Origin and Significance of New Testament Baptism*, 173f., O. Michel, *Römerbrief*, 226-28, and P. Feine, *Theologie des Neuen Testaments*, 297.

of the Pauline teaching on salvation by faith and his high estimate of the value of baptism come most nearly to solution in this verse. For Paul the inner and outer acts of the decision of faith and its expression in baptism form one indissoluble event.

5. The nature of baptism as an overt expression of faith in Christ and the confession of His name made therein are consonant with the early Christian conviction that to be baptized into Christ is to be baptized into His church.[1]

It will be seen how this saying, couched as it is in primitive Christian phraseology, introduces us to some elements of first importance for the understanding of Paul's teaching. But for his more characteristic contribution to the inter-pretation of baptism we must turn elsewhere. We begin with Rom. 6: 1ff.

Rom. 6: 1-11. Although this passage contains the pro-foundest treatment of baptism in the New Testament, and some of Paul's most characteristic utterances on it, the first question to be asked is: To what extent does it reflect Paul's own teaching and to what extent is it derived from tradition? There is no statement corresponding to that in 1 Cor. 11: 23, where Paul acknowledges his dependence on tradition in the matter of the Lord's Supper. Yet the "Do you not know?" of verse 3 seems to imply that the Roman Christians knew that baptism into Christ meant baptism into His death.[2] F. M. Rendtorff urged that the argument of this chapter would fall to the ground unless Paul could regard his statements as "current coin".[3] O. Michel has gone further and deciphered the coins. He maintains that the "we" style, following on Rom. 5, betrays the language of the confession; whereas it is only rhetorical in verses 1-2, its use in verses 4-6, 8 is formal. The expression "raised through the glory of the Father" is not Pauline and sounds as though it came from a

---

[1] So A. Schlatter, *Gottes Gerechtigkeit*, 315: "The necessity of confession arises out of the indispensability of the proclamation. A man cannot become a believer in solitude; he can become such only through fellowship with those who speak the word of faith to him. . . . For the word is the message of the Christ who calls him into His church."

[2] H. Lietzmann (*An die Römer*, ad loc.), held that ἢ ἀγνοεῖτε or ἢ οὐκ οἴδατε always hints of something already agreed on. He cites Rom. 7: 1; 11: 2, I Cor. 3: 16; 5: 6; 6: 2f., 16, 19; 9: 13, 15, 24. The contention holds good for most of these cases, but does it for 1 Cor. 3: 16; 6: 16; 9: 13? Had the Corinthians really grasped for themselves what Paul relates?

[3] *Die Taufe im Urchristentum*, 6, n.2.

confession. Neither is the key term σύμφυτοι, "united with", found elsewhere in Paul. Accordingly Michel holds that Paul is here making use of a baptismal liturgy or hymn.[1]

It must be admitted that the attempt to extract liturgical fragments from a passage like this is a delicate process and is liable to subjectivism. The strongest point in favour of the use of a baptismal hymn here seems to me to be the manifest use of a hymn, similar in content, in 2 Tim. 2: 11-13; but who can say whether or not the latter was composed by Paul himself? Moreover, we must ask, where did the liturgy originate? G. Bornkamm[2] and R. Bultmann[3] alike express the view, already adopted by H. Lietzmann,[4] that this teaching was current in the Hellenistic church, which took it over from the Greek Mysteries. It is impossible for us here to deal with the relation of Paul's theology of baptism to the Mystery Religions,[5] but it seems to me questionable to wander in Hellenistic byways in search of parallels to Paul's language when we have a plausible source at hand in his own citation of the primitive *kerygma*, I Cor. 15: 3f. There the preaching is summarized as, "Christ *died*, was *buried*, has been *raised*". If Paul wished to relate baptism to the redemptive acts of Christ, what more natural thing could he do than to employ terms reminiscent of the primitive proclamation of the facts of the Gospel, with perhaps some phrases commonly used both in the exposition and administration of baptism? It is therefore at least plausible that in Rom. 6, as in his oral instruction, Paul used both traditional and liturgical phrases, without however citing an already formulated liturgy.[6]

The difficulty of going further than this lies in the absence from the rest of the New Testament writings of the interpretation of baptism as a dying and rising with Christ, and the fact that subsequent mention of the view depends on Paul.[7] The ἢ ἀγνοεῖτε may well presume the currency of teaching *analogous to* that of Paul, without possessing the

---

[1] *Op. cit.*, 131f.   [2] *Das Ende des Gesetzes*, 37, n.5.
[3] *New Testament Theology*, i, 141.   [4] *Op. cit.*, 67.
[5] For brief but comprehensive expositions of the issues, see P. Althaus, *Der Brief an die Römer*, 54-57, and E. Gaugler, *Der Brief an die Römer*, ad loc., and for more detailed treatment, A. R. S. Kennedy, *St. Paul and the Mystery Religions*.
[6] E. von Dobschütz, "Sakrament und Symbol im Urchristentum", in *T.S.K.*, 78 (1905), 27, had already linked Rom. 6 with 1 Cor. 15: 3f.
[7] This would apply also to 2 Tim. 2: 11ff.

Pauline stamp which is so plain in Rom. 6. It would satisfy the evidence if we could take it that Paul assumed that Christians generally related baptism to the death of Christ (hence its connection with forgiveness and cleansing, 1 Cor. 6: 11); on that foundation he built his interpretation of baptism as an involvement in Christ's redemptive acts, but he could claim that it was implied by the teaching of his contemporaries.[1]

We have spoken of Rom. 6: 1ff. as an "exposition" of Paul's teaching. Yet it is an incidental exposition, containing by no means all his convictions on baptism, and it is strictly subordinated to the progress of his argument. In his setting forth of the new aeon as one of grace (Rom. 3-5) Paul felt obliged to combat the response to his teaching, "Then let us live in sin that grace may abound!" (verse 1).[2] To this he replies, "How can we, who died to sin, still live in it?" (verse 2). That this death to sin is related to baptism is indubitable in view of what follows, all of which is directed against the perverse attitude implied in verse 1. The Christian has died to sin in baptism and therefore can have nothing more to do with it.

Verse 3 fortifies this contention in two ways: the symbolism of baptism as a *burial* is appealed to;[3] and the fact that the subsequent life is of a new quality—*resurrection life*, partaking of the righteousness of the kingdom—strengthens the negative statement that a death to sin has taken place. The old life of sin has gone; the new life of righteousness has taken its place.

In passing one should note that the reference to the

---

[1] Such appears to be the view of A. Schlatter, *Theologie des Neuen Testaments*, ii, 495, H. Windisch, *Taufe und Sünde*, 171, M. Dibelius, *Paul*, 93. R. Schnackenburg (*Das Heilsgeschehen bei der Taufe nach dem Apostel Paulus*, 129) cautiously urges that Paul *insinuates* his own interpretation into that which his readers held.

[2] Cf. Rom. 3: 5-8. Whether Paul had in view Jewish Christians who regarded that as the logical conclusion from his teaching, or Gentile Christians who adopted an extreme sacramentarianism (R. Bultmann, *op. cit.*, 333, and O. Michel, *op. cit.*, 129, hesitantly) is uncertain.

[3] Despite the strong protests of A. Schweitzer (*The Mysticism of Paul the Apostle*, 19), and others, that the *rite* of baptism as such has in no way affected Paul's language, it is hard not to conclude that it has done so. Cf., e.g., the general comparison C. H. Dodd sees here: "Immersion is a sort of burial . . . emergence a sort of resurrection." That most naturally explains why Paul speaks of baptism as a burial, *before* he speaks of the death of Christ, reversing the *kerygma*, which naturally mentions the death first and then the burial. That does not mean that the idea of the new life as resurrection life is dependent on the fact of emergence from the water; that teaching is due to the *kerygma*. The *kerygma* is prior to the rite but it is effectively embodied in the rite.

believer's resurrection in verse 4 should not be controlled by the somewhat different form of it in verse 5. The lack of explicit mention of resurrection in verse 4 is due to the ethical intention of the passage. Hence it is not good enough to say with G. Bornkamm[1] that the *future* resurrection of the believer (verse 5) is reflected in his present behaviour. The changed conduct is the consequence of the new life already received in Christ. The Christian participates even now in the new creation manifested in the resurrection of Christ (2 Cor. 5: 17). On the other hand it is equally wrong to conform the future tense of verse 5 to the point of view of verse 4 and to interpret it as a merely "logical" future.[2] It is characteristic of the apostle to hold in tension a conviction of the present power of Christ's resurrection in the believer and a hope for its consummation in the resurrection at the parousia. So it would seem to be here, and the natural reference of the tenses in verses 4 and 5 should be allowed to stand in each case.[3]

Verse 5 is intended to underscore the contention of verse 4 (note the conjunction "for"). It is essential to grasp that the key term ὁμοίωμα means not simply "copy", but "likeness" or "form", in the sense that it expresses the being or essence of what is represented. Bornkamm therefore urges that "the form of his death" designates *the form of the Crucified*. "The statement really means that as we have become united with Christ as the Crucified, so we shall be united with Christ as the Resurrected."[4] It indicates that we are baptized into Christ's death because we are united with Christ the crucified, and the thought of union with Christ is carried on to its consummation in the union with Him at the Last Day.[5]

---

[1] *Das Ende des Gesetzes*, 38.

[2] Such is the procedure of J. Schneider, *Die Taufe im Neuen Testament*, 47, following Zahn, Jülicher, Lagrange in their commentaries.

[3] So P. Lundberg, *La Typologie baptismale dans l'ancienne Église*, 212. R. Schnackenburg (*Das Heilsgeschehen bei der Taufe nach dem Apostel Paulus*, 47) held that the future ἐσόμεθα of verse 5 is to be interpreted as a logical future, but in a later essay he suggested that Paul's thought hovers between a logical and genuine future in reference to the last day. See "Todes- und Lebensgemeinschaft mit Christus", in *M.T.Z.*, vi (1955), 37.

[4] *Das Ende des Gesetzes*, 42.

[5] It is unlikely that ὁμοίωμα in verse 5 is a synonym for baptism. This entails inserting a pronoun αὐτό and translating, "If we have become united *with him* by the likeness of his death . . .", a procedure condemned by most recent scholars. On the other hand it is equally certain that ὁμοίωμα must be read into the second clause, "we shall be also *in the form* of his resurrection", and there it is impossible to interpret it of baptism if the future is taken seriously.

For the first time Paul explicitly states in verse 6 that the believer suffers a crucifixion. The thought has naturally been in his mind from verse 2 on and is plainly inferred in verse 5. In one sense, as has often been pointed out, the rite of baptism is unsuitable for expressing the idea of crucifixion. But the simple thought of death and burial with Christ in baptism is understandable enough and has been set forth in verses 3ff. The nature of the death is now mentioned by Paul, in accordance with his parenetic purpose, to stress the completeness of the believer's break with sin: his "old man" has been *crucified*, that the new man in Christ might live the life of the new age.[1]

Similarly we find for the first time in this chapter a mention of faith in verse 8. O. Michel[2] holds that "we believe" here virtually means "we confess"; but confession is the utterance of faith, and, as R. Bultmann has pointed out in reference to this saying, this is a knowledge that can be appropriated only in an obedient, comprehending faith, as in Rom. 5: 3 the knowledge that "suffering produces endurance" is the knowledge of those who are justified by faith. W. F. Flemington has further urged that this faith in the God who raises from the dead both Jesus and believers with Him must be presumed as the background of the whole passage from verse 2 on.[3] In view of Paul's teaching elsewhere, that is hardly to be denied. This chapter has the convert in mind, and all that Paul says of baptism presumes a faith responsive to the grace of God operative in it.

The conclusion of the argument is, "Reckon yourselves to be dead to sin but living to God in Christ Jesus" (verse 11). This demands, not an exercise of imagination, endeavouring to live *as if* such a thing were so in order to produce the effect, but a recognition of what has taken place in baptism into Christ: "Realize that in your union with Christ you were freed from the sovereignty of sin and death and entered the kingdom wherein you live unto God in Christ Jesus."

In the foregoing summary of Rom. 6: 1-11 I have deliberately avoided the cardinal issue of the passage until the whole

---

[1] The "old man" connotes the man who belongs to the age prior to Messiah's coming and the new age of his kingdom. The "body of sin" is an analogous expression, wherein we are to think of "body" as person rather than physical organism.

[2] *Römerbrief*, 318.

[3] *The New Testament Doctrine of Baptism*, 80f.

has passed under review. The question is: How does Paul conceive of the relation between death and resurrection with Christ and baptism? The answer given by W. Sanday and A. C. Headlam is characteristic of British New Testament scholarship in this century: "When we took the decisive step and became Christians we may be said to have died to sin." That is to say, the death to sin and resurrection to life took place in baptism.[1] Similarly James Denney wrote of baptism in this passage, "If we have really died in it as Christ died, then we shall have a corresponding experience of resurrection",[2] and W. F. Flemington characterizes baptism as "a re-enactment for the believer of what once happened to our Lord".[3] This view, however, is almost unanimously rejected by Continental scholars. G. Bornkamm insists that Paul never describes baptism as involving an analogous relationship between Christ and the baptized. The death which the baptized man and Christ die is one, namely the death of Christ on the cross. He notes that Paul speaks of our being baptized into Christ, not into Jesus: the death of Jesus ended the old aeon and began the new, and it is the eschatological power of that Christ event that makes the baptismal event effective.[4] Similarly F.-J. Leenhardt maintains that the believer is not invited to die to himself but to believe that he has died with Christ and to seize this reality as an accomplished fact.[5] E. Fuchs, indeed, stated that to say that we ourselves "die" would mean to crucify Christ again; our participation in the death and resurrection of Christ is sheer miracle.[6] For A. Nygren the whole is explained by the parallel between Adam and Christ in Rom. 5. As we participate in Adam's sin and death, so we participate in Christ's death and righteousness. "That of which Paul speaks is a simple and unmystical reality. God has made Christ the head of a new humanity; and into that new organic relationship he has brought us through baptism."[7]

In the light of this conflict of opinion Rom. 6 can be read

[1] Such is the meaning of the statement in the context. *Epistle of Paul to the Romans* (I.C.C.), 154.
[2] On Rom. 6: 5, in his commentary in the *Expositor's Greek New Testament*.
[3] *Op. cit.*, 59.
[4] *Das Ende des Gesetzes*, 235-37.
[5] *Le Baptême chrétien*, 63.
[6] *Die Freiheit des Glaubens*, 29, 37.
[7] *Commentary on Romans* (E.Tr.), 237.

in two different ways: the aorists of verses 2, 4, 5, 6, 8 relate either to the death the believer died in Christ on Golgotha or to the death he dies in baptism. But is it not apparent that both these views are inadequate and that both are embraced at once by Paul? Naturally there is no virtue in baptism apart from Christ and His redemptive acts, but few believe that the personal appropriation of the grace of God is irrelevant; least of all would Paul have done so. It is the old problem in a new guise of relating the objective work of redemption to the personal appropriation of it; we do as great a disservice to theology when we over-emphasize the former as when we disproportionately magnify the latter.

We have therefore to recognize a tension in Paul's thought concerning the relation of Christ's redemptive acts and the believer's response thereto in baptism. On the one hand a work of reconciliation has been wrought independently of the will or power of the believer, yet which has included him potentially in its scope from the beginning. It is that work of grace which gives baptism any significance. The believer gratefully recognizes the mercy of God and into that death and life from death he is baptized. From this point of view it is legitimate to stress the passives of Rom. 6: the believer is *buried*, is *united* with the form of Christ's death, is *crucified* with Him, etc. A baptized man is no more able to produce this effect for himself than he is able to raise himself from death to the incorruptible life of the kingdom. Here also belongs the recognition of the representative nature of Christ's relation to mankind. It is no accident that the exposition of baptism in Rom. 6 follows upon the comparison of Adam and Christ in Rom. 5, and that comparison has gained in power for us since our understanding of the Semitic concept of corporate personality: the perpetual significance of the redemptive acts of the Head become effective for us when we are incorporated by baptism as members of His new humanity.[1]

But not alone the "for us", the "with Him" is of importance. Here is the second aspect of the tension of which we have spoken. Baptism leads to union with the *crucified* Christ. That union involves being united with Him in His

---

[1] See the exposition of this aspect of Paul's teaching in E. Best, *One Body in Christ*, 34ff.

destiny. As R. Schnackenburg put it, the being "in Christ" involves sharing the passion "with Christ"—the believer has not only to receive the fruits of Christ's suffering but to share it with Him.[1] From this angle the school of thought that lays weight exclusively on the passivity of the believer in baptism is mistaken. This is freely admitted by P. Althaus, whose loyalty to Lutheranism is unquestioned. His position may be summed up in his dictum, "God so works *on* man that He works *with* him." The grace of God operative in redemption becomes effective only as it is seized by the judgment of faith.[2] This viewpoint is given further expression in Althaus' exposition of Gal. 5: 24, a significant saying in the context of our discussion. In his commentary on Galatians he writes:

> The event in baptism is not naturalistic but entirely personal. What the baptismal act wrought in them (the baptized) they themselves confessed and made their own act—it is the missionary, adult baptism of which Paul thinks. Hence it comes about that *that which is designated in Rom. 6: 2ff. as a happening (Widerfahrnis), which a man suffers in baptism, is here spoken of as his personal act: he has crucified the old man with his passions and desires, has renounced him—a fundamental, once for all decision*, which then admittedly becomes the perpetual task for the whole life of the Christian.

The receptivity and submission of the believer in baptism is thus matched by his renunciation of his old self and identification of himself with Christ in death to sin. The statement cannot be avoided—*as* Christ died for sin, *so* he dies to sin. The same thought is present in Col. 3: 9f., if we regard the participles as past and not as equivalents to the imperative mood: "Do not lie . . . seeing that you put off the old nature with its practices and put on the new nature." The idea of stripping off the old man is fundamentally the same as renouncing him or crucifying him; and the baptismal experience is to be followed by a life in accord with it.

All this admittedly must be considered in the light of the determinative character of Christ's redeeming acts and

---

[1] *Das Heilsgeschehen bei der Taufe nach dem Apostel Paulus.* Schnackenburg's discussions of this matter, both in his book and the article that followed it, constitute the profoundest treatment I have seen of this element in Paul's baptismal theology and are worthy of closest study.

[2] *Op. cit.*, 51.

grace, but it ought to show that the rejection, often uttered in contemptuous terms, of so-called "baptismal experience" is not justified by appeal to Paul. A. Oepke may be right in asserting, "Every representation of the Pauline view of baptism is mistaken that starts out from a subjective-naturalistic 'baptismal experience' and not in the first instance from the objective situation of the salvation history."[1] But what has been outlined above is not "naturalistic", nor has the subjective aspect been made the starting point, nor has it been exalted above the objective redemption history: on the contrary, the personal experience has been grounded upon the objective redemption. F. M. Rendtorff long ago pointed out that the chief purport of Rom. 6: 3-4 is: "We were baptized into Christ . . . in order that we should walk in newness of life."[2] Christian baptism has an ethical import in its very structure. Any interpretation of it which minimizes that element is false to the thought of Paul.

Gal. 3: 27. It has already been mentioned that the idea of baptism as a "putting on" Christ (like a garment) is similar to that of Rom. 6; to "wear" the garment which is Christ presupposes a discarding of the garment which is the sinful self (Rom. 13: 12-14, Col. 3: 9ff.). In both Rom. 6: 2 and this passage the prime characteristic of baptism is its introduction "into Christ". Paul's parenetic purpose in Romans caused him to stress the negative consequence of that relationship—it involves the death of self; here the positive consequences are drawn—union with Christ involves sharing His sonship and oneness with the church.

The nature of the union with Christ is noteworthy. Most British exegetes link the phrase "in Christ Jesus" of verse 26 with the verb, not with "through faith": "You are all, through faith, sons of God in Christ Jesus." This was bestowed through faith, but not alone so: "*for* all you who were baptized into Christ did put on Christ". The union was realized in baptism. It is evident that baptism *into* Christ results in being *in* Christ, which is a *putting on* Christ. Paul then speaks of the breaking down of earthly distinctions among those "in Christ Jesus", in whom all are "one man". Baptism brings unity with Christ and His church. *And in that order of precedence.* In reaction from the individualism of

[1] Βάπτω, in *T.W.N.T.*, i, 540.   [2] *Op. cit.*, 30, n.2.

Deissmann, the pendulum has swung in the other direction and "in Christ" is now viewed as primarily a social concept.[1] Even where the personal aspect of the relationship is not denied, it is commonly regarded as secondary, as in the statement of C. H. Dodd, "The baptized person has been baptized into the Church, into the body of Christ, *and so* into Christ."[2] This is surely to reverse the situation. While it is true that for Paul Christ and the church are inseparable, the stress of his baptismal utterances is chiefly on the relationship of the believer with Christ the redeemer (1 Cor. 12: 13 is otherwise). The position is eased if we appeal to the concept of corporate personality; being "in Christ" involves personal relationship with the Head and unity with the members of the Body. But it remains that it is the Redeemer who reconciled us to God and gives life from the dead, not the church.

Consonant with this conception, Paul declares that baptism with faith bestows the status of sons of God in Christ. The thought of sonship is uppermost in Paul's mind in this passage. He goes on to draw a parallel between the situation of the race before Christ and that of an heir before attaining his majority (Gal. 4: 1ff.). God sent His Son "to deliver those under the law, that they might receive the adoption as sons". That became of personal moment to us when "God sent forth the Spirit of His Son into our hearts, crying, Abba, Father" (Gal. 4: 6). The striking parallel between Gal. 3: 26f. and 4: 6, together with its aorist tense, justifies us in thinking that the latter relates to what was done once for all in the union with the Son of God in baptism.[3]

Col. 2: 11-12. The formulation of this passage, as in those we have already considered, is due to the dogmatic purpose of the letter. In opposition to the exaltation of circumcision in the teaching of the heretics at Colossae, Paul declares that his readers have already undergone a more radical one in baptism. The conjunction of aorist tenses demands that "You were circumcised" relates to the time of

---

[1] "The expression 'being in Christ' is merely a brachylogy for being partakers in the mystical Body of Christ" (A. Schweitzer, *op. cit.*, 122f.). "'In Christ', far from being a formula for mystic union, is primarily an ecclesiological formula" (R. Bultmann, *op. cit.*, 311).

[2] *The Epistle of Paul to the Romans*, 87f.

[3] So W. F. Flemington, *op. cit.*, 58.

baptism indicated in the participle of verse 12. But not only so, Paul virtually says, "You were circumcised . . . in the circumcision of Christ and by being buried in baptism." The "circumcision of Christ" denotes His death on the cross; it is not a synonym for baptism.[1] The "circumcision" of the Colossian Christians occurred *in Christ on the cross* and *in their baptism into His death*. The objective and subjective elements of dying with Christ, which we saw in Rom. 6, here lie on the surface.[2] This fusion of the two elements is under-scored by the addition, "*in which* you were raised *through faith in the operation of God* who raised Him from the dead". The resurrection of the believer occurs in baptism through faith. Thus the passage under review brings to clearer expression three elements of baptismal experience which we saw in Rom. 6: it makes plain both the objective relation of Christ's death to baptism and the believer's subjective confession thereto in the consigning of his "old nature" to death; it substitutes for an implicit mention of resurrection with Christ in baptism an explicit statement of that factor; it replaces an indirect intimation of the relationship of faith to baptism by an unambiguous declaration concerning it.

It does more. It places circumcision alongside baptism. What is the significance of this juxtaposition? It is commonly considered that baptism has simply replaced circumcision and is to be understood in like manner.[3] The former proposi-tion is conceivable, though whether it may legitimately be deduced from this *ad hominem* argument is dubious. The latter

---

[1] The contrary is held by J. B. Lightfoot, *St. Paul's Epistle to the Colossians, and Philemon*, 181 ff., O Cullmann, *Baptism in the New Testament*, 59, J. Jeremias, *Hat die Urkirche die Kindertaufe geübt?*, J. Schneider, *op. cit.*, 48. But agreement with the position here maintained is expressed by F. M. Rendtorff, *op. cit.*, 44, A. Peake, *Epistle of Paul to the Colossians* (E.G.T.), iii, 525, A. Schlatter, *Erläuterungen zum Neuen Testament*, 7 Teil, 277, E. Lohmeyer, *Die Briefe an die Kolosser und an Philemon*, 109; the reference to the cross is maintained, but different deductions drawn, by P. Ch. Marcel (*The Biblical Doctrine of Infant Baptism*, 157), and the Church of Scotland, *Interim Report of the Special Com-mission on Baptism*, Part I (1955), 39.

[2] So G. Bornkamm: "What happened in the death of Christ on a cosmic scale is fulfilled existentially in baptism. The overthrowing of the powers, the stripping off of their might, is appropriated by the believer in the stripping off of his 'Body of flesh'." ("Die neutestamentliche Lehre der Taufe", in *T.B.*, xvii (1938), 51.)

[3] So O. Cullmann, *op. cit.*, 56 ff., The Church of Scotland, *Interim Report of the Special Commission on Baptism*, Part I (1955), 13, J. Jeremias, *op. cit.*, 40 f., P. Ch. Marcel, *op. cit.*, 84 ff. ("There is no essential or fundamental difference between the sacraments of the Old Testament and those of the New", p. 89.)

conclusion not only goes beyond the evidence, it seems to many to go against it. G. W. H. Lampe is surely right in urging that in Col. 2: 11f. baptism is *contrasted* rather than compared with circumcision.

> The real correspondence to which St. Paul points is between the Christian possession of the Spirit as the result of his faith-response to the grace of God in Christ, and the inward "circumcision of the heart" to which the great prophets had looked forward.[1]

When we consider the "existential" nature of baptism as described by Paul and the importance of faith for its efficacy, it becomes difficult to believe that Paul placed circumcision on a comparable level with baptism, or interpreted the latter in the light of the former. However understandable it is that the comparison of the two rites encouraged the church to baptize the infant children of Christian parents, as the Jews circumcised theirs, we ought to be candid enough to recognize that, on the basis of Paul's own declarations, the idea of baptizing infants involves a departure from his baptismal theology.[2]

Other Passages. The utterances we have considered contain the foundation teaching of Paul on baptism. We must now briefly mention certain other sayings that have significance for it.

1 Cor. 6: 11 certainly relates to baptism.[3] The terms "you had yourselves washed" (cf. Acts 22: 16), "in the name of the Lord Jesus Christ", the immediate mention of the Spirit in similar terms, the aorist tenses—all are best explained on the assumption that Paul here has baptism in mind. The

---

[1] *The Seal of the Spirit*, 5. The same point is made by H. Windisch, *op. cit.*, 197. H. G. Marsh (*op. cit.*, 192f.) also warns against concluding from this saying that Paul thought of the ritual act of baptism after the manner of circumcision.

[2] Compare the restrained remarks on Col. 2: 11 in M. Dibelius's commentary, *An Die Kolosser, Epheser, an Philemon*, 3rd edition revised by H. Greeven (in H. Lietzmann's *Handbuch zum Neuen Testament*), 30f.: "The analogy here affirmed by Paul between the two rites of reception must not be taken as proof that infant baptism, like circumcision, was already practised at that time when parents came over into the community (this against Jeremias). . . . The immediate application of the parallelism is directed solely to the character of baptism as an initiatory sacrament, as something ordained of the Lord, a sign of exclusive attachment to Him. The treatment of children who may have been present can have been different. It is as little in view here as the significant distinction that circumcision applies solely to men."

[3] The attempt of C. Anderson Scott to interpret otherwise illustrates the difficulty of the denial. See his *Christianity According to Paul*, 120.

chief significance of the saying is its linking of baptism with justification and sanctification.[1]

1 Cor. 12: 13. The analogy of Gal. *3: 27f.* forbids interpreting this saying as implying a Spirit baptism distinct from the experience of baptism in water.[2] It indicates, rather, that through the activity of the Spirit in baptism the rite becomes an initiation into the One Body. The corporate significance of the formula "in Christ" is to the fore here. The last clause of the sentence, acutely translated by Moffatt "we have all been imbued with one Spirit", relates to being "watered" by the Spirit, in accordance with the prophetic promises of an outpouring of the Spirit in the last days, not to drinking in the Lord's Supper.[3]

In *2 Cor. 1: 22, Eph. 1: 13; 4: 30* we find the idea of the believer being "sealed" with the Holy Spirit. In view of the exhaustive researches of G. W. H. Lampe on the meaning of this conception, it is unnecessary to attempt a further demonstration of its connection with baptism. The central idea appears to be that believers, through faith-baptism, are stamped as God's possession. "This stamp is the presence and activity of the indwelling Spirit of God, the 'first instalment' of the ultimate total redemption which is yet to come at the parousia."[4] The conception is therefore eschatological. Baptism, like the Lord's Supper, looks on to the Last Day as well as back to the first Easter.

Of *Eph. 4: 5* it is unnecessary to say more than that its inclusion of baptism in the great "unities of the Church" indicates the importance it had for the church of the New Testament. Attempts to show that the "one baptism" denotes the baptism of Christ in the Jordan and on the cross, in which we share through our own baptism, do not commend themselves and cannot be considered here.[5]

---

[1] So W. F. Flemington, *op. cit.*, 56. If, however, Paul is reproducing the common Christian view of baptism in traditional terms, they would have to be reduced in their significance. (H. Windisch, e.g., *op. cit.*, 130, regards the Spirit here as the power that brings about sanctification. See further R. Bultmann, *op. cit.*, 136.)

[2] Against E. Best, *op. cit.*, 73.

[3] So R. Schnackenburg, *Das Heilsgeschehen bei der Taufe nach dem Apostel Paulus*, 80, G. W. H. Lampe, *op. cit.*, 56.

[4] *Op. cit.*, 5f.

[5] See The Church of Scotland, *Interim Report of the Special Commission on Baptism*, Part I (1955), 7-10, J. A. T. Robinson, "The One Baptism as a Category of New Testament Soteriology", in *S.J.Th.*, 6 (1953), 257ff.

Eph. 5: 25-27 is unique in that it speaks of the church as the subject of baptism. "Christ loved the Church . . . that he might sanctify and cleanse her . . ." It is doubtful whether we ought to press this language and make it refer to a single occasion on which the church was "baptized", as, e.g., its blood baptism on the cross.[1] Paul gathers up the individual baptisms of Christians into a collective whole, implying, however, that the purpose of baptism is the calling of a holy community. The addition at the end of verse 26, "with a word" (or "*the* word"), is important. This "word" it is, apparently, that gives baptism its significance. Whether it denotes the Gospel, or the pronouncement of the Name over the baptized person, or the confession of the Name by the baptized, remains uncertain. The last alternative is most likely; it implies the other two, since it is a confession of faith in the *Lord* according to the promise of the *Gospel*.

The meaning of *Titus 3: 5-7* depends in part on the background assumed for it. It is most usually regarded as moving towards the later theology of the Catholic church.[2] This may be so, but we cannot be sure. Note first that it is probably a citation from a baptismal hymn or liturgy, as the formula at the beginning of verse 8 indicates:[3] it therefore represents a stage of tradition earlier than the writing of the Pastoral Epistles. Secondly, the term παλινγενεσία, "regeneration", while possibly deriving from Hellenistic religion, has an eschatological reference in Matt. 19: 28 and could well preserve it here also, signifying the life of the new world. That is precisely the idea of 2 Cor. 5: 17, and the presence of eschatological elements in our passage (the appearance of grace, justification, outpouring of the Spirit, inheritance of eternal life) strengthens the view that it is present in this saying also.[4] Its central conception is that in baptism the corresponding event occurs in the life of the individual as happened to the church at Pentecost: the Spirit is "poured out" through the risen Christ—an idea in direct line with the

[1] So Théo Preiss, "Le Baptême des enfants et le Nouveau Testament", in *V.C.*, i, 115.
[2] So A. Oepke, *op. cit.*, 541, R. Bultmann, *op. cit.*, 142, E. F. Scott *The Pastoral Epistles* (Moffatt Commentary), 174ff.
[3] Cf. E. F. Scott, *op. cit.*, 177f., B. S. Easton, *The Pastoral Epistles*, 99ff., J. Jeremias, *Die Briefe an Timotheus und Titus*, 66.
[4] See H. Windisch, *op. cit.*, 247, and compare C. H. Dodd, *The Fourth Gospel*, 304.

earliest interpretation of baptism, Acts 2: 33, 38.[1] Certainly the saying implies a realistic rather than symbolic understanding of baptism, but that applies to most of the Pauline utterances on baptism.

It may be well to add some consideration of *1 Cor. 7: 14; 10: 1ff.; 15: 29*. Each of these passages has been regarded as a cardinal baptism utterance of Paul, but it is doubtful whether any has much light to throw on our subject.

Taking them in reverse order, *1 Cor. 15: 29* has been claimed as of paramount significance, since it apparently involves a highly sacramental view of baptism. R. Bultmann,[2] for example, considers that there is no distinction in this saying between a sacramental and magical act; if Paul did not introduce baptism for the dead into Corinth, neither did he criticize it, for it was essentially one with his own mode of thought. Against this unwelcome conclusion attempts are continually made to eliminate the sacramentalism of the saying. Baptism for the dead may be a proleptic reference to the baptized themselves, whose bodies must die but whose baptism is in hope of resurrection;[3] or it is out of affection or respect for the wishes of the dead;[4] or it is in hope of reunion with the beloved dead.[5] Against all such views, one is inclined to agree with A. Oepke,[6] that interpretations which try to avoid the vicarious baptism for the dead lead astray. Once the idea of vicarious baptism is admitted, little is gained by the insistence that the νεκροί are Christian dead, nor can one admit with F.-J. Leenhardt[7] that our ignorance of the practice in Paul's time forbids our drawing any kind of conclusions from it; baptism for dead people is an operation on a *corpse*, or performed for an absentee, a sub-Christian perversion of the sacramental idea as set forth by Paul. If Paul tolerated it, it was by way of concession to a practice

[1] Thus G. Bornkamm, "Die neutestamentliche Lehre von der Taufe", in *T.B.*, xvii (1938), 52; L. S. Thornton, *The Common Life in the Body of Christ*, 190.

[2] *Op. cit.*, 135ff.

[3] G. W. H. Lampe, *op. cit.*, 94.

[4] A. Robertson and A. Plummer, *I Corinthians* (I.C.C.), 359.

[5] G. C. Findlay, *I Corinthians* (E.G.T.), 93f. This view is revived by Maria Raeder, a pupil of J. Jeremias, in "Vikariatstaufe in I Cor. xv. 29?" in *Z.N.W.*, 46 (1955), 258f., and by J. Jeremias himself in "Flesh and blood cannot inherit the Kingdom of God", in *N.T.S.*, ii (1955-56), 151ff.

[6] *Op. cit.*, i, 540, n. 63.

[7] *Op. cit.*, 60.

at variance with his own teaching. But, as is widely recognized, "the vital link is missing to show whether this doctrine had anything to do with Paul's teaching".[1] It is reasonable to suppose, with E. von Dobschutz,[2] that Paul here combats the Corinthian deniers of the resurrection with their own weapons: they assented to a practice whose significance was negated by their repudiation of the resurrection! While the evidence is insufficient to prove that this practice existed in the mystery religions, the material presented by J. Leipoldt[3] and F. M. Rendtorff[4] illustrates clearly enough the pagan milieu from which it sprang. It would be a dangerous weapon for advocates of infant baptism to use for the strengthening of their own position.

1 Cor. 10: 1ff. is increasingly cited as a source for Paul's baptismal teaching. O. Cullmann, for instance, finds support in it for his peculiar deduction from Rom. 6, that baptism is in two acts, first the divine action, secondly the understanding of baptism: "That prototype of baptism, the crossing of the Red Sea, is mentioned by Paul only to show that in the first act God is active and in the second man must respond."[5] The Scottish Report of May 1955[6] points out that Paul stresses that *all* were baptized, hence men, women *and children*; if Paul had not intended children to be baptized, he would have corrected the Old Testament example and explicitly excluded children from baptism. E. Best[7] follows the commentary of T. C. Edwards on 1 Corinthians and considers that, since Moses represented Christ, the baptism of the Fathers was no mere allegory but "a true baptism unto Christ", hence possessing an even deeper significance than the baptism of John. P. Lundberg[8] compares Rev. 15: 2 where John links the Red Sea crossing with the conception of a celestial sea that has to be crossed before entering heaven; so too, the passage through the Red Sea in 1 Cor. 10 implies the idea of baptism as a crossing the sea of death in order to attain the promised land.

All these interpretations suffer from an identical error:

[1] H. G. Marsh, *op. cit.*, 148. [2] *Op. cit.*, 36.
[3] *Die urchristliche Taufe im Lichte der Religionsgeschichte*, 50ff.
[4] *Op. cit.*, 33ff.
[5] *Op. cit.*, 49.
[6] The Church of Scotland, *Interim Report of the Special Commission on Baptism*, Part I (1955), 28.
[7] *Op. cit.*, 72. [8] *Op. cit.*, 145.

they put Paul's words to a use never intended by him. The writers have made of a subsidiary introduction (vv. 1-5) to an ethical appeal (vv. 6ff.) a dogmatic statement concerning the nature of the sacraments. As E. von Dob-schutz[1] said, to make of this passage a source for Paul's sacramental thought, instead of concentrating on the Old Testament story, is to make the verbal clothing of the thought the chief matter. In this connection one should note that Paul's employment of the word τυποί, types, in verse 6 covers not alone the quasi-sacraments of the sea and desert but the other experiences of the Israelites, mentioned in vv. 7ff. Naturally there is a correspondence between the experiences of the Fathers and the situation of the church, but it is not intended to be pressed. So A. R. S. Kennedy[2] wrote, "The nature of the reference to baptism clearly shows that here we have to do with a somewhat daring analogy, and warns us against reading into the language more than it contains." The mischief that ensues when this caution is not observed is sufficiently illustrated in the above-mentioned expositions. Paul's purpose was to warn against a superstitious evaluation of the sacraments that made of them a charm against the judgment of God. Under no circumstances should 1 Cor. 10: 1ff. be used to modify the teaching of Paul contained in such cardinal passages as Rom. 6: 1ff., Gal. 3: 27ff., etc.

The recent employment of *1 Cor. 7: 14* in Paedo-Baptist apologetic owes much to J. Jeremias.[3] He holds that the saying reflects customs attaching to proselyte baptism: children born of a proselyte woman before her conversion were baptized, but those born later were not; so here, just as the non-Christian partner is sanctified by the Christian, the children, too, are "holy", hence they do not need baptism. At the time of writing 1 Corinthians, the baptism of children born Christian was not practised. Cullmann[4] agreed with Jeremias. He added that the saying presupposes the idea of collective holiness: the children of Christian parents are taken up into the Body of Christ purely by reason of their birth. From this conception of holiness there is a direct line to infant baptism, but none to a baptism based on a later decision of such children. The Scottish Report of

[1] *Op. cit.*, 10ff.   [2] *Op. cit.*, 267.   [3] *Op. cit.*, 37ff.   [4] *Op. cit.*, 43f.

May 1955[1] hesitates about the idea of "holy" children being unbaptized (the holiness may be due to their baptism), but in any case such a condition demanded baptism, since there is no hint in the New Testament of two kinds of church members, the baptized and the unbaptized.

Such views labour under a grave difficulty: the "holiness" ascribed to the children of a Christian parent is apparently akin to that of the non-Christian parent (the children are ἅγιοι, the non-Christian parent ἡγίασται). If the children are holy as members of the Body of Christ, the same applies to the non-Christian partner: he or she is "in Christ" by virtue of marriage to a believer. A. Schweitzer[2] unblushingly assents to this conclusion: the non-Christian partner is a member of Christ, a recipient of His powers of life and death which fit one for the Messianic kingdom; to him this is clear proof that life in Christ is a purely physical notion. Both Théo Preiss[3] and E. Best[4] admit that the unbelieving partner and the children of the marriage are members of the Body of Christ, while denying that this means that the "unbeliever" is a Christian. It is not to be wondered that Johannes Schneider[5] indignantly asked, "Who can impute to Paul this grotesque conception of the Church?"

The clue to the exegetical difficulties of this saying is surely to be found in the exceptional use of the terms expressive of holiness. ἡγίασται and ἅγιοι evidently do not bear here their normal Pauline connotation. The verb has been used in the preceding chapter with reference to baptized Christians (6: 11), a meaning excluded from this passage. The only comparable use of the adjective that I can find in Paul occurs in Rom. 11: 16, which significantly employs a ritual conception of holiness and applies it in a derivative way to the totality of Israel. So, too, it is likely that a ritual conception of holiness is employed in 1 Cor. 7: 14. But as truly as "holy" Israel must turn to the Lord for its salvation (Rom. 11: 26ff., 2 Cor. 3: 14-16), so is it with the "sanctified" unbeliever and "holy" children: the path of faith and baptism is the appointed way into the Body of Christ.

Conclusion. An adequate discussion of the items of baptismal

---

[1] The Church of Scotland, *Interim Report of the Special Commission on Baptism*, Part I (1955), 27.

[2] *Op. cit.*, 127f.   [3] *Loc. cit.*, 118.   [4] *Op. cit.*, 77f.   [5] *Op. cit.*, 56.

instruction we have reviewed would require as much space as we have taken, which is not possible, but the chief elements have emerged with clarity. With his predecessors and contemporaries, Paul saw in baptism a *sacrament of the Gospel*. That we deduced from Rom. 10: 9f., but it is basic to all his utterances on the subject. Behind and in baptism stands the Christ of the cross and resurrection, bestowing freedom from sin's guilt and power, and the Spirit who gives the life of the age to come in the present and is the pledge of resurrection at the last day. Beyond his predecessors and contemporaries, however, Paul saw in baptism the *sacrament of union with Christ*. Because it was that, it involved union with Him in His redemptive acts, both in the rite and in subsequent life which should conform to the pattern of the passion and resurrection (Phil. 3: 10f.). And because it was that it involved union with His Body, making the believer a living member, partaking of the life of the whole. Baptism was thus an effective sign; in it Christ and faith come together in the meeting of conversion.

Here Baptists and Paedo-Baptists come to a decisive issue. To those of us in the former tradition, it seems clear that whether one thinks of baptism as a sacrament of the Gospel or as a sacrament of union with Christ, in either case faith is integral to it. The Gospel exercises its radical influence in a man's life when he receives it in faith; he becomes one with Christ when he submits to Him in faith; for Paul the decisive expression of such faith is baptism. This is fully understood by many non-Baptist exegetes. Significantly, two men who have written competent monographs on Paul's conception of faith have reached similar conclusions in this respect. W. H. P. Hatch[1] wrote:

> Faith and baptism go together, as is clear from the following passage (Gal. 3: 27) . . . The two constitute a single act of which faith is the subjective and baptism the objective side.

W. Mundle[2] repeatedly expresses himself in like terms, e.g.:

> If one takes seriously the insight that the Pauline πιστεῦσαι designates the 'becoming Christian', the adherence to the Christian Church, as it is accomplished in baptism, then the conclusion cannot be avoided that this coming to faith also

[1] *The Pauline Idea of Faith in its Relation to Jewish and Hellenistic Religions*, 43.
[2] *Der Glaubensbegriff des Paulus*, 170.

signifies the entry into the fellowship of Christ through baptism and *both must be understood as a unified act.*

This point of view seems to be consistently maintained by Paul in his baptismal teaching. Rom. 6: 1ff.; 10: 9f., Gal. 3: 27, Col. 2: 11f., 1 Cor. 6: 11 set forth a unified baptismal theology wherein the presence of faith is presumed, operative as the "instrument of surrender", if the phrase may be allowed, of the convert to Christ. Accordingly it appears to us to do violence to exegesis when the Pauline teaching concerning the baptism of believing converts is applied to infants who are incapable of such faith. Nor is there evidence that Paul possessed another baptismal theology which he applied to infants. Not a few Paedo-Baptist scholars recognize this, particularly commentators. Some of them[1] concede that infant baptism involved a fall from the heights of Paul's conception of faith. But is it necessary for the church to persist in a lowered baptismal practice and theology? It needs a baptism which can convey the fulness of meaning which its greatest apostle ascribed to it. To regain such a baptism would require adjustment on the part of all the churches, including the Baptists, although theirs is an easier task compared with the revolutionary measures which the Paedo-Baptist churches would have to take to secure it. Though there is no prospect on the horizon of any such revolution taking place, it remains that it will be a great day for the church if she finds enough courage to regain the treasure of baptism according to the teaching of Paul.

E. BAPTISM IN THE FOURTH GOSPEL AND THE FIRST EPISTLE OF JOHN

by D. R. Griffiths

In considering the interpretation of baptism in the Johannine writings, we have to deal with problems of a somewhat different order from those which confront us in other parts of the New Testament. While there is abundant scope for discussion in the baptismal teaching of other books, most of the references are direct and unmistakable, whereas

---

[1] A. Schlatter, *Theologie des Neuen Testaments*, ii, 499.

in the Johannine literature the material is very largely allusive rather than explicit, and in regard to a number of significant passages there is the utmost diversity of opinion as to whether any reference to baptism is intended.

We cannot discuss here the general background of thought of the Fourth Gospel and the First Epistle of John, but before passing on to particular passages, it may be well to emphasize the familiar fact that radically diverse views are held by scholars on the question whether a stress on the sacraments is congruous with the Johannine teaching as a whole. Thus, A. Schweitzer interprets the Fourth Gospel as a thoroughly sacramental document, deeply affected by Hellenistic mysticism.[1] It is typical of his approach to say, "The sacramental stands for so much, in the Johannine mysticism of union with Christ, that the main significance of the death of Jesus is, according to it, the provision of the sacraments."[2] More recently, O. Cullmann has argued that the Fourth Gospel is packed with liturgical and sacramental references, many of which are extremely subtle and allusive.[3] On the other hand, R. Bultmann takes the view that the gospel is non-sacramental in its teaching, though in its present form it includes a number of ecclesiastical interpolations; "the sacraments play no role in John".[4] A. N. Wilder refers to the gospel and the First Epistle of John as sanctioning "a Christian freedom in all that concerns church, office and sacrament which is needed to-day". "These writings were not only anti-gnostic, but they were also anti-ecclesiastical."[5] Henri Clavier suggests that in the Fourth Gospel there is a "diffusion of sacramental reality" which "might explain to some extent the writer's reluctance to crystallize that reality into two concrete ceremonies: Baptism and Eucharist".[6]

[1] *The Mysticism of Paul the Apostle*, 334-75. For a good summary and discussion of Schweitzer's standpoint, see W. F. Howard, *The Fourth Gospel in Recent Criticism and Interpretation* (revised by C. K. Barrett), 149-56.

[2] *Op. cit.*, 364.

[3] *Les Sacraments dans L'Évangile Johannique* (E.Tr. in O. Cullmann, *Early Christian Worship*, II, 37ff.).

[4] *Theology of the New Testament*, ii, 58. Cf. 59 ("though in John there is no direct polemic against the sacraments, his attitude toward them is nevertheless critical or at least reserved").

[5] *New Testament Faith for Today*, 162f.

[6] "Mediation in the Fourth Gospel", in S.N.T.S., Bulletin, i (1950), 22.

These brief citations serve to illustrate the sharp conflict of opinion as to whether the Johannine literature gives us the climax of New Testament sacramental teaching or the most trenchant corrective of a developing sacramentalism. Any general conclusion on this question must be assessed by its adequacy in the exegesis of particular passages, and we now turn to the explicit or supposed references to baptism in the gospel and the First Epistle of John.[1]

1. *The Fourth Gospel*

(a) John the Baptist and his rite (1: 19-34; 3: 22-30; 4: 1-3).

It is instructive to compare and contrast 1: 19-34 (the main theme of which is the witness of John to Christ) in some detail with the Synoptic parallels. The following points briefly indicate some of the most significant emphases in the Johannine record.

(i) The Fourth Gospel, even more emphatically than the Synoptics, subordinates John to Jesus, and this is, doubtless, one of the polemical aims of the early chapters. In response to the deputation from Jerusalem, John disclaims being the Messiah, or Elijah or "the prophet" (of Deut. 18: 15), and so his right to baptize is challenged. The Baptist simply states that his is (merely) a water baptism, but that there is among them One who is far greater than he is, hitherto unknown to them. We should expect to find here the contrast between baptism with water and baptism with the Spirit, which in fact occurs later in the chapter (verse 33); it is to be observed also that there is no reference to John's rite as one of repentance.

(ii) The baptism of Jesus by John is not explicitly described as in the other gospels (though it may be that a knowledge of it is assumed on the part of the readers). Emphasis is laid on

---

[1] For general discussions of the question of the sacramental teaching of the Fourth Gospel, or of baptism in the gospel, in addition to the works of Schweitzer, Cullmann and Howard already cited, see W. Michaelis, *Die Sakramente im Johannes-evangelium*, M. Barth, *Die Taufe—Ein Sakrament?* 378-453, W. F. Flemington, *The New Testament Doctrine of Baptism*, 85-96, W. H. Rigg, *The Fourth Gospel and its Message for Today*, 218-44, C. T. Craig, "Sacramental Interest in the Fourth Gospel", in *J.B.L.*, 58 (1939), 31-44, C. K. Barrett, *The Gospel According to St. John*, 60-71, Ph. H. Menoud, *L'Évangile de Jean d'après les recherches récentes*, 53-56, C. H. Dodd, *The Interpretation of the Fourth Gospel*, 133-43.

John's witness to Jesus, on the descent of the Spirit and its dwelling with Christ as an abiding endowment, in contrast, perhaps with fitful "possession".[1]

(iii) The contrast between baptism with water and Jesus' baptizing with the Holy Spirit is clearly made in verse 33. In this passage they are mentioned as contrasted modes of baptism, whereas it is probable that in 3: 5 "water" and the Spirit are brought into close relationship with baptism in a single complex of thought. (Cf. also 7: 37-39 for the association of "water" and the Spirit.)

(iv) It has been argued by Cullmann and others that the Evangelist wishes to point out, by means of the saying attributed to John the Baptist in 1: 29 ("Behold the Lamb of God") that Jesus' baptism was a vicarious and redemptive event, or at least that it foreshadowed the redemptive effect of His death. If we are to take 1: 29 as very closely linked to the general baptismal setting of this passage as a whole, then it is suggested that Jesus' baptism is His commitment to a sacrificial and redemptive career of the kind indicated in Isaiah 53.[2]

It may be questioned, however, whether such a close association between the baptism of Jesus and His death is intended here. C. H. Dodd in his examination of 1: 29 makes no reference to the baptismal setting; his conclusion is that the expression "The Lamb of God" primarily denotes Messianic leadership rather than sacrificial suffering. It is the lamb as a symbol of the leader of the flock of God which is in mind, as the apocalyptic symbolism taken over by the Apocalypse would suggest; the reference to "taking away" sin refers to "abolishing" rather than "bearing" it. It is not impossible that John the Baptist himself may have had such apocalyptic Messianic ideas in mind. Dr. Dodd's interpretation of this passage does not appear to have won wide

---

[1] So C. K. Barrett, op. cit., 148 (though with a caution against over-emphasizing the word μένειν).
[2] For the detailed discussion of 1: 29 we must refer to the standard commentaries. The following are some of the recent discussions: C. H. Dodd, op. cit., 230ff., O. Cullmann, Baptism in the New Testament, 20f., Early Christian Worship, 63ff., C. K. Barrett, "The Lamb of God", in N.T.S., i (1955), 210-18, W. Zimmerli and J. Jeremias, The Servant of God, 82ff. (and see their index), G. W. H. Lampe, The Seal of the Spirit, 37ff., W. Michaelis, op. cit., 4, 55. O. Cullmann and Zimmerli-Jeremias are favourable to Burney's equation of "Lamb" with "Servant"; C. H. Dodd and C. K. Barrett criticize the suggestion, which must be regarded as very conjectural.

support, but at least it reminds us of the fact that the background of John 1: 29 may well be a complex one, and that we cannot assume that Isaiah 53 and Old Testament references to the Passover lamb are necessarily the most immediate clues to its meaning.[1]

W. Michaelis[2] has strongly challenged Cullmann's argument that a connection is intended in this passage between the death of Christ and Christian baptism. He contends that Cullmann makes far too much of the baptismal background in the preceding verses, whereas 1: 29 is an introduction to a new section which gives us the witness of the Baptist to the person of Jesus. Even in 1: 26, the slight emphasis laid upon the baptism of John, as a function of his personal office as the Forerunner, and without any direct reference to Christian baptism, forbids us from finding in 1: 29 a connection between Christian baptism and the death of Christ. It is a mistaken view to find indirect evidence here, as Cullmann does for the interpretation of Christian baptism as baptism into the death of Christ.

One might add that these points made by Michaelis gain in force when we note that the Fourth Gospel's references to the baptism of Jesus are allusive rather than direct. Again it is not without significance perhaps that, in Christian worship, the words of 1: 29 (interpreted sacrificially) are connected, not with baptism, but with the celebration of the Lord's Supper.

So that it seems a precarious procedure, to say the least, to make far-reaching theological deductions from the very uncertain association between this verse and the theme of baptism.

(v) It has often been observed that the reference to the Sonship of Jesus (which is a part of the Divine utterance to Him according to the Synoptic record of the baptism), is here in the Fourth Gospel (1: 34) given as the final statement in the Baptist's witness to Christ. The effect

---

[1] C. K. Barrett ("The Lamb of God", in *N.T.S.*, i (1955), 218), suggests that whereas John the Baptist, or the earliest Christians, thought of the Messiah as the apocalyptic lamb, destined to overthrow evil, by virtue of subsequent developments in Christian theology and liturgy John the Evangelist was able to use the term "Lamb of God" in a greatly enriched significance.

[2] *Op. cit.*, 4. Cf. the comments in Neville Clark, *An Approach to the Theology of the Sacraments*, 31, on Cullmann's "unguarded equation of Christ's baptism with Christ's death".

is again to accentuate the subordination of John to Jesus.[1]

The main interest in 3: 22-30 and 4: 1-3 is perhaps literary and historical rather than theological, but there are some points that call for comment.

Ch. 3: 22 (cf. 26 and 4: 1—contrast 4: 2) is the only passage in the gospels which represents Jesus as baptizing in the course of His ministry, and that simultaneously with John the Baptist.

In 3: 25-30 (the Baptist's comment on Jesus' baptizing activity and His large following) we may note how the Baptist's words do not refer specifically to the two baptisms as such, they are concerned with the comparative significance of the two persons. (Cf. the comments above on 1: 29.) John reiterates his own subservience; he is simply the forerunner and the "friend of the bridegroom". The introduction to the narrative may be designed to suggest that John's baptism is to be regarded as belonging to the realm of Jewish "purifications".[2]

The passage 4: 1-3 is a difficult one, in which there seems to be good reason to suspect editorial activity.[3] This applies in particular to verse 2, which contradicts 3: 22, 26 and 4: 1. We may conjecture that the motives for this editorial correction were: (i) the desire to discriminate more emphatically between John and Jesus by removing the administration of baptism from the hands of the latter, and (ii) the desire to suggest the fact that "Christian baptism" cannot be experienced in the fulness of its significance until the death and resurrection of Christ have taken place. In imitation of 7: 39 we might say that "as yet baptism had not been given, because Jesus was not yet glorified", and perhaps there is some real connection between the two passages, in the sense that Christian baptism in its richest significance includes the bestowal of the Spirit.[4]

---

[1] C. H. Dodd (*op. cit.*, 228) takes "Son of God" to be the correct reading in 1: 34 without discussion of the variant "Chosen One of God" (cf. Is. 42: 1). Zimmerli-Jeremias (*op. cit.*, 61) regard the originality of "Chosen One" as having been demonstrated by Harnack. C. K. Barrett (*The Gospel According to St. John*, 148-49) inclines toward "Chosen One" as more likely to be changed to "Son" than the reverse.

[2] Cf. C. K. Barrett, *The Gospel According to St. John*, 182.

[3] C. H. Dodd (*op. cit.*, 311, n. 3) describes 4: 2 as having "a better claim to be regarded as an 'editorial note' by a 'redactor' than anything else in the gospel except the colophon, 21: 24-25".

[4] Cf. G. W. H. Lampe, *The Seal of the Spirit*, 41.

Perhaps the most significant points which emerge from our discussion of these passages are:

(i) the emphasis on the subservience of John to Jesus,
(ii) the suggestion that Christian baptism in its complete implication is not yet possible, since the Spirit is not yet given, and
(iii) the uncertainty of any connection between 1: 29 and the theme of baptism.

(*b*) Ch. 3: 5. The saying at the interview with Nicodemus.

This is probably the most important reference to baptism in the Fourth Gospel, though we must reckon with the fact that some scholars question whether any sacramental allusion is intended.

Thus it has been argued by some scholars, like Kirsopp Lake[1] and Rudolf Bultmann,[2] that the original reading here ran, "Except a man be born of the Spirit he cannot enter into the kingdom of God", and the words "of water and" are a later ecclesiastical gloss introducing a sacramental reference. This suggestion may at first sight be rendered plausible by the fact that the remainder of the passage gives an antithesis between "flesh" and "spirit" and that verses 6 and 8 refer to "birth of the Spirit", but the removal of reference to "water" in verse 5 is after all little other than an act of textual surgery dictated by pre-suppositions as to the author's outlook and purpose.[3]

But though we accept the familiar form of the text, we still cannot assume that there is a reference to baptism; there are some interpretations which take the reference to "water" to be non-sacramental. Thus, H. Odeberg[4] has argued that in this connection "born of water" means "born

[1] See the summary of Lake's lecture, *The Influence of Textual Criticism on the Exegesis of the New Testament* in W. F. Howard, *The Fourth Gospel in Recent Criticism and Interpretation*, 204-5.

[2] *Das Evangelium des Johannes*, 98; cf. *Theology of the New Testament*, ii, 58. B. W. Bacon (*The Gospel of the Hellenists*, 168) also argues that the reference here to baptism is redactional.

[3] Cf. C. K. Barrett, *The Gospel According to St. John*, 174 ("There is no textual ground whatever for the omission of ὕδατος καί as an interpolation"). The fact that Justin Martyr quotes verse 5 without referring to "water" and that certain MSS. include a reference to water in verse 8 (thus indicating textual disturbances in the passage as a whole) can hardly be regarded as strong evidence.

[4] *The Fourth Gospel Interpreted in its Relation to Contemporaneous Religious Currents*, 48-71.

of the Divine efflux, or semen". Odeberg gives a large number of parallels from Rabbinic literature and elsewhere for this symbolic use of the term "water" to denote the Divine creative principle. He makes much of the fact that baptism is not mentioned or alluded to in the rest of this section, whereas such expressions as "from above", "of God", "from heaven", are dominant in the context.

This interpretation has been given a sympathetic reception by some scholars,[1] but others regard it as artificial, and question the relevance of the parallels adduced.[2]

It seems less forced to take the reference as being to baptism, especially if we may stress the fact that *entrance* into the kingdom is mentioned in the context. As has often been suggested, it is difficult to envisage any Christian writer of the late first century, or the early second century, using such an expression without having in mind the sacrament of initiation into the Christian community. In view of what has been said earlier in the gospel (1: 26 and 1: 33) regarding John's water-baptism and Jesus' spirit-baptism, it is natural to see here a reference to the earlier rite as transcended and fulfilled in something greater than itself, especially as Nicodemus is a representative of Judaism (3: 1, 10).

For the author and his readers, there can be little doubt that the primary reference in 3: 5 is to Christian baptism with an underlying polemical allusion to John's baptism, of the type which forms so marked a feature of these early chapters. As to the reason why baptism is not more unmistakably indicated, C. H. Dodd makes a suggestion which he applies also to a number of other sacramental allusions in the gospel.

The evangelist appears to have deliberately exercised reserve about the Christian sacraments in writing for a public which includes pagans whom he wished to influence towards the Christian faith. So he would not say plainly that initiation into the higher order of life is by way of baptism accompanied by the gift of the Spirit. Indeed, he may well have felt that

---

[1] E.g. by R. H. Strachan (*The Fourth Gospel, Its Significance and Environment*, 134-5), who, however, combines a reference to Christian baptism with Odeberg's view. Cf. J. A. Findlay, *The Fourth Gospel*, 58. W. L. Knox on the other hand emphatically rejects Odeberg's view as "quite untenable" (*Some Hellenistic Elements in Primitive Christianity*, 91).

[2] This applies especially to the parallels from Mandaism.

to put it in that way would risk misleading such readers as he had in view. But he could bring in the idea of baptism allusively.[1]

In referring to the desire to avoid misleading pagan readers, Dodd presumably has in mind the danger of suggesting a crass and materialistic conception of regeneration as dependent upon a cultic act alone. Some scholars have suggested that in fact the Johannine teaching at this point is a definite approximation to the thought of the mystery religions and of other contemporary movements.[2] But it seems much more probable that the language used in 3: 5 tends in the opposite direction, by virtue of the reference to the Spirit (cf. the similar reference to the Spirit in 6: 63).[3]

It is not surprising perhaps, in view of the reference to the kingdom of God (here only as such in the Fourth Gospel), that some scholars have argued for a close relationship between John 3: 3, 5 and the Synoptic sayings on little children and the kingdom (Mark 10: 15, Luke 18: 17, Matt. 18: 3). J. Jeremias[4] puts all these texts in parallel columns to draw attention to the similarities. Formally, it is true, all the sayings had much in common; all begin with a solemn "verily" ("amen") clause, proceed to an exceptive clause, and end with the clause referring to entering (or seeing in John 3: 3) the kingdom. Jeremias argues that in the Synoptic sayings baptism is already implied (and draws attention especially to the word "infants" in Luke 18: 15); in John 3: 5 baptism is explicitly mentioned, the language is "hellenized" somewhat ("except a man be born from above, (or again)" in place of "as a child"), and the emphasis is more on the divine side of the process than on the human condition.

The Interim Report of the Special Commission on Baptism

---

[1] C. H. Dodd (*op. cit.*, 310f.) makes some illuminating comments on the relation between our passage and 1: 26, 31, 33 (the references to John's baptizing with water) on the one hand and 3: 22-36 (in which Jesus is described as baptizing) on the other hand. He concludes that "the evangelist's intention is to link the ideas of ὕδωρ and πνεῦμα through the idea of baptism, and in particular baptism by Jesus (the Church's baptism) in contrast to John's baptism".

[2] M. Barth (*op. cit.*, 436ff.) gives a full account of the history of interpretation. Loisy is perhaps the best-known advocate of a "mystery-religion" interpretation.

[3] Cf. C. H. Dodd, *op. cit.*, 305.

[4] *Hat die Urkirche die Kindertaufe geübt?*, 43ff.

of the Church of Scotland refers to Jeremias and follows a very similar line of interpretation.[1]

It must be said that, in spite of certain formal similarities between all these sayings, the attempt to correlate the Synoptic and Johannine teaching at this point is highly questionable, and the reading of a baptismal motif into the Synoptic sayings is altogether unconvincing. It is significant that C. H. Dodd[2] explicitly rejects the idea (which he cites from Origen) that the antecedent of the Johannine doctrine of regeneration is in such ideas as that expressed in Matt. 18: 3. He suggests that the teaching of John 3 "moves in a different sphere of thought" and continues "the real approach in Judaism and primitive Christianity to the Johannine doctrine of rebirth is by way of the eschatological conception of the transfiguration of the blessed into forms of heavenly glory in the Age to Come". Dodd argues that the apocalyptic expectation of a future "rebirth" (as represented e.g. by Matt. 19: 28) is in John 3 transmuted into a condition of entering the "Kingdom of God" (or eternal life) here and now.

The positive teaching of 3: 5 is thus, very briefly, that *entrance into the kingdom of God is impossible except by means of the rebirth in baptism which is both a water-baptism and a bestowal of the Spirit*; the very form of the construction suggests their indissoluble connection. Though the terminology used by Paul is different, and the imagery of death and resurrection is used by him rather than that of rebirth, it is questionable whether the difference between Paul and John over this matter is as radical as Schweitzer for instance makes out.[3] Paul's teaching as to the "new creation" bears a closer similarity to that of John 3 than he suggests, and baptism

---

[1] 24f. Contrast the noteworthy comment of R. H. Strachan (*op. cit.*, 135) on 3: 5. "Adult baptism alone is referred to, based on the conception fundamental to the evangelist's thought, that believers are begotten by a kind of spiritual 'seed' (1 John 2: 9), begotten of God into a new kind of life." Cf. also his point that it is psychologically intelligible how baptism and the gift of the Spirit should be so often conjoined in the New Testament in view of the revolutionary significance of baptism for early Christian converts (134, n.1). Cf. also the earlier section of the present work, "Baptism in the Synoptic Gospels", 98-115.

[2] *Op. cit.*, 304.

[3] *The Mysticism of Paul the Apostle*, 15. J. Schneider (*Die Taufe im Neuen Testament*, 59, n.118) appears to agree in general with Schweitzer, but stresses that Paul's teaching on this point has nothing to do with the *idea* of rebirth (as distinct from the experience implied?).

is for Paul as for John a critical moment in the transition to the new order of life. The Fourth Gospel apparently assumes the universality of baptism in a more definite way than does, for example, the Acts of the Apostles.[1]

It is not surprising, perhaps, that our passage has been taken recently as containing a polemic against the Essene (?) sect of Qumran, which undoubtedly laid a good deal of stress on ceremonial washings; but we share the cautious attitude of Millar Burrows[2] and Raymond E. Brown[3] toward this suggestion, especially as Nicodemus is unambiguously described as a Pharisee.

(c) Ch. 13: 1-11 (especially vv. 8-10). The Washing of the Disciples' Feet.

This incident is one in which commentators have found a many-sided significance.

(i) It has its ethical aspect as an acted parable of Christ's self-abasing humility, which is commended to the disciples (so vv. 14-20 interpret it).

(ii) It seems probable that the idea of participation of the apostles in the cleansing effects of Christ's death is also present.[4]

(iii) Sacramental allusions have been suggested in verses 8-10 with reference to baptism in particular, or, as some scholars have argued, with reference to both the main sacraments.

Again we must acknowledge that some scholars emphatically deny any sacramental interest in the passage. R. Bultmann,[5] W. Michaelis,[6] and Ph. H. Menoud,[7] among others, consider that the essential meaning of the passage stands out more clearly when it is interpreted without any reference to the sacraments.

---

[1] Cf. *supra*, 116.
[2] *The Dead Sea Scrolls*, 339.
[3] "The Qumran Scrolls and the Johannine Gospel and Epistles", in K. Stendahl (ed.), *The Scrolls and the New Testament*, 203.
[4] E. Hoskyns (*The Fourth Gospel*, 437) refers to the incident as fundamentally "resting upon and interpreting the death of the Lord", rather than conveying an ethical lesson, or interpreting the sacraments, though it does cast some light upon them.
[5] *Das Evangelium des Johannes*, 355-61. Cf. *Theology of the New Testament*, ii, 58. It is suggested in the commentary (359) that the narrative contains opposition to sacramental cleansings, including baptism.
[6] *Op. cit.*, 29-32.   [7] *Op. cit.*, 54-56.

But while the primary emphasis in the passage may well be on the self-abasing love of Christ and on identification with Him as He goes forward to His death, it is entirely in the Johannine manner to include another allusion in a narrative of this kind. The declaration to Peter of an underlying significance in this event may also be intended by the Evangelist for his readers.

Cullmann is one of those scholars who find an allusion to the Lord's Supper as well as to baptism in verses 8-10.[1] He comments thus:

> These words can surely have only this meaning—he who has received baptism, even when he sins afresh needs *no second baptism*, for one cannot be twice baptized. The reference of the word 'bathed' to baptism is the more convincing in that baptism in early Christianity did actually consist of dipping the whole body in the water.[2]

It should be noted that Cullmann accepts the longer form of the text in verse 10 ("He that is bathed needeth not *save to wash his feet*, but is clean every whit") and argues that the phrase "save to wash his feet" refers to the Lord's Supper, which, unlike baptism, is meant to be repeated.[3]

Commenting on this interpretation, Ph. H. Menoud[4] (who himself does not find either sacrament in this context) says that to represent the eucharist by the washing of feet would be to use a symbol which is not simply "defective" (Loisy) but "grotesque" (Bultmann), and we feel we must agree.

Some other scholars who also accept the longer and more familiar form of the text in verse 10, have argued that verses 6-10 reflect controversy in the early church as to the relative merits of baptism by immersion and baptism by affusion, for which the candidate would stand with only his feet in the water.[5] The implication according to von Campenhausen

---

[1] *Early Christian Worship*, 105ff. A number of scholars had earlier suggested that both sacraments are in mind (e.g. G. H. C. Macgregor, *The Gospel of John* (Moffatt Commentary) 276, W. Heitmüller, *Das Johannes Evangelium*, 145, and W. Bauer, *Das Johannes Evangelium*, 167).

[2] *Early Christian Worship*, 108.   [3] *Ibid.*, 109f.

[4] *Op. cit.*, 55. Cf. also J. A. T. Robinson, "The One Baptism, as a Category of New Testament Soteriology", in *S.J.Th.*, 6 (1953), 265n.

[5] H. von Campenhausen, "Zur Auslegung von Johannes xiii. 6-10", in *Z.N.W.*, 33 (1934), 259-71. His discussion is briefly summarized by Menoud (*op. cit.*, 55-6). Cf. also Holtzmann's interpretation summarized and criticized in J. H. Bernard, *St. John*, ii (I.C.C.), 463-64.

would be that Jesus is described as authorizing a baptism by affusion, and verse 10 would mean "He that is washed (i.e. cleansed by the word of Christ) need only be baptized by the 'foot-baptism'."

But this is an extremely conjectural interpretation, and we consider that it should be rejected both on exegetical grounds, and for the inconclusive nature of the archaeological evidence which is submitted.[1]

The original form of the text in verse 10 is a difficult problem, over which scholars are sharply divided, but it seems that a strong case may be made for the shorter reading as found in Codex Sinaiticus ("He that has been bathed has no need to wash, but is clean all over"),[2] and thus, in so far as baptism is in mind, by way of indirect allusion, the implication is that once baptism has been received "further washings are pointless".[3] If so, the teaching may well have the effect of counteracting tendencies toward the repetition of baptism in the early church.[4]

Schweitzer's view[5] that in the foot-washing the disciples are baptized in water by Christ, then later, by means of the insufflation (20: 22, 23) equipped with the Spirit, and consequently empowered to administer baptism "with water and the Spirit" to others, is surely too mechanically conceived.

J. A. T. Robinson[6] puts forward an unusual interpretation of vv. 8-10, based partly on the conception, made familiar by Cullmann in particular, of a "general baptism" undergone by Christ in His death. He suggests that of the two terms "to

---

[1] Cf. O. Cullmann (*Early Christian Worship*, 108, n.2), and Ph. H. Menoud, (*op. cit.*, 56), for detailed criticisms along these lines. C. T. Craig, (*loc. cit.*), accepts von Campenhausen's interpretation.

[2] Though the longer reading has stronger manuscript support, the shorter reading may be regarded as being intrinsically superior. (So M.-J. Lagrange, *L'Évangile selon Saint John*, 353-55.) Cf. R. Bultmann, *Das Evangelium des Johannes*, 357-61, J. H. Bernard, *op. cit.*, ii, 462-64, E. Hoskyns, *The Fourth Gospel*, 436-39, C. K. Barrett, *The Gospel According to St. John*, 367-69, R. H. Lightfoot, *St. John's Gospel*, 273. M. Goguel (*L'Église Primitive*, 33) and J. H. Bernard prefer the longer reading; E. Hoskyns, C. K. Barrett and R. H. Lightfoot while acknowledging the complexity of the textual problem, regard the shorter reading as preferable.

[3] C. K. Barrett, *The Gospel According to St. John*, 368. The words quoted are used with a somewhat wider reference by Barrett.

[4] Cf. O. Cullmann, *op. cit.*, 108.

[5] *Op. cit.*, 360-62.

[6] *Loc. cit.*

bathe" (λούεσθαι) and "to dip" (νίπτεσθαι), it is the latter which is "the symbolic, sacramental act to which the promise of incorporation is attached, i.e. Christian baptism". Robinson argues that the expression "he that is bathed" (ὁ λελουμένος) must be taken to refer to "the act of general baptism which Jesus is about to accomplish in His death". The death of Jesus is to be "the great washing which will give the water-baptism of the Church its efficiency, and also its necessity (for without it there will be no incorporation in the person and work of Christ)".

It is very difficult to accept this interpretation of verse 10. Robinson's attempt to invert the significance usually given to the two verbs is not convincing. As far as New Testament usage outside this passage is concerned, it would suggest that λούεσθαι is the more appropriate term for baptism; it is used, in simple or compound form, for baptism or in close association with it in Acts 22: 16, 1 Cor. 6: 11, Heb. 10: 22, whereas there is no specific use of νίπτειν for baptism (of persons). It is interesting to note a comment by C. H. Dodd[1] on the use of these two verbs in the LXX of the Pentateuch. He writes: "In the cultic regulations of the Pentateuch λούεσθαι is generally used of the ceremonial bath which forms part of the ritual of consecration to the priesthood, and νίπτειν of ad hoc ablution before officiating." Dodd suggests that there may possibly be a clue in this usage to the interpretation of the foot-washing narrative. If that is so, it is clear that its implication goes against Robinson's interpretation.

Thus, we consider that an underlying sacramental reference was in the author's mind as he wrote this passage, and that it was related to baptism rather than the eucharist. As R. H. Lightfoot[2] says of the incident, it was "a cleansing bound to recall the Church's rite of baptism by water". We find it preferable to accept the shorter reading, and it seems that in so far as the author is alluding to baptism,

---

[1] Review of O. Cullmann, *Les Sacrements dans L'Évangile Johannique*, in *J.E.H.*, iii (1952), 218-21. W. F. Arndt, and F. W. Gingrich, *A Greek-English Lexicon of the New Testament and Other Early Christian Literature*, 482, comment on ὁ λελουμένος: the one who has bathed (in contrast to the one who has his feet washed), and with allusion to the cleansing of the whole body in baptism. H. Windisch, *Johannes und die Synoptiker*, 26, 77, is referred to as taking a different view.

[2] *St. John's Gospel*, 261.

he is pointing out that it need not be repeated, rather than discussing its precise mode of administration.

(d) Ch. 19: 31-37 (especially verse 34). The issue of blood and water.

This is presented as a most significant event. The solemnity with which the passage closes has often been indicated; after the events narrated in verses 31-34, verse 35 is a strong asseveration of the fidelity of the witness whose testimony underlies the record, and verses 36 and 37 cite the Scriptures which have been fulfilled in the events just described. There is thus every reason to think that the Evangelist attached very great significance to the fact that Jesus' legs were not broken, and that from His lanced side there came forth blood and water.

It is probable that here again several truths are suggested. Thus (i) an anti-Docetic emphasis may well be present in the sense that it is stressed that Jesus was in no way spared from physical death.[1] But this theme is hardly meant to be the most prominent, for there is more emphasis in the passage as a whole on the distinctive features of the death of Jesus than on those aspects which He shares with others.

(ii) The fulfilment of Old Testament passages has already been briefly referred to. In verse 36, the fact that Jesus' legs remained unbroken is seen as a fulfilment of references in the Pentateuch to the un-mutilated paschal lamb.[2] In verse 37 the piercing of His side is claimed as a fulfilment of Zech. 12: 10 ("When they look on Him whom they have pierced"). It would be possible to argue, in the case of a less subtle and allusive work than the Fourth Gospel, that the issue of water and blood is simply recorded in order to emphasize with what grim reality this prophecy was fulfilled

---

[1] F. Büchsel (*Das Neue Testament Deutsch*, 4, 174) lays most stress on the anti-Docetic element ("Jesus was really dead and was a man like other men"), and the Messianic emphasis ("for John the spear-thrust is a proof of the Messiahship of Jesus"). He regards a sacramental reference as "improbable but not impossible".

[2] The primary reference seems to be to Exod. 12: 46; cf. Num. 9: 12 of the Passover sacrifice, though C. H. Dodd argues that in view of the presence of other quotations from the Psalms in vv. 24 and 28, Ps. 34: 20 is in mind here. (Cf. R. H. Lightfoot, *St. John's Gospel*, 327: the Pentateuchal passages are more pertinent, but there is closer verbal correspondence with the Psalm, and perhaps St. John is willing to let his readers see here a fulfilment of both passages.)

at the crucifixion. But it appears that more than this is intended.

(iii) It seems very probable that a sacramental implication is in mind, the "blood" and "water" representing the two sacraments. If so, it is meant to indicate that the crucified Christ is the originator of the two sacraments in their full significance. His redemptive death gives content and significance to them both; they are the creation of Him who "came by water and by blood" (1 John 5: 6). There are hints of this earlier in the gospel: "the reference to 6: 55 and 7: 38 is inevitable".[1]

In view of 7: 38 and other associations of "water" and "spirit" in the Fourth Gospel, it may well be that the bestowal of the Spirit is also in mind here. (Cf. the association of the Spirit, water and blood in 1 John 5: 8 as Hoskyns indicates.)[2]

While it seems that the majority of commentators find some measure of sacramental reference in this incident, there are those who dissent. Bultmann again regards this passage as including an ecclesiastical gloss[3] (i.e. the words "and at once there came out blood and water"), supplied to give a deeper meaning to the incident of the spear-wound. He concedes, however, that this deeper meaning "can only be that both sacraments, Lord's Supper (blood) and baptism (water) are founded upon Jesus' death".[4] There is no manuscript evidence for omitting the phrase which Bultmann regards as redactional.

The objections have often been made against a sacramental interpretation that "blood" is not a very apt way of referring to the Lord's Supper, and that the order "blood and water" is unexpected if the two sacraments are in mind. In this particular setting, however, both the use of the term "blood" and its prior occurrence in the expression are almost inevitable,[5] and it is entirely in accordance with Johannine allusiveness to have both the terms used with their literal significance and with a more far-reaching reference.

[1] C. H. Dodd, *op. cit.*, 438.

[2] *Op. cit.*, 532.

[3] *Das Evangelium des Johannes*, 525; cf. *Theology of the New Testament*, ii, 54.

[4] *Ibid.*

[5] So G. H. C. Macgregor (*The Gospel of John*, 350); W. H. Rigg, *op. cit.*, 228f.

We conclude that, while no unmistakable clue is given as to a symbolic reference in the "blood" and the "water", it is entirely in accordance with Johannine allusiveness to have both terms used with their literal significance and with a more far-reaching suggestion. The implication is, as has been indicated earlier, that the death of Christ is the sacrificial and redemptive act which constitutes the two sacraments.

(*e*) Other possible allusions.

There remain a number of passages in the Fourth Gospel containing possible allusions to baptism, which we can only indicate very briefly. Thus, A. Schweitzer[1] and O. Cullmann[2] suggest that the "living water" of 4: 14 refers to baptism, but this is unconvincing, in view of the widespread use of "water" as a religious symbol quite apart from baptism, and the difficulty of fitting the idea of baptism into a context which refers to the "drinking" of water. Cullmann's observation that "in many gnostic baptist sects in the ancient world the baptismal water was drunk" is not very pertinent.[3]

There is more to be said for an underlying reference to baptism in the healing narratives of 5: 1-19 and 9: 1-39, whilst 7: 37-39, though it does not directly refer to baptism, is of great significance indirectly, in that it points forward to the glorified Christ as the giver of the Spirit, and so as the author of "baptism with water and Spirit" (cf. 1: 33; 3: 5; 19: 34).[4]

2. *The First Epistle of John*

In the First Epistle of John (which we take to be from the same hand as the Fourth Gospel), we have a background which might well have elicited from the author a body of definite sacramental teaching. The false teaching of the Docetic heretics, which required the author to lay such a pronounced emphasis on the incarnation and on the

---

[1] *Op. cit.*, 355f.

[2] *Op. cit.*, 80-84.

[3] W. Michaelis (*op. cit.*, 15-19) rejects a number of Cullmann's arguments, and his general approach to this incident.

[4] G. W. H. Lampe, *The Seal of the Spirit, passim.* Cf. his "'Baptisma' in the New Testament", in *S.J.Th.*, 5 (1952), 163-74.

historical basis of the gospel, might well have led him to give a full statement of the sacramental principle.

But, in fact, here, as in the Fourth Gospel, the sacramental teaching is indirect and allusive, and there is again considerable controversy over the exact meaning of the relevant references.

(a) Ch. 2: 20, 27. The "anointing".

The most familiar view is that this is a reference to the Holy Spirit.[1] But C. H. Dodd in discussing this passage says that "it is reasonable to suppose that the chrism is something connected with baptism". He himself considers that the "chrism" is a kind of teaching which is an indwelling power in believers, and suggests that, rather than identifying it with the Holy Spirit we should think of it as "the Word of God, that is, the Gospel, or the revelation of God in Christ, as communicated in the rule of faith to catechumens, and confessed in baptism. This is the Christian's initiation, by water and the Word."[2] Such a reference to the Gospel rather than to the Spirit at this point would be more objective in emphasis, Dodd argues, and more in harmony with the teaching of such a passage as 4: 1-6.

On either view, it appears that baptism lies in the background of this reference, whether as the supreme occasion for the bestowal of the Spirit, or as the outstanding occasion on which the truth of the Gospel was confessed by the believer.

G. W. H. Lampe, who takes the reference to be to "the Messianic unction of the Spirit", suggests that the author here means to recall Christ's "anointing" and that there is a play upon the idea of believers as Χριστοί contrasted with heretics as ἀντίχριστοι.[3] He discusses fully the question as to whether there was any ceremony in the early practice of the church, which, as a supplementary rite added to baptism, would specially indicate the gift of the Spirit. After the New Testament period, with the elaboration of the baptismal rite, the ceremony of "chrismation" came to be associated with the reception of the Spirit, but Lampe

---

[1] So B. F. Westcott, *The Epistles of St. John*, 73. Cf. A. E. Brooke, *The Johannine Epistles* (I.C.C.), 57.
[2] *The Johannine Epistles* (Moffatt Commentary), 63.
[3] *The Seal of the Spirit*, 61.

concludes that there is no evidence for such an act of unction in New Testament times.[1] He emphasizes the fact that it is "through baptism in water" and not through any other ceremony, such as a physical anointing, that "the believer enters into the possession of the Spirit",[2] according to New Testament teaching, and speaks of "the totally un-Scriptural tendency to divorce baptism of the Spirit from baptism in water".[3] John 3: 5 may be regarded as significant in this connection.[4]

(b) Ch. 5: 5-8. The Three Witnesses.

This passage has given rise to voluminous discussion which cannot be even summarized here.[5] The interpretation which we accept as most probable is that which takes verse 6 as giving *primarily* a chronological summary of the whole historic ministry of Christ from His baptism to His cross, with an implied correction of Docetic views; a secondary allusion to the two sacraments (cf. John 19: 34) may also be present. In verse 8 we take the "water" and the "blood" to be references to the two sacraments in their function of rendering perpetual testimony to Christ in the on-going life of the church (cf. Paul's teaching on baptism in Rom. 6, and his reference to the Lord's Supper as "proclaiming" the Lord's death, in 1 Cor. 11: 26). It does not seem to be essential that we should maintain a single unvarying reference for the terms "water" and "blood" throughout the whole passage.[6]

T. W. Manson[7] has raised the question whether this passage, taken in conjunction with 2: 20, may not point to a

---

[1] *Op. cit.*, 81; cf. B. F. Westcott on 2: 20.　　[2] *Op. cit.*, 45.　　[3] *Op. cit.*, 303.

[4] *Op. cit.*, 60. Cf. J. Schneider, *op. cit.*, 59. Note Lampe's comments on John 3 in relation to Hellenistic and Gnostic ideas.

[5] See A. E. Brooke, *op. cit.*, 131-38, C. H. Dodd, *The Johannine Epistles* (Moffatt Commentary), 127-33 and W. F. Flemington, *op. cit.*, 88-92.

[6] A. E. Brooke (*op. cit.*, 132-34) argues for an "historical" rather than a "sacramental" interpretation throughout. So Bultmann and Michaelis. Contrast B. F. Westcott, *op. cit.*, 182, and J. Denney, "He that came by Water and Blood", in *The Expositor* (1908), 423. ("It is to the writer quite incredible that any Christian reader should ever have heard John 3 without thinking of baptism or John 6 without thinking of the Supper, or this passage without thinking of both.") Denney finely draws out the significance of the sacramental reference in this contrast. W. F. Flemington (*op. cit.*, 89f.) argues that there is a secondary sacramental reference, but to baptism only.

[7] "Entry into Membership of the Early Church", in *J.T.S.*, xlviii (1947), 25-33.

form of initiation rite in which an anointing (reception of the Spirit) precedes baptism. He shows that we have literary evidence going back to at least the third century, and probably attesting a practice of much greater antiquity, in the Syrian or Syriac-speaking churches, in which anointing and imposition of hands precede baptism.

Manson approves of the reading, "he who came by water, blood, *and Spirit*", in verse 6,[1] and takes the reference there to be to Pentecost as an event in the past. He points out the significance of the term "$\chi\rho\hat{\iota}\sigma\mu\alpha$" in 2: 20 in view of its later ritual associations, and raises the question whether, if "water" and "blood" in verse 8 correspond to the laver and the chalice, the "Spirit" (in verse 8) does not likewise point to a ritual anointing, a physical "$\chi\rho\hat{\iota}\sigma\mu\alpha$". He argues that perhaps originally the Christian order of initiation followed a pattern similar to that adopted in the Jewish initiation of proselytes, so giving, in a Christian setting, the sequence: (i) reception of the Spirit (imposition of hands, unction), (ii) baptism, (iii) admission to the congregation and the Lord's Table. But this sequence was changed in the practice of the church to one in which the reception of the Spirit became the consummation of the initiation rite, a change which Manson regards as in some ways an unfortunate one, possibly influenced by ideas found in the Hellenistic mystery-cults.

This is an interesting approach to 1 John 2 and 5, but there is a good deal of the conjectural in it. Thus the attempt to associate the witness of the Spirit (verse 8) with a rite is by no means necessary, and in view of other Johannine teaching on the witness of the Spirit (e.g. in the gospel, chs. 14-17 and in the First Epistle), may be deemed unconvincing. The way in which the Spirit is connected with the sacraments in the gospel of John (3, 6) seems also to tell against the idea that it represents itself a ritual act in this context. G. W. H. Lampe takes the view that it is improbable that three stages of initiation are referred to

---

[1] This reading is found in Codices Sinaiticus and Alexandrinus, and is adopted in Moffatt's translation, and defended by C. H. Dodd, *The Johannine Epistles* (Moffatt Commentary), 128, n. 1. We think that H. Windisch (*Die Katholischen Briefe*, 132) is probably right in regarding the reference to the Spirit in verse 6 as an addition. The whole passage is one in which there has been intense textual activity and "glossing", culminating in the notorious "Three Heavenly Witnesses" interpolation in verse 8.

here[1] and, as we have indicated earlier, emphasizes the lack
of evidence for any rite signifying Spirit-baptism in New
Testament times. With this view we have shown ourselves
to be in complete agreement.

(c) "Little Children" in 1 John.

It should not be necessary to discuss the use of this expression in 1 John in connection with baptism, but recent
attempts have been made to suggest that certain uses of the
term are indirect evidence for Paedo-Baptism.

Thus the Interim Report of the Special Commission on
Baptism of the Church of Scotland[2] speaks of John as
(in 2: 12) specifically addressing little children ($\pi\alpha\iota\delta\iota\alpha$)
and later, "in distinction from little children infants ($\tau\epsilon\kappa\nu\iota\alpha$)
as well". It is then argued that to both of these who are born
of God (2: 29) he speaks of their "anointing from the Holy
One", which can only refer to the gift of the Spirit in
baptism.

We can only say that we find this exegesis quite unconvincing. In 2: 12, 13 the reference to various groups in the
community is probably merely rhetorical,[3] and in view of the
fact that in 4: 1-4 $\dot{\alpha}\gamma\alpha\pi\eta\tau o\iota$ and $\tau\epsilon\kappa\nu\iota\alpha$ are used interchangeably in a context which speaks of the "testing of spirits"
and the dangers of heresy, one cannot surely imagine that any
literal meaning can be attached to the use of these terms
(i.e. $\tau\epsilon\kappa\nu\iota\alpha$ and $\pi\alpha\iota\delta\iota\alpha$). They are caritative terms expressing the author's loving concern for his readers and his
authoritative standing. We may note that Paul also used
$\tau\epsilon\kappa\nu\iota\alpha$ of his readers (Gal. 4: 19), where there can be no
thought of children or infants in the literal sense. The term is
also used in the Fourth Gospel with reference to the disciples.[4]

---

[1] Op. cit., 91f.
[2] 26. P. Ch. Marcel (The Biblical Doctrine of Infant Baptism, 206, n. 4)
refers to Jer. 31: 33ff., and also argues that Rev. 11: 18; 19: 5 and 20: 12
should be taken as "referring to little children and not to the 'little people'
or the 'humble of the earth' as opposed to the rich and powerful". But it is
surely unconvincing to press for any precise sense in such a stereotyped expression. Cf. W. F. Arndt and F. W. Gingrich, op. cit., 523, and A. M. Honey-
man, "Merismus in Biblical Hebrew", in J.B.L., 71 (1952), 12. (The frequent
phrase פקטן ועד-גדל does not refer particularly to "great and small" or
"young and old" but generally to "everyone, regardless of rank or of age.")
[3] So C. H. Dodd, The Johannine Epistles (Moffatt Commentary), 37-39.
[4] Cf. the comment by W. F. Arndt and F. W. Gingrich (op. cit., 815) on
$\tau\epsilon\kappa\nu\iota o\nu$: "used by Jesus in familiar loving address to his disciples, or by a
Christian apostle or teacher to his spiritual children".

It will be clear from the course of our discussion that we regard sacramental teaching as harmonious with Johannine doctrine in general, and that we find references to baptism in most of the passages which we have discussed.

At the same time we must confess that a good deal of the teaching is indirect and allusive in form, and therefore capable of being interpreted in a variety of ways. In view of the symbolism and the fondness for double meanings which are characteristic of our author over the wider field of his work in general, it seems probable that he has introduced a number of allusions to the rites of the church in a some-what cryptic fashion. The reason for his indirectness, apart from his own literary habits, may well be that he is aware of a constituency which might respond readily to certain widespread images and turns of speech, while he does not feel called upon to disclose fully to such readers the inner-most experiences of the Christian community.

The most significant aspects of the Johannine teaching on baptism appear to be:

(*a*) The persistent stress on the activity of the Holy Spirit; a feature of the sacramental teaching in general which safeguards it from the materialistic and the magical.

(*b*) The firm connection which is maintained between baptism and the historic basis of the Gospel. The Spirit, the water and the blood bear their constant witness to Him who came by water and blood, who was Himself the creator of the sacraments, and who is still the theme of their proclamation.

F. BAPTISM IN OTHER NEW TESTAMENT WRITINGS

by S. I. Buse

To dismiss the witness of the rest of the New Testament as of comparatively little importance would be a great mistake. We must guard against the danger of allowing the comparative extent of, say, the Pauline writings to lead us to exaggerate their significance in the total New Testament picture. The treatment of baptism in the "other writings" represents facets of life and belief in the first-century Christian church which must be given their full weight in any attempt to present a balanced picture of the New Testament teaching about baptism.

1. *1 Peter* is clearly of the greatest importance for our purpose. A number of scholars regard the greater part of it as originally a baptismal homily. The two most recent English commentaries on the epistle are constructed upon the basis of this assumption.[1] The theory is usually associated with the name of R. Perdelwitz,[2] but it was advanced independently by W. Bornemann.[3] In the view of Perdelwitz, 1: 3—4: 11 was a baptismal sermon, and in that of Bornemann 1: 3—5: 11. Perdelwitz connected the hypothesis with the rather questionable idea that 1 Peter shows acquaintance with the terminology of the mystery cults, but this in no way invalidates the truth of his main contention: in fact it was made in the earlier part of his work before he discussed the relation to the mystery religions, and Bornemann's statement involves no suggestion of the influence of the mysteries. There are good grounds for seeing a baptismal sermon in 1: 3—4: 11.

(*a*) A number of indications point to the conclusion that it is a homily originally independent of the rest of the letter. That there is a clear break at 4: 12 is shown by the doxology and the "Amen".[4] Perdelwitz argued conclusively[5] that, whereas the sufferings of 4: 12ff. were already being experienced by the readers, the persecution in the earlier part of the epistle was just a hypothetical possibility, as we see from 1: 6; 3: 13, 14, 17. To these considerations may be added the fact that 1: 3—4: 11 has no genuine epistolary characteristics, lacking, as it does, references to places and people. The polished style, long sentences, impressive opening and ending are homiletic in character. Ch. 4: 12f., on the other hand, "has the quick and nervous language of a letter written in haste and under tension".[6]

(*b*) There are many signs that the address was delivered at

---

[1] F. W. Beare, *The First Epistle of Peter*; C. E. B. Cranfield, *The First Epistle of Peter*.

[2] *Die Mysterienreligionen und das Problem des 1 Petrusbriefes*, 146.

[3] "Der erste Petrusbriefe—eine Taufrede des Silvanus?" in *Z.N.W.*, xix (1919-20), 143ff.

[4] C. F. D. Moule, "The Nature and Purpose of 1 Peter", in *N.T.S.*, iii (1956), 2.

[5] *Op. cit.*   [6] F. W. Beare, *op. cit.*, 7.

the time of a baptism. The hearers were fresh converts who were finding their new faith an "unspeakable joy" (1: 8). Ch. 2: 1ff. makes this perfectly clear. The force of verse 3 is best brought out by rendering it "Seeing that you have responded to the Psalmist's words, 'taste and see that the Lord is good' ", a reference to the fact that they "have taken the initial step of adherence to Christ"[1] and a reminder that their new experience of divine action in Christ was the promise of greater thrills to come. "In coming to Him you are being built" is a description of their conversion and addition to the church. Clearest of all is the employment of the image of newborn babes who were to be fed on pure milk so that they might grow, a picture that comes readily to mind in relation to the newly-baptized, as the usage both of the mysteries[2] and of Christians of the time of Tertullian and Hippolytus proves.[3] The explicit reference to baptism in 3: 21 says: "Baptism now saves you", and, while it would be absurd to make every "now" in the epistle point to a baptism happening at that time, it is the most natural way of interpreting 3: 21. All these indications are strengthened by the use of the aorist tense in commands such as those to hope (1: 13), to love (1: 22) and to be holy (1: 15) with the implication that these are new obligations involved in their new life.

Another line of research linking 1 Peter with baptism has been pursued by a number of scholars, the best known in the English-speaking world being P. Carrington[4] and E. G. Selwyn.[5] After a detailed study of closely similar passages in 1 Peter, the Pauline epistles and James, they have concluded that the likenesses are due not to dependence of one writing upon another, but to the use of common primitive catechetical material. In the light of the terminology and practices associated with proselyte baptism, these scholars connect most of this material with baptism. Selwyn outlines two baptismal catechetical patterns, one reflecting the Gentile needs and Jewish fears which we meet in the Council of Jerusalem and another dating from A.D. 50-55.

[1] E. G. Selwyn, *The First Epistle of St. Peter*, 157.
[2] Cf. R. Perdelwitz, *op. cit.*, 155f.
[3] F. L. Cross, *1 Peter: a Paschal Liturgy*, 33.
[4] *The Primitive Christian Catechism.*
[5] *Op. cit.*, 363ff.

Yet another thesis has been advanced by Herbert Preisker in his edition of the Windisch commentary.[1] It is that 1 Peter is the record not simply of a baptismal homily but of a baptismal service, which included hymns, teaching, exhortation, prayers, blessing and doxology, and of which part preceded and part followed the actual baptismal rite. In support of his theory Preisker argues that, whereas 1: 3-21 talks of the sanctification as future, 1: 22f. regards it as something accomplished—the converts are sanctified, are reborn. Moreover different parts of the epistle reveal differences of style. The service, on Preisker's hypothesis, began with an introductory prayer (1: 3-12), the eschatological stress of which provided a keynote of joy. The present participle, "being kept for", linked this with the baptismal act as the moment when the convert was taken into divine protection. The next section of the epistle (1: 13-21) was made up of teaching which portrayed the way of living of the Christian community against the background of the Levitical Law of Holiness. That the actual baptism took place between 1: 21 and 1: 22 is indicated by the change in the verses that follow: the converts have now sanctified their souls (1: 22), have been reborn (1: 23), are like new-born babes (2: 2), have tasted that the Lord is gracious (2: 3). Ch. 1: 22-25 represented the baptismal vow; 2: 1-10 was basically a hymn in three strophes, built up on the Old Testament. There followed in 2: 11—3: 12 a fresh exhortation, with a new beginning, "beloved" and "I beseech", with its peak in a hymn to Christ (2: 21-24). This address was succeeded by another, apocalyptic in character (3: 13—4: 7). Ch. 4: 7b-11c was based on what originally would have been the final prayer. Joined to the baptismal service, in the view of Preisker, was a concluding service for the whole congregation. It included an eschatological address (4: 12-19), an exhortation to the elders and younger church members, and finally the whole church (5: 1-9), rounded off by a concluding blessing and a congregational doxology.

Preisker's theory has been accepted with some modifications by F. L. Cross.[2] His agreement is due in no small

---

[1] *Die Katholischen Briefe*, 3rd edition, edited by H. Preisker (*Handbuch zum Neuen Testament*).

[2] *Op. cit.*, 28ff.

measure to a comparison of the analysis with the account of baptism in the Apostolic Tradition of Hippolytus. In view of the pastoral setting for which he contends, he believes that what we find in 1 Peter was the celebrant's part in the Easter baptismal service. He suggests that the first communion followed 2: 10.

Regarded as a whole, the Preisker-Cross theory is hardly acceptable. Most readers will agree with C. F. D. Moule that it is not easy to imagine "how a liturgy-homily, shorn of its rubrics . . . but with its changing tenses and broken sequences all retained, could have been hastily dressed up as a letter and sent off (without a word of explanation) to Christians who had not witnessed its original setting".[1] We have only to compare the work of Cross with that of Preisker to see how little they really support one another. All they have in common, apart from the baptismal homilies, is the opening prayer, which as J. W. C. Wand remarks "is not a very normal sort of prayer",[2] and the doxology of 4: 11, together with the assumption that the baptism took place between 1: 21 and 1: 22. Cross's treatment of all the addresses as the work of one person and his apparent ignoring of Preisker's "hymns" remove a great deal of the argument for a baptismal service, leaving what is in effect "not so much the liturgy itself as the Bishop's running commentary on it".[3] Moreover, Preisker realizes quite rightly that, if his thesis is to be maintained, he has to account for the whole epistle except a brief introduction and conclusion necessary to create the epistolary form. It is one thing for a homily to be incorporated into a letter; it is quite another for a service to be joined to heterogeneous material and then despatched, without explanation, as an epistle. Cross feels that Preisker's treatment of the passages from 4: 12 to the end is not convincing, but is unable to offer a satisfactory alternative. Such a failure to fit in the latter part of the epistle is a serious flaw in the argument.

Rejection of the Preisker-Cross theory, however, does not necessarily involve rejection of the view that 1 Peter is made up to a great extent of baptismal homiletic material.

---

[1] "The Nature and Purpose of 1 Peter", in *N.T.S.*, iii (1956), 4.
[2] "The Lessons of First Peter", in *Interpretation*, ix (1955), 389.
[3] *Ibid.*, 396.

In the article already mentioned, C. F. D. Moule[1] states a convincing case against the position of Cross but has surprisingly little to say against the thesis of Perdelwitz and Bornemann. On "now", all he says is: "The other occurrences would fit perfectly well into a baptism already in progress—especially 3: 21. But not one of them is out of place in a simple 'dispensational' view of things as in 1: 12: once *thus*, now *thus*: *once* the Flood, *now* (in the present dispensation) baptism", and on the conclusion drawn from the description of the recipients as "newborn babes": "The argument is certainly not without force, and I admit that it would be impressive cumulatively. But it needs more grains to go with it before it forms a heap." His own view of the letter as having been written in two forms, one for those actually suffering persecution and another for those for whom it is a future possibility, is far less conceivable than the assumption that the epistle incorporates a baptismal sermon or sermons.

The conclusion to which we are driven, therefore, is that 1 Peter includes two baptismal homilies, one delivered before and the other after the rite,[2] which means that not just the explicit reference to baptism in ch. 3 but practically the whole epistle becomes relevant to our discussion of the baptismal teaching of the work.

A characteristically baptismal concept occurs at the very beginning of the first homily. The Christian had been "begotten again" by God through the resurrection of Christ (1: 3). A little later the converts are described as "newborn babes" (2: 2). The seed from which they had now sprung was "incorruptible, through the word of God, which liveth and abideth". They had thus been given an immortality which was in marked contrast to natural human life which was like grass that soon withered and perished (1: 23-24). Many have regarded these ideas as importations out of the mystery religions,[3] drawing attention to quotations like the one from Sallastius: "after this we are fed on milk as though being reborn". There are however Rabbinic parallels to the language, showing its use with reference to newly converted

---

[1] "The Nature and Purpose of 1 Peter", in *N.T.S.*, iii (1956), 6.

[2] This would not rule out the possibility that elements of baptismal catechisms were used: for the occasion would encourage the repetition of such instruction.

[3] F. W. Beare, *op. cit.*, 17f.; H. Windisch, *Die Katholischen Briefe*, 59; R. Perdelwitz, *op. cit.*, 42ff. See particularly the discussion in E. G. Selwyn, *op. cit.*, 308.

proselytes, and J. Jeremias has drawn attention[1] to the evidence from cemetery inscriptions, which show that a new name was given the proselyte as to one newly born.

Whatever be the origin of the terms, *1 Peter insists on the essentially moral implications of this new life of the Christian.* He is a "child of obedience" (1: 14)—his new birth must result in obedience to the will of God. What God has done for him is bound up with imperatives, as often in New Testament teaching: in coming to Christ, he has purified his soul unto unfeigned love of the brethren, yet he is still commanded to love the brotherhood; he has been sanctified, yet he is bidden to be holy; he has been born to a new hope, and yet he is urged to hope.

One of the effects of baptism was purification. ἡγνικότες (1: 22) points to the definite moment of baptism when the cleansing took place.[2] The writer went to great pains, however, to guard against misunderstanding. It is souls that have been cleansed, and the purification should lead not to individualistic piety, but to love of the brethren. Baptism does not save by a "putting away", as one would divest oneself of a garment, of "the filth of the flesh" or "the flesh of filth" (3: 21).

The positive clause that follows in 3: 21, συνειδήσεως ἀγαθῆς ἐπερώτημα εἰς Θεόν, is notoriously difficult to translate, but we are fortunate now to have the help of the investigations of C. A. Pierce[3] into the meaning of συνειδήσις. After a painstaking examination of the use of the word and its cognates, he has found that it relates principally to specific acts, always past, and, unless the contrary is clearly stated, always evil. "The fundamental character of the συνειδήσις group of words is that man is by nature so constituted that, if he overstep the moral limits of his nature, he will normally feel pain—the pain called συνειδήσις (conscience)." Conscience is not a teacher of morality, but a protector from danger, and, as a kind of punishment, the inner counterpart to the divine wrath. A "good conscience" is thus basically the absence of the pain of conscience, the absence of the consciousness of having committed an evil act. The "good

[1] *Hat die Urkirche die Kindertaufe geübt?*, 21f.
[2] C. E. B. Cranfield, *op. cit.*, 41.
[3] *Conscience in the New Testament.*

conscience" of our passage, therefore, must be a reference to the realization of the reality of divine forgiveness.

The other word, ἐπερώτημα, however, is still a riddle. It occurs nowhere else in the New Testament, and Greeven[1] has to confess that occurrences outside the New Testament fail to throw much light on its meaning in 1 Peter. Normally the word means "inquiry" or "question". There is some slight evidence of its use for "prayer". Once in the Theodotion Version of the Greek Old Testament it seems to denote "decision". There is a papyrus example of the noun and a number of occurrences of the related verb which provide evidence for their employment in the formal query and agreement confirming a contract, thus giving the meaning "stipulatio", "pledge".

It is not surprising that a great number of translations have been offered of 3: 21. In the light of the meaning of "conscience" as indicated by C. A. Pierce, only two remain really possible: "prayer for a good conscience", a pleading for the realization of divine forgiveness, or "pledge of a good conscience", a pledge of God's forgiveness. Our only means of choosing between the two is to relate the clause to the passage as a whole. To say that "baptism saves as a prayer" hardly makes sense. The introduction of the clause "through the resurrection of Jesus Christ" is strange if simply a prayer is involved. Something from the divine side rather than from the human seems to be in the writer's mind. Thus, in spite of both the Bauer and Kittel dictionaries, the better translation here is "pledge of a good conscience". *Baptism gives more than outward bodily cleansing: it is God's pledge that a man may stand before Him without qualms of conscience.* This is assured by the resurrection of Christ, who bore our sins, and by the subjection to Him of all those who might possibly be our accusers. It is difficult not to see in this passage striking parallels to the teaching of Paul on baptism in Rom. 6, particularly when we look at the verses that follow. It is true that E. G. Selwyn, commenting on 4: 1, remarks:

> those who can see little in this epistle except Paulism naturally regard this phrase as an echo of St. Paul's baptismal teaching in Rom. 6: 3-11. It is true that both Apostles, like the primitive church generally, regard the ethical obligations of baptism

---

[1] "Eperotema", in *T.W.N.T.*, ii, 686.

in the same light. But the mysticism of Rom. 6 is conspicuously absent from St. Peter's teaching about baptism here, which in its firm historical reference is far more like that of 1 Cor. 10: 1, 2; and the Pauline idea of justification, essential to the argument in Rom. 6: 6, 7, nowhere occurs in 1 Peter.[1]

The strength of the evidence, however, must not be underestimated. We may compare 4: 1 "whoever has suffered in the flesh has ceased from sin" with Rom. 6: 7, "He who has died is freed from sin". Selwyn himself draws attention to the constant insistence in Paul's writings on the subordination of the supernatural powers to Christ.[2] C. A. Pierce's interpretation of the meaning of "good conscience" removes the objection of the absence of the idea of justification: "pledge of a good conscience towards God" is almost a statement in other words of justification. There is, therefore, an overwhelming case for some connection, direct or indirect, between the Pauline teaching and that of 1 Peter.

This may help us to elucidate the passage preceding 3: 21, on which B. Reicke quotes Luther's words with which everyone who has wrestled with the verses sympathizes: "as dark as any saying in the New Testament. I don't yet know for certain what St. Peter means."[3] The textual problem can quickly be solved in favour of δ: $\hat{\omega}$ is very weakly attested and is obviously due to the difficulty of understanding the sentence with the nominative. Grammatically the verse can be treated in a number of different ways, of which only the more likely need be mentioned.[4] ἀντίτυπον can be an adjective used adverbially, "antitypically", but this can hardly be the meaning here in view of the definite statement that "baptism saves". Selwyn puts "antitype" in apposition to "you", thus producing "which now saves you, who are the antitype of Noah and his company", but his discussion does not allay our suspicions that the author would never have regarded his fellow-Christians as the "antitype" of Noah and his company. Perhaps the most satisfactory approach is that of Reicke,[5] who devotes a whole chapter of his monograph to a detailed proof that from Homeric times down to the late Hellenistic period it was possible to incorporate an

---

[1] *Op. cit.*, 209.   [2] *Op. cit.*, 207.   [3] *Disobedient Spirits and Christian Baptism*, 1.
[4] Cf. discussion in E. G. Selwyn, *op. cit.*, 203ff., 298ff.; M. Barth, *Die Taufe—Ein Sakrament?* 498ff.
[5] *Op. cit.*, 143ff.

appositional antecedent into a relative clause, and who offers the translation "which antitypical baptism now saves you", thus making the family of Noah passing through the flood and the Christian going through the waters of baptism one and the same antitype.

The presence of the water is the common feature, and it is not surprising that many have seen in the water the means of salvation. But the waters of the Flood are always a picture of destruction rather than of salvation. "Through the water" must be a local rather than an instrumental expression. In spite of the advocacy of E. G. Selwyn and C. E. B. Cranfield, it is not likely that the writer had both senses in mind, with something of a Johannine double meaning. Cranfield's words[1] may be quoted:

> the little company in the Ark were saved through water, in the sense that they were brought to safety through the element which was destroying others; it is also true that in a sense water was the means of their safety, for it bore the ark. In the case of baptism the water is the means of salvation, though it is also true that it symbolizes the death into which we are buried with Christ.

The epistle does not say that the water saves: the relative pronoun refers to the whole preceding clause and not simply to the one word "water". Once more we have an approximation to the kind of teaching we find in the Pauline letters: *the Christian dies with Christ in the waters of baptism, and in that experience he finds salvation.* I Peter says this explicitly in 4: 1. As F. W. Beare has pointed out, "arm yourselves with the same mind" means "reckon yourselves as having 'suffered in the flesh', as having died to this present life, as He did".[2]

The reference to Noah occurs in a still wider context, that of Christ's preaching to "the spirits in prison", on the interpretation of which there are wide divergences of view among scholars. The main standpoints that have emerged in the history of the discussion still have representatives in contemporary scholarship. C. F. D. Moule,[3] F. W. Beare[4]

---

[1] *Op. cit.*, 86f.

[2] *Op. cit.*, 152f. Cf. the close association of Flood, death and baptism as shown by P. Lundberg, *La Typologie baptismale dans l'ancienne Église*, 86ff., 112ff.

[3] "The Judgment Theme in the Sacraments", in D. Daube and W. D. Davies (eds.), *The Background of the New Testament and its Eschatology*, 478.

[4] *Op. cit.*, 144f.

and C. E. B. Cranfield[1] still maintain that Christ is portrayed as preaching to the dead of Noah's generation after the crucifixion. M. Barth[2] thinks that the writer is saying that before the Flood, during the time of God's longsuffering, Christ preached to Noah's compatriots through the patriarch himself, not so much by what Noah said as by his action of building the ark. The independent and weighty arguments of B. Reicke[3] and E. G. Selwyn,[4] however, seem likely to swing opinion over to the conviction that 1 Peter is dealing with Christ's proclamation of His victory to the spirit-world, the angelic beings, who were mentioned in connection with the Flood. πνεῦμα is used as a rule of supernatural beings rather than of the dead. The distinction drawn between the time of the proclamation and the time of disobedience ("once disobedient") is proof enough that the period envisaged is not the time before the Flood but after the Lord's death. ἐκήρυξεν means "proclaim" rather than "preach" in this passage. The connection between verse 18, "Christ also died for sins once for all, the righteous for the unrighteous, that he might bring us to God; being put to death in the flesh but made alive in the spirit" and verse 19, "who went and preached to the spirits in prison" is best understood as "in which process", "on which occasion".

1 Peter thus sets baptism against a cosmic background. To see the full significance of the rite the converts were to take into account the subjection of all evil powers to the Christ who died on their behalf. "The good conscience" of which it was the pledge to them was in danger of no challengers. Once again we recall Rom. 8: 33ff.: "Who shall bring any charge against God's elect? it is God who justifies; who is to condemn? it is Christ Jesus who died, yes, who was raised from the dead, who is at the right hand of God, who indeed intercedes for us . . . I am sure that neither death, nor life, nor angels, nor principalities . . . will be able to separate us from the love of God in Christ Jesus our Lord." They could fearlessly repudiate the evil supernatural powers at their baptism and could face courageously any resultant persecution at the hands of the earthly minions of the fallen angels. The Christ into whose death and resurrection they were being baptized had triumphed over all.

[1] *Op. cit.*, 85.　[2] *Op. cit.*, 489ff.　[3] *Op. cit.*, particularly 42ff.　[4] *Op. cit.*, 314ff.

Throughout the whole of 1 Peter the eyes of writer and readers are very much on the future. Their baptism involved being born again "unto a living hope . . . unto an inheritance . . . reserved in heaven". They were to set their "hope perfectly on the grace that is to be brought unto" them "at the revelation of Jesus Christ". As a result of their baptismal experience they were strangers in their own countries. To borrow the language of another New Testament writer, "their citizenship was in heaven". What they had already experienced of the blessings of Christ was a mere foretaste of what was to come: they were to await "a salvation ready to be revealed at the last time".

Nothing in 1 Peter suggests the possibility of the baptism of infants. Only the most naïve would think of the phrase "newborn babes" as an indication of the actual age of the neophytes: for it would be impossible to preach to infants about the significance of their baptism. The whole argument involves the assumption that those who were baptized had consciously accepted the Christian Gospel with its implications: the preacher appealed to the experience through which they were passing and urged them to keep in mind the ethical consequences of the step they were taking. He reminded them of the "passions of" their "former ignorance" (1: 14), and of "the time that is past" when they walked in "licentiousness, passions, drunkenness, revels, carousing, and lawless idolatry" (4: 3). They had been "straying like sheep", but had now "returned to the shepherd and guardian of their souls" (2: 25). Two of our greatest authorities on 1 Peter make this point. Windisch,[1] after a discussion of a number of passages including 1 Peter, said that

> the apostolic teaching on baptism . . . clearly refers to mature people, who have knowledge of good and evil and a consciousness of their sin and guilt, to whom one can give commands and insist on their duty to alter their life and to obey the Lord's command. Infant baptism in this milieu is an impossibility.

F. W. Beare[2] explains to his readers that

> the persons to whom the discourse is addressed are of course not the children of Christian parents, baptized in infancy, but

[1] "Zum Problem der Kindertaufe im Urchristentum", in *Z.N.W.*, xxviii (1929), 129.
[2] *Op. cit.*, 53.

converts from paganism for whom baptism is the seal of conversion, the act of public profession, and the symbol of admission to all the privileges of a Christian society. For such as they, baptism and confirmation are one; and the instruction to be given corresponds, *mutatis mutandis*, to that which would follow confirmation in circumstances akin to our own.

Submission to baptism was described as an act of obedience. The majority of recent commentators[1] agree that the perfect participle, ἡγνικότες, "cannot suggest a *process* of purification" and that in consequence the "obedience" is to be understood not of a continuing attitude, but of a particular act.

> The converts' baptism, which is the response of faith to the proclamation, the public confession of their adherence to the truth, is the act of "obedience to the truth", by which their souls have been sanctified.[2]

The baptizands were not infants who some day might come to believe: they were people who already believed in One they had not seen (1: 8) and whose faith might be tested in the fires of persecution (1: 7) before it found its goal in the salvation of their souls (1: 9). It was their belief that made the stone, that was a stumbling block to others, to them a ground of pride.

Our conclusions on the teaching of baptism found in this letter are:

(a) there is nothing to suggest the possibility of the baptism of infants. On the contrary, the whole argument involves the assumption that those who were baptized had consciously accepted the Christian Gospel with its implications,

(b) the reference to a "good conscience" shows that baptism implies the realization of the divine forgiveness,

(c) the Christian dies with Christ in the waters of baptism, and in that experience he finds salvation,

(d) the whole epistle insists on the essentially moral implications of this new life of the Christian.

2. *Hebrews*. It is fitting that 1 Peter and Hebrews should be considered together: for the affinities between the two

---

[1] F. W. Beare, *op. cit.*, 83f.; C. E. B. Cranfield, *op. cit.*, 41; E. G. Selwyn, *op. cit.*, 149.

[2] F. W. Beare, *op. cit.*, 84.

epistles are very pronounced.[1] We are not surprised, therefore, to discover among C. A. Pierce's conclusions from his investigation into the meaning of "conscience" in the New Testament that the teaching on baptism in Hebrews is a very real development of what we find in 1 Peter.[2]

> This interpretation (in 1 Peter) of the relation of conscience to the mystery of redemption is here suggested rather than stated—and that obscurely and in passing. It is fully expounded and developed, as one of its key themes, by the Epistle to the Hebrews, which sees conscience against the background of the same theme—the once-for-all efficacy of Christ's death and Christian initiation.

In 10: 22 the tense of the participles, "sprinkled" and "washed", justifies us in regarding them as references to baptism. Christian initiation is pictured as succeeding where the older Levitical rites failed: it gives the cleansing essential for men's approach to God. Two processes are regarded as working one with the other: the washing of the body with pure water and the sprinkling of the personality with the blood of Christ which removes the stains of "an evil conscience".[3] Such cleansing is not achieved by human repentance or human resolve: the passive voice makes it clear that it is God who sprinkles and washes, not men themselves. *The writer of the Epistle to the Hebrews thus regards baptism as the point in Christian experience where the results of the death of Christ are made effective by entry into that close fellowship with God which is represented as the Holy of Holies.*

It will be remembered that P. Lundberg, from his own standpoint, also regards Heb. 10: 22 as closely analogous to the teaching of 1 Peter, but feels that "this character of purification presents itself at the expense of certain essential parts of the baptismal concept according to which baptism is considered above all as a sacramental death and a new creation".[4] It is significant, however, that, as C. Spicq[5] and E. G. Selwyn[6] have shown in such convincing detail, there are the closest resemblances between Heb. 13: 20-21 and 1 Peter. This is of interest because Heb. 13: 20-21

---

[1] E. G. Selwyn, *op. cit.*, 463ff.; cf. C. Spicq, *L'Épître aux Hébreux*, i, 139ff.
[2] *Op. cit.*, 98ff.   [3] J. Schneider, *Die Taufe im Neuen Testament*, 65.
[4] *Op. cit.*, 113ff.   [5] *Op. cit.*, i, 142f.   [6] *Op. cit.*, 464f.

throws light on the baptismal teaching of another writing associated with Rome and with St. Peter, the Gospel according to St. Mark. The writer of Hebrews quotes with reference to the death of Jesus precisely the passage which influenced the form of the story of the baptism of Jesus which we find in Mark's Gospel.[1] There is yet another link between the two. The writer to the Hebrews refers in the baptismal context of 10: 19f. to "the way which he dedicated for us, a new and living way, through the veil, that is to say, his flesh". Mark, it will be recalled, stresses that at the moment of the death of Jesus the veil of the temple was torn, using the same word as he employed when he talks of the "splitting" of the heavens at the time of our Lord's baptism.

The prominence of the theme of baptism in Hebrews is due to the peril of apostasy which the writer is trying to avert. To leave the Christian fold would be to renounce all that baptism meant. The readers are called to remember their baptism and the profession of faith they then made (4: 14; 10: 23). On the one hand, the author tries to bring to memory the joy of the first days (6: 9; 10: 32f.), listing "the most captivating elements of the first religious experience to show the monstrosity of a voluntary rejection of the faith".[2] It was then they were "enlightened",[3] a term used in both the baptismal passages 6: 1f. and 10: 32f. and understood as referring to the baptismal experience by the Peschitta, which reads "gone down for baptism", an interpretation supported by the fact that it took place "once"—teaching, which could also be the cause of enlightenment, would be a continuous process rather than something that took place once and for all.

They had had the thrill of tasting the word of God and had already received some of the blessings of the age to come. Their baptism was also associated with their reception of the Holy Spirit and their experience of the new powers and joy that His presence brought. It was little wonder that, in

---

[1] Cf. my note, "The Markan Account of the Baptism of Jesus and Isaiah LXIII", in *J.T.S.*, vii (1956), 74f.

[2] C. Spicq, *op. cit.*, ii, 152.

[3] E.g. H. G. Marsh, *The Origin and Significance of New Testament Baptism*, 151f.; R. Bultmann, *Theology of the New Testament*, i, 143; per contra, J. Schneider, *op. cit.*, 65n.

the days immediately following their baptism, they had thought the endurance of persecution worth while. They took joyfully the spoiling of their possessions, confident that they had a better inheritance which could not be destroyed. They shared the sufferings of others who were being persecuted. "Therefore do not throw away your confidence which has a great reward", cries the writer of the epistle (Heb. 10: 35).

On the other hand, he makes baptism the ground of solemn warning. He stresses the possibility of post-baptismal apostasy. C. Spicq[1] has shown movingly that the author treats this not as a mere theoretical speculation, but as a real danger confronting both his readers and himself. In itself apostasy is shown to be revolting: it means treating the blood of Christ "in which the neophyte is as it were bathed in baptism" as a common thing, and is insolence towards the Holy Spirit he received. Its effects are the cancellation of all the benefits of conversion and baptism, the loss of the reward for which so much has been endured. What makes the threats even more frightening is the denial of the possibility of a renewal of repentance and forgiveness. The baptismal context of 6: 6 supports the interpretation of the Greek Fathers which asserts the impossibility of a second baptism. C. Spicq, who rejects this exegesis of 6: 6, says when he comes to deal with 10: 26f.:[2]

> The argument takes for granted the radical union of Christ and the Christian realized in the baptismal act. The neophyte has been crucified, is dead, has been buried with Christ. One doesn't die the second time (9: 25; 10: 18). Just as Jesus cannot die anew, baptism cannot be repeated.

Baptism is linked in 6: 6f. with a number of other "first principles of Christ", all of which are closely associated with it. The plural "baptisms" is used. Many explanations have been offered for this: it has been related, for example, to the triple immersion in the name of the Trinity and to washing of body and washing of soul.[3] The most likely implication of the plural is that the converts would have been taught to differentiate between the significance of Christian baptism and rites such as Jewish washings, the baptisms of the mystery cults and perhaps the baptism of

---

[1] *Op. cit.*, 321-22.   [2] *Op. cit.*, ii, 321.   [3] Cf. C. Spicq, *op. cit.*, ii, 148.

John the Baptist.[1] Only in contrast to other customs which were outwardly and apparently similar could the Christian sacrament properly be understood.

It is interesting to find "laying on of hands" in the list of "first principles". H. G. Marsh[2] complains that "the context gives no indication of what is meant by" it. "It may be the post-baptismal act or it may refer to something different— a kind of ordination." "A kind of ordination", however, could hardly be included among "first principles" and the use of $\tau\epsilon$ rather than $\kappa\alpha\iota$ implies that "laying on of hands" is here joined firmly with baptism, probably at the same ceremony.[3] L. S. Thornton[4] wishes to make the "enlightenment" and the "tasting of God's good word" baptismal gifts as over against the "tasting of the powers of the age to come" which he holds were given by the laying on of hands, but there is really no support for such a distinction in the passage.

What is very significant about the list of "first principles" is that both by the order in which they are stated and by the nature of what is included *no room seems given for infant baptism*. The list begins with repentance and faith and then goes on to baptism and the laying on of hands.[5] This fits in with the whole argument of the baptismal passages. For the writer of this epistle, baptism involved repentance and confession of belief in Christ: it was the expression, as far as the human side was concerned, of conscious decision.

[1] Cf. J. Schneider, *op. cit.*, 65.   [2] *Op. cit.*, 170f.   [3] C. Spicq, *op. cit.*, 148.
[4] *Confirmation, Its Place in the Baptismal Mystery*, 169f.
[5] J. Schneider, *op. cit.*, 64.

5

BAPTISM IN THE EARLY CHRISTIAN CENTURIES

by A. W. Argyle

IN the New Testament, as we have seen in the last chapter, Christian baptism is administered to those who have confessed repentance towards God and faith in Jesus Christ. "The theology of baptism therein presented to us is concerned with the baptism of adults alone."[1] Even in the fourth-century church Fathers like Gregory Nazianzen, Gregory Nyssen, Basil and Rufinus, though born of Christian parents, were not baptized till manhood. Yet in the meantime there had grown up the rite of infant baptism, which by the fifth century had become the general practice of the church.

A. Factors which Contributed to this Change

1. There was a tendency to place an unscriptural materialistic interpretation upon Christ's own baptism, alleging that His immersion in the Jordan conferred upon baptismal waters a sanctifying potency, which Ignatius[2] associated with His passion, later writers with the sinlessness of His person. In the eighth century John of Damascus[3] links the sanctifying power of baptismal water with the water that proceeded from the Saviour's side as He hung upon the cross (John 19: 34), though he still attributes to the Lord's baptism in the Jordan a purifying and exorcizing effect upon the water of baptism, "breaking the heads of the dragons

---

[1] G. W. H. Lampe, *The Seal of the Spirit*, 93.
[2] *Eph.*, 18. 2.
[3] *De Fide Orthodoxa*, iv. 9 (P.G. 64, 1120).

on the water" (Ps. 74: 13).[1] As the idea that the baptismal water in itself had a sanctifying power prevailed, emphasis upon the necessity for conscious repentance and faith in the recipient of baptism naturally declined.

2. "The materialistic decadence of much of the post-biblical theology of baptism"[2] may be associated with a failing grasp of the Biblical doctrine of grace.[3] In the New Testament, Divine grace is the personal prevenient love of God which freely gives and forgives. It is God Himself taking the initiative in spontaneously saving unworthy sinners. In the patristic period it tends more and more to be represented as an impersonal and quasi-material force or a sub-personal pneumatic power conveyed through specially ordained channels, till Ambrose can say that unless a person is baptized he cannot receive the remission of sins nor imbibe the gift of spiritual grace;[4] and John of Damascus can speak of "the water by the grace of the Spirit cleansing the body from sin and delivering it from corruption".[5]

3. Along with this defective doctrine of grace is found an imperfect grasp of the full Pauline conception of the faith-union of the penitent believer with Christ through personal self-committal to a personal Saviour. Faith tended to be regarded chiefly as intellectual assent to a creed.[6] If the candidate was an adult, he recited or assented to a credal formula before his baptism; if an infant, sponsors said that he believed in this sense; though, as Augustine[7] found when challenged by Boniface, it is not easy to explain how this can be. Ideally, as Origen[8] saw, the whole life and spiritual progress of a Christian should be the unfolding of what is

[1] "In spite of the very great prominence given in popular devotion from early times to the Epiphany feast, at which Christ's baptism was commemorated, and despite the importance for early Christology of the Spirit-anointing, the Fathers are too often content either to moralize on the humility shown by our Lord in receiving baptism, or to enlarge upon the theme of the sanctification of baptismal water effected by His immersion in the Jordan—a theory for which there is no warrant in Scripture" (G. W. H. Lampe, *op. cit.*, 34).

[2] G. W. H. Lampe, *ibid.*

[3] Cf. T. F. Torrance, *The Doctrine of Grace in the Apostolic Fathers*, 140f.

[4] *De Myst.*, 20.

[5] *Loc. cit.* Cf. Cyprian, *Ep.*, 76, where he says that as the Red Sea drowned Pharaoh, so baptism drowns the devil out of a man.

[6] "The time and original use of creeds, their primary *raison d'être*, was to serve as solemn affirmations of faith in the context of baptismal initiation" (J. N. D. Kelly, *Early Christian Creeds*, 31).

[7] *Ep.*, 98 (P.L. 33, 360). Cf. *infra*, 216.

[8] *Hom.*, 10. 4, in Exod. (P.G. 12, 373 B).

implicit in baptism. This can be truly so only if baptismal experience includes the moral repentance, the willed decision and self-dedication of the candidate.

4. Another factor in the rise and growth of infant baptism was popular sentiment, expressed in a concern for the welfare of the children of Christian parents. The belief that the baptismal water, previously consecrated, possessed in itself a mysterious sanctifying potency would greatly encourage some parents to have their children baptized as soon as possible; though upon other parents this belief had precisely the opposite effect, leading them to delay the baptism of their children as long as possible through fear of post-baptismal sin. In both classes the notion that the baptismal water in itself could sanctify obscured the need for conscious repentance and faith on the part of the recipient.

5. The doctrine of original sin, while it does not appear to have been a cause of the introduction of infant baptism, nevertheless helped to establish it. Those who defended the baptism of infants could appeal to this doctrine in support of it, claiming that, although the new-born infant had no sins of its own to be remitted, yet it needed the forgiveness of sin biologically inherited from Adam and the human race through its parents. In turn the practice of infant baptism helped to strengthen the doctrine of original sin and to add to it the unscriptural doctrine of original guilt, alleging the infant's share in responsibility for Adam's sin. It was held by Ambrose and Augustine, for instance, that the baptism even of infants secured the cancelling of this guilt. The New Testament insistence upon the candidate's personal penitence and conscious faith as conditions of baptism was ignored.

Together with a failing grasp of the New Testament doctrine of baptism we find an increasing concentration upon typological exegesis of Scripture in regard to baptism. Many passages relating to water in the Old Testament are interpreted as prefiguring Christian baptism; but in view of the conception of Christian salvation as a new exodus, a new deliverance from the worse than Egyptian bondage of sin and a new entrance into a new Canaan effected by the death, burial and resurrection of Christ which are symbolized in Christian baptism, special emphasis is laid upon the baptismal interpretation of the crossing of the Red Sea and of

Jordan.[1] In keeping with this typological exegesis milk and honey were administered to the newly-baptized[2] as a symbol of spiritual entrance into the promised land "flowing with milk and honey".[3]

The patristic doctrine remained faithful to the Pauline teaching that Christian baptism portrays the death, burial and resurrection of the Lord. The close association of both baptism and the eucharist with the cross of Christ brought it about that when infant baptism arose communion also was administered to babes. The newly-baptized infant, having received chrism and the imposition of hands, which rites were as a rule still part of the baptismal ceremony, was admitted to the Lord's Table.[4] This is still so in the eastern church, and it continued to be so in the west till the eighth century, and sometimes even later. The earliest extant copy of the Gregorian Sacramentary[5] provides for communion of baptized infants even if they have not yet received chrism and confirmation. The *Ordo Romanus* (c. A.D. 730), 46, insists that infants baptized on Easter eve shall take no food nor be suckled after their baptism before they communicate of the sacrament of the body of Christ.[6]

Up till the fifth century baptism was administered as a rule[7] by the bishop, or at least in his presence, but after that usually by the presbyters, often in the absence of the bishop. Since in the west confirmation had to await the arrival of the bishop, an interval tended to arise between baptism and confirmation. In the *De Ordine Baptismi* of Theodulph, bishop of Orleans in the eighth century, episcopal confirmation

---

[1] E.g. Origen, *Hom.*, 4. 2, *in Jos.*, iii. 7 (P.G. 12, 843 D).

[2] Tertullian, *De Coron. Milit.*, 3; *Adv. Marc.*, i. 14.

[3] Hippolytus, *Apostolic Tradition*, 23. 2. Cf. J. Crehan, *Early Christian Baptism and the Creed*, 171ff. In the *De Ordine Baptismi* of Theodulph (eighth cent.), salt (cf. Matt. 5: 13) is administered to the infant after insufflation and exorcism, but before baptism (P.L. 105, 225). The use of milk and honey is not mentioned by Theodulph.

[4] Cyprian, *De Lapsis*, 25 (P.L. 4, 500). Augustine, *Serm.*, 174, 6 (P.L. 38, 944); *Contr. Julian*, op. imperf., ii. 30 (P.L. 45, 1154). *De Pecc. Mer.*, i. xx. 26 (P.L. 44, 123); i. xxiv. 34 (P.L. 44, 129). Gennadius of Marseilles (A.D. 495), *De Eccl. Dogm.*, 22. The Gelasian Sacramentary (lib. i, n. 75). Council of Toledo (A.D. 675), Canon 11. *Const. Apost.*, 8. 13 (P.G. 1, 1109). Pseudo-Dionys., *De Eccl. Hierarch.*, 7. 11 (P.G. 3, 565). Evagrius (A.D. 594), *Hist. Eccl.*, 4. 36 (P.G. 89, 276Q). John Moschus (A.D. 630), *Pratum Spirit.*, 196 (P.G. 87, 3, 3081).

[5] *Liturgia Rom. Vet. Murat.*, tom. ii, col. 158.   [6] *Musae Ital.*, tom. i, 28.

[7] Others could baptize in exceptional cases (Tertullian, *De Bapt.*, 17), especially in clinical baptism (Cyprian, *Ep.*, 69. 13; the anonymous *De Rebaptismate*, 10; Cf. Jerome. *Dial. adv. Lucif.*, 7).

by the imposition of hands is separated from baptism (c. 17).[1] As this separation became usual, communion tended to be deferred till after confirmation. But it was not till the thirteenth century that baptism and confirmation (followed by first communion) became permanently separated in the west by an interval of from seven to fourteen years.[2] The western church thus broke away from a centuries-old tradition which the eastern church retained.[3] The sacraments of baptism and communion are so closely linked by their association with the death of Christ and the faith-union of penitent believers with Him in His saving work that to admit infants to the former and exclude them from the latter is doctrinally inconsistent.

The admission of infants to baptism inevitably resulted, as far as infants were concerned, in the disappearance of the catechumenate as a period of instruction before baptism, though inconsistently infant candidates were still called "catechumens". In the Dark and Middle Ages, as whole nations were subjugated by invading Christian armies, baptism was often a symbol, not of faith, but of submission to the jurisdiction of the ecclesiastical power of the conquering state, and the baptism of so-called converts resembled that of infants in so far as systematic teaching concerning the faith followed baptism instead of preceding it. This practice violated Canon 2 of the Council of Nicea (A.D. 325) which was directed against premature baptism and demanded ante-baptismal instruction. Baptism as a mode of entrance into the *corpus christianum* was frequently a mere concomitant of entrance into citizenship of a Christian state, and was sometimes compulsory.[4] *Thus baptism, through its application*

---

[1] P.L. 105, 235. In Rabanus Maurus, *De Cler. Instit.*, i, 28-30, though chrismation by a presbyter follows immediately upon baptism and is itself followed by first communion, confirmation takes place at the end of youth that the receiver "may be strengthened by the Holy Spirit to preach to others the same gift which he himself received in baptism" (P.L. 107, 314).

[2] E. H. Plumptre, "Confirmation", in *Dictionary of Christian Antiquities*, i, 425. Cf. G. Dix, *The Theology of Confirmation in Relation to Baptism*, 21ff.

[3] In the east presbyters are allowed to confirm by chrism with oil consecrated by the bishop. The baptized infant then receives communion.

[4] See H. H. Milman, *History of Latin Christianity*, 4th revised ed. (1867), ix, 226: "Charlemagne was a Teuton warring on Teutons: he would need no interpreter for the brief message of his evangelic creed to the Saxons—'Baptism or death'." In the assembly of Paederborn (A.D. 785) he also commanded the Saxons, under penalty of a heavy fine, to have their infants baptized during their first year. See A. Lagarde, *The Latin Church in the Middle Ages*, 37, and the references there.

to infants, progressively lost its New Testament significance till it could be used as a mere outward sign without any inward spiritual significance.

Our purpose now is to trace the development of the church's teaching on baptism in the early centuries, so as to substantiate the claims which we have made, and to emphasize particularly those aspects of the subject which are still relevant to the whole of our discussion.

B. *Historical Development in the Early Centuries*

1. The First and Second Centuries. The First Epistle of Clement to the Corinthians (*c.* A.D. 96) provides little evidence on the subject of baptism, apart from a reference to the outpouring of the one Spirit of grace,[1] which probably alludes to the bestowal of the Holy Spirit in baptism, and two further possible allusions in the description of the deluge which Noah proclaimed as "regeneration" (παλιγγενεσία)[2] and the phrase "through Him our foolish and darkened mind springs up into the light".[3] These two latter passages have been claimed as referring to baptism,[4] but it is doubtful whether they do. The ideas of regeneration and illumination are, it is true, closely associated with baptism, but not invariably so. The technical terms for baptismal illumination (φωτισμός, φωτίζω) are lacking in 1 Clement.[5]

The Homily of unknown date and authorship, called the Second Epistle of Clement to the Corinthians, explicitly teaches that the Spirit is received in baptism, for it refers to baptism as "the seal",[6] recalling St. Paul's conception of the seal of the Spirit bestowed sacramentally in baptism,[7] though the author has given a quasi-materialistic turn to the Pauline teaching, implying that baptism sets upon the mortal flesh of the believer a seal which brands him as the property of God and which must be kept inviolate by good

[1] I Clem., 46. 5. [2] 9. 4. Cf. 1 Pet. 3: 21.

[3] 36. 2. Cf. Heb. 6: 4 (φωτισθέντας), 10: 32 (φωτισθέντες), 1 Pet. 2: 9.

[4] A. Benoit, *Le Baptême chrétien au Second Siècle*, 84, 89.

[5] It is possible that the references to "light" and "illuminated" in the Odes of Solomon (e.g. 36. 3, 41. 6, 32. 1, 34. 3, 10. 7) are to be associated with baptism, and that the Odes are Jewish-Christian baptismal hymns of the first half of the second century. (See J. H. Bernard, "The Odes of Solomon", in *J.T.S.*, xii (1910), 1ff.)

[6] 2 Clem., 6. 9, 7. 6, 8. 6.

[7] 2 Cor. 1: 21-22, Eph. 1: 13-14; 4: 30. See G. W. H. Lampe, *op. cit.*, 3ff.

conduct. "The significance of baptism lies therefore not so much in the change introduced as in the obligations laid upon the believer. There would be no obligation were there no change, for obligation means preserving the new status of the soul, or the seal of baptism."[1]

The so-called Epistle of Barnabas (early second century) relates baptism to Old Testament typology. The Jews are declared to have rejected the baptism which brings remission of sins, inasmuch as they abandoned God, "the fountain of life".[2] Blessed are they who go down into this water, for they have set their hopes on the cross. The author interprets the "river" of Ezekiel 47: 1-12, as the water of baptism into which "we go down laden with sins and filth", and from which we rise "bearing fruit in the heart, resting our fear and hope on Jesus in the spirit".[3] The effect of baptism is to exorcize the demons who have dwelt in the heart.[4] That the recipients of baptism are thought of as believers is shown by the declaration of salvation by faith based upon instruction received: "Whosoever, saith He, shall hear these things spoken and shall believe, shall live for ever."[5] The conception of baptism which emerges here is a thoroughly spiritual one, being closely related to an inward moral regeneration resulting from remission of sins and the gift of the Spirit.

Ignatius of Antioch (c. A.D. 110) devotes less space in his writings to baptism than to the eucharist. He does, however, stress the purpose of Christ's baptism "to fulfil all righteousness",[6] and elsewhere he asserts that it had another purpose, "to purify the water by His passion" ($\tau\hat{\omega}$ $\pi\acute{a}\theta\epsilon\iota$).[7] This difficult phrase has been variously interpreted.[8] It probably means that the baptism of Jesus prefigured and inaugurated His passion and death which gave purifying effect to the baptismal waters.[9] Here we see already the unscriptural teaching that the baptism of Jesus gave a mystical sanctifying

---

[1] T. F. Torrance, op. cit., 129.

[2] Barn. 11. 2. Cf. Jer. 2: 12-13, Ps. 1: 3.

[3] Barn. 11. 11. The water of Ezek. 47: 3 appears in the LXX as ὕδωρ ἀφέσεως, "the water of remission", and many of the Fathers interpret it of the water of baptism. Cf. Odes of Solomon, 6. 7f.

[4] Barn. 16. 7.   [5] 11. 11.   [6] Smyrn., 1. 1. Cf. Matt. 3: 15.

[7] Eph., 8. 2.   [8] See A. Benoit, op. cit., 63ff.

[9] Cf. J. B. Lightfoot, The Apostolic Fathers, Part ii, second edition, ii, 75.

N

potency to the baptismal water itself. This teaching frequently appears in subsequent Fathers,[1] with the difference that they attribute the sanctifying effect of Christ's baptism upon the water not to His passion, but to the sinlessness of His person. Ignatius further describes Christian baptism as affording us weapons for spiritual warfare,[2] and declares that baptism is the rite of admission into the church and is therefore not to be administered "apart from the bishop".[3]

The *Didache* ("The Teaching of the Twelve Apostles")[4] describes baptism as being administered "into the name of the Father, and of the Son, and of the Holy Spirit"[5] or "into the name of the Lord" (i.e. Christ),[6] thus showing that these two formulae were interchangeable and had essentially the same meaning. The *Didache* is important as distinguishing *four* varieties in the mode of baptism. The four methods are given in order of preference as follows: immersion in a stream, immersion in standing water, either cold or warm, and triple affusion, or pouring.[7] The directions for baptism make it clear that the candidates had reached years of understanding. The moral instruction known as "The Two Ways", which forms the first part of the treatise, is to be repeated by the administrant before baptism. Another direction reads: "But before baptism let him that baptizeth and him that is baptized fast, and any also that are able; and thou shalt order him that is baptized to fast a day or two before."[8] The institution of the fast before baptism was doubtless inherited from Judaism, where it was frequent,[9] and the moral instruction presents parallels to that which preceded Jewish proselyte baptism.[10]

The *Didache* shows that affusion was recognized as a valid mode of baptism at an early date, although immersion was preferable where possible. Affusion would be more convenient in cases of sickness; but, as the evidence both literary and archaeological shows, immersion was the normal mode in the

[1] E.g. Tertullian, *Adv. Jud.*, 8 (P.L. 2, 615), *De Bapt.*, 9 (P.L. 1, 1210). Clement Alex. *Eclogae*, 7 (P.G. 9, 701). Ambrose, *Exp. Ev. Luc.*, 2, 83 (P.L. 15, 1583). Bede, *Exp. Ev. Luc.*, 3. 21, lib. i. 3 (P.L. 92, 358).

[2] *Polyc.*, 6. 2. Cf. 1 Th. 5: 8, Eph. 6: 11f.   [3] *Smyrn.*, 8. 2.

[4] The problem of the date of the *Didache* cannot be discussed here; it probably belongs to the first half of the second century.

[5] *Did.*, 7. 1, 2.   [6] 9. 5.   [7] 7. 1.   [8] *Ibid.*   [9] Cf. A. Benoit, *op. cit.*, 11.

[10] Cf. F. Gavin, *The Jewish Antecedents of the Christian Sacraments*, 43f., and *supra*, 68, 74f.

first four centuries,[1] and the immersion seems to have been accomplished by the administrant standing with the candidate, who knelt in the water, and bowing him forward.[2]

In the Shepherd of Hermas (*c.* A.D. 140), the church, represented in a vision as a tower, is said to be builded upon water, "because your life is saved and shall be saved by water".[3] Those who receive baptism are admitted into the tower and are arrayed in white robes[4] as wearing the name of the Son of God.[5] The robe which the baptized put on is the Holy Spirit,[6] which is bestowed upon the believer and must be preserved intact.[7] The water of baptism is the seal of the Spirit, and the baptized receive from their sealing the fruit of the Spirit, one faith and love.[8] Through baptism they pass from death to life. "So these likewise that had fallen asleep received the seal of the Son of God and entered into the kingdom of God. For before a man has borne the name of the Son of God he is dead; but when he has received the seal he lays aside his deadness and receives life again. The seal then is the water; so they go down into the water dead and they come up alive."[9] Baptism is here thought of as administered to people who have reached years of understanding, to whom "this seal was preached",[10] and it is conceived in New Testament fashion as a means whereby the believer is buried and raised again to newness of life. In the *Mandates* it is declared that penitence is a precondition of baptism, and remission of sins and a holy life are its results.[11]

Justin Martyr (*c.* A.D. 150) clearly understands Christian baptism to be administered in the Threefold Name to

---

[1] C. F. Rogers (*Baptism and Christian Archaeology*) sets out to prove from the archaeological evidence that the normal practice in the early church was baptism by affusion. But the evidence which he adduces hardly supports his arguments. He describes twenty-nine of the early baptisteries which have been excavated (322f.). Their average depth is 3 ft. 2 in., fully sufficient for immersion of a kneeling candidate. That early baptism was by immersion seems clear from the language of Rom. 6: 3f., and Col. 2: 12.

[2] W. N. Cote, *The Archaeology of Baptism*, 31. Cf. H. Wheeler Robinson, *Baptist Principles*, 42f. There is abundant evidence both in literature and in art that open air baptism—especially in running water—persisted till a comparatively late period. Cf. Tertullian, *De Bapt.* 4: *nulla distinctio est mari quis an stagno, flumine an fonte, lacu an alveo diluatur.*

[3] *Sim.*, 3. 3. (Cf. 1 Pet. 3: 20-22.)   [4] *Sim.*, 8. 2, 2-3.
[5] *Ibid.*, 9. 13, 2-3, 7.   [6] 9. 24, 2.   [7] 9. 32, 4.   [8] 9. 17, 4.
[9] 9. 16, 3-4.   [10] 9. 16, 4.   [11] *Mand.*, 4. 3.

believers only.[1] The recipients of baptism are they who "are
persuaded and believe" the Christian teaching to be true
and promise to live in accordance with it. They have fasted
and prayed. The regeneration, or new creation, which they
are said to receive in baptism is represented not as something which takes place apart from conscious faith, but as the
result of self-dedication to God[2] whereby "the children of
necessity and of ignorance" become "the children of choice
and knowledge". The candidate "chooses to be born again"
and, having repented, obtains in the water "remission of sins
formerly committed". "And this washing is called illumina-
tion ($\phi\omega\tau\iota\sigma\mu\acute{o}s$), because they who learn these things are
illuminated in their understandings."[3] Justin further con-
trasts the Jewish baptism which cleanses the body alone
with the inward and ethical significance of Christian
baptism, which is a "washing" of repentance and of the
knowledge of God, "the water of life",[4] a baptism with the
Holy Spirit,[5] "the laver of regeneration".[6] It is a spiritual
circumcision, bringing forgiveness of sins through the mercy
of God.[7] The water-baptism and the Spirit-baptism are one,
the former being the outward sign of the latter. The description of baptism as a spiritual and effective circumcision
implies that it is "the seal" of the Spirit, though Justin does
not actually use the term.[8]

Justin's reference to the current use of the technical term,
the noun "illumination" ($\phi\omega\tau\iota\sigma\mu\acute{o}s$), as a synonym for
baptism is the earliest in Christian literature and calls for
special comment. The association of baptism with enlightenment had already occurred in Heb. 6: 4; 10: 32, probably

---

[1] An attempt has been made to prove the existence of infant baptism from
Apol., I, 15. 6: "Many men and women, who have been disciples of Christ
since their childhood ($\grave{\epsilon}\kappa\ \pi\alpha\acute{\iota}\delta\omega\nu$), have remained pure till sixty and seventy
years of age." Ph. H. Menoud ("Le Baptême des enfants dans l'Église ancienne",
in *V.C.*, ii (1948), 15-26) thinks that only a baptized person could be described
as a disciple of Christ. But the term "disciple of Christ" is too general to have
the precise meaning "baptized", and, on the other hand, the word $\pi\alpha\hat{\iota}\delta\epsilon s$ is
capable of being applied to children who are old enough to answer questions,
as well as to babes. Cf. A. Benoit, *op. cit.*, 152.

[2] *Apol.*, I, 61. 1. $\grave{\alpha}\nu\epsilon\theta\acute{\eta}\kappa\alpha\mu\epsilon\nu\ \acute{\epsilon}\alpha\upsilon\tau\upsilon\grave{s}\ \tau\hat{\wp}\ \Theta\epsilon\hat{\wp}\ \kappa\alpha\iota\nu\omicron\pi\omicron\iota\eta\theta\acute{\epsilon}\nu\tau\epsilon s$.

[3] I, 61. 2, 65. 1.   [4] *Dial.*, 14. 1.   [5] *Ibid.*, 29. 1.

[6] *Apol.*, I, 61, 66.   [7] *Dial.*, 19. 2, 43. 2.

[8] The conception of baptism as the seal which marks the believer for redemption is further illustrated in *Acts of Paul and Thecla*, 32, 34, 40; the *Acts of Paul*,
3, 24, 31ff. (Schmidt, 32f.), the *Acts of Peter*, 5 (Lipsius-Bonnet, 50-51), the
Acts of Xanthippe, 13, 28. See G. W. H. Lampe, *op. cit.*, 106ff.

also in 1 Peter 2: 9, and possibly in 1 Clem. 36. 2. For Justin "illumination" is especially associated with the teaching of the Gospel,[1] and its suitability as a name for baptism arises both from the fact that those who are baptized are instructed believers and from the fact that they receive in baptism the Holy Spirit of wisdom and understanding whose work it is to guide them into all truth and the vision of God.[2] Although Justin says that at the baptism of Jesus a fire was kindled in Jordan,[3] this is not the reason why he describes baptism as illumination.

No writer of the second century, except in Gnostic sects, draws a distinction between a rite of water-baptism and another of Spirit-baptism, nor does any writer before Tertullian afford indisputable evidence of infant baptism. It is true that, according to the letter of the church of Smyrna describing the martyrdom of Polycarp (A.D. 155), ix.3, the martyr just before his death claimed to have been in the service of Christ for eighty-six years. But this does not prove that Polycarp was baptized in infancy, for he may have served Christ before being baptized, since he was the son of Christian parents. Even after infant baptism became established, several of the late Fathers, though born of Christian parents, were not baptized till manhood (e.g. Gregory Nazianzen, Gregory Nyssen, Basil, Ephraim Syrus and Rufinus). The evidence from early Christian inscriptions, adduced by J. Jeremias[4] to prove the very early practice of infant baptism, is similarly inconclusive.

It has been claimed by some[5] that infant baptism is alluded to by Irenaeus (c. A.D. 180). The evidence cited is indirect, occurring in a passage which asserts, in reply to Gnosticism, the reality and completeness of Christ's human experience, in infancy, childhood, youth and old age. "He came to save all through Himself; all, I mean, who through Him are born again unto God, infants and little children,

---

[1] *Dial.*, 122.

[2] Cf. *Dial.*, 39. 2, 4. 1. It is interesting to note that in the LXX "enlightenment" is associated with repentance and salvation. Thus whereas the call for conversion at Hos. 10: 12 runs in the Hebrew: "break up your fallow ground", the LXX has "enlighten yourselves with the light of knowledge" (φωτίσατε ἑαυτοῖς φῶς γνώσεως).

[3] *Dial. c. Trypho*, 88.   [4] *Hat die Urkirche die Kindertaufe geübt?*, 25ff.

[5] E.g. F. Loofs, *Dogmengeschichte*, ed. 4, 212; H. Wheeler Robinson, *op. cit.*, 36.

and boys, and young men and old men."[1] It is argued that this indicates infant baptism, because in some other passages[2] Irenaeus means by "being born again" baptismal regeneration.[3] But this argument is not wholly convincing, for Irenaeus frequently speaks of regeneration without reference to baptism. Too much weight should not be placed upon an isolated passage which appears to be somewhat rhetorical, and, as the reference to Christ's old age shows, is not to be taken altogether literally. "It is not clear whether Irenaeus speaks of infant baptism, though it must have been coming into the church about this time, as Tertullian objected to it a little later."[4]

In any case, the teaching of Irenaeus presupposes the baptism of adult believers. It is the man who has faith and is beginning a full Christian life who receives baptism,[5] in which is imparted the "Rule of Truth",[6] the confession of the Threefold Name, and the incarnation, passion and resurrection.[7] The believer receives the indwelling presence of the Holy Spirit as the inward counterpart of baptism in water,[8] and the soul experiences a resurrection, being raised up by the power of the Holy Spirit, and entering the kingdom of God.[9] Baptism effects remission of sins, and is the seal of eternal life and the new birth unto God.[10]

2. The Third Century. Tertullian (*flor. c.* A.D. 197-225), is important for our subject inasmuch as he was the first Father of the church to devote a whole treatise to baptism. He assumes at the opening of *De Baptismo* (written before his professed adherence to Montanism) that the candidate has received some instruction in the Faith.[11] The catechumen is also described as having been prepared by fasting, prayer and vigil.[12] The mode of baptism indicated is that of immersion: "a man is lowered into the water, and, with intervals for a few words, is dipped (*tinctus*) and rises up

---

[1] *Adv. haer.*, 2. 22. 4.   [2] *Ibid.*, 1. 21. 1; 3. 17. 1.

[3] Irenaeus adopts Justin's description of baptism as "the laver of regeneration", 5. 15. 3.

[4] J. Lawson, *The Biblical Theology of Saint Irenaeus*, 267.

[5] *Adv. haer.*, 4. 23. 2.

[6] 1. 9. 4. "This appears to be an allusion to the confession of Christian belief by custom made at baptism" (J. Lawson, *op. cit.*, 266). Cf. Tertullian, *De Coron. Milit.*, 3.

[7] *Demonstration of the Apostolic Preaching*, 41.   [8] *Ibid.*, 42.   [9] *Ibid.*, 89.

[10] *Ibid.*, 3.   [11] *De Bapt.*, 1: "*eos qui cum maxime formantur*".   [12] *Ibid.*, 20.

again".[1] But Tertullian lays more stress on the inward meaning than on the outward mode. He chose a new term which he often uses to signify "baptize". The Greek word $\beta\alpha\pi\tau\iota\zeta\omega$ suggested two ideas, roughly equivalent to "dip" and "dye". The Latin word for the former ("dip") was *mergere*, and for the latter ("dye") *tingere*.[2] Tertullian chose the latter as more fitted to stress the importance of spiritual regeneration.[3] He describes baptism as *intinctio paenitentiae*,[4] *intinctio Dominica*.[5]

From Tertullian's writings we can piece together the form that was used in baptism. First, in the presence of the congregation (*ecclesia*) and under the hand of the president (*sub antistitis manu*) the candidate solemnly renounced the devil and his pomp and his angels.[6] Then he was thrice immersed in the name of the Father, the Son and the Holy Spirit[7] in water which was previously consecrated.[8] Some form of creed was recited by the candidate[9] in the presence of the congregation and of sponsors.[10] According to *De Corona Militis* (3) milk and honey were administered to the newly-baptized,[11] a practice which Hippolytus interprets as signifying entrance into the new inheritance, the new Canaan, "the land flowing with milk and honey".[12] Tertullian is the first writer who clearly mentions the sponsors (*sponsores, susceptores, arbitri*), the post-baptismal administering of unction, the anointing with olive-oil, followed by the laying-on of hands,[13] together with the making of the sign of the cross on the forehead of the baptized.[14]

The order which we find in Tertullian, whereby baptism is followed by anointing and imposition of hands, was the common practice of the church. But another order was observed in Syrian or Syriac-speaking churches, in which

---

[1] *De Bapt.*, 2.   [2] Or *tinguere*, e.g. *tinguimur, Adv. Prax.*, 26.

[3] Cf. J. Morgan, *The Importance of Tertullian in the Development of Christian Dogma*, 81-2.

[4] *De Paenit.*, 2.   [5] *Ibid.*, 12.

[6] *De Coron. Milit.*, 3. Cf. *De Idol.*, 24, *De Spec.*, 4, *De Cult Fem.*, 1. 2.

[7] *Adv. Prax.*, 26: *nam nec semel, sed ter, ad singula nomina in personas singulas tinguimur.*

[8] *De Bapt.*, 4. Cf. Cyprian, *Ep.*, 70. 1.

[9] *De Coron. Milit.*, 3; *De Virg. Vel.*, 1; *De Praes. Haer.*, 13.   [10] *De Bapt.*, 6.

[11] Cf. *Adv. Marc.*, i. 14.   [12] *Apostolic Tradition*, 23. 2.   [13] *De Bapt.*, 7.

[14] *De Coron. Milit.*, 3: *frontem signaculo. De Spec.*, 24: *signaculo fidei. De Idol.*, 19: *signo Christi.*

the anointing and imposition of hands preceded the baptism.[1]
This order may have been very early,[2] but in the rest of
Christendom the usage which we find in Tertullian prevailed.

Tertullian interprets the "seal" of the Spirit, by which the
believer's response of faith to God is sacramentally sealed,
as the water-baptism itself, "the laver of regeneration",[3]
the "sacrament of sanctification".[4] The post-baptismal
signing with the cross on the believer's forehead is also called
a "seal"[5] but only in the sense of "a mark of Christian
service, a sign of the Christian *militia*, a seal set upon the
elect of God, and a defence against the power of the devil;
it is not the sacramental sign of the bestowal upon the
baptized of the Holy Spirit".[6] There is, however, some
confusion in Tertullian's teaching concerning the relation
of baptism to the gift of the Spirit. Sometimes he appears to
say that the gift of the Spirit is bestowed in baptism itself;[7]
at other times he speaks as if it were bestowed in the post-
baptismal imposition of hands.[8]

The great African teacher stressed the connection of
baptism with repentance and a change of heart, declaring:
"We are washed, not in order that we may cease from
sinning, but because we have ceased, since in heart we have
been bathed already."[9] Yet he regards the water itself as
washing away sin and possessing spiritual potency through
the intervention of an angel who prepares the water for the
coming of the Holy Spirit and the gift therewith of eternal
life: "the spirit is bodily washed in the waters and the flesh
is spiritually cleansed in the same".[10] He insists that faith
is not sufficient without baptism, and that baptism cannot
be repeated, the only second laver (*secundum lavacrum*) being

---

[1] This is the order found in the *Didascalia*, the *Liturgical Homilies* of Narsai,
the *Acts of Judas Thomas*, the *History of John the Son of Zebedee*, the *Life of Rabbula*,
Ephraim's Hymns on the Epiphany. See R. H. Connolly, "The Liturgical
Homilies of Narsai", in *C.T.S.*, viii (1909), xlii-xlix, and *Didascalia Apostolorum*,
xlixf., 146f.

[2] Dom Gregory Dix (*The Theology of Confirmation in Relation to Baptism*, 15)
thinks that the Syrian practice was the earliest of all; but in most churches it
was reversed at an early date. Cf. T. W. Manson, "Entry into Membership of
the Early Church", in *J.T.S.*, xlviii (1947), 25ff.

[3] *De Pud.*, 1.   [4] *De Bapt.*, 1.   [5] *De Res. Carn.*, 8.

[6] G. W. H. Lampe, *op. cit.*, 159.   [7] E.g. *Adv. Marc.*, i. 28.

[8] *De Bapt.*, 6, 8. Cf. *De Res. Carn.*, 8.   [9] *De Paenit.*, 6.

[10] *De Bapt.*, 4-5. Yet elsewhere he declares that the soul is sanctified not by
water, but by the response of renunciation and faith (*De Res. Carn.* xlviii).

martyrdom, the baptism of blood.[1] In the case of those who have not been baptized by water, it takes its place, and to those who have lost it, this restores it.[2]

Tertullian attacked the practice of infant baptism, denying that the dominical saying "Forbid them not"[3] gave any basis for it, and declaring that the benefits of baptism are best reserved for later years. "Let them come, then, while they are growing up; let them come while they are learning, while they are being taught whither to come; let them become Christians when they have become able to know Christ. Why does the innocent period of life hasten to the remission of sins?"[4]

The reasons which Tertullian gives for delaying the baptism of young children may be summarized as follows:

(*a*) They have no need of the remission of sins. Though they inherit a bias towards evil, infants have not actually sinned.

(*b*) Baptism involves great responsibilities which should be undertaken only by persons of mature intelligence and established character. Post-baptismal sin exposes the sinner to graver condemnation.

(*c*) The baptism of very young people exposes their sponsors to some danger. In Tertullian's day sponsors undertook serious responsibilities, being required to give assurance of the reality of the candidate's faith, repentance and renunciation of sin, and also to promise to watch over the candidate's life and direct his steps in the way of righteousness and truth.

Tertullian recommends the delaying of baptism for adults also, because hasty action involves risk of deception or self-deception, and post-baptismal sin will be visited with the heaviest condemnation.

It cannot be said that Tertullian expressed clearly the essential objection to infant baptism, viz. that the recipients of baptism, in the New Testament sense, must evince conscious faith and repentance, whereas infants have neither. Yet, as we have seen, he does in general stress the close connection of baptism with penitence and faith, and his emphasis upon the serious responsibilities involved in

---

[1] *Op. cit.*, 16.   [2] *Ibid.*   [3] Mark 10: 14; Matt. 19: 14; Luke 18: 16.
[4] *De Bapt.*, 18.

baptism and his insistence upon the importance of the candidate's knowledge of Christ were valid grounds for rejecting the rising practice of infant baptism. As A. Harnack observed: "Complete obscurity prevails as to the Church's adoption of the practice of child baptism, which, though it owes its origin to the idea of this ceremony being indispensable to salvation, is nevertheless a proof that the superstitious view of baptism had increased."[1] The unscriptural idea that the baptismal water in itself possessed sanctifying potency probably contributed in no small measure to the rise of infant baptism.

In the writings of Clement of Alexandria, contemporary of Tertullian, most of the references to baptism imply believer's baptism, preceded by catechetical training.[2] "We are washed from our sins and no longer entangled in evil. This is the one grace of illumination ($\mu\acute{\iota}\alpha$ $\chi\acute{\alpha}\rho\iota\varsigma$ $\alpha\H{\upsilon}\tau\eta$ $\tauο\hat{\upsilon}$ $\phi\omega\tau\acute{\iota}\sigma\mu\alpha\tau\sigma\varsigma$) that our characters are not the same as before our washing."[3] There is no repentance nor rational baptism nor "blessed seal" apart from free choice.[4] In baptism the seal of the Holy Spirit is conferred upon the believer, translating him from an earthly condition to a heavenly one,[5] and protecting him from evil spirits.[6] The baptismal illumination is associated with learning, revelation and the vision of God.[7] There appears to be one cryptic reference to infant baptism in an allegorical passage of the *Paedagogus*.[8]

The teaching of Hippolytus, who belongs to the early third century, is on the whole in accordance with New Testament doctrine in that he associates baptism with the remission of sins, regeneration, admission into the church, and the gift of the indwelling Spirit, though it is not clear whether he connects the bestowal of the Holy Spirit with water-baptism itself or with the post-baptismal rite of anointing. Sometimes he appears to teach the former,[9] sometimes the latter.[10] But, in any case, the baptism which he describes

---

[1] A. Harnack, *History of Dogma* (E.Tr.), ii. 142.

[2] The *Protrepticus* is addressed to the unbaptized, the *Paedogogus* to the baptized. See R. B. Tollinton, *Clement of Alexandria*, ii, 139.

[3] *Paed.*, 1. 6 (P.G. 8, 285).   [4] *Strom.*, ii. 3 (P.G. 8, 941 C).

[5] *Eclogae*, 24 (P.G. 9, 709). Cf. 1 Cor. 15: 49.   [6] *Op. cit.*, 12 (P.G. 9, 704).

[7] *Paed.*, 1. 6 (P.G. 8, 281). *Strom.*, v. 10 (P.G. 9, 97).

[8] III, ii (P.G. 8, 633), $\tau\hat{\omega}\nu$ $\grave{\epsilon}\xi$ $\H{\upsilon}\delta\alpha\tau\sigma\varsigma$ $\grave{\alpha}\nu\alpha\sigma\pi\omega\mu\acute{\epsilon}\nu\omega\nu$ $\pi\alpha\iota\delta\acute{\iota}\omega\nu$.

[9] E.g., *Homily on the Theophania*, 8-10 (P.G. 10, 860-61).

[10] Dan. 1. 16. 4 (P.G. 10, 693 A).

is that of the penitent believer who "comes down in faith to the bath of regeneration, and renounces the devil, and joins himself to Christ; who denies the enemy, and confesses that Christ is God; who puts off the bondage, and puts on the sonship" and who "comes up from the baptism brilliant as the sun, flashing forth the beams of righteousness, and, which is the chief thing, he returns a son of God, and joint-heir with Christ".[1]

In the *Apostolic Tradition of Hippolytus*, which probably represents the practice of the Roman church at the beginning of the third century, we find our earliest full liturgical text of the baptismal rite, comprising an account of the selection of fit catechumens, their three-year period of instruction (which, like that of the *Didache*, has some affinities with the teaching which preceded Jewish proselyte baptism), exorcism,[2] "insufflation" and sealing by the bishop with the sign of the cross on foreheads, ears and noses,[3] marking the catechumen for God and putting to flight the evil powers. Then an unction with "oil of exorcism" follows the catechumen's renunciation of Satan and all his works.[4] The candidates are then baptized, professing their faith in answer to questions before each of three immersions. Then they are anointed with the "oil of thanksgiving" by a presbyter, and led into the congregation, where the bishop lays his hand upon them with prayer, anoints them with "holy oil in God the Father Almighty, and Jesus and the Holy Ghost",[5] seals them on the forehead and gives them the kiss of peace. Though provision is made for the baptism of little children, parents or relatives acting as sponsors,[6] the baptism here set forth is mainly that of adult instructed believers. It is a matter of dispute whether the bestowal of the Spirit is here associated with the immersion in water or with the episcopal imposition of hands and sealing with chrism.[7]

We turn now to the teaching of Origen (A.D. 185-254), head of the Catechetical School of Alexandria in succession to Clement, and subsequently, on his dismissal from this office, resident at Caesarea for the last twenty years of his

[1] *Homily on the Theophania*, 10.　　[2] 20. 8.　　[3] *Ibid.*　　[4] 21. 10.
[5] 22. 1-2.　　[6] 21. 4.
[7] See G. W. H. Lampe, *op. cit.*, 128ff. for a discussion of the question, and a critical examination of the views of Dom Gregory Dix in *The Apostolic Tradition of Hippolytus*.

life. His writings thus fall into two groups, those of his Alexandrine and those of his Caesarean period.

In the former his teaching on baptism shows no knowledge of the practice of infant baptism. He declares baptism to be the seal of faith and repentance and renunciation of the devil.[1] His emphasis lies upon the inward, ethical and spiritual significance of the rite, and he insists upon sincere penitence, faith and humility in the catechumens as the necessary preparation for their reception of the remission of sins and the gift of the Spirit, which they will receive in baptism.[2] Origen uses 1 Cor. 10: 1-4 to illustrate the baptism by immersion of a penitent adult believer, who ascends from the water a new man (*homo novus*) ready to sing a new song.[3] "Those who are born again through the divine baptism are placed in paradise, that is, the church, to do spiritual works that are within, and they receive commandments to love all their brethren."[4] Origen likens the baptism of Jesus to Joshua's crossing of the Jordan,[5] and repeats the New Testament doctrine that in baptism the believer is united to Christ in His death, burial and resurrection,[6] is born again, and becomes a member of the church. Origen repudiates any *ex opere operato* theory of the efficacy of baptism when he says that some, being insincere, are baptized to condemnation,[7] and therefore do not receive the Holy Spirit. Whilst, however, Origen normally associates the gift of the Spirit with water-baptism he also says, when he is expounding Paul's teaching on the ἀρραβών, or "earnest" of the Spirit, that it is to be acquired by making the response of faith to the teaching of the Gospel of salvation.[8] The essential feature of baptism itself is the right disposition of the candidate, his faith and repentance, in response to which the Holy Spirit is given. The inner significance of baptism is revealed in the entire spiritual

---

[1] *Hom.*, 12. 4, in Num. (P.G. 12, 665 C).

[2] *Hom.*, 6. 2, in Lev. (P.G. 12, 468 B). Cf. *De Princip.*, 2. 10. 7 (P.G. 11, 239 B). *Hom.*, 5. 5, in Exod. (P.G. 12, 330 D).

[3] *Hom.*, 5, in Exod.   [4] *Comm. in Gen.*, tom. iii, 28 (P.G. 12, 100).

[5] Josh. 3.

[6] *Hom.*, 19. 14, in Jer. (P.G. 13, 493 C). Cf. *Hom.*, 4. 2, in Josh. 3: 7 (P.G. 12, 843 D).

[7] *Hom.*, 6. 5, in Ezek. (P.G. 13, 713 D).

[8] *Eph.*, 8 (*J.T.S.*, iii (1901-2), 243), cited by G. W. H. Lampe, *op. cit.*, 164.

progress of the baptized, which is an unfolding of what he received in baptism.[1]

In his later, Caesarean, period Origen became acquainted, probably for the first time,[2] with the practice of infant baptism, which he describes not only as a custom of the church,[3] but as an apostolic custom. "The church", he writes, "has received a tradition from the Apostles to give baptism even to little children."[4] Origen infers that the purpose of infant baptism must be the remission of original sin, inherited from Adam's fall, or a mysterious sinfulness inherent in birth.[5] Thus the practice of infant baptism, which probably arose partly out of popular sentiment, helped to foster the growth of the doctrine of original sin. (Previously, in his Alexandrian period, Origen had taught a different doctrine of the origin of sin, that of the pre-existence of the soul, its sin in the pre-existent state, and its punishment for that sin by becoming incarnate in the person of an individual man.)[6]

Cyprian, bishop of Carthage, a contemporary of Origen, directs that infants should be baptized as soon as possible on the ground that this secures the forgiveness of original sin, the taint inherited by descent from Adam.[7] He finds infant baptism prefigured in Jewish circumcision.[8] He teaches that baptism effects regeneration because it is the means whereby the Holy Spirit is bestowed[9] even upon infants, according to their capacity.[10] The normal mode of baptism for Cyprian is immersion, but he allows affusion for those who are baptized in sickness, and claims that those who have been baptized by affusion (*perfusi*) have received the gift of the Spirit no less than their fellow-Christians who were baptized by immersion (*loti*).[11]

The growth of infant baptism inevitably obscured the New Testament significance of baptism as a sacrament of penitence and faith in which the Holy Spirit is received. It easily led to an unscriptural distinction between water-baptism as a cleansing

---

[1] *Hom.*, 10. 4, in Exod. (P.G. 12, 373 D).

[2] See C. Bigg, *The Christian Platonists of Alexandria*, 246; A. Harnack, *op. cit.*, ii, 365, n. 5; N. P. Williams, *The Ideas of the Fall and Original Sin*, 219-20.

[3] *Hom.*, 8. 3, in Lev. (P.G. 12, 496).   [4] *Comm. in Rom.*, v.9 (P.G. 14, 1047).

[5] *Ibid.*, citing Ps. 51: 5. Cf. *Hom.*, 14 in Luc. (P.G. 13, 1834), citing Job 14: 4-5. Cf. N. P. Williams, *op. cit.*, 224ff.

[6] *De Princip.*, ii. 8ff. See N. P. Williams, *op. cit.*, 210ff.   [7] *Ep.*, 64.

[8] *Ep.*, 64. 4.   [9] *Ep.*, 63. 8.   [10] *Ep.*, 64. 3.   [11] *Ep.*, 69. 13-14.

from original sin and confirmation[1] by the episcopal imposition of hands as a means of conferring the Holy Spirit. This tendency was reinforced by an undue emphasis upon Acts 8: 17; 9: 17 and 19: 6, superficially interpreted.[2] Cyprian, however, strenuously asserted that the Holy Spirit is given in baptism itself, provided it is Christian baptism within the true church, and not heretical or schismatic baptism, which, like Tertullian,[3] he refused to regard as valid baptism. There can be no true baptism without the Spirit.[4] Water alone is not able to wash away sins and to sanctify a man, unless he have also the Holy Spirit.[5] Sometimes Cyprian inconsistently associates the gift of the Spirit with the imposition of hands,[6] but even then he regards the baptism and the confirmation as forming one ceremony for the gift of the Spirit.[7] Firmilian of Caesarea similarly associates the gift of the Spirit with baptism.[8] Where he appears to associate it with the imposition of hands, he insists that the laying-on of hands must not be divorced from baptism.[9] Augustine, however, unlike Cyprian and Firmilian, recognized the validity of "heretical" baptism, but taught that its virtue was realized only when the baptized person passed into the one true church.

The growing tendency to dissociate water-baptism from the bestowal of the Spirit, and to unite the latter with the imposition of hands, is illustrated in the anonymous work *De Rebaptismate*, where baptism is little more than outward lustration in preparation for a subsequent Spirit-baptism by the rite of laying-on of hands, which may follow immediately upon the water-baptism, or may be delayed for a longer interval.[10] This doctrine is based on Acts 8: 17 and 19: 6. On the other hand the anonymous writer adduces Acts 10: 44 as evidence that the Holy Spirit may be bestowed without

[1] The actual term *confirmatio* "occurs first in Can. 2 of the South French Council of Orange in A.D. 441". G. Dix, *The Theology of Confirmation in Relation to Baptism*, 21.

[2] See G. W. H. Lampe, *op. cit.*, 64ff.

[3] *De Bapt.*, 15.

[4] Cyprian quotes John 3: 5 in support of this contention.

[5] *Ep.*, 70. 1, 74. 5.

[6] *Ep.*, 73. 9.

[7] *Ep.*, 72.

[8] *Ep.*, 75. 12.

[9] *Ibid.*, 8.

[10] 10. Cf. 11, 18, 5, 6.

either baptism or imposition of hands. He shows no sign of having appreciated the profound Pauline doctrine of baptism as the union of believers with Christ, their self-identification with the redemptive acts of His death and resurrection, their dying to sin and being raised to newness of life, and their "sealing" by the "earnest" of the Spirit.

3. The Fourth Century. A failing grasp of the New Testament significance of baptism helped to promote the custom of baptizing infants. But even when infant baptism was fully established, it was far from being universal. *Baptism was often delayed until adult life.* Eusebius tells us that Novatian was not baptized till he became sick and seemed about to die, whereupon he received baptism by affusion on the bed where he lay; "if indeed we ought to say that such a one did receive it".[1] The Emperor Constantine postponed his baptism till his death was imminent (A.D. 337), believing that "whatever errors he had committed as a mortal man, his soul would be purified from them through the efficacy of the mystical words ($\lambda\acute{o}\gamma\omega\nu$ $\mathring{a}\pi o\rho\rho\acute{\eta}\tau\omega\nu$ $\delta\upsilon\nu\acute{a}\mu\epsilon\iota$) and the salutary waters of baptism".[2] Augustine's baptism, too, was deferred, as he himself tells us. In view of a severe illness in his boyhood, preparations were made to baptize him; but as he suddenly recovered, his baptism was deferred lest he should incur greater guilt by post-baptismal sin. Indeed, there was a prevalent saying: "Let him alone, let him do as he will; for he has not yet been baptized."[3] It is not on such unworthy grounds that Baptists reject infant baptism, but because Christian baptism, in the New Testament sense, is intended for those who are penitent and consciously believing.

It was the false belief that water-baptism in itself washes away all former sin that led some, who were already convinced of the truth of the Gospel, to delay the rite till the close of their life so as to die free from guilt and secure admission to heaven. Such baptism was called "clinic" baptism, from the Greek $\kappa\lambda\acute{\iota}\nu\eta$, a bed; and the persons thus baptized were known as the *clinici*.[4] This custom was

---

[1] *E.H.*, vi, 43. Eusebius questions whether he received the Holy Spirit, because, though he recovered, he did not receive the "sealing" at the hands of the bishop.

[2] Eusebius, *Life of Constantine*, iv. 61.

[3] *Confess.*, i. 11.   [4] Cyprian, *Ep.*, 76.

vigorously attacked by Gregory Nazianzen,[1] Gregory Nyssen,[2] Basil,[3] and others.

Believers' baptism continued alongside infant baptism. Athanasius taught that the Holy Spirit is granted to those who believe and are born again through the laver of regeneration.[4] And in the fullest account that we possess of fourth-century practice, the *Catechetical Lectures* of Cyril of Jerusalem (*c.* A.D. 315-86), the candidates for baptism are instructed catechumens, and they are baptized by immersion. He insists that those who come to baptism must have honesty of purpose[5] and sincerely renounce sin and Satan,[6] for only such are "enlightened" by the sacrament.[7] The effects of baptism are twofold: forgiveness and sanctification, the cleansing of the soul from sin, and the gift of the Holy Spirit. In Pauline words the rite is described as burial with Christ unto death (Rom. 6: 3).[8] It is "ransom for the captives, remission of offences, death of sin, and regeneration of the soul, the garment of light, the holy, indissoluble seal".[9] But while "remission of sins is bestowed equally upon all", "the communication of the Holy Spirit is bestowed according to each man's faith".[10] With regard to the baptism of heretics, Cyril agreed with Cyprian and Firmilian that heretics are to be "re-baptized", because their former washing was not true baptism.[11]

While Cyril sometimes associates the gift of the Spirit with baptism,[12] at other times he connects it with chrisma-tion. But as the latter occurred almost immediately after the baptismal immersion, it is doubtful how far Cyril regarded it as a distinct rite. He interprets it as symbolic of the anointing ($\chi\rho\hat{\iota}\sigma\mu\alpha$) with the Spirit which makes the believers true Christs ($\chi\rho\iota\sigma\tau\sigma\acute{\iota}$) and invests us with the panoply of the Holy Spirit.[13] While he seems to distinguish between the opera-tion of the Spirit in baptism, and the full gift of the Spirit in the ensuing chrismation, it is anachronistic to use Cyril's language as evidence for the doctrine that this gift

---

[1] *Orat.*, 60, 28.   [2] *Adversus eos qui differunt Baptismum Oratio.*
[3] *Hom.*, in Bapt., 3-4.
[4] τὸ Πνεῦμα τὸ ἅγιον τὸ διδόμενον τοῖς πιστεύουσι καί ἀναγεννωμένοις διὰ λουτροῦ παλιγγενεσίας, *Serap.*, i. 4 (P.G. 26, 537 B).
[5] ἡ πρόθεσις γνησία, *Procat.*, I.   [6] *Cat.*, 19. 2.   [7] *Procat.*, 2.
[8] *Cat.*, 20. 6.   [9] *Procat.*, 16.   [10] *Cat.*, I. 5.   [11] *Procat.*, 7.
[12] *Cat.*, 21. I.   [13] *Cat.*, 21. I.

becomes the full possession of the Christian only at confirmation, and that in baptism the Holy Spirit is bestowed only in a restricted sense.[1]

Cyril's *Catechetical Lectures* throw considerable light upon the fourth-century practice and mode of baptism in Jerusalem. All but the last five were addressed to candidates looking forward to baptism at the coming Easter. The last five, known as the *Mystagogical Catecheses* (19-23), addressed to Christians recently baptized, treat of the sacraments; the first three deal with baptism, including the accompanying chrismation, the fourth with eucharistic doctrine, and the fifth with eucharistic liturgy.

From the first three we can reconstruct the baptismal rite in detail. First the candidates gathered in the vestibule of the baptistery (ὁ προαύλιος τοῦ βαπτιστηρίου οἶκος) and, facing west with outstretched hands, formally renounced the devil and all his works and pomp and service. Then, turning to the east, they said: "I believe in the Father, and in the Son, and in the Holy Spirit, and in one baptism of repentance."[2] Going thence into the inner chamber (ὁ ἐσώτερος οἶκος), they took off their clothes and were anointed with exorcized oil. Then, one by one, they were led by the hand to "the holy pool of divine baptism" (τὴν ἁγίαν τοῦ θείου βαπτίσματος κολυμβήθραν), where after a second profession of their faith they were immersed three times in the blessed baptismal water to symbolize the three days' burial of Christ.[3] Next they received the post-baptismal chrismation, and after putting on white garments the "neophytes"[4] proceeded, carrying lighted tapers, from the baptistery into the church where they were greeted with psalm-singing[5] and received their first Holy Communion.[6] The baptism described by Cyril is, from first to last, the baptism of penitent, instructed believers.

Gregory of Nazianzus (c. 325-90), advises the baptism of infants in case of danger, but thinks that where there is no danger, baptism should be deferred until they can hear and answer questions.

---

[1] See F. L. Cross, *St. Cyril of Jerusalem's Lectures on the Christian Sacraments*, xxxif.

[2] *Cat.*, 19.   [3] *Cat.*, 20. 4.   [4] νεοφώτιστοι, lit. "newly enlightened".

[5] *Procat.*, 15. Cf. Gregory Nazianzen, *Orat.*, xl. 46 (P.G. 36, 425).

[6] *Cat.*, 21-22.

o

Shall we baptize infants also? Certainly, if danger threatens. For it is better to be sanctified unconsciously than to depart from this life unsealed and uninitiated. Our argument for this is the circumcision after eight days, which is a kind of typical seal, and is applied even to those who are still without reason; as also the anointing of the door posts (Exod. 12: 7f.), which was applied to insensible objects, brought salvation to the first-born. But if there is no danger, my judgment is that they should wait till they are three years old (or a little more or a little less) when it is possible for them to hear and answer something about the sacrament. For then, even if they do not completely understand, yet they will receive the outlines.[1]

Baptism is "illumination" (τὸ φώτισμα) and a "change of life" (βίου μετάθεσις), the "support of faith" (ἔρεισμα πίστεως), the "perfecting of the mind" (νοῦ τελείωσις):[2] he compares the seal of Christian baptism with the blood of the Passover, teaching that the effect of baptism is analogous to that of the Passover seal, preserving the baptized from destruction and stamping them as the elect people of God and inheritors of "a second life". But he is obliged to distinguish in this respect between the significance of adult baptism and that of infant baptism. For infants baptism is only a "seal", but for adults, who have sinned, it is a "cure" (ἄκος) as well as "the best seal" (σφρηγὶς ἀρίστη),[3] for it is a bestowal of grace and restoration of the image of God lost by sin, effecting a purging (κάθαρσιν) of sin.[4] Thus Gregory Nazianzen "draws a sharp distinction between the effects of adult and those of infant baptism, affirming the former to include both dedication to God and remission of sin, but the latter to consist in dedication only".[5] Gregory himself, like his namesake of Nyssen and like Basil, was not baptized till manhood.

Gregory of Nyssa (c. 335-95), an intimate friend of Gregory Nazianzen, and a brother of Basil, developed the conception of Origen that the whole spiritual progress of a Christian is the unfolding of what he received in baptism, in

---

[1] Orat., xl. In Sanctum Baptisma, 28 (P.G. 36, 400).

[2] Ibid., 3 (P.G. 36, 361).

[3] Carmina, i (poemata theologica), sect. i. 9 (de testamentis et adventu Christi), lines 91-92 (P.G. 37, 464):

σφρηγὶς ἀλεξικάκοιο Θεοῦ τόδε, νηπιάχοις μὲν
σφρηγὶς, ἀεξομένοισι δ' ἄκος καί σφρηγὶς ἀρίστη.

[4] Orat., xl., 6-7 (P.G. 36, 365-68).   [5] N. P. Williams, op. cit., 290.

which the Holy Spirit secures for the believer participation in a life no longer subject to death. But, like Cyril of Jerusalem, Gregory wavers on the question whether the Spirit is received in baptism or in chrismation, sometimes asserting the former,[1] sometimes the latter.[2] He stresses the part played by the believer's own choice in the process of regeneration,[3] and denies that baptized persons are regenerated unless water-baptism is followed by transformation of character.[4] He does not regard a babe who dies unbaptized as subject to God's wrath or tainted with any kind of sin. In his treatise *On the untimely deaths of infants*[5] he teaches that the soul of an infant who has died before attaining the age of reason will receive such blessing as it is capable of receiving, which, though less than that to which an adult saint can look forward, is nevertheless true blessing; and such child-souls may grow in the knowledge of God till at last they achieve full intellectual and spiritual maturity.

Basil of Caesarea (*c.* 329-79), sometimes called Basil the Great, teaches that instruction should precede baptism, and that the catechumens should resolve to live a good life.[6] Christians, he says, are saved through faith and by being made regenerate through the grace received in baptism in the name of the Trinity.[7] "Faith and baptism are two ways (τρόποι) of salvation, cognate to one another and inseparable."[8] He stressed the importance of immersion as a symbol of Christ's death, burial and resurrection, and deplored the prevalent tendency of the Christians in the churches of the east to delay baptism till old age.[9] He associates baptism especially with the gift and operation of the Holy Spirit.[10] The presence of the Spirit within the soul begins when the convert is regenerated in baptism.[11]

Chrysostom (*c.* 345-407), who was born at Antioch of a Christian mother and became bishop of Constantinople, recognized the practice of infant baptism and regarded it with favour, but that it was not the general practice of the

---

[1] *Vita Moys.* (P.G. 44, 361 D).   [2] *Maced.*, 16 (P.G. 45, 1321 A).
[3] *Or. Catech.*, 39 (P.G. 45, 100).   [4] *Ibid.*, 40 (P.G. 45, 101).
[5] *De infantibus qui praemature abripiuntur* (P.G. 46, 161-92).
[6] *De Baptismo*, I, 1f. (P.G. 31, 1513f.).
[7] *De Spiritu Sancto*, 26-28 (P.G. 32, 113-17).   [8] *Ibid.*, 28.
[9] *Hom.*, xiii, *in Sanctum Baptisma*, 5f. (P.G. 31, 432f.).
[10] *De Spirit.*, 35 (P.G. 32, 129 C).   [11] *Hom.*, in Ps. 28 (P.G. 30, 81 B).

eastern church is proved by the fact that he himself was not baptized till he was over twenty years of age, and also by his own teaching concerning the significance of baptism. He insists that the seal of the Spirit, by which the believer is recognized by God to be His own, is goodness of moral character,[1] and he associates the seal of the Spirit with baptism,[2] for which a synonym is illumination ($\phi\acute{\omega}\tau\iota\sigma\mu\alpha$).[3] In baptism, which is closely linked with the cross of Christ,[4] the Christian becomes prophet, priest and king, and is sealed by the Spirit as a soldier receives a seal or tattoo-mark to stamp him for military service. Whereas the Jews had circumcision as a seal, Christians have the inward earnest ($\dot{\alpha}\rho\rho\alpha\beta\acute{\omega}\nu$) of the Spirit, given in baptism.[5] The close connection between baptism and the death, burial and resurrection of Jesus is brought out by the comparison, common in the Fathers, between water-baptism and the martyr's baptism of blood, in which he shared literally, and not in a figure, in Christ's death and resurrection.

In treating baptism as the counterpart of circumcision, Chrysostom unwittingly exposes the weakness of infant baptism. Describing baptism as the painless circumcision made without hands (cf. Col. 2: 11), he says that it has no fixed season, as the Jewish circumcision had, but may be received by infants, or the middle-aged, or those in old age, thus being purged of sins and receiving pardon for past offences.[6] Of the Jewish circumcision of infants he says that it was without spiritual value. "For what benefit to his soul can an infant derive from it, since he has no knowledge of what is done to him, and has no sense?"[7] Clearly this ground of condemnation would be equally valid in the case of infant baptism.

The writings of Ambrose, bishop of Milan (d. 397), enable us to reconstruct the rite of baptism as practised in Milan in the latter half of the fourth century.[8] Catechumens

---

[1] *Hom.*, 5. 3, in 2 Tim. (P.G. 62, 627).

[2] *Hom.*, 2. 2, in Eph. (P.G. 62, 18-19). *Hom.*, 6. 2, in Col. (P.G. 62, 339-40).

[3] *Hom.*, 3. 4, in Phil. (P.G. 62, 203): $\chi\omega\rho\grave{\iota}\varsigma$ $\phi\omega\tau\acute{\iota}\sigma\mu\alpha\tau\sigma\varsigma$ . . . $\chi\omega\rho\grave{\iota}\varsigma$ $\sigma\phi\rho\alpha\gamma\hat{\iota}\delta\sigma\varsigma$.

[4] "Not only is baptism called the Cross, but also the Cross is called baptism". *Hom.*, xxv, in Joan. (Jn. 3: 5), 2 (P.G. 59, 151). Cf. Rom. 6: 5f., Col. 2: 12, Mark 10: 39, Luke 12: 50.

[5] *Hom.*, 3. 7, in 2 Cor. (P.G. 61, 418).

[6] *Hom.*, 40, in Gen. (P.G. 53, 373).   [7] *Ibid.*

[8] Cf. F. H. Dudden, *Saint Ambrose, His Life and Times*, i, 336ff.

were divided into two classes: (a) "hearers" who listened to the lessons and sermon before the eucharist, but were dismissed before the eucharist itself began; they might remain in the probationary stage as long as they chose; (b) "competents"[1] or "elect"[2] who had given in their names to the bishop as candidates for baptism.[3] Public baptism was usually administered on the night between Easter eve and Easter day.[4] "The candidates, who at this epoch were normally adults, entered their names at the beginning of Lent, and devoted themselves, during the whole of this season, to elaborate preparation for the holy rite."[5] This discipline included rigorous fasting and abstinence from the use of marriage.[6] On all week-days in Lent except Saturdays, at the third and ninth hours, special services were held for catechumens, consisting of lessons, psalms and sermon, at which the candidates received instruction on Christian morals and on the elements of the Christian religion.[7]

The actual baptism late on Easter eve started with the ceremony of the Effeta, or "the mystery of the opening", in which the bishop touched the ears and nostrils of each candidate, symbolizing the opening of the faculties to the effective reception of the sacraments.[8] Next, the candidates stripped naked,[9] and in response to the bishop's questions renounced first the devil and his works, then the world and its pleasures.[10] After the renunciation the bishop consecrated the water, which he signed with the cross.[11] The candidate then descended into the baptistery and was asked: "Dost thou believe in God the Father Almighty?" "Dost thou believe in our Lord Jesus Christ and in the Cross?" "Dost thou believe also in the Holy Spirit?"[12] To each question the candidate, facing towards the east,[13] replied: "I believe", and after each response was immersed. The candidate was then assisted from the font, dried with linen cloths, and led to the bishop who anointed his head with chrism, thus consecrating him to the priesthood of all believers.[14] Next came the foot-washing, the bishop washing the feet of a few of the baptized, the presbyters washing those of the remainder,

[1] Ambrose, *Ep.*, 20. 4.   [2] *De Elia*, 34.   [3] *De Abraham*, i. 23.
[4] *De Elia*, 34.   [5] F. H. Dudden, *op. cit.*, i, 336.   [6] *De Elia*, 79, 81.
[7] *De Myst.*, 1.   [8] *Ibid.*, 3, 4.   [9] In Ps. lxi *enarr.*, 32.
[10] *De Myst.*, 5, 8.   [11] *Ibid.*, 8, 14, 20.   [12] *Ibid.*, 21, 28.
[13] *Ibid.*, 7.   [14] *Ibid.*, 30.

while the gospel lesson, John 13: 4f., was read.[1] Then the newly-baptized were robed in white garments, which they continued to wear throughout Easter week,[2] and were brought to the bishop to receive the spiritual seal of the signing of the cross,[3] which signified, according to Ambrose, that conformation to the likeness of Christ in His death and resurrection which is effected in him by the indwelling of the Holy Spirit,[4] who regenerates, sanctifies and "seals" the soul, restoring the divine image.[5]

The effect of baptism, according to Ambrose, is remission of sin and guilt,[6] and regeneration through the Holy Spirit.[7] Ambrose himself advocated baptism in infancy[8] for the remission of original sin and guilt.[9] He further rebuked unbaptized adults who continued to postpone the rite.[10] He insisted upon the necessity of baptism, declaring that unless a person is baptized in the name of the Father, and of the Son, and of the Holy Spirit, he cannot receive the remission of sins nor imbibe the gift of spiritual grace.[11] He evidently thought of "grace" as some impersonal entity conveyed mechanically, and not, in New Testament fashion, as the personal, prevenient, love and forgiveness of God. Ambrose asserted that no one could enter the kingdom of heaven except through baptism, not even an infant or a person prevented by necessity.[12] He makes an exception, however, to this rule in the case of martyrs who have undergone the baptism of blood.[13]

It was Augustine of Hippo (354-430) who first gave to infant baptism a systematic theological basis. His wise Christian mother, Monica, refused to let him be baptized at an early age, because she thought him unprepared to maintain a Christian life, and feared that he would incur greater guilt by post-baptismal sin.[14] For this refusal Augustine was inclined to blame her, believing that if he had been baptized in early years he would have escaped the pollution of guilt which rested upon him in youth.

---

[1] *De Myst.*, 31-33.   [2] *Ibid.*, 34.   [3] *Ibid.*, 42.
[4] *De Sacramentis*, 6. 2-6. 7 (P.L. 16, 455).
[5] *De Spir.*, 1. 6; 3. 10 (P.L. 16, 722f., 791f.).   [6] *De Poenitentia*, 1. 36.
[7] *De Spir.*, 1. 80.   [8] *De Abraham*, ii, 81, 84.
[9] Cf. In Ps. xxxvi *enarr.*, 63; *Expos. Ev. Luc.*, i, 37.
[10] *De Elia*, 84, 85; *Expos. Ev. Luc.*, vii, 221.   [11] *De Myst.*, 20.
[12] *De Abraham*, ii, 11 (P.L. 14, 497).   [13] *De Obitu Val.*, 53.
[14] *Confess.*, i, 11, 17.

For his justification of the practice of infant baptism Augustine turned to the doctrines of original sin (the theory that all men inherit sinfulness from Adam's "fall") and original guilt (the theory that all men inherit the guilt of Adam's sin, sharing the responsibility for it and the pollution of it).[1] Augustine held that baptism cancelled the guilt (*reatus*) of Adam's sin, but left its activity (*actus*), which Augustine identified with concupiscence, still in existence.[2] The grace received in baptism was regeneration by the Holy Spirit, divine forgiveness and the remission of guilt,[3] but complete salvation could be achieved only by a transformation of character. "The sacrament of baptism is one thing, the conversion of the heart is another, but man's salvation is made complete through the two together."[4] "When either of these requisites is omitted unintentionally, God Himself supplies it."[5] That is, in a case like that of the penitent thief on the cross, where conversion took place, but the converted man could not be baptized, God supplied the baptism and so the dying Saviour assured him of paradise. Here Augustine clearly means a spiritual baptism, not a water-baptism. In the case of an infant receiving water-baptism, God Himself supplied the converted heart, so that a baptized infant who died in infancy was a saved soul. Augustine associated the gift of the Holy Spirit in the baptismal rite with the post-baptismal imposition of hands, which, he held, bestowed the Spirit even upon infants.[6]

He taught that baptism corresponds to the Jewish circumcision, which, being administered on the eighth day, prefigured Christ's resurrection and our regeneration through the risen Christ.[7] Thus circumcision was reckoned under the old covenant for baptism,[8] which is as necessary for Christians as circumcision was for the ancient people of Israel.[9] Unlike Cyprian and the Donatists, Augustine regarded baptism in

---

[1] The theory of original guilt rested in part upon a false exegesis of Rom. 5: 12, where ἐφ'ᾧ, mistranslated by the Latin *in quo*, was taken to mean "in whom", i.e. all sinned in Adam. Cf. N. P. Williams, *op. cit.*, 308.

[2] *De nupt. et conc.*, i. 29f. (P.L. 44, 431f.).

[3] *Ep. ad Boniface, Ep.*, 98. 2 (P.L. 33, 360).

[4] *Bapt.*, iv. 25, 32 (P.L. 43, 176).   [5] *Ibid.*

[6] *Bapt.*, iii, 17, 22 (P.L. 43, 149).

[7] *Op. imp. c. Julian.*, 6. 18 (P.L. 45, 1541). Cf. *Pecc. Orig.*, 32. 37 (P.L. 44, 403).

[8] *Ep.*, 187. 11. 34 (P.L. 33, 845).   [9] *Ep.*, 265. 4 (P.L. 33, 1087).

the name of the Trinity as true baptism even when administered by an unworthy person.[1] Baptism is one and unrepeatable, the seal by means of which the baptized is stamped with an indelible character. Augustine added, however, that baptism received outside the church is incomplete, and that baptism administered in schism has to be made effective by the imposition of hands within the true church before the schismatically baptized can be incorporated in the fellowship of the Spirit and receive the supreme gift of charity (*caritas*).

Light is thrown upon Augustine's understanding of the significance of infant baptism by his correspondence (*Ep.*, 98) with Boniface, who asked him two questions: (*a*) Do parents harm their baptized infant children when they try to heal them in time of sickness by sacrificing to the false gods of the heathen?[2] (*b*) How can the parents of a child presented for baptism declare: "he believes"?

To the first question Augustine replied that the baptized infant would not lose the benefit of his baptism, for he received regeneration through the operation of the Holy Spirit in himself and in his parents. When his parents turn to sin, he does not share their fault.[3] When the grace of Christ has been once received, the child does not lose it otherwise than by his own impiety if, when he grows older, he turns out so badly.

To the second question Augustine answered that, while infants do not actually believe in the sense of perceiving and assenting to the truth, nevertheless they are said to believe because they receive the sacrament of faith. So that the sponsors do not speak falsely, because "an infant, although he is not yet a believer in the sense of having that faith which includes the consenting will of those who exercise it, nevertheless becomes a believer through the sacrament of that faith".[4] A less convincing answer it would be difficult to imagine, though it was erected into a dogma by

[1] *Bapt.*, 3. 10. 15 (P.L. 43, 144).

[2] The question continues: "If they do not harm, how does the faith of the parents benefit them when they are baptized, if the parents' lack of faith can be no detriment to them?"

[3] "*Regenerans Spiritus in majoribus offerentibus et parvulo oblato renatoque communis est: . . . quando majores peccant . . . non est anima utrorumque communis ut etiam culpam possint habere communem.*"

[4] *Ep.*, 98 (P.L. 33, 359f.).

the Council of Trent (Canon 13), decreeing that little children, "though they have not actual faith, are ... after having received baptism, to be reckoned among the faithful".
But nothing can alter the fact that, at the time of receiving baptism, the infant has no Christian faith, and the New Testament significance of baptism as the immersion of those who are already penitent believers has disappeared.

Under the impetus of Augustinian doctrine, infant baptism spread throughout the church, though of course adult baptism continued for adult converts. Pelagianism opposed the doctrines of original sin and original guilt, but fostered infant baptism none the less. For Pelagius taught that baptism was a sacramental mystery which *ex opere operato* imparted regeneration and salvation to its recipients, and his followers sanctioned its administration to infants.[1] Julian, the Pelagian bishop of Eclanum, held that in baptism infants receive spiritual illumination, the adoption of sons, the heavenly citizenship, sanctification, membership in the body of Christ, and possession of the kingdom of heaven, but no remission of sins, for they have no sins to be remitted.[2]

4. The Fifth Century and After. By the fifth century infant baptism had become the general practice of the church. It was challenged only by a few isolated communities like those of the Paulicians of the ninth century and the Petrobusians of the twelfth. These will be considered in the next chapter.

The superstitious notion that water-baptism itself was regenerative had triumphed. A document of the Syrian Church, dated about A.D. 450, reads: "Let the lambs of our flock be sealed from the first, that the Robber may see the mark impressed upon their bodies and tremble. Let not a child that is without the seal suck the milk of a mother that has been baptized. ... Let the children of the kingdom be carried from the womb to baptism."[3] The administration of

---

[1] Pelagius, *libellus fidei*. Cf. Pelagius in Rom. 6: 4 (A. Souter's text, in *C.T.S.*, ix (1926), 49). In this passage, however, Pelagius has adult believers' baptism in mind (*renuntiantes pristinae vitae*).

[2] Op. imp., *c. Julian.*, i. 53 (P.L. 45, 1075f.).

[3] Assemani, Bib. Orientalis, i, 221: quoted in *Dictionary of Christian Antiquities*, i, 170. Cf. Narsai's *Homily on Baptism* (*c.* A.D. 500), Homily xxii, in *C.T.S.*, viii (1909), 36.

baptism to infants was made compulsory by an edict of the
Emperor Justinian, who reigned from A.D. 527 till 565.

Photius, patriarch of Constantinople (A.D. 858-867,
878-886), repeats this law in his Nomocanon, and adds to it
a similar one concerning the Samaritans: "That though they
themselves were not to be baptized till they had been two
years catechumens, yet their little ones, who were capable of
instruction, might be admitted to baptism without any such
delay or prorogation."[1] The term catechumen was still used
to describe even newborn infants who were candidates for
baptism. Theodulph, bishop of Orleans in the eighth
century, defends the description of infants as *audientes* and
catechumeni simply on the ground that it was apostolic custom
first to instruct those whom they were about to baptize.[2]

The fullest representative exposition of the doctrine of
baptism in the Middle Ages is that of St. Thomas Aquinas
(d. A.D. 1274). His teaching on baptism is given in *Summa
Theologiae*, Part III, Questions 66-69, with some preliminary
observations in the preceding Questions on the sacraments in
general. He teaches that baptism is not a mere washing, but
something permanent, being a vehicle of the life of divine
grace, which he conceives as an impersonal power flowing
through the sacraments, whereas in the New Testament the
grace of God is God Himself personally loving, forgiving,
strengthening those who personally respond. Aquinas
declares that baptism is necessary for salvation, though a
man who wishes to be baptized, but is forestalled by death,
will obtain salvation without being actually baptized, on
account of his desire for baptism. God "whose power is not
tied to visible sacraments" sanctifies a man inwardly. This
remedy, however, would not avail for an infant who died
unbaptized. Hence baptism should not be deferred. Aquinas
did not pause to inquire what sort of a God he would be who
damned infants because they died unbaptized.

An infant, declares Aquinas, must be baptized in order
to be made regenerate and loosed from original sin. He
admits that baptism is a sacrament of faith, and that the
infant has no personal faith, but he claims that the faith

---

[1] J. Bingham, *Church Antiquities*, xi, IV, sect. 19. Quoted by W. N. Cote,
op. cit., 121.

[2] *De Ordine Baptismi*, i (P.L. 105, 224).

and intention of the parents and the church avail on behalf of the infant. "It is not the custom of the church to baptize the children of unbelievers against their parents' will." By the baptism of faith the baptized are incorporated in Christ and in His passion and death, are absolved from all sin, and become inheritors of eternal life. It may be questioned whether such language is appropriate unless applied to penitent believers who consciously dedicate themselves to Christ, dying to sin and rising to newness of life.

Aquinas reveals that "in many parts of the world the ordinary way of baptizing is by immersion". He comments that "Christ's burial is more clearly represented by immersion; wherefore this manner is more frequently in use and more commendable". He holds that both single and triple immersion are lawful, since one immersion signifies the oneness of Christ's death, and of the Godhead, while threefold immersion signifies the three days of Christ's burial and also the Trinity of Persons in the Godhead.

After the fourth century immersion had begun to be replaced in some churches by a copious affusion on the head, the person to be baptized standing in the water.[1] Affusion had been permitted earlier, when immersion was inconvenient, as we know from the *Didache*. In cases of sickness, no doubt, affusion was practised in preference to immersion. The latter, however, was still the mode of baptism upheld in the fourth century, as we have seen, by Cyril of Jerusalem, for example, who emphasized threefold immersion in the water of the baptistery, as symbolic of Christ's three-days' burial.[2] Basil[3] and Augustine[4] similarly stressed the importance of immersion as a symbol of Christ's death, burial and resurrection.

As Aquinas testifies, even after the spread of affusion, immersion continued to be widely practised and advocated. In Britain the early converts were immersed or dipped in rivers[5] or in baptisteries;[6] and dipping remained the standard mode of baptism here until the middle of the

---

[1] See P. Drews, "Taufe III Liturg Vollzug", in A. Hauck, *Realencyclopaedie für Protestantische Theologie und Kirche*, ed. 3, xix, 432.

[2] *Cat.*, 20. 4.   [3] *De Baptismo.*   [4] *De Mysterio Baptismatis.*

[5] Bede, *H.E.*, ii, 14.   [6] See W. N. Cote, *op. cit.*, 27.

sixteenth century, as is shown by the rubrics of "The Book of
Common Prayer". Threefold immersion was prescribed by
the Sacramentary of Gregory the Great (d. A.D. 604), one as
each Person of the Trinity was invoked; but the fourth
Council of Toledo, held in A.D. 633, decreed that one
immersion was sufficient.[1] But both the single and triple
forms of immersion continued to exist side by side in the
Latin Church, while the Greek Church persisted, and still
persists, in the practice of triple immersion.

The *Ordo Romanus*, a ritual composed in the eighth
century, prescribes triple immersion in terms similar to
those of the Sacramentary of Gregory the Great, but for St.
Bernard of Clairvaux (d. A.D. 1153) triple immersion signified (as it did for St. Cyril of Jerusalem) the three-day so-
journ of Christ in the sepulchre.[2]

The mere sprinkling of the head, familiar to-day in infant
baptism, first became the generally recognized custom in the
western church after the thirteenth century, but even then
the eastern church retained, and still retains, complete
immersion of infants.

One among many unfortunate consequences of the general
practice of infant baptism was *the disappearance of the catechu-
menate period of pre-baptismal instruction*. It is true that lip-
service is paid to the principle that Christian baptism is
believers' baptism. John of Damascus, in the first half of the
eighth century, declared that baptism into Christ signifies
the baptism of those who believe in Him, and have been
instructed in the Christian Confession.[3] Theophylact,[4] three
centuries later, also writes: "It is impossible for one who has
not believed to be baptized."[5] But practice was not consistent

---

[1] *Non oportere ter mergere eum qui baptizetur*, Can. vi. The reason for rejecting
triple immersion was that, as practised by the Arians, it was made to signify a
difference, or degrees of divinity, in the Divine Persons of the Trinity, whereas
the single immersion emphasizes their unity.

[2] *In Coena Domini*. So also in Narsai's *Homily on the Mysteries of the Church and on
Baptism*, Hom. xxi, in *C.T.S.*, viii, 51: "Three days was our Redeemer with the
dead: so also he that is baptized: the three times are three days." Cf. St. Cyril
of Jerusalem, *Cat.*, 20, 4, and John of Damascus, *De Fide Orthodoxa*, iv, 9 (P.G.
94, 1120).

[3] *De Fide Orthodoxa*, iv. 9.

[4] Archbishop of Bulgaria in the second half of the eleventh century.

[5] βαπτισθῆναι δὲ τὸν μὴ πιστεύσαντα ἀδύνατον, *In Joan.*, viii (P.G. 124, 20). He
also writes that no unbaptized person may partake of Holy Communion
(οὐδεὶς ἀβάπτιστος μεταλαμβάνει, *In Matt.*, xiv).

with this principle. The belief that baptism itself effected a change in the recipient, and made him a Christian, led to the practice of admitting heathen peoples into the church by the mere act of baptism, without any regard to the question whether they had received a moral and spiritual conversion.

> When infant baptism became general, and men grew up to be Christians as they grew to be citizens, the maintenance of the earlier standards became impossible in the church at large. Professing Christians adopted the current morality; they were content to be no worse than their neighbours . . . that which had been the ideal standard of qualifications for baptism became the ideal standard of qualifications for ordination; and there grew up a distinction between clerical morality and lay morality which has never passed away.[1]

The degeneration and moral decay of many professing Christians, including even some clergy, in the medieval church was facilitated by the unscriptural practice of infant baptism, supported as it was by the unscriptural doctrine of original guilt and the belief in the mechanical power of the outward rite of baptism, irrespective of the disposition of its recipient, to confer regeneration by the Holy Spirit. It was inevitable that some who yearned to see a church characterized by a sincere, inward, spiritual Christianity, and who read the Scriptures with reverent understanding and obedient hearts, should have felt the difficulty which has been clearly stated by an Anglican scholar:

> that the custom of baptizing unconscious infants (in virtue of the exclusive emphasis which it seems to lay upon the *ex opere operato* aspect of the sacred action, and the complete absence from it of the subjective and *ex opere operantis* aspect) is not unattended by theoretical difficulties, such as do not arise in connection with the normal administration of the other sacraments.[2]

The western church rightly refused to admit infants to Holy Communion, on the ground that personal faith is necessary for a proper reception of this sacrament. On the same ground infants should have been excluded from

---

[1] E. Hatch, *The Organization of the Early Christian Churches*, 140. (Quoted by H. W. Robinson, *op. cit.*, 39f.)

[2] N. P. Williams, *op. cit.*, 221.

Holy Baptism. The eastern church, though in error, was more consistent in admitting infants not only to baptism, but to confirmation and communion as well. In the New Testament both baptism and the observance of the Lord's Supper are on the same footing, both being linked with Christ's death, and both being administered to penitent believers only.

Chapter

6

THE ANABAPTISTS AND THE RISE OF THE BAPTIST MOVEMENT

by W. M. S. West

A. *Medieval Attempts at Baptismal Reform*

WE have seen in the previous chapter how the practice of infant baptism became established in the church by the fifth century and how the meaning of infant baptism became interpreted in terms of baptismal regeneration. Baptism worked *ex opere operato*; it effected salvation. An infant through its baptism was assured of salvation and life eternal. An infant dying unbaptized had no hope of salvation and faced an eternity of punishment. True, there were various refinements of this doctrine, but they did not affect the basic issue.[1]

From time to time in the Middle Ages voices of protest were raised against such teaching. In the eastern church, at the beginning of the ninth century, the Paulicians appear to have denied the validity of infant baptism and with it the doctrine that infants have original and operative sin. There is extant a document of the Paulicians edited and translated by F. C. Conybeare under the title of *The Key of Truth* (1898). From this document it is quite clear that the Paulicians practised believers' baptism. In their catechism one of the answers reads:

I have true witness from the holy Gospel which our Lord enjoined on the holy Church, saying after His resurrection: "Go ye into all the world, and preach the gospel to all creatures. He that shall believe and be baptized shall live; and he that

---

[1] Augustine (*Enchiridion*, 93) suggests, for example, concerning the unbaptized infant who dies: "Surely, the lightest of all punishments will be laid on those who have added no further sin to that originally contracted."

believeth not shall be judged". Behold, my reverent ones, first did he enjoin faith, repentance, and then he gave the command of holy baptism.[1]

This quotation could be multiplied many times and the remarkably interesting description of the actual ceremony of baptism leaves no doubt but that the candidate is one able to make his own confession of faith prior to being baptized.[2] It is worth while remarking that the Paulicians also had a ceremony for the blessing of infants.[3] This was held on the eighth day after birth and in the home of the child, in the presence of members of the congregation. After saying the Lord's Prayer the minister and the congregation together offered a prayer for the blessing of the child and prayed that he might be "brought through" to reach holy baptism. The minister, too, is given his responsibility towards the growing children:

> Again ye, the elect ones, must observe the utmost care that they receive before baptism, instruction and training, both of body and soul, as St. Paul saith: "Practice thyself in godliness." So must ye without delay bring those who come unto faith, hope, love and repentance, and with extreme care and testing practice them, no matter who they be, lest peradventure anyone should be an impostor . . . like Simon in Acts 8: 13.[4]

Yet, whilst in the eastern church the Paulicians seem to have been an isolated group of oriental Christians, in the west at the beginning of the twelfth century a similar and more sustained protest appeared in a group gathered around Peter of Bruys. This group was active chiefly in the area around Toulouse and became quite influential. The teaching of Peter of Bruys comes to us chiefly through the statement of Peter the Venerable, Abbot of Cluny, and for our purpose it is sufficient to note that he denied infant baptism and held to believers' baptism.

> But we await a time suitable to faith, and baptize a man, after he is ready to recognize his God and to believe in Him; we do not, as you charge us, rebaptize him, because the man who

---

[1] F. C. Conybeare, *The Key of Truth*, 118.
[2] *Ibid.*, 97.   [3] *Ibid.*, 90.   [4] *Ibid.*, 91.

has not been washed with the baptism by which sins are washed away ought never to be called baptized.[1]

We are told that the Petrobusians also rejected prayers for the dead, denied the sanctity of church buildings and carried out a certain amount of iconoclasm. These emphases appear to have been gathered up by the Waldensian Movement of Peter Waldo and the Poor Men of Lyons, who were driven by persecution from Lyons out into southern Europe and northwards to Germany and possibly to England. Wherever they went they preached and taught these doctrines and they must have helped, in some small measure at least, to prepare the ground for the reception of all shades of Reformation opinion.

There was, however, another development in the Middle Ages which, for our purpose, is of prime importance; namely the involvement of church with state and state with church. This involvement was especially evident in the western church with which, of course, we are chiefly concerned. It is manifest in the growth of the idea of the *Volkskirche*, i.e. the church of the community, in which community and church are two ways of looking at the same thing. Ideally, the medieval world constituted a spiritual world-empire which was based upon "the one Christian religion and in which christendom and humanity as a whole were regarded as identical".[2] But as in the old dispensation circumcision had been the initiatory rite into the society, now, infant baptism, viewed as we should say to-day sociologically, whatever may have been its theological meaning, was reckoned to bring the child into membership of the community. Quite clearly the door was wide open for the involvement of sociological thinking with theological in respect of any discussion of baptism—infant or believers'. The doctrine of the state became involved with the doctrine of the church and we shall have cause to suggest that this involvement inevitably clouded thinking on the question of baptism. In the Middle Ages, therefore, infant baptism became thought of

[1] Quoted by H. W. Robinson, *Baptist Principles*, 63, from Neander, *Church History*, viii, 339.

[2] P. Peachey, "Social Background and Social Philosophy of the Swiss Anabaptists 1525-1540", in *M.Q.R.*, xxviii (1954), 102ff. This article is a summary of Peachey's larger work *Die soziale Herkunft der Schweizer Täufer in der Reformationszeit*.

not only as effecting salvation from sin but also as making the child a member of the community.

B. *The Dawn of the Reformation*

Such was the thinking concerning infant baptism when, in the late autumn of 1517, Luther strode through the streets of Wittenberg to nail his 95 Theses to the door of the Castle Church, and when Zwingli in December 1518 took up his work as People's Priest at the Gross Münster in Zürich. In the years following, the movement known as the Reformation gathered speed. Luther and Zwingli, from their very different backgrounds and spiritual experiences, fiercely attacked the Roman Catholic doctrines and practices which, they felt, obscured at every turn the truth of the Gospel concerning salvation. They set at the heart of their theology God's gift of grace in Jesus Christ apprehended by the faith of the individual believer.

This basic emphasis was naturally reflected in the Reformers' teaching on the sacraments. Luther, in his *Babylonish Captivity of the Church*, lays down that in a sacrament there is contained a divine promise which is apprehended by the faith of each Christian.[1] Zwingli also places great emphasis upon the need for faith on the part of the Christian receiving the bread and wine.[2] Certainly, in their doctrine of the Lord's Supper, the application of the general principle is manifest, but in their thought on baptism it is by no means so evident. It is outside the scope of this study to undertake a detailed critique of the baptismal teaching of the two Reformers. It must suffice at this point to say that, whilst both rejected the medieval *ex opere operato* doctrine, and whilst both felt the need for faith of some sort on the part of the recipient, they nevertheless finally held to the practice of infant baptism. The word "finally" is used advisedly, for, as we shall see, both Luther and Zwingli, especially the latter, had some hesitation on this matter.

It was against this background that there arose amongst followers of the Reformers those who believed that Scripture taught the doctrine and practice of believers' baptism, and

---

[1] H. Wace and C. A. Buchheim (eds.), *Luther's Primary Works*, 324ff.

[2] See, for example, Zwingli's comments upon John 6: 56f., in his "De vera et falsa religione commentarius", in C.R., 88 (1900), Zwingli's *Sämtliche Werke*, iii, 780f.

who, applying the principle of the absolute authority of the Bible which they had learned from the Reformers, put their belief into practice. So began the movement known as Anabaptism. It is the aim of this chapter to tell the story of the rise of this movement and to indicate its place in the life and thought of the church.

C. *Who were the Anabaptists?*

In the past generation the Anabaptists have emerged from the cloud of general condemnation under which they had lain for more than three centuries. It can now be seen that most of them did not merit the severe treatment meted out to them by church historians. But more than that, it has become plain that not only were they undeserving of condemnation but also that they represent a movement of considerable significance and importance in the Reformation. They constitute a third group which emerged from the Reformation alongside the Lutheran and Reformed churches. Rufus Jones, writing nearly fifty years ago, said of the movement:

> It is the spiritual soil out of which all Nonconformist sects have sprung, and it is the first plain announcement in modern history of a programme for a new type of Christian Society which the modern world, especially in America and England, has been slowly realizing—an absolutely free and independent society, and a state in which every man counts as a man, and has his share in shaping both Church and State.[1]

The name "Anabaptist" means, of course, rebaptizer and was the title given to the movement by its opponents. As far as can be ascertained the title originated in Switzerland from the pen of Zwingli in the year 1525. In the May of that year he wrote his work entitled *Von dem touff, von widertouff unnd vom Kindertouff*,[2] thus, in its title, coining the German equivalent of Anabaptism. This should not surprise us, for the work was published four months after the first definite evidence we have of believers' baptism (or re-baptism) taking place within the context of the Reformation movement.

---

[1] R. M. Jones, *Studies in Mystical Religion*, 369.
[2] C. R. (Zwingli), iv, 206.

One of the chief problems facing any student of the Anabaptist movement is that the name "Anabaptist" came to be used to cover a multitude of men. It seems clear that Zwingli's original use of the word was directed against those who were baptizing again, i.e. practising believers' baptism, but the word was extended to include others. As the epithet "a Red" has been applied, in modern times, to those holding extreme views about anything, so the name Anabaptist was extended to cover all sorts of enthusiasts on the left wing of the Reformation movement. Our first task must therefore be to suggest some criteria by which it is possible to disentangle those who really merit the name of Anabaptist from the other groups which have been conveniently classified as Anabaptist by church historians from, at least, Henry Bullinger onwards.

From the research of recent generations, and following E. Troeltsch partly,[1] it seems reasonable to suggest that we may find a working hypothesis if we divide up those loosely called Anabaptists into three groups: the evangelical Anabaptists, the Spiritualists and the Anti-Trinitarians. This grouping is in the main accurate, especially for the earlier years of the Reformation, but there are inevitably some people whose ideas and writings would seem to put them in more than one group. The distinction between the last group and the first two is obvious. The distinction between the evangelical Anabaptists and the Spiritualists may perhaps be made in their attitude to the Bible, the Word of God.

The *evangelical Anabaptists* were Biblicists. They took as the basis of their reform the literal interpretation of the Bible; it was God's Word, and man stood under its authority to interpret it with the aid of the Holy Spirit. Their interpretation of the Bible led them to a belief in the visible church manifesting itself as a fellowship of believers, disciples living according to the Word of God; a fellowship, the entrance to which was by believers' baptism, and in which the believers alone sat down together round the Lord's Table. To this

---

[1] E. Troeltsch, *The Social Teaching of the Christian Churches*, ii, 691ff. C. H. Williams and A. M. Mergal (eds.), *Spiritual and Anabaptist Writers* (Library of Christian Classics, xxv, Documents illustrative of the Radical Reformation), have attempted a detailed classification of those called Anabaptists. They use "Evangelical Anabaptists" to denote a somewhat narrower group than here suggested. This terminology goes back to Robert Friedmann's article, "Conception of the Anabaptists", in *Church History*, ix (1940), 341-65.

group belong Conrad Grebel (1489-1526), Felix Manz (d. 1527), George Blaurock (d. 1529), Balthasar Hubmaier (1481-1528), Jacob Huter (d. 1536),[1] and many others.

The *Spiritualists*, as their name suggests, set the authority of direct revelation from God to the individual through the Holy Spirit above the Word of God, although some of them used the Bible to check and confirm their revelations. This group owed, in fact, much to the medieval mystics. They tended to play down any emphasis upon a visible community—a church—and naturally had no great interest in, nor set much store upon, the sacraments. To this group belong Thomas Müntzer (? 1490-1525), Caspar Schwenckfeld (1489-1561), Sebastian Franck (1499-1542), and almost certainly—eventually—Andreas Carlstadt (1481-1541).

The most famous names among the *Anti-Trinitarians* are Miguel Servetus (? 1510-53) and Faustus Socinus (1534-1604). But it is the life and thought of the evangelical Anabaptists which will mainly concern us and in this chapter the word "Anabaptist" will, in future, normally be used in the narrower sense as referring to this group.

The Anabaptists were not, numerically, a hole-in-the-corner sect as is so often imagined. As early as May 1525, Zwingli wrote to Vadian, the Reformer of St. Gall, and told him of the gravity of the Anabaptists' challenge.[2] By 1530, Sebastian Franck wrote of three definite movements: Lutheran, Zwinglian and Anabaptist. And in the following year he recorded: "The Anabaptists spread so rapidly that their teaching soon covered the land. . . . They soon gained a large following and baptized thousands, drawing to themselves many sincere souls who had a zeal for God."[3] In the same year H. Bullinger wrote that "The people were running after them as though they were living saints."[4] The authorities took the challenge of the Anabaptists very seriously, the Diet of Speier in 1529 summarily passing sentence of death upon all Anabaptists.

---

[1] For these men see articles in C. Hege and D. C. Neff (eds.), *Mennonitisches Lexikon*, and in C. H. Smith, H. S. Bender et al., *Mennonite Encyclopaedia*.

[2] C. R. (Zwingli), viii, 331f.

[3] Quoted by J. Horsch, *Mennonites in Europe*, 293, from Sebastian Frank's *Chronica, Zeitbuch und Geschichtbibel*.

[4] *Von dem unverschampten frafel—*, folio 2v.

The question may well be asked as to why, if the Anabaptists were so strong numerically, their influence upon the contemporary Reformation movement was not more obviously marked and recorded. A partial answer is not far to seek. It is twofold. First, they had little organization, and although they had some form of ministry they had no ecclesiastical hierarchy; they sought no state support. Secondly, and this leads on from the first point, they had no great leader, at least no leader left alive. Most of the outstanding Anabaptists were removed by state persecution before 1530. The leaders were harried from pillar to post, with the reverse result from that intended, in that persecution spread the movement and after the Diet of Speier general persecution was applied—spasmodically certainly, but effectively. The number of Anabaptists put to death in the years 1525-40 seemingly runs into many thousands. The attempt to obliterate the movement nearly succeeded, but a remnant remained. And the principles for which so many suffered were preserved. We turn now to indicate what those principles were.

D. *Principles of the Anabaptists*

It is now generally taken as proven that the Anabaptists were children of the Reformation—that is, that they were not a revival of the evangelical religion of the Middle Ages. We shall consider the problem of their origin later, but the older view of Ludwig Keller[1] (followed in part by T. M. Lindsay)[2] that the Anabaptists were nothing else than the continuation of the medieval movements, such as the Waldensians, is generally rejected. It is true that in the past five years an attempt has been made to revive this theory in relation to the Bernese Anabaptists, but this is not held to have succeeded.[3] The evidence points the other way. The Anabaptists held that the way of salvation for man, from the very beginning, depended upon grace and is appropriated by faith. This is the decisive emphasis of the Reformation. The dependence of the Anabaptists upon the Reformers,

---

[1] *Die Reformation und die älteren Reformparteien.*

[2] *History of the Reformation*, ii, 430ff.

[3] Theory revived by D. Gratz (*Bernese Anabaptists*), criticized by P. Peachey (*op. cit.*), and in a review by R. Kreider (*M.Q.R.*, xxviii (1954), 313ff.), also J. Städke, "Die Anfänge des Täufertum in Bern", in *T.Z.*, 11 (1955), 75ff.

especially Zwingli, for their sacramental doctrine is demon-
strable. But our present task is not to describe the thought
which the Anabaptists learnt from the Reformers, but rather
to show where they differed or went beyond their teachers.
For clarity we will take five points and deal with each
separately, though in fact they are inter-related.

  *1. That the Bible is the Word of God and therefore absolutely
authoritative.* This, of course, was typical of the whole
Reformation movement, but the appeal to the Bible by the
different Reformers varied in degree. They agreed that for
doctrine it was the absolute norm, but for church practice
it is safe, though somewhat inaccurate, to say that Luther
accepted practices as long as they were not contrary to the
Bible, whilst Zwingli felt that only practices explicitly
specified in Scripture should be followed. The Anabaptists
learned from Zwingli, but their interpretation was even
more literal. They tended to make the New Testament their
court of appeal and to distinguish between the old and new
covenants, the new abrogating the old. This led Zwingli to
reintroduce the covenant theology of the unity of the old and
the new and it was he and Bullinger[1] who chiefly laid the
foundations for the edifice of covenant theology subsequently
built.

  There is abundant proof to support the contention that the
evangelical Anabaptists were men of the Word, Biblicists
rather than Spiritualists.[2] Hubmaier wrote: "The Word of
God is water to all those who thirst for salvation and is
made alive in us through the Spirit of God."[3] They were
men of the Bible first and acknowledged the Holy Spirit's
work in making the Word live. A contemporary writer
records the cry of the Anabaptists in Zürich: "Do you have
Zwingli's word, we want God's word."[4] This emphasis is
acknowledged in the writings of both German and Swiss
historians. Walter Köhler comments: "The Anabaptists
wanted to be Bible Christians and they were on the whole
precisely that."[5] L. Von Muralt, one of the leading Swiss

---

  [1] Zwingli, *op. cit.*, and in *In Catabaptistarum Strophas Elenchus*, C. R. (Zwingli), vi,
i f. and Bullinger, in *De Testamento seu Foedere Dei Unico*, emphasize the covenant
theology. The matter is discussed in detail in G. Schrenck, *Gottesreich und Bund
im älteren Protestantismus*.

  [2] W. Wiswedel, "The Inner and Outer Word: a Study in the Anabaptist
Doctrine of Scripture", in *M.Q.R.*, xxvi (1952), 171ff.

  [3] Quoted by W. Wiswedel, *loc. cit.*   [4] *Ibid.*   [5] *Ibid.*

historians of to-day, says: "The Anabaptists stand on the platform of scripture."[1] It is necessary that we should establish this point clearly as it has a definite bearing upon our later discussion of the origins of the Anabaptists.

It is necessary also to comment that although there is considerable research still to be done on the Anabaptist doctrine of the authority of the Bible, present indications suggest that they appear to be guilty of the two faults mentioned by Mr. Winward in chapter 2.[2] First, in that they "jump from Scripture to to-day as if nothing of value had been preserved in between". Secondly, in their apparent failure to distinguish between Biblical practices which are essential because they arise out of the very nature of the Gospel itself, and those practices which are indifferent, arising as they do from temporary circumstances existing at the time of the apostles. These two tendencies will become self-evident as we proceed.

2. *That the true church-type is that of a fellowship of believers, free from state control.* When the Anabaptists measured the Church of Rome against the pattern of the church they found in the New Testament they were convinced that almost everything was wrong. When they measured the church ideal of the Reformers against the pattern of the New Testament they found that, although it was a great improvement on Rome, nevertheless it fell short of the New Testament ideal. It is suggested that the Anabaptists were convinced by the New Testament that what was required was not a *reformation* of the church but a *restitution*. They viewed the Constantinian Settlement as the point at which the true church "fell" and they looked upon Luther and Zwingli as half-way men because they did not really free the church from her ancient bondage. F. H. Littell writes: "The Anabaptists conceived of their historical significance as a restitution of the true church, a recovery of the discipline and mobility which characterized the Christian people before the church went a-whoring from her Lord."[3] But care must be taken as to the content of the word "restitution". There is considerable weight of evidence to suggest

[1] Quoted by W. Wiswedel, *loc. cit.*   [2] *Supra*, 53.
[3] "The Anabaptist Doctrine of the Restitution of the True Church", in *M.Q.R.*, xxiv (1950), 38ff., and also *The Anabaptist View of the Church.*

that the ideal of the Anabaptists was not so much a historical re-establishment of something previously lost, as a continuation of the true church, the timeless and perennial community of genuine believers.[1] This matter is still in debate amongst scholars, but whether restitution or continuation be the right conception it is quite certain that their ideal was the church of the New Testament.

The Anabaptists claimed to find in the New Testament local churches in the pattern of companies of believing men and women with the wider church as the union of these local fellowships. Their ideal was to set up such fellowships. It may be suggested that as Luther's teaching centred upon *sola fide* and Zwingli's and Calvin's upon the sovereignty of God, so the Anabaptists' thought centred upon the New Testament *ecclesia*—separated, of course, from state control. It is becoming more and more generally accepted that in this conception of the church as a separated fellowship of believers we are close to the heart of Anabaptist thought. Their conception of the church was that of sinners called out of the world, who by baptism were brought into the fellowship of believers, into membership of one body—Christ—which membership was expressed in brotherly love and in the celebration of the Lord's Supper. They undoubtedly thought of themselves as the "covenant people"[2] and in view of later developments of the covenant idea it must be said that the Anabaptists, at least at first, thought of this covenant between God and the individual as being made in and through believers' baptism. They quote 1 Peter 3: 21, which Luther's translation rendered as: "Baptism is the covenant of a good conscience with God (*Der Bund eines guten Gewissens mit Gott*)". The most recent Anabaptist research appears to suggest that the conception of this fellowship of believers, covenant people, led the Anabaptists with the New Testament in their hands to a conviction of the rightness of believers' baptism and the rejection of infant baptism.

3. The true baptism is that of believers. It is clear that rejection of, or doubts concerning, infant baptism cannot be a criterion for judging who is and who is not an Anabaptist. During the

---

[1] R. Friedmann, "Recent Interpretations of Anabaptism", in *Church History*, xxiv (1955), 132ff.

[2] R. Friedmann, *loc. cit.*

Reformation many people had serious doubts about the practice of infant baptism. Luther himself wrote to Melanchthon in 1522 concerning infant baptism: "I have always expected that the devil would touch this sore point . . . we ourselves are in great conflict concerning it".[1] Luther had some reason to be concerned, for it was by no means an easy thing for him to reconcile his sacramental teaching with infant baptism. His emphasis on the necessity of faith at the reception of the sacrament we have already noted, and he worked this out logically enough in his teaching of the individual believer receiving the Lord's Supper in faith. In baptism, however, he had either to posit implicit faith in the child as of the faith of a man asleep, or else to take the faith of the sponsor as satisfying the condition of faith for the infant.

Zwingli hesitated longer than Luther and at one point appeared to reject infant baptism. Balthasar Hubmaier later wrote to Zwingli reminding him of this. "In 1523 . . . I conferred with you in Graben Street upon the scriptures relating to baptism; then and there you said that I was right in saying that children should not be baptized before they were instructed in the faith; this had been the custom previously and therefore such were called catechumens. You promised to bring this out in your exposition of the Articles . . . anyone who reads it will find your opinions clearly expressed."[2] In fact, when we turn to Zwingli's exposition of his eighteenth Article[3] we find that he does assert that in the earlier church the baptism of infants was not so common as at present and that those to be baptized were instructed as catechumens, being baptized only after making their personal confession of faith. Although Zwingli at this point does not go on to reject infant baptism he certainly admits the possibility of believers' baptism. That Zwingli was at one time inclined towards believers' baptism he himself admits when, in 1525, writing concerning believers' baptism, he said: "This error misled me also some years ago, so that I thought it much better to baptize children after they have come to a riper age."[4]

---

[1] L. Enders, *Dr. Martin Luther's Briefwechsel*, iii, 276.
[2] Quoted in C.R. (Zwingli), iv, 228, n.21.
[3] C.R. (Zwingli), ii, 123.   [4] *Ibid.*, iv, 228.

If we ask why, in spite of doubts and apparent inconsistencies, Luther and Zwingli came down on the side of infant baptism, at least part of the answer must be that they held to the medieval social order in which, as we have suggested earlier, society was considered "as a single universal, mystic body viewed now as *ecclesia universalis*, now as *respublica generis humani*".[1] For the Reformers, the religious and the secular order were one in the *Corpus Christi*. The pattern of the *Volkskirche* prevailed. Infant baptism brought the child into the church and into society. It is obvious why rejection of infant baptism was so severely punished. To reject it inevitably undermined the medieval conception of the *Corpus Christianum* and to maintain the rightness of believers' baptism was to replace the medieval conception by one of the church as the *Corpus Christi* of believers. This helps to explain the accusation of anarchy against the Anabaptists and why they suffered so much persecution. As we have said, the Anabaptists dated "the fall" of the church from the time of the Constantinian Settlement when the change to the medieval concept of the fusion of *imperium* and *sacerdotium* was set in motion. Zwingli, on the other hand, dated the fall of the church from the sixth century with the rise of papal hierarchy and domination. Hence, Zwingli opposed only the abuses of the medieval concept, whilst the Anabaptists attacked the concept itself. The significance of this difference cannot be overestimated, and it helps to explain why the battle of Zwingli with the Anabaptists centred in the main upon baptism.

4. That Christianity is a way of life rather than a system of belief. The Anabaptists applied Christian principles to their personal lives. They had a strict discipline within the church and were aggressively missionary in their own lives to win men out of the sinful world. H. S. Bender has characterized their life as "existential discipleship".[2] The term "existential" means here, above all, an extreme concreteness of the Christian experience. It is not doctrinal understanding, nor emotion. What the Anabaptist accepted as truth, that he put into practice in life forthwith. To profess the new birth

---

[1] Quoted by P. Peachey, "Social Background and Social Philosophy of the Swiss Anabaptists", in *M.Q.R.*, xxviii (1954), 102ff., from O. von Gierke, *Das deutsche Genossenschaftsrecht*, 517.

[2] "The Anabaptist Theology of Discipleship", in *M.Q.R.*, xxiv (1950), 25ff.

meant a new life. To promise obedience to Christ meant actually to live out and to carry through His principles and do His works. To claim the cleansing and redemption from sin which baptism symbolized meant to leave the sins and lusts of the flesh and to live a holy life. We should not think of the Anabaptists as groups of pious Bible-reading Christians who gathered to sing hymns and rejoice together in the forgiveness of sins, content to show in their lives a somewhat insipid moralism. After baptism they set out to live with the Holy Spirit's help a sinless life; they knew they would fail, but they believed that there should be no compromise with sin. They were not perfectionists; they did not believe that after baptism a man could not sin, but rather that he should not.

It is easy to understand, however, how the accusation of perfectionism could be levelled at them as it was later notably by Calvin. They went out into the world as disciples of Christ uncompromisingly; that they would collide with the world was inevitable—they expected that—they even had their conception of the church as the suffering church; their conception of Christ and the faith was of the uncompromising command to deny themselves and to take up the cross and to follow; they even developed what has been called "a theology of martyrdom".[1] Their literal interpretation of Christ's teaching led most of them to pacifism and to the consequent position that a Christian could not be a magistrate, for that would involve the use of the sword. A similar literal interpretation of the New Testament led to the refusal of most of them to swear any oaths.

Now this is a very different picture of the Anabaptists from that which was presented until relatively recently. The deplorable episode of Münster, involving a small group of them, coloured all writing and thinking about the Anabaptists for three hundred and fifty years. Yet it appears that our picture is a true one. Even Zwingli and Bullinger had to admit, however grudgingly, the apparent excellence of their lives.[2]

5. *That there should be no compulsion in things of religion but rather religious toleration.* The Anabaptists claimed religious

---

[1] E. Stauffer, "The Anabaptist Theology of Martyrdom", in *M.Q.R.*, xix (1945), 179ff.

[2] C.R. (Zwingli), vi, 24, and Bullinger, *Der Widertoufferen Ursprung*, fol. 15v.

toleration from the beginning,[1] they claimed it for themselves and they claimed it for other people. The plea for
toleration echoed throughout the whole Anabaptist movement. It was not simply that they were persecuted and
demanded the right for their case to be heard and claimed
the right to exist; it was more than that. They based their
plea upon several grounds, of which we may enumerate four:

(*a*) The teaching and example of Christ and His apostles
showed no compulsion in bringing men to the faith.

(*b*) The obligation that was given to all Christians to love
all men including unbelievers. This was also a ground of
their pacifism.

(*c*) They emphasized the principle of voluntarism and free
commitment in church membership. The Anabaptist
churches were free churches both in the sense of being free
from state control and of being made up only of those who
became members of their own free will.

(*d*) They believed that faith was a gift from God and
therefore was impossible to create by compulsion of man.
They believed that if you burn a heretic you may be pre-
maturely uprooting the harvest of a soul God planned to
reap to-morrow.

E. *The Origins of the Anabaptist Movement*

We turn now to consider the origins of the Anabaptist
movement. Various theories have been suggested. Karl Holl
believed the origins were to be found in Zwickau and
Wittenberg during the winter months of 1521-22 when the
Zwickau Prophets moved into Wittenberg and caused
considerable disturbance.[2] Ernst Troeltsch placed the
beginning of the movement in Zürich in the years 1524-25
when Grebel, Blaurock and Manz broke finally with
Zwingli.[3] Walter Köhler suggested a combination of these
views, saying that the idea of re-baptism and the separation
of the fellowship of believers from the *Volkskirche* originated
amongst the Zwickau group, whilst the first adult baptism
and the first Anabaptist congregation was in Zürich.

[1] H. S. Bender, "The Anabaptists and Religious Liberty in the 16th
Century", in *A.R.G.*, xliv (1953), 32ff.

[2] "Luther und die Schwärmer", in *Gesammelte Aufsätze*, i, 420ff.

[3] *Op. cit.*, 703ff.

Köhler further suggested that the Zürich group maintained contact with Zwickau and Wittenberg without having been called into existence by the Wittenberg fanatics.[1] Which of these theories is accepted depends, in part, at least, upon the definition given to the word "Anabaptist".

Space forbids a detailed examination of every aspect of this problem of Anabaptist origins. The events at Zwickau and subsequently in Wittenberg, where the returned Luther soon restored order, appear to suggest that we are here dealing with an outbreak of Spiritualism. The Zwickau Prophets claimed to be prophets of the Lord; there was no longer need for the Bible, but only for the Holy Spirit who spoke through them. Outward forms, including infant baptism, were indeed rejected, but evidence is lacking which might suggest that they advocated believers' baptism or a church conception of a separated fellowship of believers.[2]

This is as true of Thomas Müntzer[3] as of the other Zwickau enthusiasts. He certainly had doubts concerning infant baptism but he does not seem ever to have re-baptized believers. There is good reason to believe that his doubts were not simply concerning infant baptism but had to do with the sacrament of baptism itself. When he was in Basle in September 1524 he was still baptizing infants and at this time published a baptismal liturgy, and Conrad Grebel, on reading this, immediately became suspicious that Müntzer was on the way to a repudiation of baptism. This is the logical outcome of Müntzer's thought. As far as his ecclesiology is concerned, until the end of his life, he was in and out of pastorates within the state churches, being appointed pastor of St. Mary's church at Muhlhausen as late as February 1525. His ideal was to build the kingdom of God on earth, by force if necessary, not in the form of a separate fellowship of believers but as a Christian state in which the

---

[1] *Die Religion im Geschichte und Gegenwart* (2nd edition, 1931), v, col. 1915.

[2] There does appear to have been what may be called a "conventicle Christianity" in Zwickau amongst the textile workers. But these seem not to have been Anabaptists but evangelical Lutherans studying the Bible for themselves. Luther did himself at different times encourage the idea of an *ecclesiola* in the *ecclesia*.

[3] For Thomas Müntzer and his part see H. S. Bender, "The Zwickau Prophets, Thomas Müntzer, and the Anabaptists", in *M.Q.R.*, xxvii (1953), 3ff., and M. M. Smirin, *Die Volksreformation des Thomas Müntzer und der grosse Bauernkreig*, and sources quoted by Bender and Smirin.

godly elect were to compel the ungodly with the sword. When he preached before the princes at Weimar he appealed to them to be the instruments for carrying out the prophet's word.

It seems therefore that Thomas Müntzer was far from the thought and spirit of Anabaptism. So far no evidence has come to light to suggest that, before Müntzer's death, believers' baptism was practised in Saxony or Thuringia, where his influence was strongest, neither is there evidence at this time for the existence of the theory or practice of the church as a fellowship of believers separated from the state. Yet, in spite of this, to suggest that Müntzer may be *entirely* rejected as an influence upon the beginnings and the subsequent history of the evangelical Anabaptists is surely to claim too much,[1] and probably his opposition to the established practice of infant baptism may help to explain the speed with which Anabaptist views spread in the years following 1525.

Whilst Luther had been dealing with the situation in Wittenberg, and the discontent of the peasants had been growing stronger, Zwingli in Zürich was facing his own problems.[2] And as we have in mind especially the evangelical Anabaptist movement it is necessary to examine events in Zürich in more detail.

In January 1523, after the First Disputation, Zürich had accepted Reformation teaching by virtue of a decree of the city council. But Zwingli and his supporters were still a relatively small group in the city. Yet what they lacked in numbers they made up for in enthusiasm. Amongst the group around Zwingli at this time were Conrad Grebel and Felix Manz, both young men and both enthusiastic for speedy reformation. Grebel was a humanist scholar, but like Manz he had been converted by Zwingli to the evangelical faith. Zwingli, in August 1523, allowed Grebel to write a Latin poem as an epilogue to the Zürich reformer's work *Archeteles*.[3]

---

[1] For Müntzer's influence, however, cf. G. Mecenseffy, "Die Herkunft des oberösterreichischen Taufertums", in *A.R.G.*, xlvii (1956), 252ff., and especially Lowell H. Zuck, "Anabaptism: Abortive Counter Revolt within the Reformation", in *Church History*, xxvi (1957), 211ff., where he attacks current Mennonite attempts to dissociate Thomas Müntzer entirely from the Anabaptist movement.

[2] F. Blanke, *Brüder in Christo*, gives a full account of Zwingli's troubles with the Anabaptists, as does H. S. Bender, *Conrad Grebel*.

[3] C.R. (Zwingli), i, 327.

By the autumn of that year, however, it became clear to Zwingli that he was going to find it difficult to control the enthusiasm of Grebel, Manz and certain other of his supporters. At the Second Disputation held at the end of October 1523 it was agreed that the Roman doctrine which made the Mass a repetition of the sacrifice of Christ was false and contrary to the Word of God. When it was suggested that the discussion should turn to another subject Conrad Grebel asked permission to speak. He begged the council to give instructions to the pastors, while they were gathered together, concerning the manner of future celebrations of the Lord's Supper. Zwingli replied that it was necessary to leave to the city council the decision as to the timing and the ways and means of carrying out the proposed reform. Grebel maintained that this reform should be carried out immediately; Zwingli counselled caution.

There are two seeds of possible disagreement here of which the first is immeasurably the more important. Firstly, Zwingli's statement that the city council should decide matters of reform. This was not unnatural, as it was the council who had initiated the Disputation and in their invitation had reserved the right of ultimate decision to themselves. But in reply to Zwingli's statement Simon Stumpf, one of Grebel's supporters, said: "Master Ulrich, you do not have the right to place the decision on this matter in the hands of my lords, for the decision has already been made, the Spirit of God decides . . . if my lords adopt and decide on some other course that would be against the decision of God, I will ask Christ for His spirit and will preach and act against it."[1]

It is difficult to know whether Zwingli and Grebel at that moment saw the far-reaching effects of Zwingli's policy and of the opposition to it. H. S. Bender thinks Grebel had seen the issue, and comments: "It was a major issue of policy for the Reformation. Zwingli and Grebel made opposite decisions and their ways separated. One road led by way of Zwingli into the State Church, while the other road led by way of Grebel into the Free Church."[2] Whether, in fact, Grebel had seen the issue clearly is perhaps doubtful, but it was obviously inherent in the situation. The second point of

[1] C.R. (Zwingli), ii, 784. [2] *Conrad Grebel*, 99.

disagreement arises from the first. Zwingli felt that reform, especially liturgical reform, should proceed gradually. Grebel and his friends thought that when any doctrine or practice had been shown to be contrary to Scripture then it should be discontinued forthwith, without tarrying for any city council decision or for fear of popular prejudice.

From October 1523 onwards the relationship between Zwingli and Grebel became more and more strained. In the next months strenuous attempts were made by the Grebel group to persuade Zwingli to urge the city council on, and they even suggested the election of a new city council which would proceed more quickly. But Zwingli understandably refused to countenance any such suggestion. Ecclesiastical decisions must be taken by the city council when it felt the time was ripe. Grebel and Manz became more and more disillusioned and during the spring and summer of 1524 began radically to rethink the situation. It is probable that we may gain some evidence as to the way their thoughts were turning from an exposition of the New Testament epistles from Ephesians to Hebrews published about the end of June 1524 by Ludwig Hätzer, at that time a member of their group.[1] Hätzer criticizes Zwingli's reformation for not having adhered to the Word of God with all strictness. The booklet indicates that a second reformation is expected which would produce the true church of confessing Christians. This appears to be confirmation that the split between Zwingli and Grebel was due at first to a difference in ecclesiology, and what that involves is hinted at by a marginal note on Eph. 5: 26 which gives the first literary evidence that the practice of infant baptism was becoming suspected by Grebel and his friends.

That this was so is confirmed beyond any doubt by a letter written by Grebel, in his own name and that of his friends, on September, 1524, to none other than Thomas Müntzer in Saxony.[2] In this letter the writer, after criticizing Zwingli, puts forward a new statement concerning the church. He envisages the restoration of a form of church

[1] G. Goeters, "Ludwig Hätzer, A Marginal Anabaptist", in *M.Q.R.*, xxix (1955), 251ff.

[2] Printed as Document 14 in L. von Muralt and W. Schmidt (eds.), *Quellen zur Geschichte der Täufer in der Schweiz*, 13ff. (E.Tr., C. H. Williams and A. M. Mergal (eds.), *Spiritual and Anabaptist Writers*, 73ff.).

nearer to the model of the primitive church, a church made up of a small number of those who have confessed to a personal faith in Christ and who have received baptism on account of that faith. From this moment the Zürich State Church of Zwingli is explicitly rejected. Grebel sees it only as "everybody's" church in which the herd instinct and superficial faith predominated. The Lord's Supper is to be a simple meal held in the evening at which only the words of institution are to be read, and the meeting is to be held, not in churches with priests in sacerdotal vestments, but in the homes of believers—the only alternative places to churches. The meal should symbolize the fellowship of Christians with one another and with Christ. Baptism should be administered, as in the early church, only to believing adults and should signify the cleansing from sin. It is undoubted that Grebel is arguing for the creation of a fellowship of believers, a fellowship independent of the State Church, in fact a Free Church. There also appears in this letter the claim that a Christian should not make war— which appears to be a criticism of Thomas Müntzer— and this means, in effect, that a Christian may not take office in the state.

This important letter was never received by Thomas Müntzer, for it apparently only reached St. Gall and is now in the archives there. It speaks of these matters only in theory; the principles are stated but not yet put into practice, although in Zürich there were already fathers, Grebel amongst them, who were refusing to present their infants for baptism. Grebel and Manz strove to convince Zwingli, and through him the Zürich Council, of the rightness of believers' baptism. Two discussions were held with Zwingli and the other ministers, but they broke down and each side blamed the other for the breakdown.

Probably about the beginning of December 1524 Manz wrote a long statement to the Zürich Council[1] setting out the arguments against infant baptism and asked that Zwingli should reply in writing. Although Zwingli did not accept this challenge directly, he did state his arguments in favour of infant baptism in a work which appeared in the same month

[1] C.R. (Zwingli), iii, 368-72. Until recently this document has usually been attributed to Grebel.

under the title *Wer Ursache gebe zu Aufruhr*.[1] Zwingli enumerates seven distinct groups who are causing him trouble and it is important to notice that the opponents of infant baptism are enumerated as one group and the peasants who refused to pay tithes and taxes as another. Zwingli, from the first, looked upon Grebel's group as being purely religious in character, and not involved with economic factors.

The city council ignored Manz's call for a written discussion and instead summoned the representatives of the two opposing groups to a Disputation on January 17, 1525, at the city hall. Each side was to put forward its views on baptism and the council was to make the decision as to who was right and to act upon it. It is probably not too much to say that the matter was decided before a word was spoken. As a result of the Disputation it was decreed that all infants must be baptized in the eight days after birth and that all who did not bring their infants to baptism would be banished. A second decree followed on January 21, 1525, which forbade the opponents of infant baptism from meeting together and Grebel and Manz from speaking in public. Those members of the group who were not natives of Zürich were to be banished.

It was now clear to Grebel and his friends that the crisis was upon them. They must either turn back and abandon their position or go forward to translate their theory into practice. On the evening of January 21, 1525, they met together, probably in Felix Manz's house, and after prayer together George Blaurock stood up and invited Grebel to baptize him by affusion on profession of his faith. Grebel did this, and Blaurock then baptized the other brethren. It does not seem unreasonable to say that at that moment the evangelical Anabaptist movement was born. The Hutterite account of this historic meeting says: "and so they together dedicated themselves in the high fear of God to the name of the Lord, confirmed one another in the service of the Gospel and began to teach and hold the faith".[2] And although it is clear that at times these Anabaptists were too literal in their interpretation of the Bible, in this fundamental and essential issue of baptism they surely acted in absolute accord with

[1] C.R. (Zwingli), iii, 373ff.
[2] *Geschichtbuch der Hutterischen Brüder* (1923), 35.

Biblical thought and practice as reflected by the conclusions drawn in chapter 4 of this present work.

We are fortunate in being able to reconstruct, from the records of later judicial proceedings, something of the life and thought of this group in Zürich in the days immediately following the first re-baptism.[1] The Anabaptist activity centred upon Zollikon, a village on the eastern shore of the Lake of Zürich, some three miles from the city. In this village they met for evening meetings in private houses and there are eyewitness accounts of at least two meetings.

They began with Bible reading, followed by an exposition which challenged the hearers and was designed to lead to conversion. There then followed baptism on profession of repentance and faith of those converted. The baptism was performed by affusion in the name of the Trinity. As far as can be discovered, the meaning of baptism was twofold. It was a visible sign of God's grace which brought forgiveness, and it was a sign of the power which was sent to the pardoned sinner to enable him to live the new life demanded of a Christian.

After baptism the company proceeded to celebrate the Lord's Supper in the simplest manner with the reading of the words of institution, the breaking of the bread and the pouring out of the wine. The Anabaptists thought of the Lord's Supper as a fellowship meal of those who in faith believed themselves redeemed, and to share in it meant to accept the obligation to love God above all and to live a life of discipleship. It is worth recalling that at this time, January 1525, Zwingli was still celebrating the Roman Mass (except the sacrifice) in Zürich and here in Zollikon, therefore, was indeed reformation without tarrying for any. During the week January 22-29, 1525, there is evidence of thirty-four baptisms at least. The Zürich authorities could not let this Anabaptist activity go unchecked, especially when George Blaurock claimed the right to preach in the village church on the Sunday. All those known to have been involved were arrested and from that moment on, and down the years, the Anabaptists were a hunted people.

---

[1] F. Blanke, *Brüder in Christo*, 22ff., based upon L. von Muralt and W. Schmidt (eds.) *op. cit.* For an English translation of Blanke's reconstruction see "Zollikon, 1525", in *B.Q.*, xv (1953-54), 147-65.

The background of this Anabaptist movement in Zürich is clear. The leaders had been followers of Zwingli and they held to the same basic Reformation principles.[1] In their sacramental doctrine they stood near to Zwingli and they shared very many other ideas of Zwingli, including the heart of all his preaching, which Oscar Farner has shown to be the call to repentance and salvation.[2] What little evidence there is of the attitude of these first Anabaptists towards Luther and the Reformation in Wittenberg is almost entirely critical. In fact these Anabaptists themselves claimed that "Zwingli had led them into this thing"[3] and this was spoken specifically concerning baptism. They were children of the Reformation in general and of the Zwinglian Reformation in particular. Professor Blanke, the Swiss church historian, has written:

> The Anabaptists wished to build further upon the foundations which Zwingli laid. The deviations from Zwingli go in the direction of a yet more literal and strict adherence to the Holy Scripture. The authority of the Bible is for Zwingli, and for the Anabaptists who parted from him, the rule of conduct, but in the application of this rule of conduct the Anabaptists think in details more literally and more biblically.[4]

Such a statement from so outstanding a scholar pin-points again the vital importance of the question of authority. It is no accident, therefore, that this work begins with a chapter on this subject, and perhaps no mere coincidence that some of the earliest challenges to the practice of infant baptism in recent years came from that champion of the return to "Biblical Theology", Karl Barth.

We have suggested that Zwingli viewed the issues involved in the rise of Anabaptism in Zürich as entirely religious. Traditionally, however, there has been an ever-present tendency to suggest that there were social and economic factors involved in the Anabaptist origins in Switzerland, and that Anabaptists were implicated in the Peasants' Revolt. In the early days there is scarcely any evidence to

---

[1] F. Blanke, *Brüder in Christo*, 42ff.   [2] *Huldrych Zwingli*, iii, 142ff.
[3] L. von Muralt and W. Schmidt (eds.), *op. cit.*, 90, and Heinold Fast, "The Dependence of the first Anabaptists on Luther, Erasmus, and Zwingli", in *M.Q.R.*, xxx (1956), 104ff.
[4] *Brüder in Christo*, 45f.

support this. Of the thirty-four who were baptized during the first week in Zollikon only four were of the class reckoned as "peasant". In the records of the court proceedings against them it is the religious issues which are debated.[1] It has recently been shown beyond all doubt that the movement was born in an academic and theological milieu and had immediate success amongst the middle classes and only then did it spread to the peasantry, but not until months, and in some cases years, after the Peasants' Revolt had collapsed.[2] An examination of the cases in which individual Anabaptists were allegedly implicated in the Peasants' Revolt in Switzerland shows that, while inter-action of certain ideas is clear, and in a few cases known participants in that Revolt later entered Anabaptist ranks, "it is simply untenable historically to attribute to Anabaptism a causative role in the Peasants' Revolt".[3]

The question as to whether there is a connection between events in Wittenberg and Zürich admits of no easy answer. We have suggested that the events in the two cities were very different in character; Spiritualism in Wittenberg as against Biblicism in Zürich. But there was opposition to infant baptism in both places. Of the men involved in the Zwickau and Wittenberg occurrences only Müntzer and Carlstadt are likely to have had either personal or literary contact with the Zürich group in the crucial years 1522-24. The contact between Carlstadt and the Zürich group, though indisputable, is unlikely to have been either close or continuous, for Zwingli welcomed him in Zürich in the winter of 1524 and Bullinger later commended him to Myconius in Basle. This is unlikely treatment for a friend of the Anabaptist group!

The evidence for the Zürich Anabaptists' contact with Müntzer is more definite,[4] but the effect of such contact is not easy to estimate. There is the irrefutable evidence of the letter which, as we have already seen, Grebel wrote to Müntzer. It is addressed to "The true and faithful proclaimer of the Gospel T. Müntzer at Alstedt, on the Harz, our faithful

---

[1] *Brüder in Christo*, 46f.

[2] P. Peachey, "Social Background and Social Philosophy of the Swiss Anabaptists", in *M.Q.R.*, xxviii (1954), 102ff.

[3] *Ibid.*, 113, n.19.

[4] H. S. Bender (*Conrad Grebel*, 115ff.) has a full discussion of this matter.

and beloved brother in Christ". The letter appears to suggest that they had only recently become acquainted with Müntzer by means of five pamphlets he had written. It criticizes Müntzer for using force, even in protecting Christians. There is, however, also a note of acknowledgment to the effect that, of all the baptismal writings Grebel had read, all except Müntzer's advocate infant baptism.[1]

This does not suggest that it was Müntzer who brought Grebel and his friends to their position concerning baptism, for although Grebel admits that Müntzer's work is the best he has read, the pamphlet does not specifically demand believers' baptism as a *sine qua non*—and Grebel suspects that for Müntzer the outward form of baptism is, in the final analysis, unimportant. This was probably true; certainly Müntzer was never a re-baptizer. The total impression gained from this letter is that Grebel and his group had already reached their position on the church, the sacraments, the use of the sword, etc., before they read Müntzer's pamphlet, but that when they read it they recognized him as a possible supporter and wrote to him stating their point of view[2] and criticizing him on certain points where they suspected him of being "unsound". As things turned out they would find that Müntzer differed from them on almost every issue.

In view of what we have written we may suggest four conclusions concerning the origins of evangelical Anabaptism.

1. That this Anabaptist movement was a child of the Reformation in general and the Zwinglian Reformation in particular.

2. That the origins of such Anabaptism were fundamentally entirely religious though with its challenge to the accepted church/state relationship it had certain political implications.

3. That the idea of a separated fellowship of believers and the connected practice of believers' baptism were first put into practice in the Reformation context in Zürich in January 1525.

[1] G. Mecenseffy (*loc. cit.*) differs from Bender on the interpretation of this letter from Grebel to Müntzer.

[2] G. Goeters (*loc. cit.*) indicates that the Grebel group had reached a clear position in the early summer of 1524.

4. That there was opposition to infant baptism amongst the Wittenberg radicals, and this may have both encouraged the Zürich group in their stand and also have helped to prepare the ground for the reception of Anabaptism as it spread beyond the borders of Switzerland.[1]

This is a somewhat radical modification of the view of Köhler indicated at the beginning of this section. It is the conclusion towards which available evidence points at the moment; but there is much material concerning the Anabaptists hidden away in archives, and evidence may yet be discovered which will cause a revision of the conclusions so far suggested.

F. *The Spread of the Anabaptist Movement*

It is outside the scope of this present work to give a detailed history of the subsequent spread of the Anabaptist movement throughout Europe. The briefest of summaries must suffice.

From Zürich, persecution sent the Anabaptists in several directions. Northwards, William Reublin went to Schaffhausen and on to Waldshut, where Balthasar Hubmaier and a hundred and ten others joined the movement on Easter Sunday 1525. From Waldshut Jacob Gross seems to have been one of the earliest Anabaptist ambassadors to carry the movement to Strasbourg. Here too in 1526 came Michael Sattler, who is the most likely author of the earliest Anabaptist confession of faith, the seven Schleitheim Articles.[2] From Waldshut, Hubmaier moved on to Augsburg where there were soon flourishing Anabaptist congregations. In Augsburg, Hubmaier baptized Hans Denck,[3] a man of considerable personality and education, who took over the leadership of the Anabaptist congregation when Hubmaier moved to Nikolsburg.

Eastwards the movement went from Switzerland to the mountainous regions of the Tyrol, carried thither possibly by George Blaurock. Severe persecution in the Tyrol and south

[1] The influence of the Waldensian movement in helping to prepare the ground for Anabaptism cannot be ruled out.

[2] B. Jenny, *Das Schleitheimer Täuferbekenntnis 1527*.

[3] See article in C. Hege and D. C. Neff (eds.), *op. cit.*, and G. Baring and W. Fellmann, *Hans Denck, Schriften*, xxiva and xxivb, in series *Quellen und Forschungen zur Reformationsgeschichte*.

Germany drove the Anabaptists still further eastwards to Nikolsburg in Moravia, which became a vast Anabaptist refugee centre—at one time it was estimated that there were twelve thousand Anabaptists there. Hubmaier arrived in 1526 and before long there was a split in the Anabaptist camp on the question as to whether they should pay the war tax levied by the authorities. Hubmaier led the party which said they should. Jacob Wiedemann led the pacifist opponents to Hubmaier. Wiedemann's group also advocated the institution of community of goods. This latter group moved on eastwards to the village of Bogeneitz in neighbouring Austerlitz and here Wiedemann laid down his cloak in a field to receive all that the community possessed. This was the beginning of the chequered career of a remarkable community known as the Hutterian Brethren, after Jacob Huter who succeeded Wiedemann as leader. This group preserved many Anabaptist records, not the least important of which is the confession of faith of Peter Rideman, produced in 1541 and published in English for the first time in 1950.[1] There can be little doubt that this 200-page confession represents fairly accurately the theology of the Anabaptists.

It is clear that there was also a southward movement into southern Switzerland and northern Italy, though this movement is not so easy to trace. But before long Anabaptism appears near Venice and in this area seems to have been quickly influenced by the anti-Trinitarian views set forth by Servetus in 1531 in his first book on the Trinity.[2]

The Anabaptist apostle who travelled throughout northern Germany and the Low Countries was Melchior Hofmann.[3] He was a man of considerable zeal, but unfortunately his teaching was vitiated by tenets which helped to lead to the discrediting of the whole Anabaptist movement. His Christology was Docetic. He found it impossible to believe that Christ bore anything of man's sinful flesh from Mary and he taught that Christ was born out of Mary but not of

---

[1] This confession contains an article on Original Sin with a doctrine not dissimilar to that of Zwingli (English edit.), 56ff. C.R. (Zwingli), v, 372f. R. Pfister, *Das Probleme der Erbsünde bei Zwingli.*

[2] *De Trinitatis Erroribus.*

[3] Article in *Mennonitisches Lexikon*, ii, 326ff.; also H. J. Schoeps, *Von Himmlischen Fleisch Christi*, 38ff., and C. H. Williams and A. M. Mergal (eds.), *op. cit.*, 182ff.

Mary. So we find time and again the accusation of defective Christology being levelled at Anabaptists from the area in which Hofmann travelled. To make matters worse, Hofmann was also an apocalyptic visionary. He was convinced of the nearness of the second coming of Christ and that he himself was the prophet Elijah, the first of the two witnesses of the approaching end, which Hofmann dated 1533 in Strasbourg. This sort of teaching proved to be potentially dangerous; for when, in the Netherlands, the movement underwent severe persecution as the result of the startling advances it had made under Jan Matthys, the idea became prevalent that the saints were called to set up the kingdom by force in preparation for the returning Lord. So there took place the fantastic events in the city of Münster from 1533 to 1534 when a group captured and held the city which they believed to be the scene of the coming kingdom of God.

The facts of the Münster episode are too well known to need repetition here. We would only suggest that three factors produced the situation. The quite incredible persecution of the Anabaptists in the Netherlands in the early 1530s when to be buried alive was a relatively pleasant way of dying; the apocalyptic violence to which an extension of Hofmann's teaching .might lead; the fact that such a situation usually produces a leader, unbalanced, who can turn it to the exaltation of himself and lives a short life of glory—and of madness. So it was in Münster with Jan of Leiden (John Bockelson)—who was scarcely sane. It was he who instituted polygamy in Münster in the face of considerable opposition and against all the strict morality of the general Anabaptist movement.[1] The frantic, stricken Anabaptists fled from the Low Countries to Münster, there to enact an episode which besmirched the name of the Anabaptist movement for three hundred and fifty years. Yet only a very small group within the Anabaptist movement was involved and the methods they adopted were contrary to the teaching of earlier and later Anabaptism. Even in Holland, at that time, there were Anabaptists led by Obbe and Dirk Phillips who rejected the enthusiastic excesses of Jan Matthys. The affair of Münster does not stand in the

---

[1] Against even the *Bekenntnis des Glaubens und Lebens der Gemeinde Christi zu Münster*, published earlier in 1534.

main stream of Anabaptist thought and practice, and whilst it is certainly not right to divorce Münster entirely from Anabaptism, neither is it correct to judge the whole Anabaptist movement by Münster.

The immediate result of Münster was to bring to an end the Anabaptist movement as an effective force in Europe. Anabaptism became equated with Münster. The whole movement stood condemned by the excesses of the minority driven frantic by persecution and led by a near madman. Persecution of the Anabaptists became more and more severe and in the years 1535 to 1546 it is estimated that many thousands were put to death in Holland and Friesland alone. Some fled to England and in these years evidence of Anabaptist activity in Kent and Essex begins to appear. A further result of Münster was its effect upon Calvin. He could never again keep cool about baptism, nor about Anabaptism, and, building upon the foundations laid in Reformation times by Zwingli and Bullinger, he erected an edifice of covenant theology to support the practice of infant baptism.[1]

Yet after Münster a remnant of Anabaptism remained. The Hutterian communities in Moravia survived. And even in Holland and north Germany all was not lost. For in Holland there arose a new leader named Menno Simons, an ex-Roman Catholic priest whose brother had been killed in Anabaptist riots in Holland at the time of Münster. Menno left the Roman Catholic Church in 1536 and took office in one of the groups associated with Obbe and Dirk Phillips. He became a travelling missionary and gathered together the Anabaptist remnants of northern Europe into a new movement which still bears his name—the Mennonites. With a group of these Mennonites at least one exile English Separatist congregation later had contact. Severe persecution drove the anti-Trinitarian elements out of north Italy and southern Switzerland eastwards until eventually they reached Poland where, under the influence of Faustus Socinus, a strong Unitarian movement developed, whose tenets were summed up in the Racovian Catechism of 1605 and whose subsequent persecution and banishment in 1651 led to the appearance in England of Unitarian theology and churches.

[1] *Institutes*, iv, 16.

G. *The Forerunners of English Separatism*

We must now turn to events in England, and indicate the main outline of the much better known story of the rise of the Separatist movement and the beginning of the English Baptist Separatists.[1]

No description of the background of any Reformation movement in England in the sixteenth century can be complete without, at least, a passing reference to Lollardy. In the fifteenth century Lollardy had declined, certainly in the academic circles, but its strength amongst the people in the land during the first decades of the sixteenth century is one of the many tantalizing unknowns of history. What can be said is that in 1512 and 1521 the bishops had to take action against Lollardy and that it is known to have been stronger in the south of England and especially in the south-east. It was into this part of England that many of the Anabaptist refugees from the Continent came in the 1530s and it is in this part of the country that we hear most of the authorities grappling with the Anabaptists. This is to be expected, but whether they found a welcome in Lollard groups we can never tell for certain. But ground prepared by Lollardy for the reception of Reformation ideas, and extreme Reformation ideas especially, can never be ruled out.

With the persecution in the Netherlands and Germany in the years after 1534 intensifying, Anabaptist refugees begin to appear in England. On May 25, 1535, twenty-five Dutch Anabaptists were examined at St. Paul's and from their statements it is clear that, in addition to denying infant baptism and holding Zwinglian views of the Lord's Supper and probably of original sin also, they accepted Hofmannite Christology.[2] Fourteen of them were burnt, two at Smithfield, but the rest were sent to other towns to suffer, which may suggest the need for widespread warning concerning the faith of Anabaptists. At the Anabaptist Synod held at Bockhold in Westphalia in 1536 there were representatives from England and some of the expenses of the Synod are said to have been borne by someone from England. When

---

[1] Cf. C. Burrage, *The Early English Dissenters* (2 vols.), and A. Peel, *The First Congregational Churches*.

[2] J. Stow, *Chronicles of England*.

participants in the so-called Pilgrimage of Grace presented their demands to Henry VIII, included was the request to stamp out heresies—especially those of the radicals. The king was forced to appoint a commission of clergy with Cranmer as chairman, in 1538, to search for Anabaptists and their books and later in the same year more Dutch Anabaptists were burnt. All this evidence indicates that during Henry's reign Anabaptists were in England and the measures taken against them tend to suggest that their numbers were not negligible.

During the reign of Edward VI there is considerable evidence for so-called Anabaptist activity. "So-called", for in fact it is by no means certain that those labelled Anabaptists were anything more than "half-way Anabaptists" as M. M. Knappen suggests.[1] In 1547 Ridley and Latimer were appointed to deal with Anabaptists in Kent and in the following year there appeared in English the first of many works of the Swiss Reformers written against Anabaptism.[2] During 1549 John Hooper published probably the first work written against the Anabaptists by an Englishman,[3] and he complains in a letter to Bullinger of Anabaptist hecklers at his public lectures at St. Paul's.[4] Hooper was, in fact, sent down to Kent and Essex in 1550 seemingly to deal with the increase of Anabaptism in that area.

At this time there appear evidences of groups of English sectaries in Kent and Essex, at Faversham and at Bocking. J. Strype recorded that "these were the first that made separation from the reformed Church of England, having gathered congregations of their own". He also suggested that they held the opinions of the Anabaptists and Pelagians.[5] In spite of this it does not appear that they were either Anabaptists or committed Separatists. Records of the examination of members of these groups are still extant[6] and it is plain that the members were certainly Englishmen and that they denied the doctrine of predestination, believed that

---

[1] *Tudor Puritanism*, 149.

[2] C. Burrage (*op. cit.*, i, 55) discusses the background of this work.

[3] *A Lesson on the Incarnation of Christ.*

[4] *Original Letters* (Parker Society), i, 65f.

[5] *Ecclesiastical Memorials*, ii, 1, 369.

[6] *Acts of the Privy Council of England* (New Series), iii, 53ff., and C. Burrage, *op. cit.*, 52ff.

Christ died for all men, rejected original sin, refused to communicate with known sinners, and absented themselves from communion in the parish churches. There is no reference to any practice of re-baptism.

These groups have been variously labelled. Gilbert Burnet called them "probably some of the Anabaptists".[1] R. W. Dickson (following Strype), called them "the first English Separatists".[2] C. Burrage suggested "that these early English conventicles . . . were merely Nonconformists (in the early meaning of that term) of a rather peculiar type".[3] Certainly they had not worked out any theory of Separatism and perhaps we may call them rather more than Nonconformists and rather less than Separatists. They were imprisoned but not burnt as was a Dutch Anabaptist in 1551. It is worthy of note that when the forty-two Articles were finally produced just before the death of Edward VI in 1553, no fewer than seventeen of the Articles can be construed as striking at some aspect of Anabaptist teaching, including, of course, Hofmannite Christology, denial of original sin and predestination, and the rejection of infant baptism.[4]

When it became clear that Queen Mary was going to lead the English church along the road that led to Rome, there appeared in London and elsewhere congregations which met secretly to worship according to the rites of the Edwardine church. These secret conventicles of Mary's reign are of interest to our study because there is clear evidence that they were viewed, by later Separatists, as setting a precedent. Evidence for these congregations is supplied chiefly by Foxe, but is confirmed by other sources. J. Foxe lists the places where the congregations met and these included Aldgate, Cheapside, Thames Street, Pudding Lane and on board a ship.[5]

From the examination of the records of proceedings taken against members of a congregation apprehended by the authorities, it is quite plain that they were indeed members of a group which met for worship, separated from, and

[1] *History of the Reformation*, iv, 48.
[2] *History of the Church of England*, iii, 206ff.   [3] *Op. cit.*, 51.
[4] Cf. C. Hardwick, *A History of the Articles of Religion*, 2nd ed., 84ff.
[5] J. Pratt (ed.), *Acts and Monuments*, viii, 558.

contrary to, the usages of the realm of England as then established. Several of the congregations paid for their Separatism with their lives. Evidence suggests that there was more than one of these congregations and the imprisoned John Hooper seems to have been in contact with one of them.[1] It is possible that Hooper encouraged these congregations in their stand, and this need not surprise us, for the same bishop had earlier written that when the ministry is corrupt and the sacrament used contrary to the institution of Christ, then "every man may, in his private room, with his Christian and faithful brothers, communicate according unto the order of scripture".[2]

The question as to whether there is any relationship between these Marian congregations and the Bocking and Faversham groups of Edward's reign is not easy to answer. C. Burrage thinks that a member of one of the Kent and Essex groups appears as a deacon in one of the London congregations.[3] It is certain that the Kent and Essex congregations were active during Mary's reign and for obvious reasons now appear as the "Freewillers". We find them in controversy with some of the Protestant prisoners in London gaols. But a close examination of the evidence provided by personnel and by theology seems to suggest that Burrage is mistaken. The truth of the matter appears to be that in Mary's reign we are dealing with two distinct types of sectaries, one the so-called Freewillers, whom we have met before in Edward's reign, and the other, the various congregations meeting secretly in London and following the orthodox doctrine and liturgy of Edward VI. There appears to be no evidence of continuity between the Freewillers and the later Separatists who denied the doctrine of predestination. As Knappen says, the movement seems to have been "overwhelmed by the waves of predestinarian orthodoxy which rolled in from the Continent in the early years of Elizabeth's reign".[4] Yet, in the last resort, who can say whether some trace of the Freewillers' thought did not perhaps survive the flood-tide of Calvinism?

In assessing the strength of Anabaptism, or certain strains

---

[1] *Later Writings of Bishop Hooper* (Parker Society), 588ff., 614ff.
[2] *Early Writings of Bishop Hooper* (Parker Society), 61.
[3] *Op. cit.*, 53. Cf. J. Foxe, *op. cit.*, viii, 454ff.   [4] *Op. cit.*, 151.

of Anabaptist teaching in England at this time, we need to remember the suggestion of Philip Hughes[1] that, of the some two hundred and eighty martyrs in Mary's reign, a considerable percentage of them were not in fact reformers pure and simple but were Anabaptists. This would mean a consideraable hold of Anabaptism upon Englishmen. Hughes can make out a strong case to support his suggestion, though whether he proves his main thesis (i.e. that therefore most of them would have been burnt by any monarch, Catholic or Protestant), may be doubted. Nor, for our purpose should we forget that while Protestants stood together in the flames at Oxford and elsewhere, their brethren in relative freedom in exile at Frankfort were quarrelling bitterly about church government and church liturgy. Of these factions, one group advocated, at least in theory, that ultimate authority was vested not in the ministers and elders but in the congregation. Clearly then, in recording the forerunners of the movement known as Separatism, there come into the reckoning the Anabaptists, the secret conventicles of Mary's reign, and the troubles of the church in Frankfort.

H. *The Formative Period of English Separatism*

When we come to the reign of Elizabeth I we enter upon the formative period of English Separatism. The Queen was resolved to steer the English Church on a middle course between Rome and Geneva. The result was very nearly an ecclesiastical shipwreck on the rocks of compromise. The enthusiastic Protestant exiles, returning to build Geneva's version of the early church in England's green and pleasant land, soon found that Elizabeth would countenance no such construction, partially, one feels, because the architect was John Calvin. Some of the exiles accepted the situation, agreed to fill some of the many vacant bishoprics, and hoped for better days—but others refused. Then came the Convocation of Canterbury of 1563. The would-be reformers both in and out of bishoprics hoped that a Puritan programme might be pressed through the Houses. But the Puritan party was defeated by one vote (59-58). After this rebuff, signs of a division within the Puritan ranks became clearer. Some of those within the establishment, notably

[1] *The Reformation in England*, ii, 254ff.

the returned exile bishops, although still sympathetic and still hopeful, grew daily more conservative; especially on the issue of ceremonies. Some of those not in office grew more and more impatient and extreme. We may see the writing on the wall and it reads "Nonconformity and Separatism".

In the two years following, the situation as far as uniformity of liturgical practice in the church was concerned can only be described as chaotic.[1] Matthew Parker, archbishop of Canterbury, very much desired to bring about uniformity, but it was a difficult and unpopular task. The Queen equally desired uniformity but at the same time was determined that somebody else should take the blame for the repercussions of such enforcement. At length, in 1566, Parker produced what have become known as *The Advertisements*.[2] These were Articles enforcing uniformity, and, in a cleverly written preamble, the archbishop veiled the fact that they were issued without royal authority. Every minister was to subscribe to them, and, as they included articles demanding vestments abhorrent to the Puritans, there was bound to be trouble.

Of the London clergy, 37 out of 100 refused to subscribe, and after a period of three months some of them were deprived. All over the country ministers suffered the same fate. There developed a pamphlet warfare on the questions of the Prayer Book and vestments. This grew more and more bitter. The deprived ministers grew more and more aggrieved. They could not hold office, they were in want, and, worst of all, the shortage of ministers was such that inefficient and ignorant men were appointed in their places. Not only the deprived clergy, but also some of the people, thought little of the church settlement to which the bishops demanded subscription. Quite clearly here was a situation ready made for the appearance of Separatism and, sure enough, evidence for groups meeting outside the established churches reappears from 1566 onwards.

In August 1566, Grindal, bishop of London, wrote to Bullinger giving an account of the situation and indicated

[1] J. Strype (*Life of Matthew Parker*, i, 302) preserves a report from Cecil entitled "Varieties in the Service and Administration used".

[2] H. Gee and W. J. Hardy (eds.), *Documents Illustrative of English Church History*, 467ff.

R

that some, both ministers and lay, had it in mind to separate.[1] From the years 1567 and 1568 various sources supply us with evidence of a growing number of congregations worshipping apart from the parish churches. Stowe's *Memoranda* even list the places where these congregations met, including Aldgate, Pudding Lane, Thames Street and on board a ship, which were some of the places in which the Marian congregations had met.[2] A letter from Grindal in 1568 indicates that these congregations had got as far as electing their own officers and exercising discipline. He says that these people have "openly separated from us".[3] There is evidence, in London, of several such congregations with a total membership of several hundreds. One of the earliest congregations apprehended, that known as the Plumbers' Hall congregation, agreed that they had worshipped separately and had their own ministers, and when asked what made them act as they did replied: "We remembered that there was a congregation of us in this city in Queen Mary's day."[4] This could well suggest that they separated and worshipped in the same places as the earlier secret congregations because some of the members from Queen Mary's days were members now.

Are we to call these early Elizabethan congregations Separatists? They are certainly Separatist in the negative sense, i.e. in that they refused to attend their parish churches, worshipping apart from the Church of England in private houses and using another form of service. But they appear to have no positive teaching concerning a church being made up of believers, covenanted together, gathered out of the world and denying the authority of temporal power over it. Perhaps we should not be far wrong if we called them "liturgical Separatists" as against the more clearly defined "doctrinal Separatists" such as Robert Browne who appeared a decade later.

Yet there is another link in the chain of development of Separatism before we reach Robert Browne, and that is the congregation of Richard Fitz. This is the first-known

---

[1] *Zürich Letters* (Parker Society), i, 168.

[2] *Three 15th Century Chronicles with Historical Memoranda* (Camden Society), 143.

[3] *Zürich Letters*, i, 201, "*apertam defectionem a nobis fecerunt*".

[4] *Grindal Remains* (Parker Society), 203.

congregation in England which had a covenant. To obey this covenant each member separately pledged himself and then took communion as a ratification of his consent. A further document, dated 1571, connected with this congregation, is the most advanced Separatist manifesto of the earlier Elizabethan sectaries—part of one sentence reads "according to the saying of the Almighty our God, Matt. 18: 20, where two or three are gathered in my name there am I so (are) we a poor congregation whom God has separated from the churches of England and from the mingled and false worshipping therein used. . . ."[1] This is on the way to anticipating Robert Browne. Dr. Albert Peel believed that Richard Fitz's church "was in practice, a true congregational church".[2] Certainly later Separatists wrote of Richard Fitz's church that it "professed and practised that cause (Brownism) before Mr. Browne wrote for it".[3]

Robert Browne is generally reckoned to be the father of English Separatism,[4] although, as we have seen, implicit Separatism ante-dates him. It was in the year 1581 that the first Brownist congregation was gathered at Norwich. The path by which Browne was led to his clear doctrinal Separatism is fairly clear to see. He first found himself in conflict with the bishops, not because he objected to the episcopal office as such but for at least four reasons. He believed that the bishops possessed usurped power in that the people had no choice as to the bishops and ministers.[5] He believed that the bishops forced their own laws and practices upon the people, contrary to the authority and Word of God.[6] He claimed that the bishops dressed themselves and the ministers in the marks of the Antichrist.[7] He maintained that the bishops allowed known sinners to mingle with the faithful in partaking the Lord's Supper.[8]

Quite clearly the first and fourth reasons are of considerable importance, involving as they do the question of authority in, and doctrine of, the church. For all these reasons Browne advocated Separatism. "For where open

---

[1] C. Burrage, *op. cit.*, ii, 16f.   [2] *Op. cit.*, 41.

[3] Miles Micklebound, *Mr. Henry Barrowe's Platform*, i, 7 verso.

[4] A. Peel and L. H. Carlson (eds.), *The Writings of Robert Harrison and Robert Browne*, N.C.T., ii.

[5] N.C.T., ii, 400.   [6] *Ibid.*, 414.   [7] *Ibid.*, 419.   [8] *Ibid.*, 402.

wickedness is incurable and Popish prelates do reign up-
holding the same, there is not the Church and kingdom of
God."[1] There must be immediate reformation without tarrying for any, not even for those who would wait for the
magistrates' permission to reform.[2] This attitude clearly
echoes that of the Zürich Anabaptists more than half a
century earlier. The magistrate is not to interfere in ecclesiastical matters. "How then should the Pastor, which hath
the oversight of the magistrate, if he be of his flock, be so
overseen of the magistrate, as to leave his flock when the
magistrate shall unjustly and wrongfully discharge him?"[3]
There is evidence, however, that Browne was not absolutely
certain about the magistrate having no control over the
church. He feels that the magistrates should look to the
"outward provision and outward justice" of it. "But to
compel religion, to plant churches by power and to force a
submission to ecclesiastical government by laws and penal-
ties belongeth not to them."[4]

Browne put his Separatism into practice in Norwich. He
gathered his people together out of the world. They covenanted together and they elected their officers.[5] His definition
of the church runs thus: "The church planted or gathered,
is a company or number of Christians or believers, which by a
willing covenant made with their God, are under the
government of God and Christ, and keep his laws in one
holy Communion."[6] It is a fellowship of believers. Browne
gave detailed instructions for the election and ordination of
church officers and for every aspect of church life and
thought. Although each congregation could make its own
decisions, under God, Browne did not believe that it should
ignore all other congregations, and he advocated what may
be termed a loose form of connexionalism.[7]

In Robert Browne we have set before us a pattern and
idea of church life which we have come to know as the
congregational type. His church was a covenanted fellowship
of believers outside the authority of the magistrate. But he
held fast to infant baptism. "The children of the faithful,
though they be infants, are to be offered to God and the
Church, that they may be baptized. Also those infants or

---

[1] N.C.T., ii, 405.   [2] *Ibid.*, 413, 153.   [3] *Ibid.*, 154.
[4] *Ibid.*, 164.   [5] *Ibid.*, 422f.   [6] *Ibid.*, 253.   [7] *Ibid.*, 270f.

children which are of the household of the faithful and under their full power. Also all of discretion which are not baptized, if they hold the Christian profession and show forth the same."[1] Infant baptism, yet not indiscriminate infant baptism but only baptism of those children of believing parents, is here indicated. The theological implication of this distinction between the children of believing and non-believing parents, which is still made to-day, must needs be examined in a later chapter.[2]

Robert Browne recanted his Separatism and conformed. Yet he had stimulated a movement which could not simply cease when its chief spokesman deserted. It was a movement which issued in the English Free Churches.

Before going on to trace the origins of the English Baptists we must glance very briefly at events in London. In spite of the appointment of the determined John Whitgift to the See of Canterbury in 1583, Separatism in London in the years after 1585 took on a new lease of life with congregations meeting in Aldgate and elsewhere. Whether this increased activity had anything to do with the presence in the city of Robert Browne—supposedly now submissive to the established church—is not certain. It certainly coincided with the coming of John Greenwood and Henry Barrow. Barrow himself set out four reasons for Separatism which are identical with those we noted in Robert Browne.[3] The covenanted congregations with which Barrow and Greenwood were connected reflected all the views of Separatism that we have already indicated together with three additional points worthy of comment. Now that the office of the apostles had ceased, public ministers are no longer required; any private man, who is a brother, whatever his calling, may preach.[4] All prayer is to be extempore, none is to be read, and even the Lord's Prayer is not to be used.[5] In view of the unsatisfactory ministry in the Church of England, children are to be left unbaptized until a suitable minister can be found.[6] It is not surprising that this group was accused of re-baptizing, i.e. Anabaptism, but there is no evidence that they did in fact re-baptize.

---

[1] N.C.T., ii, 256ff.   [2] *Infra*, 321f.
[3] *Transactions of Congregational Historical Society*, ii, 292ff.
[4] C. Burrage, *op. cit.*, i, 126.   [5] *Ibid.*   [6] *Ibid.*

Barrow, Greenwood and Penry, a Separatist sympathizer, were all hanged for their stand. Francis Johnson assumed charge of the congregation in 1592 with a four-fold Genevan order of ministry. In spite of increased numbers, or perhaps because of them, they forsook their dangerous existence in London for the precarious life of a congregation in exile and finally settled in Amsterdam.

During these formative days of Separatism Anabaptist activity in England continued. In 1560 and 1562 the Queen had to take action against them, the Proclamation in the latter year banishing them, "whether they were natural-born people of the land, or foreigners". Does this mean that there were English Anabaptists? If taken at its face value it does. But the other available evidence is silent about English Anabaptists. At Easter 1575 thirty Anabaptists were arrested in Aldgate, but these were all Dutchmen with the familiar Hofmannite Christology. In 1589 the Master of Peterhouse, Cambridge, spoke of several Anabaptist conventicles in London and added that some of their members had been educated at the universities. But when he goes on to describe their tenets it appears that he is most certainly describing congregations such as that led by Greenwood and Barrow. Anabaptists in England there certainly were, yet irrefutable evidence of English converts to Anabaptism or an English Anabaptist congregation during the reign of Elizabeth I there certainly is not.

I. *The English Baptist Separatists*

We come finally to outline the story of the origins of the English Baptist Separatists. In the main we shall be concerned with the spiritual pilgrimage of John Smyth[1] from Anglican to Puritan, from Puritan to Separatist, and from Separatist to Baptist Separatist.

Like most of the Separatists, Smyth was a Cambridge man. He matriculated at Christ's in 1586 and the tutor to whom he was first assigned was Francis Johnson of whom we have already heard. After graduating Smyth became a Fellow and was ordained in 1594 by the bishop of Lincoln.

---

[1] W. T. Whitley, *The Works of John Smyth*, i, ii. Research into the life of John Smyth is at present being actively pursued and there are indications that certain of Whitley's conclusions concerning Smyth may have to be challenged.

In 1600 he was elected Lecturer to the city of Lincoln, which meant, in fact, that he would be city preacher. From his sermons of this time it appears that he had adopted the position of a moderate Puritan. He held to the Genevan pattern of the ministry yet at the same time seems to have accepted the necessity of bishops to govern. In his sermons on the Lord's Prayer he makes it plain that he is aware of Separatist activity, notably that in London, for he comments on those who reject the use of the Lord's Prayer or any other prescribed form of prayer.[1] Smyth lost his position in Lincoln in 1602 owing to the defeat of his supporters on the city council. He was dismissed on the technical point of his failure to obtain a bishop's licence to preach and for "personal preaching". For the next few years he apparently travelled about, visiting London and Cambridge. By 1606 he was living in Gainsborough and struck up new friendships notably with Thomas Helwys of Broxtowe Hall in Basford, Nottingham. The vicar of Gainsborough was a permanent absentee and Smyth on one occasion conducted an unorthodox form of service in the Parish Church. When an episcopal visitation brought this occurrence to light Smyth received no commendation for his enthusiasm and concern for the people—rather the reverse.

Events were conspiring to drive the now Puritan Smyth towards Separatism. James I was on the throne and the ecclesiastical authorities were striving more strongly than ever for conformity and issued new Canons. The outcome of the Hampton Court Conference, from which the Puritans had hoped for so much, had been unsatisfactory and more than a few of the nonconformists within the establishment were being forced to face up to the issue of Separation. A group of ministers, including Smyth, met in Coventry in 1606. Smyth was by this time arguing for Separation and did so at this conference. Whitley indicates Smyth's argument thus:

> He took the bold line that the result of Hampton Court and the new Canons was to refuse all reformation, that it revealed the Church of England as an institution corrupt, and contentedly corrupt, with ministers corrupt, worship corrupt;

[1] W. T. Whitley, *The Works of John Smyth*, i, 81.

therefore it behoved every man who would not himself be corrupted to linger no longer but depart out of Babylon.[1]

Such discussions went on in many places and from Suffolk there came to Smyth a request for his advice on the matters in hand. Smyth's reply shows that by this time he was quite certainly a Separatist.[2] The church should consist of saints only. Each congregation should elect its own minister. The true worship needs no outward help of devised forms of prayers and ceremonies. The primitive form of church government was by a college of pastors or presbytery. None of these conditions holds good in the Church of England so all the faithful must make Separation. The echo of Browne and Barrow is surely too strong to be so coincidental.

With this position Smyth's next step must be to gather a congregation in the Gainsborough area. This he did, sometime in 1606. They covenanted together "to walk in all his [the Lord's] ways, made known or to be made known unto them, according to their best endeavours, whatsoever it should cost them, the Lord assisting them".[3] They were indeed faithful to their covenant. Smyth renounced his ordination and was elected and ordained minister by the congregation. The movement spread and was joined by John Robinson, who assisted Smyth in the care of the widespread congregation. The thought of Smyth and his congregation was typically Separatist; one point only needs to be mentioned. The fourfold pattern of ministry was absent. Two types only were instituted: the elders (pastors) to deal with the spiritual affairs and the deacons (or widows) to deal with material affairs. This ministry was not thought to be of the *esse* of the church; merely of the *bene esse*, it added nothing except order. During 1606 and 1607 the ecclesiastical authorities intensified their attack upon Separatism and eventually in 1607 or 1608 the Lincolnshire groups left for Amsterdam in an emigration largely organized, and probably financed, by Thomas Helwys.

In Amsterdam the congregation settled in the bakery of Jan Munter, a Mennonite. Soon after their arrival they were followed by John Robinson, who took part of the group to Leiden and gathered a new congregation there. It was part

[1] W. T. Whitley, *The Works of John Smyth*, i, lviii.
[2] *Ibid.*, ii, 557ff.   [3] *Ibid.*, i, lxii. (Quoted from Bradford.)

of this same group that in 1620 emigrated to the New World, achieving undying fame as the Pilgrim Fathers.

The church of Francis Johnson was also in Amsterdam but before long the two congregations were in conflict over several matters. Smyth published his account of this conflict in his pamphlet *Differences of the Churches of the Separation*.[1] It is not necessary for us to go into the dispute in detail, but one matter calls for mention. There was a difference of opinion on the question of the authority of the ministry *vis-à-vis* the church. Smyth put the ultimate authority on the shoulders of the church, i.e. all the church members. If the majority of the church agree about anything and the elders disagree, the matter nevertheless is accepted. Anybody may bring anything to the church without first referring the matter to the elders. The task of the officers is to lead and to moderate. But the church can function without officers and the church does not delegate her authority to the ministry when she ordains them. Yet important though this issue was—and is—a matter of even greater import arose at the same time: that of baptism.

We have seen that Smyth argued that if the worship, ministry, government and constitution of the Church of England were not of apostolic institution the faithful should separate. We have seen that Smyth renounced the ordination he had received from the bishop. We have seen that his church rejected the worship, government and constitution of the Church of England; the question was now raised as to the validity of the baptism and confirmation they had received from a ministry not of apostolic institution in a church from which they had now separated. They felt that logic demanded the rejection of such a baptism. But more than that, their reading of the New Testament suggested to them that the apostolic practice was not infant baptism, but believers' baptism. The New Testament section of this present work would seem to confirm that, like the Anabaptists of Zürich before them, Smyth and his friends did not misinterpret either the theology or the practice of the apostolic days. The result was the writing of the first statement by an Englishman arguing for believers' baptism. It is Smyth's pamphlet *Character of the Beast*.[2]

[1] W. T. Whitley, *The Works of John Smyth*, i, 269ff.   [2] *Ibid.*, ii, 563ff.

It argues two propositions; that infants are not to be baptized and that anti-Christians converted are to be admitted into the true church by baptism. Smyth argues that the true church was that of believers entered by baptism after confession of repentance and faith. The churches that baptized infants are of false constitution. In this respect the Separatist churches are of the same false constitution as the Church of England,

> therefore the Separation must either go back to England or go forward to true baptism: and all that shall in time to come separate from [the church of] England must separate from the baptism of [the church of] England and if they will not separate from the baptism of [the church of] England there is no reason why they should separate from [the church of] England as from a false church.[1]

This argument again clearly raises theological issues which must be considered in a later chapter. Is there any ecclesiological reason for churches practising infant baptism to remain separate from the Church of England?

Some time in 1609 Smyth put his theory into practice. The congregation, together with Smyth, acknowledged their previous errors, even of covenanting in Gainsborough, and went back to the beginning again, viewing themselves as anti-Christians converted. They desired now to form a church of believers through believers' baptism. But who was to do the baptizing? Eighty-four years previously the Zürich group were faced with the same problem; then Grebel baptized Blaurock and Blaurock the rest. But now Helwys and Smyth discussed the matter and finally Smyth baptized himself by affusion and then baptized the others. Thus the first English Baptist church was formed—albeit on foreign soil.

Naturally the whole affair and notably Smyth's action in baptizing himself was the subject of much criticism. One critic asked why, if he desired re-baptism, he did not apply to the Mennonites who practised believers' baptism.[2] Possibly this struck home to Smyth, for he began negotiations on behalf of his church with the Waterlander Mennonites to whom Jan Munter belonged. As the result of his approach

[1] W. T. Whitley, *The Works of John Smyth*, ii, 567.

[2] J. H. (John Hetherington or Joseph Hall) in *A Description of the Church of Christ with her peculiar privileges* (1610), 23.

Smyth received a confession of faith from the Mennonites
to study and before long Smyth's church replied with a
confession of twenty articles.[1] This Confession is of considerable interest for, in addition to asserting believers'
baptism, it departs still further from orthodox Calvinistic
Puritan Separatist doctrine, in which Smyth had been
nurtured, in that it denies the extreme doctrine of original
sin and also asserts that the grace of God is for all men and
that He desires all men to be saved. From this time onwards
the Arminian strain becomes explicit in Baptist thought and
gave the name to the General Baptists. It is possible that
Smyth and his congregation learnt these emphases from their
contact with the Mennonites. Certainly Smyth would have
heard something like it from Peter Baro in his Cambridge
days; certainly, too, the Arminian controversy was raging in
Holland at that very time; yet its sudden appearance at this
point in Smyth's thought is suggestive of Mennonite influence.

It is interesting that the plea for religious toleration, so
dear to the hearts of the Anabaptists and their descendants,
also appears almost immediately in Smyth and Helwys.
Whether the Mennonite practice of believers' baptism had
any prior influence on the Englishmen's decision to institute
that rite is very uncertain. The decision, as we have seen,
looks very much like the logical working of Smyth's mind,
though his thinking may have been stimulated by the
knowledge that certain individual English exiles had earlier
gone over to Anabaptism. That there was some Mennonite
influence on the Baptist groups is surely vouched for by the
practice of foot-washing, which appeared soon after the
Baptists returned to England.

It was not long before Helwys and certain others began
to have doubts concerning the application which Smyth was
now making for membership with the Mennonites, and they
tried to prevent negotiations going forward. They hesitated
on two scores. They were concerned at the suggestion that
the Mennonites held a Hofmannite doctrine of the Incarnation, but whether this is so is not clear; their tendency
was not to be too explicit in trying to explain the paradox of
God becoming man. More important, however, was the disagreement with the Mennonites' emphasis on the need for

[1] W. T. Whitley, *op. cit.*, ii, 681f.

some succession in the ministry. The Mennonites insisted that elders should be ordained by elders. Helwys and others could not accept this. They believed that it was the task of each local church to elect and ordain its own officers, with the natural corollary that the officers so elected and ordained had authority only in the congregation in which they ministered. These reasons seemed sufficient for Helwys and fifteen others to separate from Smyth. Smyth and some thirty others proceeded with their negotiations, but things moved slowly. Smyth never lived to see the request for membership granted, for he died in 1612, but granted it was, and on January 21, 1615, those remaining of his group were admitted to membership of the Mennonite church and their separate identity disappeared.

Meanwhile, towards the end of 1612, Helwys and his group returned to England where they founded the first known Baptist church in England at Spitalfields in London. This was the beginning of the General Baptists in England. We have commented upon their theology as it developed in Amsterdam, notably after contact with the Mennonites, yet it must be remembered that it was a difference of opinion with the Mennonites that was a contributory factor to the refusal of Helwys to support Smyth in his application.

It only remains for us to mention Helwys's famous contribution to the literature of the time, his work entitled *The Mystery of Iniquity*. This was addressed to King James I and is generally acclaimed as the first thorough-going plea for universal religious toleration made in England. It reminded the king that he was mortal and not God and therefore had no authority over the immortal souls of his subjects. The plea fell on deaf royal ears. Helwys was imprisoned and died sometime before 1616. The leadership of the group fell to John Murton, who was a native of Gainsborough and an original member of Smyth's church. He, too, deserves mention in connection with his plea for religious toleration.[1] He echoes, almost exactly, arguments used by Balthasar Hubmaier a century earlier in the first known plea for universal religious toleration, *Concerning Heretics and those that Burn Them*.

The General Baptist movement spread and by 1626 we

[1] W. K. Jordan, *Development of Religious Toleration in England*, ii, 299.

find clear evidence for the existence of four other churches, at Lincoln, Coventry, Salisbury and Tiverton. The five churches approached the Mennonites again and were received in friendly fashion, but negotiations broke down, chiefly on the issue of the ministry, the Mennonites maintaining that no unordained person could lead the worship.

Soon after this date a second strain of Baptist thought and life appeared in England. As far as can be ascertained, this movement arose independently of the General Baptists and without direct contact with the continental Anabaptist movement. In 1616 Henry Jacob returned from exile to form, traditionally in Southwark, what is usually called the first Independent church.[1] Jacob belonged to the type designated by Burrage, "Independent (or Congregational) Non-Separatist Puritan". In essence, this meant that each congregation in the Church of England was capable of determining its own policy and affairs without the oversight of the episcopacy or of synods. Hence, the apparently paradoxical Independent Non-Separatist title is given. The pattern of ecclesiastical life at the time, however, meant that in spite of this theory the church of Jacob was in practice Separatist. Nevertheless it is noteworthy that the Barrowist congregation in London viewed them with considerable suspicion, largely because members of Jacob's congregation sometimes attended parish churches. Jacob's church was founded on a covenant basis and the outline history of the subsequent life of this church is preserved, mainly in the Gould Manuscript[2] housed in the Angus Library of Regent's Park College, Oxford.

As early as 1620 the question of the rights and wrongs of complete separation began to be agitated in Jacob's church, for during this year a group came from Colchester to join the church although, the manuscript says, an old church of the separation was there. If this refers to a Colchester church of the Brownist-Separatist type, this group presumably desired an independent church order without entire separation. When, in 1624, Jacob emigrated to Virginia he was succeeded as pastor by John Lathrop and six years later there began a series of secessions from the church. In 1630, Mr. Dupper, who had been a member of

---

[1] C. Burrage, *op. cit.*, i, 281ff.   [2] Printed in full in *T.B.H.S.*, i, 193ff.

the Colchester group, decided that parish churches could on no account be regarded as true churches, and, when a member of the Jacob-Lathrop church had a child baptized in a parish church, Mr. Dupper and some others seceded and became Separatists in communion with the Barrowist church. There was a further secession from the mother church three years later led by Samuel Eaton who, with others, received a further baptism. By whom and why is not clear. It is not certain whether they rejected infant baptism as such or whether they were re-baptized because they viewed their baptism in the parish church as null and void. Very probably they rejected infant baptism as such, for in 1638 another group left the Jacob-Lathrop church because they agreed with Eaton, and this group is specifically said to have been convinced that baptism was not for infants but for professed believers.

It looks then as though 1633 may be reckoned as the date for the first-known group of Particular Baptists, so-called because, coming as they did direct from Calvinist Puritan stock, they held to the doctrine of predestination and believed that Christ died, not for all men, but only for the elect. We cannot be absolutely certain of the correct dating for the origin of this Particular Baptist movement, as the 1638 secession did not join with Eaton as might have been expected, but with a Mr. Spilsbury who appears here for the first time. A. C. Underwood conjectured that either Mr. Spilsbury had become pastor in the group which had contained Eaton, or had, independently since 1633, become pastor of an anti-Paedo-Baptist church.[1] A further possibility would be to suggest that Eaton and his group in 1633 received their baptism from Mr. Spilsbury, who might have been already functioning as an anti-Paedo-Baptist prior to 1633.[2] If this be true then the origins of the Particular Baptists are thrown still further back into obscurity! Whatever may be the truth, sometime before 1638 the first Calvinistic Particular Baptist church was founded.

So we have two strains of Baptist life in England on the eve of the Civil War. How they fared and how their life and

[1] *A History of the English Baptists*, 58.
[2] *T.B.H.S.*, i, 221, and n. 224, gives a quotation from a scurrilous rhyme which states that Spilsbury re-baptized Eaton.

thought developed in the subsequent years will be told in the next chapter.

J. *Baptism and the Church*

We have now traced the rise of the practice of believers' baptism during the century of the Reformation. It has involved us in telling the story of the rise of two movements, the Anabaptist on the mainland of Europe in the sixteenth century and the Baptist Separatists in England and Holland at the beginning of the seventeenth. We have seen that at one definite point the two movements were in contact and have suggested that some influence passed from the earlier to the later. Whether there was any influence at any other point can only be conjectural. We have shown that there is much more involved in the two movements than a return to the exclusive practice of believers' baptism; there is, for example, the doctrine of the church as a fellowship of believers, which in both cases seems to have arisen, in practice, prior to the return to believers' baptism. This was the church doctrine of the English Separatists, of Browne and of others.

We know that the Anabaptists were active in England from 1534 onwards—was there then perhaps influence on the Separatists? We are faced with the undeniable fact that so far no link at all has been discovered either in Norwich, where there was known to be a group of Dutch Anabaptists, or in London, where the Dutch Anabaptists met, as did the Separatists of Mary and Elizabeth's reigns, in Aldgate. M. M. Knappen sums up the position, "the available facts concerning the origin of the English Separatists have defied the best efforts of modern scholars to connect them with the continental sectaries".[1] It sometimes seems as if the silence is almost too complete! The pattern of events in Zürich in the 1520s and in England some half a century later was strangely parallel, but then, in many respects the situations which produced the pattern were similar. Yet as Dr. Payne has recently said on this issue: "Ideas had legs in the sixteenth and seventeenth centuries as they have to-day."[2]

---

[1] *Op. cit.*, 315. A dissertation by Irwin B. Horst on the Anabaptists in England has been submitted to the Free University of Amsterdam, but the present writer has thus far been unable to gain access to it. Cf. also "England", C. H. Smith, H. S. Bender et al., *Mennonite Encyclopaedia*, ii, 215ff.

[2] "Who were the Baptists?" in *B.Q.*, xvi (1955-56), 339ff.

The contact of the General Baptists with the descendants of the Anabaptists is undoubted. As far as Anabaptist contact with early Separatism is concerned, it seems that we shall never know the answer. But one wonders, if Anabaptism had not had such a bad name, whether Browne and others might have been willing to admit that they had, at least, heard of the Anabaptist doctrine of the church! Can it be that we are dealing with a case of unavowed origins?

Most important, however, for our purpose, is to see that both on the Continent and in England the return to the practice of believers' baptism was accompanied by a definite ecclesiology and attitude to the challenge of the Christian life. The theological relevance of such matters must needs be examined afresh in the light of present-day ecumenical discussions. The Baptist historian does not write his chapter only to show how the Baptist movement arose, but in order that he may illumine the work of the theologian.

Chapter

7

BAPTISMAL CONTROVERSIES, 1640-1900

by D. M. Himbury

IT is the task of this chapter to outline the development of what can be considered the classical arguments used in the baptismal controversy. These revolve around two main topics: the true subjects for baptism, and the valid mode.

The former question usually presupposed a difference in view concerning the relationship of the new covenant and the old, and the significance of the practice of proselyte baptism. Concerning the mode it is strange that it was the Paedo-Baptists who spoke of baptism as "dipping" in the sixteenth and early seventeenth centuries, rather than the Baptists. In the nineteenth century the positions were reversed. The Baptists would now go to almost any lengths to prove the necessity of baptism by immersion, as is seen in F. W. Gotch's *A Critical Rendering of the Word* βαπτίζω (1841), a study of the translations and renderings of the word in thirty-three ancient and modern languages, while the Paedo-Baptists became equally aggressive in the advocacy of the opposite point of view. However, towards the end of the period there are signs of another change on the part of Baptists. J. Leonard Russel, in *Baptism, its Mode and Subjects* (1877), is not prepared to demand that immersion is the only valid mode of the rite.

The baptismal controversy in these years divides itself into three periods. First, the lively debates of the Commonwealth and Restoration periods, when the subject had a political as well as a religious significance. Second, followed the calmer, more academic consideration of baptism in the late seventeenth and eighteenth centuries, when all the available evidence, especially the relevant Biblical and patristic passages, was carefully sifted and made to uphold the view of one party or the other. Third, the nineteenth century saw the revival of active, and often bitter strife, reflecting the ecclesiastical and intellectual turmoil of the mid-century. In some respects it is not one of the most interesting or important periods of history, but it has been felt necessary to include and critically to survey these years in order to help the reader to appreciate the way in which the modern Baptist views the subject.

Dr. J. R. C. Perkin, to whom I am greatly indebted for valuable suggestions regarding this survey, points out that for the Baptists of the eighteenth and nineteenth centuries the greatest problem lay in the definition of the relationship between baptism and the doctrine of the Holy Spirit. This led some, at the close of our period, to stress a more "sacramental" view. In baptism, they held, God really acts; by it the believer enters the church and receives new power by the gift of the Spirit. This view emphasized the God-to-man aspect of baptism, rather than the man-to-God, which had characterized much of Baptist thinking. The volume of literature produced by the controversialists is quite enormous, and this study can refer only to a small part of it.

A. *The Commonwealth and Restoration Periods*

The two groups of Baptists, General and Particular, demonstrated clearly their similarities, as well as the distinctive features in their respective attitudes towards baptism, in the clauses dealing with that subject in their Confession of Faith, issued in the seventeenth century. The Particular Baptist Confession of 1644, reprinted in 1646, 1651 and 1652, first speaks of *baptism in its relation with the church*, which

> as it is visible to us, is a company of visible Saints, called and separated from the world by the Word and Spirit of God, to the visible profession of the faith of the Gospel, being baptized into that faith, and joyned to the Lord, and each other, by mutual agreement, in the practical enjoyment of the Ordinances commanded by Christ their Lord and King.[1]

Such baptism is

[1] W. J. McGlochlin, *Baptist Confession of Faith* (1911), 183.

to be dispensed only upon persons professing faith or that are Disciples, or taught, who upon a profession of faith ought to be baptized.[1]

The following clause is devoted to *the mode of the ordinance*, this being the first direct reference of its kind to immersion in Baptist writings, unless the phrase of Leonard Busher, "dipped for dead", be given this significance.[2] This clause says:

> The way and manner of the dispensing of the Ordinance the Scripture holds out to be dipping or plunging the whole body under water: it being a signe, must answer the thing signified which are these: first, the washing the whole soul in the blood of Christ; secondly, that interest the Saints have in the death, burial, and resurrection; thirdly, together with a confirmation of our faith, that as certainly as the body is buried under water, and riseth againe, so certainly shall the bodies of the Saints be raised by the power of Christ in the day of the resurrection, to reign with Christ.

There is an interesting marginal note which says that the administrator and the subject are to wear "convenient garments", that the rite shall be conducted "with all modestie". This reflects one of the accusations brought against the early Baptists by their opponents, illustrated most graphically on the title-page of Featley's *Dipper Dipt*.

This confession goes on to say that Christ has shown that the one designed by Him to administer the ordinance is a "preaching disciple". In an Appendix to the second edition of this Confession, Benjamin Cox relates this view of baptism to his soteriology when he says that a true believer, whether baptized or not, is in a state of salvation and shall certainly be saved; yet such a believer ought, in obedience to his Lord's command, to desire baptism, for Christ makes such obedience of inestimable benefit to the believing soul, while no true believer could, in good conscience, disregard such an evidently divine ordinance.[3]

The 1656 Somerset Confession follows that of 1644 in most

---

[1] W. J. McGlochlin, *op. cit.*, 185.

[2] W. T. Whitley's discussion of this is seen in "Baptized—Dipped for Dead", in *B.Q.*, xi (1943), 177ff.

[3] See E. B. Underhill, *Confession of Faith* (1854), 57.

respects, and its clause on baptism brings together those points to which reference has been made and says

> that it is the duty of every man and woman, that have repented from dead works, and have faith towards God, to be baptized: that is, dipped or buried under the water, in the Name of our Lord Jesus, or in the Name of the Father, Son and Holy Spirit, therein to signify and represent a washing away of sin, and their death, burial and resurrection with Christ, and being thus planted in the visible Church and body of Christ, who are a company of men and women separated out of the world by the preaching of the Gospel, do walk together in communion in all the commandments of Jesus, wherein God is glorified and their souls comforted.[1]

In 1660 the General Baptists issued a Confession of Faith, which again relates baptism to "the gathered Church",[2]

> That the right and only way of gathering Churches (according to Christ's appointment) is first to teach or preach the Gospel to the Sons and Daughters of men; and then to Baptize (that is in English to Dip) in the Name of the Father, Son and Holy Spirit, or in the Name of the Lord Jesus Christ; such only of them as profess *repentance towards God and faith towards our Lord Jesus Christ*.[3]

The Confession also faces the problem of the status of the child within the visible church and of what is involved in the doctrine of salvation for the unbaptized infant. The clause we have quoted above continues by calling the sprinkling of children "a scriptureless thing" and says that those who hold it make the pure Word of God of no effect, rejecting the only way the New Testament knows of bringing members into the church. It differentiates between the old covenant, which brought children into the church by generation, and the new, which brings in believers by regeneration. Of the fate of infants it says:

> That all children dying in infancy, having not actually transgressed against the Law of God in their own persons are

---

[1] W. J. McGlochlin, *op. cit.*, 208.

[2] For a discussion on the view of baptism as an initiatory rite, held by many Baptists in this period, see J. M. Ross, "The Theology of Baptism in Baptist History", in *B.Q.*, xv (1953-54), 104ff.

[3] W. J. McGlochlin, *op. cit.*, 115.

only subject to the first death, *which comes upon them from the sin of the first Adam,* from whence they shall be all raised by the second *Adam;* and not that anyone of them (dying in that estate) shall suffer for Adam's sin, eternal punishment in Hell (which is the second death) for of such belongs the Kingdome of Heaven, not daring to conclude with that uncharitable opinion of others, who though they plead much for the bringing of children into the visible Church here on earth by *Baptism,* yet nevertheless by their doctrine that Christ dyed but for some, shut a great part of them out of the Kingdome of Heaven for ever.[1]

It was, of course, much simpler for the General than the Calvinistic Baptists, whose view of original sin and election separated them from their own Baptist brethren, to speak of the future that awaited the infant after death.

The main similarities and differences between these two groups of Baptists in their doctrine of baptism is seen as we compare and contrast the two most developed confessions, The Orthodox Creed of the General Baptists, published in 1678, and the Particular Baptist Confession of 1688 to which was added an Appendix on Baptism.

Both speak of baptism as an ordinance of the New Testament, ordained by the Lord Jesus, the only Law giver to the church, to be continued until *the end of the World.* They agree also that it is the sign of the believer's fellowship with Christ in His death and resurrection, of being ingrafted in His body, of the remission of sin and of the newness of life. The outward element of the ordinance is water and both Confessions say that baptism is to be done in the Name of the Father, Son and Holy Ghost (both omitting the earlier reference to baptism in the Name of Christ alone), "by immersion or dipping of the person", both adding that this mode is necessary to the due administration of the ordinance.[2] Neither of the Confessions is as dogmatic about who shall administer the sacrament as that of 1644: the 1678 Confession is most vague, saying simply that the act "ought by the minister or administrator, to be done in a solemn manner"; that of 1688 says of the Lord's Supper as of

---

[1] W. J. McGlochlin, *op. cit.,* clause x.

[2] A difference between these two Confessions is one of terminology. The Particular Baptists refer to baptism as an "ordinance", the General Baptists to "this holy sacrament".

baptism, "These holy appointments are to be administered by those only who are qualified and thereunto called, according (Matt. xxviii: 19; 1 Cor. iv: 1) to the commission of Christ".[1]

The great difference lies in that the Particular Baptist Confession makes no mention of infant baptism, simply saying that the proper subjects are those "who do actively profess repentance towards God, faith in and obedience to our Lord Jesus". On the other hand the Orthodox Creed explicitly condemns the "popish doctrine", "that those infants that die without baptism or have it not actually or in desire are not nor cannot be saved". It goes on to deny "their practice of admitting persons only upon an implicit faith of the Church and their superstitions and popish ceremonies of salt and spittle, and breathing on the face of the party baptized, together with their charms and hallowed lights. Neither do we believe that infants dying in infancy without baptism, go to purgatory, or *limbus infantum*".[2] In addition to this, another clause of the Confession[3] holds that little children dying before they are capable of choosing either good or evil, whether they are born of believing or unbelieving parents, shall be saved by the grace of God, the merit of Christ and the work of the Holy Spirit, and thus made members of the invisible church to enjoy everlasting life, and that baptism is not relevant to this issue. *Common to all Confessions is the belief that baptism administered to believers by immersion is the seal of the individual's covenant with Christ.*

The theological ferment of the years 1640-60 made these views one of the most controversial topics of ecclesiastical arguments, more so as many believed that the denial of infant baptism was a cause of political upheaval. In this period several histories of the Anabaptists of the Continent were published, laying stress on the happenings at Münster, and almost every one of them written simply to illustrate that the decay of the commonwealth must follow the rejection of what were regarded to be the traditional beliefs and practices of the church.[4] This lends to the debate an

---

[1] E. B. Underhill, *op. cit.*, 147.   [2] W. J. McGlochlin, *op. cit.*, 145.
[3] *Ibid.*, 157, "Of children dying in Infancy".
[4] W. T. Whitley's *Baptist Bibliography* gives the titles of nine such histories written in English, and with this purpose, between 1642 and 1660.

acrimony rooted in fear. Thus *A Short History of the Anabaptists of High and Low Germany* (1647) concludes with an appeal that the king and his parliament shall weed out all who relish Popery and suppress the growth of Anabaptism, "which is the canker of Religion and the gangrene of the State". It was this that led the early Baptists frequently to refer to themselves as those who are usually, though unjustly or falsely, called Anabaptists.[1] This political fear led to much abusive literature, supremely represented by Thomas Edwards' *Gangrena*; but over against this stood a theological factor. It was agreed by almost all in the Puritan tradition that the Scriptures contained a platform of church government, though they did not approach the Scriptures in the manner outlined for us in chapter 2 above. This led to a thorough consideration of Biblical teaching concerning baptism and caused some, such as John Tombes, John Milton and John Bunyan, to accept an anti-Paedo-Baptist view.

Typical of this concern is the chapter in which Richard Baxter, one of the great champions of the Paedo-Baptists, indicates the way in which he had grappled with this problem.[2] He tells us that when a young man he had many doubts concerning the lawfulness of infant baptism and spent much time in studying the question. He goes on

I had read Dr. Burges and (some years later) Mr. Bedford for Baptismal Regeneration, and heard it in the Common Prayer that God would bless Baptism to the infant's Regeneration (which I thought to be meant of a Real and not a Relative change). I soon discovered the error of this doctrine, when I found in Scripture that Repentance and Faith in the aged were ever prerequisite, and that no Word of God did make the end to infants which was prerequisite in others: and that signs cannot, by moral operations, be the instruments of a real change on infants, but only of a Relative: and that to dream of a Physical instrumentality was worse than Popish.

It was then he came to the conviction concerning the baptism of infants,

---

[1] Cf. the titles of the Baptist Confessions of 1644, 1646, 1660.
[2] *Plain Scripture Proof of Infants Church-Membership and Baptism* (1656).

that it might be a sign to enter them Church-members, and solemnize their Dedication to Christ, and to engage them to his people, and to take Him for their Lord and Saviour, and to confer on them remission of sins, and what Christ by the Covenant promised to the Baptized.

He was, however, still troubled by the silence of the Scriptures and the weak reasonings of many Paedo-Baptist divines. It was these scruples that prevented him from accepting a pastoral charge and he became a lecturer. While at Gloucester he had even spoken in extenuation of the Baptists against the attacks of a certain Mr. Winnel. He felt compelled, some time later, to dissociate himself from Baptist views, when he realized that the fruit of Anabaptism was Rantism. From the account we see how the theological and non-theological factors combine in creating the atmosphere for the baptismal controversies of the period.

There is little to distinguish the view of the nature of baptism held by Anglican, Presbyterian and Independents in these years. The belief expressed by the Assembly of Divines is little different from that expressed in the Thirty-Nine Articles, except in one important respect. The *Shorter Catechism* states:

> Baptisme is a Sacrament, wherein the Washing with Water in the name of the Father, and of the Son, and of the Holy Ghost, doth signifie and seal an ingrafting into Christ, and partaking of the benefits of the Covenant of Grace, and our engagement to be the Lords.[1]

This may be compared with Article XXVII of the Church of England which also speaks of baptism as a sign that distinguishes Christian men from others as also of his regeneration, new birth and grafting into the church. It is also the promised forgiveness of sins and of adoption to be the sons of God and the confirmation of faith and grace. As to the subjects of baptism, this Article adds that the baptism of young children is to be retained in the church as being most agreeable with the institution of Christ. The *Shorter Catechism* is more specific and says

> Baptisme is not to be administered to any that are out of the Visible Church, till they profess their faith in Christ and

[1] *The humble advice of the Assembly of Divines . . . concerning a Shorter Catechism* (London 1647), 15.

obedience to Him; but the infants of such as are members of the Visible Church are to be baptized.

This was one of the characteristic beliefs of the Puritans. William Perkins, for example, in the previous century, wrote that infants within the covenant are such as have at least one of their parents faithful to Christ, for such holy parents,

> though they cannot derive faith unto their posterity (for the sonnes of God are not made such by naturall generation, but by the Adoption of God the Father), yet may they believe both for themselves and others, according to the tenour of the covenant of grace . . . so then the faith of the Parents maketh those their children to be accounted in the Covenant, which by reason of their age doe not yet actually believe.[1]

This emphasis reflects the perpetual concern of all Puritanical thinkers that the essential sanctity of the church should never be violated by the admission of the unworthy. Indeed the margin of the *Geneva Bible* on Eph. 5: 26 speaks of baptism as the token that God has consecrated the church to Himself, and made it holy by His Word. The *Directory for the Publique Worship of God* (1644) justifies the baptism of the children of the faithful by claiming that they are "foederally holy" before baptism. It then goes on to consider its effect and says

> that the inward Grace and virtue of Baptism is not tyed to that very moment of time wherein it is administered, and that the fruit and power thereof reacheth to the whole course of our life: and that outward Baptism is not so necessary, that through the want thereof the Infant is in danger of Damnation, or the Parents guilty if they doe not contemne or neglect the Ordinance of Christ when and where it may be had.[2]

Christopher Love, the Cardiff-born Puritan who was executed in 1651, develops the theme of the fate of unbaptized infants. In one of his works he says that many people regard infancy as an age of innocence, as though they were harmless, or even without sin, and many women would wish to be with their children in hell. Yet while he would not claim that all infants are damned, for God has His own secret, gracious ways whereby they may be saved, yet should one live but a minute in the world, God may justly punish

---

[1] W. Perkins, *The Golden Chaine*, Works (1635), 73.   [2] *Op. cit.*, 40.

him for the sin of his nature.[1] In another work he holds that while in an adult faith comes from hearing the preaching of the Gospel, this rule does not apply to young infants; because they are not capable of understanding, God expects no more from them than they are capable of offering to Him. Children cannot exercise faith, but have "habitual faith" and "seminary grace", if they belong to the elect. If a child can have sin before he can act sinfully, so he can have grace before he can exhibit repentance.[2]

H. Hammond, the Anglican, expressed a complementary point of view in opposition to the views of John Tombes. He believes that the fact of original sin makes it essential that infants should be baptized and adds

> it was as reasonable for children to be called believers, who yet had no faith of their own, but only of their parents, etc., to bring them to Christ, as for the same children to be accounted sinners (as undoubtedly they are) which yet never committed any act of sin . . . 'tis the profession of faith, and not the possession of it, which is required as the qualification which authorized the Church to admit them to baptisme; and that being performed by the Infant's proxies in his name, the Church may very lawfully accept it of those who can performe no other in lieu of a personal profession.[3]

The sixteenth and seventeenth centuries saw also considerable discussion of the mode of baptism, among Paedo-Baptists. William Perkins expresses a generally held belief when he says that the ancient custom in baptism was "to dippe and as it were, to dive all the body of the baptized in the water"; but adds that the present accepted mode, especially in cold countries, is to sprinkle the baptized "by reason of children's weaknesses, for very few of ripe years are now adayes baptized". He claims that this change has been justified on the ground of charity and necessity.[4] Daniel Dyke says that John 3: 23 shows that baptism then was "the rite of dousing" but adds that this was more appropriate to Palestine than to a northern climate.[5] Daniel Featley makes a case for the mode of sprinkling after saying that dipping may be used in baptism and that the

---

[1] Hell's Terror (1653), 64.　　[2] The Soul's Cordiall (1653), 172.
[3] The Baptizing of Infants (1655), 5.
[4] Op. cit., 73.　　[5] Six Evangelical Histories (1617), 211.

Church of England allows and practises this, but he denies that baptism is tied to this form. He makes six points why sprinkling is a valid form of baptism.

1. Christ does not demand that His followers should be dipped, only that they should be baptized.

2. Baptism does not always mean dipping. He quotes as his evidence Matt. 3: 11, Acts 1: 5; 2: 3, Matt. 20: 23, Mark 10: 38 and Heb. 9: 10.

3. "If the thing or spiritual Act or Grace signified by baptism, may be sufficiently expressed without Dipping, then is not Dipping necessary in Baptism."

4. The outward act of baptism, representing the inward ablution of the Spirit, is expressed by sprinkling; his proof texts are Heb. 9: 13; 10: 22 and 1 Pet. 1: 2.

5. Sick people must not be excluded from baptism because of infirmity.

6. He refers to the scandal caused by men and women going together naked into rivers to be baptized.[1]

The Directory of Public Worship simply defines baptism as "Sprinkling and washing with water" and in discussing the mode is more concerned to emphasize that the rite shall not be administered by a private person, but by a minister of Christ, nor shall it take place in private houses, but before a congregation in a place of worship and there the ceremony shall not be performed at the place where the font had, in the past, been placed. It is, however, significant that many Anglicans and Puritans had recognized that *dipping* was the New Testament mode of baptism long before it became customary among Baptists.

The Baptists had also to contend with that part of the left-wing movement in English Puritanism which is usually comprehended in the title *The Religion of the Spirit*. Many in this movement found much to praise in the witness of the Baptists, though they considered that any insistence upon ecclesiastical ceremonies would stint the Spirit of God. William Erberry, the Welsh Puritan, who became associated with the mystic, Morgan Llwyd, at Wrexham said that "the baptized Churches" who are the "children of the waters" were the purest form of church-fellowship in his day, but he goes on,

[1] *The Dipper Dipt*, 7th edition (1660), 37.

> Those Churches that are in purest forms, that have not the
> appearance of the Spirit from on high, the Lord will roare in
> them, and will make every one of them to tremble . . . because
> therein they disobey the command of Christ: they tell their
> proselytes, you must be dipt, because you must obey the
> command of Christ. I say going forth to baptize, or be baptized,
> without the baptism of the Spirit on the Church, is not the
> command of Christ, but against it.[1]

He believes that mere water-baptism not only denies the
Spirit but also divides the church. He notes the lack of unity
among the Baptists themselves, which means, not simply
that they hold differing opinions on matters of doctrine,
but that one group will not "break bread" with another.
On the mode of baptism his opinion is most interesting.

> The way of baptizing in the primitive Churches was by way of
> washing the Disciples' feet, or believers going down into the
> waters up to the ankles, therefore John saith, whose shooe
> latchet I am not worthy to unloose. . . . When the Eunuch was
> baptized by Philip, 'tis said, He went down into the waters, or
> as the Greek, He went down unto the waters (up to the ankles)
> neither is it anywhere said, they put off their clothes, and
> then put them on again; never did I read of that in their
> catechisme; they say, He that is the minister must have a
> modest garbe, or garment, and those that are to be dipt must
> have garments; When Peter baptized five thousand in one
> day, where could the Apostles have so many garments at
> once? It is plain they have deceived the world and themselves,
> too, both in believing and in baptizing, and in dipping.[2]

William Dell, Rector of Yelden, the chaplain to General
Lord Fairfax, who was noted for certain inconsistencies,
including "for being professionally against Paedobaptism
and yet he had his own children baptized",[3] distinguishes
between the baptism of John and that of Christ. The former
was water-baptism, not a baptism of fire, and so was limited
in its effect to the element used and affected only the outward
man. Thus, while John's baptism heralded the kingdom of
Christ, it had no part in it.

> It is not water but Spirit Baptism that makes us Christians,
> and Water Baptisme hath been an unlawfull blending or

---

[1] *To the Children of the West* (1653), 55, printed with *The Babe of Glory*.
[2] *Ibid.*, 60.   [3] See A. G. Matthews, *Calamney Revised* (1934), 162.

mixing of the Church and World together, so that they could not be well differenced from each other, to the great prejudice of the Congregation of Christ.[1]

The apostles, he admitted, practised water-baptism but in this, he believed, they were following John rather than Jesus and this was no more a precept of Christ for the church than was the use of circumcision by some of the apostles. Christ's baptism is not concerned with material water, but with the Word. He quotes Matt. 28: 20, to attempt to identify teaching with the means whereby Christian baptism in water was effected. Like Erberry he identifies water-baptism with the disunity of the church, also quoting the breach of communion caused by those who held "closed communion" beliefs. On the other hand he says

> Spirit-baptism makes us one with Christ the Head, so with the Church the body. . . . I say not by being dipt into the same water, but by receiving the same spirit do we become one body with the Church, and it is not the being of one judgment or opinion or forme, or the like, that makes men one true Church or body of Christ, but the being of one Spirit.[2]

The Quaker view follows this spiritual emphasis, identifying spirit-baptism with the unity which they regarded as an essential feature of the true church. James Naylor expresses this: "In the world there be many sorts and forms of Baptismes; but in Christ there is but one, and that is of the Spirit."[3] Fox's *Journal* also testifies to the sometimes bitter opposition between the Quakers and both the Paedo-Baptists and the Baptists. In 1668 he argues with a Papist that there was no justification in Scripture for christening infants and adds "the one baptism by the one Spirit into one body we owned; but to throw a little water on a child's face, and say that was baptizing and christening it, there was no Scripture for that".[4] Earlier, in 1655, we find a typical argument between Fox and the Baptists, when he challenged a group of them at Dorchester whether they were sent of God to baptize as John was, or whether they had the same Spirit and power as the apostles possessed. They admitted

---

[1] *The Doctrines of Baptismes* (1648), 12.
[2] *Ibid.*, 22.   [3] *Love to the Lost* (1656), 37.
[4] P. L. Parker (ed.), *Journal*, 400.

that they had not and also agreed with Fox that only two powers existed, that of God and that of the devil. Fox then added, "If you have not the power of God that the Apostles had, then you act by the power of the devil".[1] Thus the discussion of the true nature of baptism was one of the great controversies in this period of great theological ferment, and its varying interpretations became a significant cause of offence to many Christians.

B. *The Seventeenth and Eighteenth Centuries*

These conflicting views on baptism found expression in a series of public disputations, the accounts of which have provided a large and important body of literature on the subject. J. J. Goadby compiled a convenient synopsis of some of the more important ones.[2]

The first he mentions, which was also one of the most important of the whole series, took place at Southwark on October 17, 1642, between a company of Baptists led by William Kiffin, one of the most influential leaders of the Particular Baptists, and Daniel Featley, a man despised by Baptists and later imprisoned by the Presbyterian faction. Featley argued that circumcision was to the old dispensation what baptism is to the new, and as the former is recognized by the apostle Paul to be "a seal to the righteousness of faith" (Rom. 4: 11), so baptism has the same end in view, to be a seal of the covenant of Grace, granting free remission of sin. Under the old law, children had no actual faith neither could they make profession of such, yet they were allowed to receive the sacrament of circumcision. For the same reasons, children under the Gospel, though without faith, ought to receive baptism as the seal of the covenant of righteousness by faith. This is making an analogy which Mr. Gilmore[3] has already suggested ought not to be made, and if, as John 3: 5 plainly states, no one can enter the kingdom of God but those born of water and the Spirit, then unbaptized children cannot ordinarily enter into that kingdom, though Featley would not tie God to an outward rite. He also makes

[1] P. L. Parker (ed.), *Journal*, 56.

[2] *Bye Paths in Baptist History* (1871), 139-79. This list is of course, by no means exhausted. A. S. Langley (*T.B.H.S.*, 216ff.) speaks of 91 disputations in which Baptists were involved, 26 of which deal specifically with baptism.

[3] *Supra*, 55f.

the claim, on the basis of Acts 2: 39, that children are comprehended in Christ's covenant, and quotes 1 Cor. 7: 14 to show that children are holy and, consequently, fit subjects for baptism. According to his own account in *The Dipper Dipt* the arguments of the Baptists were, for the main part, legalistically Scriptural, holding that children ought not to receive baptism simply because there is no specific command given in the New Testament to justify such a practice.

The Dipper Dipt (published in 1644) became one of the most popular and famous attacks upon the Baptists and went through seven editions by 1660. It also had the effect of provoking the Baptists to examine closely their own position. J. M. Cramp says that it was one of the factors that led the Particular Baptists to publish the Confession of 1644.[1] In 1645 Henry Denne, who had begun his own controversy with Featley when they were together in the Peterhouse prison, carried on his examination of his views in *Anti-Christ Unmasked*. Another typical answer to Featley was that of Samuel Richardson, in *Some Brief considerations on Doctor Featley in his book entitled "The Dipper Dipt"*, though this was more concerned with refuting his calumnies than with developing a doctrine of baptism.

The most distinguished and erudite of all the disputants was undoubtedly Richard Baxter. One of his first debates was with Benjamin Cox, who held, Baxter says, that ministers if they were unbaptized were no true ministers of Christ and that it was unlawful to hear them, or to join with those churches in which the members of the congregation had not received believer's baptism.[2] In 1649 Baxter debated with his greatest opponent in this matter, John Tombes, when he claimed that the great question to be decided was not the nature of the sign whereby members are admitted to the church, but the age at which this takes place, a matter fully determined in the Old Testament, and not mentioned in the New, which "speaketh more sparingly of that which is discovered in the Old". It was generally agreed that all disciples of Christ should be baptized, but Baxter holds that some infants are to be counted among His disciples, which

---

[1] *Baptist History* (1875), 267.
[2] *Op. cit.* This consists of the arguments prepared by him for his debate with Tombes.

he infers from Acts 15: 10, Luke 9: 47-49, and from the continuity of the church with the old covenant. (Acts 7: 38, Rom. 1: 17, Matt. 23: 37-39 and Rev. 11: 15.)

Moreover, he claims it would be wrong if children were the losers because Christ has abrogated the law, for if children are not in membership with the visible church we can have no sound hope that, dying at that time, they can be saved. Christ Himself, even when an infant, was the Head of the Church; it is therefore incredible that He would exclude children from it. However, following the Puritanical tradition, Baxter does not extend this privilege to all infants. He points out that only children of Israelites could be admitted to the old covenant, and so only children of believers can be accounted holy.

> But [he adds] when we buy infants, or they are left orphans wholly to us, so that they are wholly ours and at our dispose [sic] the Parents being either dead or having given up their interest to us, I doubt not though they were the children of Jews and Turks, but it is our duty to lift them under Christ, and enter them into his School, Kingdom or Church by Baptism.

Tombes argued that the practice of infant baptism would result in ignorance and there would be no solemn engagement on their part to follow Christ. To meet this Baxter suggests the revision of the *Directory* in four respects:

1. That the parents should covenant on behalf of the child as the infant is unable to covenant for himself.

2. That the ancient practice of confirmation should be reduced to its primitive state so that all persons when they come of age should be brought solemnly to face the congregation to renew or own the covenant personally, which they entered into at baptism.

3. That the church may have power to renew this covenant, as there shall be occasion, or to call any particular person to the renewing of it.

4. That the express words of the covenant may be prescribed to all Christians out of God's Word, and that no one shall have power to impose any other covenant upon the children.

This he justifies by saying that God's promises made in baptism are not absolute but conditional.

There was also discussion of the mode. He denies that dipping was the custom in Scriptural times. It was unlikely that there was sufficient water in the gaoler's house; Amon was but a small stream; the Eunuch went down into the water simply; it was a mountainous country and this proved convenient. He also adds that going down over the head into water is a breach of the sixth commandment, and being baptized naked, a breach of the seventh.

John Tombes was vicar of Leominster from 1630 to 1642 and again from 1649 to 1662, whilst holding strong anti-Paedo-Baptist views. This did not lead him to complete fellowship with the Baptists whose views he often expressed most eloquently. He was described as differing from the Church of England on the point of infant baptism, but would not separate from its communion any further than by going out of the church while that office was performed, and returning again when the ceremony was completed.[1] He disputed some nine times on the question of baptism, and first published his views in 1645.[2] His thesis was founded on the simple proposition: "That which hath no testimony of Scripture for it is doubtful. But this Doctrine of Infant Baptism hath no testimony of Scripture for it. *Ergo*, it is doubtful." He denies that baptism succeeds circumcision, for the covenant made with Abraham was not a pure gospel-covenant; many of its promises concerned only the house and lineage of Abraham himself. To deny baptism to infants cannot be made a reason for asserting, as the Paedo-Baptists claimed, that Baptists would have God's Grace more restrained under the new dispensation than under the old; for, he adds, "The Grace of God is not tied to Sacraments, neither do Sacraments give grace by the work done."

The body of this work is a consideration of the main texts used by both parties in these debates, and he concludes his reasoning with the assertion: "The last, and that a weighty reason of doubting is, because Infant-Baptisme seemes to take away awe, perhaps the primary end of

---

[1] See A. G. Matthews, *op. cit.*, 488.

[2] J. Tombes, *Two treatises; and an appendix to them concerning infant baptisme* (1645).

baptism: for many things argue that it was one end of Baptisme, that it should be a sign that the baptized shews himself a disciple, and confesseth the faith in which he has been instructed." He ends with an answer to Stephen Marshall and sums up his view in four parts:

1. Infant baptism is not so ancient as is pretended, but as now taught is a late innovation.
2. Anti-Paedo-Baptism hath no ill influence on church or commonwealth.
3. Infant baptism cannot be deduced from Holy Scriptures.
4. Infant baptism is a corruption of the ordinance of baptism.

Marshall in his book makes one interesting debating point, "All who reject the Baptizing of Infants do, and must upon the same ground reject the religious observation of the Lord's Day, as the Christian Sabbath, viz. because there is not (say they) any express institution or command in the New Testament."[1] Tombes answers that many Paedo-Baptists also reject the celebration of the Lord's Day and holds that the command in the Decalogue belongs to the moral law and, therefore, still stands. He then goes on to quote evidence from the New Testament and early Fathers of the church to justify the celebration of the first day of the week, but ends by saying that Marshall's arguments must be taken *cum grano salis*.[2] Yet he was capable of making similar attacks. An analogous debating point figured in one of the most famous debates in which Tombes took part, that which took place at St. Mary's Church, Abergavenny, on September 5, 1653, when his opponents were John Cragge and Henry Vaughan.[3] This disputation, like many others, was a trial of logicians rather than of theologians. Tombes claims that if the argument from circumcision is valid, then women must not be baptized, for, under the old covenant, only males were circumcised. Vaughan answers "In the eyes of all laws whatsoever, the women are but

[1] *A Sermon on the Baptizing of Infants* (1645), 6.
[2] J. Tombes, *op. cit.*, 31.
[3] The account of this debate is given in *The Anabaptists Anatòmized* (1653). The debate was occasioned by a sermon preached by Tombes on the text Mark 16: 16 which was answered by a sermon preached by Cragge on the same text.

ignoble creatures, and therefor the usual stile of laws and covenants is *Si Quis* and *Qui* in the masculine." Yet Tombes' main point is much more important, for he holds that in considering any point of doctrine or practice we must beware of answers drawn from analogies and, quoting John Paget's *Defence of Church Government* and John Ball's *Reply to the Answer of the New England Elders*, holds that such methods could be justly used to justify most Roman Catholic beliefs and innovations.

The arguments used in most of the other baptismal debates were similar to these and often add a certain ingenuity to passion and vituperation. This is seen even in the titles of the accounts of these issued by one party or the other. Samuel Fisher gives his account of a debate in Ashford, Kent, on July 27, 1649, *Baby-baptism meer babism* (1653); the dispute at Newport Pagnell between the Baptist, John Gibbs, and the Independent, Richard Carpenter, is described in the latter's *The Anabaptist washt and washt, and shrunk in the washing* (1653); while the considerable body of literature prompted by the Portsmouth debate of 1698-99 included *An Example of the pretences and character of Mr. W Russell (the late Portsmouth deputant) and others* (1700), and Russell's own *Infant Baptism is will-worship* (1700). Yet there were times when such debates were prohibited, particularly when Presbyterianism gained political power. In 1645 a number of Baptists published *A Declaration Concerning the Publike Dispute which should have been in the Publike Meeting-House of Alderman-Bury, the 3d of this instant month of December, Concerning Infants-Baptisme*. In this they recognize that before holding such a disputation they must "crave leave of the civill Magistrate, to have liberty to dispute in some publike place" and use the opportunity to demonstrate that, in spite of what is said and written of the Baptists, they are always ready to obey the civil magistrate and are subject to his authority in all his lawful commands.

There was also disagreement among Baptists themselves concerning aspects of baptism, and two of these can be singled out. Some, following the principle of the absolute authority of the word of Scripture, believed that baptism should be followed by the laying on of hands. This is seen in the controversy between Chillenden, D'Anvers and certain other Baptists,[1] on the one hand, and John More, who argued against them in favour of the practice in his work *A lost ordinance restored; or eight questions in reference "to the laying on of hands" lovingly answered by one of the least of saints, with a general exhortation to all baptized Churches not yet under the practice* (1654). A similar literary discussion took place between Edward Hanson, whose work was entitled *Touchstone*, and John Griffiths, the General Baptist who wrote *Laying on of hands on baptized believers no counterfeit, tryed by the touchstone, and found gold* (1654).

The other matter which led to controversy was the relation of baptism to the Lord's Supper. The Particular Baptists stressed that only baptized-believers should be admitted to the ordinance. Benjamin Cox, in his Appendix to the 1646 Confession of Faith, relates this matter to necessary church order:

> Though a believer's right to the use of the Lord's Supper do immediately flow from Jesus Christ, apprehended and received by faith; yet inasmuch as all things ought to be done not only decently but also in order, 1 Cor. xiv. 40; and the Word holds forth this order, that disciples should be baptized, Matt. xxviii. 19; Acts ii. 38; and then be taught to observe all things (that is to say, all other things) that Christ commanded the Apostles, Matt. xxviii. 20; and accordingly the Apostles first baptized disciples, and then admitted them to the use of the Supper Acts ii. 41, 42; we therefore do not admit any to the use of the supper, nor communicate with any in the use of this ordinance, but disciples baptized, lest we should have fellowship with them in their doing contrary to order.[2]

The great champion of this point of view was William Kiffin, who holds that the ordinance of baptism is the pledge of an entrance into covenant with God and of giving ourselves to Him, whereby we are completely dedicated to the service of the Trinity and therefore must, of necessity, come before that of the Lord's Supper.[3]

---

[1] *Eight questions in reference to that principle of the foundation of the doctrine of Christ termed laying of hands* (1653). For a further discussion see E. A. Payne, "Baptists and the Laying on of Hands", in *B.Q.*, xv (1953-54), 203ff.

[2] E. B. Underhill, *op. cit.*, 59.

[3] *A Sober Discourse of Right to Church Communion wherein is proved by Scripture, the Example of the Primitive Times and the Practice of all that have Professed the Christian Religion: That no unbaptized person may be regularly admitted to the Lord's Supper* (1681), 6.

His opponent was John Bunyan. He denies that baptism is the "initiating and entering ordinance" into the church. Its purpose is that faith may be strengthened in the death and resurrection of Christ figured in baptism. Its value is subjective. Persons can only be admitted to the church, "by a discovery of their faith and holiness and their declaration of willingness to subject themselves unto the laws and government of Christ in His Church".[1] It is Christ Himself and not baptism which is the door into the sheep-fold. He refused to debate with the Baptists, for he considered himself too "dull headed" to engage with them and because he feared the "heats and contentions" which might arise.[2] The one baptism referred to in Eph. 4: 4-6 is of the spirit not water and so baptism is not a prerequisite for communion in the Gospel of which the Lord's Supper is the sign. The controversy concerning closed-communion persisted till well into the nineteenth century and still persists as far as the Baptists of Wales are concerned, while a number of Strict Baptist Churches are still active in England.

After Bunyan the greatest advocate of open-communion was probably Robert Hall, who expressed his attitude to the problem in *The Terms of Communion*, published in 1815. After examining the case for closed-communion he advocates the contrary practice on four grounds:

1. The obligation of brotherly love.

2. The express injunction of Scripture respecting the conduct to be maintained towards Christians who differ in their religious sentiments. This point he argues from the decision of the apostles following the Council of Jerusalem, and from Paul's attitude towards those who were troubled by meats offered to idols.

3. Paedo-Baptists are members of the true church and therefore cannot lawfully be excluded from its communion.

4. The only justification for refusing participation in the eucharist to any professor of Christianity is some criminal action on his part. Paul was justified in excluding the incestuous member of the church at Corinth but it is impossible to ascribe criminality to all Paedo-Baptists.

[1] *A Reason of my Practice in Worship*, in G. Offer (ed.), *Works*, ii, 605ff.
[2] See J. Bunyan, *Differences in Judgment about Water Baptism, no bar to Communion* (1673), *Works*, iii, 641.

Hall accuses those who held to the belief in closed-communion of having "attempted an incongruous mixture of liberal principles with a particular act of intolerance".

He was answered by Joseph Kinghorn, minister of the church at St. Mary's, Norwich,[1] who holds that one could not expect the New Testament to prohibit the unbaptized from receiving the Lord's Supper, for no circumstances arose which made such a prohibition necessary. The unbaptized could not be received into the primitive church, and so there was no reason for them to forbid them fellowship at the table of the Lord. However, "mixed communion" in the modern church is a departure from this early practice and introduces rites and ceremonies for which there is no Scriptural authority. Baptists, he claims, must face the challenge that if they can lawfully communicate with those they believe to be in error, then their own separation is entirely without justification. He denies Hall's claim that exclusion from the eucharist is a punishment, for he claims there is a great distinction between those who are barred from the Supper as "unworthy" and those who cannot enjoy it because they are "unqualified". Kinghorn's attitude is a legal one, holding "that it is not everyone that is received of Jesus Christ who is entitled to communion at His table, but such and such only as revere His authority".[2] Hall, on the other hand, speaks for like-minded Baptists when he says in reply to this work, "our sole intention is to expose the inconsistency of supposing an involuntary mistake on this subject [Baptism] a sufficient bar to Communion, while it is acknowledged to be none to the participation of future blessedness".[3] The problem raised is still unresolved, for whereas most English Baptists practise open-communion, the contrary is the common characteristic of the majority of Baptist churches in Wales.

The atmosphere of baptismal discussion in the post-Restoration period was very different from that we have outlined in the earlier period. Controversy continued but the writings are more calmly academic in tone. In 1705 William Wall published his *History of Infant-Baptism*, a work

---

[1] *Baptism a Term of Communion* (1816).   [2] *Op. cit.*, 62.
[3] *A Reply to the Rev. Joseph Kinghorn being a further indication of the practice of Free Communion* (1818), *Works*, iii, 332.

that was regarded as one of the greatest on the subject, even by Baptists, who accepted the accuracy of much of his research while rejecting the conclusions he drew from it. Well into the nineteenth century it was regarded by many Paedo-Baptists as the most erudite apologia for their point of view. In 1711 John Gale published a refutation of his thesis, *Reflections on Mr. Wall's History of Infant Baptism*, to which Wall replied with his *Defence*, published in 1720, for which he was awarded a D.D. of Oxford University.

The *History* begins with an examination of Jewish proselyte baptism and claims that the great commission of our Lord can be understood only against this background. He then reviews the historical evidence from the *Epistles of Clement* and *The Shepherd of Hermas* to his own day and claims to have considered in detail all passages dealing with the subject in Christian authors to the time of Augustine, for his writings and those of his successors dealt so fully with the topic that they could only be examined in a more general fashion.

Some of his proofs for the practice of infant baptism in the early Fathers are more ingenious than historically accurate, depending on deductions from their soteriology. He admits that most of these writers speak of adult baptism, but points out that this is to be expected, for these were the centuries when many heathen were being converted to the Gospel. He accuses many anti-Paedo-Baptists of using, in their arguments, many forged and spurious works and of mis-understanding the context of many baptismal references in the Fathers. Wall names many famous figures in the history of the Christian church who were not baptized as infants, but claims that anti-Paedo-Baptists who refer to these have not also remarked that most of them had, at least, one un-baptized parent. As to the Celtic church, he says that it is a misunderstanding of its views to claim that it rejected infant baptism, while he believes that even the heretics either baptized their children or rejected water-baptism com-pletely. An interesting chapter deals with the fate of the unbaptized infant who dies while still innocent. He points out the varied views of medieval theologians but goes on:

> The Protestants generally have defined that the due punish-ment of original sin is, in strictness, damnation in hell. I suppose and hope that they mean with St. Austin a very

moderate degree of it in the case of infants, in whom original corruption, which is the *formes* or source of all wickedness has not yet broke out into any actual sin. But if their doctrine in this respect hath been more rigid than that of the Church of Rome, or of the ancient Greek doctors, they have in another respect, viz. in the case of Christian people's children given such a mitigating explanation of our Saviour's words as to allow better hope than either of them.

In the case of an unbaptized child of a Christian parent, he believes that God will take the intention for the act, and holds that all baptized infants, without actual sin, are in a state of salvation. After tracing the rise of anti-Paedo-Baptism, he devotes the remaining chapters to the state of the controversy in his own day and claims that as all national churches were Paedo-Baptist, the anti-Paedo-Baptists were guilty of the sin of schism, and often the mere tool of the Papists. He recognizes immersion as the primitive mode of baptism, and condemns the *Directory* for prohibiting it, but denies that the word means simply "to dip" and claims that affusion is a valid mode for the rite. The work ends with an appeal for the restoration of church fellowship which has been broken by the controversy.

Gale's *Reflections* is an equally erudite work, which is in the form of thirteen epistles. He begins by saying that Dr. Wall's moderation is merely pretended and that there is, in fact, little to distinguish him from Dr. Featley. He admits that the *History* is the best published defence of infant baptism, but claims that the author has ignored the evidence which was inconvenient for his purpose, and has misinterpreted the evidence he quotes. He also accuses Wall of being merely abusive in considering Baptist history, in that he generalizes from the failings of the few and denies that their existence is schismatic, which sin can be predicted only of "those who rashly and unjustly either give or take occasion so to separate".

Gale deals with the mode of baptism before considering the qualifications for its subjects, a fact indicative of a change of emphasis among Baptist apologists. He rejects completely Wall's arguments from Jewish proselyte baptism, claiming that the authorities he quotes are too late to give sure grounds for believing it was even in vogue in the time of the

Saviour, while there is also evidence to the contrary. In either case he claims there can be no analogy between Jewish and Christian baptism, for it is more rational and Scriptural to consider John's baptism as the pattern for that of Christ, and there is no evidence that He commended infant baptism or that the apostles practised it. He also denies Wall's main thesis, that the purpose of baptism is to wash away original sin, and when it is described as "a circumcision without hands" the reference is to a spiritual, inward experience rather than to an external rite. Parallel to this is his rejection of Wall's belief that the Fathers identified infant baptism with regeneration, which followed from the view that baptism takes the place of circumcision, and, in common with many Baptists, he argues that if this parallel must be followed in one respect, it must also be respected in others and the ordinance should be administered on the same day and denied to females. It is Gale's view that no evidence can be found for the practice of infant baptism before A.D. 250, and that Baptists are justified in maintaining their position only if it can be shown that Christ did not institute the rite and that the Scriptures do not commend it. Infant baptism is, for him, a corruption of the Scriptural ordinance and, like transubstantiation, grew up as an excess of zeal, which led to the use of extravagant hyperbole when speaking of the simple rite of the early church.

At the end of the eighteenth century another famous work was published, *Paedobaptism Explained* by Abraham Booth. He tells us that he had spent much time collecting the opinions of anti-Paedo-Baptists and was prompted to publish his researches after reading Henry's *Treatise on Baptism*. The work also contains answers to Dr. Williams and Peter Edwards. It consists largely of quotations from anti-Paedo-Baptists, which are used to justify Baptist opinions; a method often used since that time. Like Gale he first considers the mode of baptism, dealing with the significance of the word "baptize", its design in the mind of Jesus, the practice of John, the present practice of the Greek and oriental churches, together with a section giving reasons why sprinkling took the place of immersion. Though the method differs greatly from other Baptist writers of the period, the main trend of the argument is very similar. In considering the nature of the ordinance he is much concerned to deny that proselyte baptism has any relevance to the question. He makes five points:

1. Jewish baptism was a civil, not a religious, rite, and its administration was confined to proselytes and to such children born to such parents prior to their incorporation in the Jewish church.

2. Its antiquity is very doubtful.

3. The baptism of John was entirely new, for his name, the Baptizer, was sufficient to distinguish him from his contemporaries.

4. It is unthinkable that Jesus in such a vital matter would refer His disciples to the writings of His enemies.

5. To argue from proselyte baptism to Christian baptism is to claim that the latter is, like the former, of human rather than divine institution.

His general condemnation of Paedo-Baptist opinions is very similar to that of Gale, claiming that there is no express command in Scripture for its use, neither is there the example of the apostles, for there is no evidence at all for the baptism of infants before the end of the second or the beginning of the third century. It arose then, he believes, because of a wrong view of its purpose, for men came to believe at that time that salvation would be conferred upon their children by its instrumentality. The work contains a very useful examination of the main proof-texts used by both sides in the controversy as well as a section considering historically and dogmatically the parallel between infant baptism and infant communion.

By the end of the eighteenth century most aspects of the subject of baptism had been treated, in some learned work or other, in such detail that one wondered if further writing on the subject were academically justified; yet controversy in this matter had still a practical bearing on ecclesiastical life. Many Baptists were afraid that the revival led by Wesley might undermine their own position in the eyes of the people and attacked his Paedo-Baptist views. This can be seen in Cuthbert Boyce's *A Serious Reply to the Rev. Mr. John Wesley*, a typical Baptist controversial document of its period, of which A. C. Underwood says: "Boyce makes many excellent debating points about baptism, but he gives the modern reader the impression that he was more concerned to save the Baptist face than to win a religious battle."[1]

C. *The Nineteenth Century*

The nineteenth century saw a great revival in baptismal controversy. A very great volume of literature on the subject poured from the press. This varied between great academic tomes and single sheet tracts sold usually at a shilling or so a hundred.[2] Much of this controversy was inspired, directly or indirectly, by the new concern for the sacraments shown by the Oxford Movement.[3] The views of this group on baptism find expression in a series of sermons preached by John Keble in 1849–50, which were published by E. B. Pusey in 1869 under the title *Village Sermons on the Baptismal Service*. In this he speaks of baptism as a coronation in which the meanest child is made a priest and king to God the Father, and as a marriage with Christ, whereby the baptized is made bone of His bone and flesh of His flesh. When John the Baptist spoke of one who would baptize with the Holy Ghost and with fire, he meant no other baptism than that which is now practised in the church of Christ. Of the mode of this rite he says:

> In the outward part of Baptism there are two things of consequence, the element or matter, which is the water, to bury the child in, or to be poured or sprinkled upon it; and the form of words, ordained by our Lord Himself, "In the Name of the Father, and the Son and the Holy Ghost". If either of these two were wanting, i.e. if the child were washed or dipped in water, but not in the Sacred Name: or again, if the Name were said over it, but no water applied to it; then it would not be baptized.

Once a child is so baptized he is a Christian for ever, unless by his own sin he cast away the grace granted him. He rests this doctrine upon his view of original sin, and adds:

---

[1] *A History of the English Baptists*, 149f.

[2] The Baptist Tract and Book Society issued many of these tracts, designed, of course, to catch the eye of the public at large.

[3] Another factor which contributed in no small measure to this revived interest in baptism was the republication of the volumes of Wall and Gale in 1819 and 1820. These works occasioned far greater interest at their republication than when they were originally issued.

although the guilt of our birth-sin was blotted out in our Baptism, yet the sin itself remains like a spark from hell-fire within us, which may be fanned into a flame and the devil is always trying to fan it. While we are in the flesh, we are all fallen and corrupt, but the Holy Spirit entering in at baptism mends our nature and opens the door both of the Church and Kingdom.

Thus the sacrament has, for Keble, a twofold significance; it is a covenant between God and the person baptized, and a means whereby God bestows on that person His gift of grace. Being such, it is a work of faith and not of sight, for neither party can visibly confirm this covenant. The church speaks for the child, through the godparents it appoints, and God commissions His priest to speak for Him who is "but shadow and token of our Lord Jesus Christ". Thus it is Christ Himself who receives the children and signifies in the rite that He intends them not only to be of His church, but also means them to go to heaven to enjoy for ever His own presence with that of the saints and angels. Keble justifies the baptism of infants, who cannot covenant for themselves, from the words of Jesus, "Compel them to come in" (Luke 14: 23). The efficacy of baptism depends, to a great extent, on the consecration of the water.

> We may consider it as an act of our Great High Priest and Saviour, applying by the Church's prayer to the particular water that is in the Font, the sanctifying virtue, which in His Own Baptism He had conferred upon all the waters of the earth.

Following baptism the child is to be signed on the forehead with the cross, to mark him for Christ's own and to protect him from evil spirits. For Keble and his friends in the movement, baptism, like other aspects of church life, is not a matter for debate. "The Word of God, as declared by His Church, is so plain, that we are not to doubt it at all, but simply to believe it."

Such views as these caused many Baptists to take a more critical attitude towards the articles of the established church. The outstanding controversy in this regard occurred in 1864 and followed a sermon preached by C. H. Spurgeon and published in the *Metropolitan Tabernacle Pulpit* (No. 573).

It was delivered on Sunday morning, June 5, on the text, Matthew 16: 15, 16. His main theme was that baptism without faith saves no one, and this leads him to say:

> I am not aware that any Protestant Church in England teaches the doctrine of baptismal regeneration except one, and that happens to be the corporation which with none too much humility calls itself *the* Church of England.

That this is the doctrine of the Anglican church he seeks to prove from the Book of Common Prayer, quoting especially from the baptismal service and the catechism. To his own rhetorical assertion that there are many evangelical clergy within the National Church, he answers, "Why then do they belong to a Church which teaches this doctrine in the plainest of terms?" and goes on:

> I know of nothing more calculated to debauch the public mind than a want of straightforwardness in ministers, and when worldly men hear ministers denouncing the very things which their own Prayer Book teaches, they imagine that words have no meaning among ecclesiastics, and that vital differences in religion are merely a matter of tweedle-dee and tweedle-dum, and that it does not matter what a man does believe so long as he is charitable towards other people.

The doctrine of baptismal regeneration he contrasts with the spiritual religion taught by Jesus, in that it makes salvation depend upon a mere ceremony. He adds also that our own observation testifies against it, for not all who are baptized can be called children of God, and the "performance" called by the Anglicans, baptism, can help no one, for no person has any right to make such solemn promises on behalf of another. Finally, he claims that the preaching of this belief had a wrong and evil influence which was seen in the "fearful strides" Popery had made in England.

This sermon created a remarkable stir in theological and ecclesiastical circles, which prompted Spurgeon to preach, on June 26, from Hebrews 13: 13 when he spoke again of the established church as a corrupt corporation which tolerates evangelical truth, while finding room for infidels and men who deny the authenticity of Scripture. This sermon considers their doctrine of baptism to be one element of the general corruption of the Anglicans' theology. On July 24 he

preached again on the subject, his text being Mark 10:
13-15, and his title *Children brought to Christ, not to the font*.
Yet after saying "this text has not the shadow of the shade of
the ghost of a connection with baptism", he implies that his
opponents have been mis-using Scripture, and preaches a
simple evangelical sermon without further topical reference.

It is impossible in this limited space to list the replies
provoked by Spurgeon's series. W. T. Whitley says that they
numbered nearly 150[1] and a great many thousands of
copies of these were sold. It was natural that many attacked
Spurgeon's personality and purpose rather than his views.
The *London Review* for July 9, 1864, says:

> Now assuredly, this is not argument but assertion; not fair
> dealing but misrepresentation; not Christian charity but party
> zeal; and good and wise men of even Mr. Spurgeon's con-
> gregation will think so. Such questionable assumption of the
> functions of a judge will, moreover, injure him personally; it
> will damage him publicly. Already he has lost the friendship
> of influential clergy and laymen of the Church.

Letters which flowed to the religious press showed an
acrimony unsurpassed even in the seventeenth century. The
Christian World, in September 1864, carried a series of letters
from the Rev. Charles Bullock claiming that Spurgeon in
denying the place of children in the church must also deny
their right to say, "Our Father, which art in heaven".
Most of the tracts, many of which were anonymous, were
in the form of either epistles or sermons. The subject was
approached from almost every possible standpoint. R. P.
Hutchison published a tract, *Mr. Spurgeon shewn to be a
Teacher of Baptismal Regeneration*. Charles Wills, in *Baptismal
Regeneration*, called him a Socinian. W. G. Abbott, in *A Few
Words in reply to C. H. Spurgeon*, accuses him of ignorance of
the main grounds of baptismal controversy and reminds
him of the works of Wall and Gale. A few, like J. H. Titcomb
in *The Washing of Regeneration*, attempt to demonstrate
honestly the view held by evangelical clergymen of the
relationship of baptism to the doctrine and experience of
regeneration. The controversy degenerated into a distasteful

---

[1] *Op. cit.*, 321. Yet this number is far too low an estimate, as is shown in
W. Y. Fullerton's biography of Spurgeon (363-66).

literary squabble, typified by Robert Bellman's *Great is Diana: or Mother Church and the Babes*—a defence of Spurgeon and a most sarcastic attack on Charles Wills. The author of the controversy did not descend to such levels and the published correspondence between him and the Hon. Baptist W. Noel, who wrote on behalf of the Evangelical Alliance, is a model of moderation, especially on the part of the latter.[1]

The nineteenth century also saw the publication of a number of learned works on the subject of baptism. Of these the most exhaustive is undoubtedly *A Hand Book of Christian Baptism* by R. Ingham, published in 1865, a work over 600 pages long, to which he added in 1871 another work, *Baptism, Its Subjects*, a book over 700 pages long. He begins by speaking of baptism as a divine and permanent institution, which belongs only to the New Testament. It is essentially "a solemn and significant profession of discipleship to Jesus" and "the divinely-appointed way of entrance into the body of Christ". Yet he insists that to speak of it as initiatory does not imply that it precedes repentance and faith, or that it is, in itself, regenerating, but only that it is ever "the first act required of the professing recipient of the Gospel, the act in which by divine appointment, he signified his faith in Jesus and devotedness to Him, and by which he was introduced where Christians existed, into their society and privileges".

Being a positive institution of God it cannot be ascertained from the light of nature or reason but solely from revelation, and thus there is within the command to baptize and be baptized a moral obligation which comes from its author. He deals at great length with the mode of baptism and particularly with the meaning of βαπτίζω, which he claims means "to immerse" and ought to be so rendered in our English translation of the Bible. On this matter there had been some dispute, earlier in the century, between Baptists and the British and Foreign Bible Society. To demonstrate his point Ingham masses his proofs together from many different fields, from the evidence in Greek Lexicons and writers,

---

[1] Spurgeon was never abusive but has been described as writing to Baptist Noel as though he were addressing the crowded congregation at the Metropolitan Tabernacle.

the ancient versions, the practice of the Greek Church and the Jews, from the works of philologists and archaeologists, though his examination of purely literary evidence as to the use of the word is not as complete as that of Alexander Carson in his *Baptism in its Modes and Objects* (1844).

The largest section of Ingham's works deals with the "futility of all known objections to the Baptist interpretation of the rite", and it is most difficult to think of any objection, textual, historical or practical, that he has ignored. In some ways the *Addita* are more interesting than the main argument. In the first he deals with the design of baptism and says, in a way that reflects a deal of disputes in many churches at that time, "We believe that pastors of churches—not to mention many persons who are not pastors—may claim from the Scriptures a right to baptize any believer without consulting any person, although their position is different from that of apostles and evangelists. The present practice of many Baptist Churches seems to transfer this right from the preacher of the Gospel to the Church." He also denies the necessity of baptism being administered on the Lord's Day or before a large congregation, saying, "There is a medium betwixt being ashamed of Christ, and making an exhibition of our taking upon us a scriptural profession of Christianity." In apostolic times, he says, baptism was conducted "at the earliest convenient time and place". The utility of baptism rests in its confession of the one triune God and of personal sin and not in benefits conferred on unconscious babes.

Dr. Elliott-Binns has shown that the latter half of the nineteenth century saw a noteworthy revival of interest in historical and archaeological studies.[1] There was at this time abundant new material upon which the historian and theologian could work. It is strange that he does not mention the study of baptism in this regard, for which archaeology in particular became a topic of vital interest. Yet his judgment on the period is true when related to the study of these particular subjects: "A too exclusive concentration on the collection of facts was a definite weakness of the historical studies of the later nineteenth century for it was not adequately balanced by the use of imagination." The best example of this aspect of baptismal studies is Wilfred Nelson

[1] L. E. Elliott-Binns, *English Thought 1860-1900*, 93ff.

Cote's *The Archaeology of Baptism* (1876). It is natural that this work should be mainly concerned with the mode, though he also considers liturgies together with the testimonies of early writers, both orthodox and heretical. Much of the interest in the book is centred on the illustrations drawn by an American artist, Edwin M. Gardiner. These reproduce a number of early paintings depicting baptism, usually that of our Lord, showing the subject standing in water with the administrator either with his hand upon his head, or pouring water upon him. There are also a number of plans of baptisteries usually in Italy which indicate that immersion was, for a long time, the accepted form of the rite. The book ends with a study of baptism in various places in Christendom and in the different traditions of the church.

The history of baptismal controversy in Britain has not always been a happy one; it has been the cause of much bitterness and has led to extravagant denunciation on both sides. Numerous non-theological factors have influenced the course of the discussion in every period. Yet it has also produced works of great learning and has provoked all sections of the Christian community to define, with theological exactness, their own view of the church and sacraments. Many of the arguments used remained virtually unchanged from the seventeenth to the nineteenth centuries, though the late eighteenth- and nineteenth-century writers tended to lay much greater stress on the right manner of baptism than did those of the earlier period. Baptist apologists tended, throughout these years, to be legalistic in their attitude, resting much of their case upon the need for a plain Scriptural command. These centuries saw the gathering together of a great body of information about baptism, which provides the background of modern discussions, so that it is useful to re-examine this material in the light of contemporary trends, and to reconsider contemporary trends in the light of this material.

Chapter

8

THE THEOLOGY OF BAPTISM

by Neville Clark

THE eleven disciples, standing in the afterglow of resurrection glory and turning to the task of filling the vacancy in the apostolic ranks left by the defection of Judas, laid down one essential condition to be satisfied by any candidate put forward to become the twelfth witness of the resurrection of the Lord. It was necessary that such a man should be one who had companied with them "during all the time that the Lord Jesus went in and out among [them], beginning from the baptism of John until the day when he was taken up" (Acts 1: 21f.). Such is Luke's testimony.

It is a significant witness, pointing unmistakably to the crucial period of salvation-history, and delimiting the *kairos* of redemption by reference to the baptism of John on the one hand and the ascension of Christ on the other. Nor does it stand alone. For the apostolic *kerygma*, so far as we can trace it, pivots on the same segment of history.[1] True, it looks back to prophetic foreshadowing and forward to future fulfilment, but at its heart are embedded the mighty acts of God in Jesus Christ, from Jordan to Olivet. This is the clue to baptismal theology, if baptism be in very truth "the *kerygma* in action".[2] The rite is historically rooted, conformed to the pattern and limits of *Heilsgeschichte*. Its foreshadowings lie in the past, its consummation in the future; but its theology must be written round the two poles of the baptism of Jesus at Jordan and its fulfilment in His death, resurrection and ascension.[3]

[1] C. H. Dodd, *The Apostolic Preaching and Its Developments;* A. M. Hunter, *Interpreting the New Testament 1900-1950*, 34-36.

[2] W. F. Flemington, *The New Testament Doctrine of Baptism*, 73.

[3] For justification and amplification of the paragraphs immediately following the reader is referred to my more detailed exposition in *An Approach to the Theology of the Sacraments*, 9-35, 71-85.

The background provided by the Old Testament in general and Jewish proselyte baptism in particular may aid us to set the baptism of John in proper context and perspective, but, as we have seen,[1] the practice of the Baptist carries its own independent justification in the light of which it is rightly to be interpreted. Supra-national in its scope, ethical in its implication, initiatory in its purpose, eschatological in its deepest meaning—such were its primary notes and emphases. But, by His action at Jordan, Jesus ensured that the rite could never be the same again. By virtue of His participation in it, it was, at one and the same time, broken and remade, negated and fulfilled. For the righteous remnant of prophetic expectation concentrated itself in Him who was alone the true Israel of God and alone could fulfil all righteousness, and the long-awaited princely Messiah emerged from the baptismal waters as the servant of the Lord. If the old was taken and used, it was also transformed.

Nor was the fulfilment itself more than partial. The great eschatological, initiatory and redemptive themes are promulgated at the Jordan, but they still await their final sealing and ratification. To fulfil all righteousness for men involved the carrying of the sin of the world through the shadows of Calvary; to act out the vocation of the Servant-Messiah demanded the offering of a perfect life even unto death; to reconstitute the covenant-people of God necessitated an inclusive humanity available only on the other side of the cross and resurrection; and though the eschatological gift of the Spirit "descended" upon the Christ who "ascended" from the waters of Jordan, yet to make possible the pentecostal "descent" the "ascent" from Olivet had first to be completed. "I have a baptism to be baptized with; and how I am constrained until it is accomplished" (Luke 12: 50). The historical polarity remains. The acknowledgment of Messianic vocation in terms of servanthood, of baptism in terms of Calvary, means that throughout the ministry the rite remains, in some sense, a transformed yet empty vessel, waiting to be filled to overflowing.

Yet, though we assert that the baptism of Jesus involved the filling of an ancient practice with new meaning and that the full reality of the transformation waited necessarily upon

[1] *Supra*, 71f.

His cross, His resurrection and His ascension, we may not therefore denude the ministry of all significance. The people of God are in process of being reconstituted and the birth-pangs of the church made known, as the Messiah summons, commissions and empowers His disciples. They also are called to share in His vocation, to tread His way, to shoulder His cross, to know His sufferings. But those who stand on the hither side of the cross-resurrection event can share only partially and proleptically. "With the baptism with which I am baptized, you *will be* baptized" (Mark 10: 39). Only after the resurrection is Christian baptism a reality; for the rite finds its essential rationale in the self-offering of the Servant-Son. The baptism of Jesus at Jordan is incomplete precisely because His baptism is, in the end, His cross. It is from His side that the water flows (cf. John 19: 34); it is His crucified and risen body that links Johannine and Christian baptism together and bridges the gulf between them. The Matthaean command of the risen Christ which has traditionally provided the church with its baptismal charter may be historically suspect, but theologically it is unimpeachable. The initiation of the baptizing mission of the people of God belongs inevitably to the *risen and ascending* Lord.

This means, at least, that it is at the ascension of our Lord that Christian baptism becomes possible. It belongs between Pentecost and parousia, to the "time" of the church, to the overlap of the "ages". Grounded in the atoning work of Christ, which it applies and extends, its theology must always be an inference from Christology transposed into its true eschatological key. So it is that the passing of the baptism at Jordan through the cross-resurrection by those who live in the light of the ascension produces the constant threefold emphasis of New Testament baptismal theology. Baptism, in this normative period, implies, embodies and effects forgiveness of sin, initiation into the church and the gift of the Holy Spirit. Each and all stem from John's baptism and the participation of Jesus in it; each and all are transfigured by the fulfilment that the cross and the resurrection provide; each and all are marked by the tension between the "now" and the "not yet" which characterizes the Christian era. The baptism of Jesus was "a baptism of repentance for the forgiveness of sins" (Luke 3: 3), and this emphasis is taken up in the Acts and unwarrantably heightened in the early Fathers;[1] but the epistles of Paul subject this note to the richer and more positive concept of new life in Christ, as the Christological criterion begins to overwhelm the inheritance of the past and the original symbolism of the baptismal act (Rom. 6: 3, 4).

The washing at Jordan marked initiation into the remnant reconstituted for and expectant of the coming of Messiah, and this note sounds ever more plainly in the New Testament interpretation of Christian baptism as incorporation into the new community of the crucified and risen Lord, who alone was true Israel and alone fulfilled its mission. The gift of the Holy Spirit, which descended upon the Christ at His baptism, is poured out by the ascended and glorified Lord upon His people, and those who respond to the Gospel proclamation receive the power and presence as they, too, share in the baptismal experience. Yet through it all the eschatological tension remains. Because the Christ who has come is the Christ who will come, to the end the forgiven sinner is *simul justus et peccator*, the church is the broken body under the cross, the Spirit is but the "earnest" of the inheritance (Eph. 1: 14).

Because the pattern of New Testament baptismal interpretation is Christological through and through, these diverse strands and emphases come together into a rich and coherent unity. Baptism effects initiation into the life of the blessed Trinity and all the blessings of the new "age", and so embodies the wholeness of redemption. It is "into Christ", into the crucified, risen and ascended Lord, into the whole drama of His redemption achievement. We are incorporated into Christ that we may be crucified with Christ. We are crucified with Christ that we may share His resurrection. But " 'in Christ' . . . is primarily an ecclesiological formula".[2] That is to say, our incorporation is into the crucified and risen body of the Lord, the organic unity animated by the Holy Spirit, Christ in His church, *Totus Christus*, the whole Christ, head and members.

It is only against a background such as we have outlined

---

[1] Cf. A. Benoit, *Le Baptême chrétien au Second Siècle*, 36ff., 121ff., 148ff., 188ff.

[2] R. Bultmann, *Theology of the New Testament*, i, 311. Cf. C. H. Dodd, *Gospel and Law*, 36-37; K. L. Schmidt, *The Church*, 21.

that any relevant judgment can be made in connection with the burning controversy within the church as to the rightful recipients of baptism; but it must at once be admitted that no immediately obvious or conclusive answer to this question is provided by an appeal to the practice of the New Testament age. To point out that the constant concern of the earliest Christians is with the rite as applied to adult believers may be to advance an irrefutable claim; but in the end it is not clear that this is to do more than register the necessary conditions of every missionary situation, when the Gospel is first proclaimed. In any event, evidence for the baptism of adult believers of the second generation is lacking. It has, indeed, been claimed that there are signs that within the New Testament period the practice of infant baptism was not unknown, and confirmation both of a direct and of an indirect nature has been adduced to support such a case. On the one hand, Lydia is baptized "with her household" (Acts 16: 15), the Philippian jailer is baptized "with all his family" (Acts 16: 33; cf. 18: 8), children are among those for whom Christian conduct is laid down (Col. 3: 20, Eph. 6: 1) and to whom the title "saints and faithful brethren in Christ" (Col. 1: 2) is given. On the other hand, if Jewish proselyte practice could be taken as a guide, baptism would certainly be administered to children born before the conversion of their parents.

The weight to be attached to this evidence varies with the presuppositions of the adjudicator; perhaps this is the measure of its ambiguity. The direct evidence from the New Testament seems best characterized by the adjective "flimsy"; the indirect evidence from Jewish practice points in too many different directions at once for any accurate assessment of its significance easily to be made. No simple line can be drawn from proselyte to Christian baptism; and if the former practice had been strictly normative for the latter the result would have been neither infant baptism nor believers' baptism but the restriction of baptism to first generation believers and the children already born to them.[1] Thus far, the very utmost that could be claimed would be a presupposition in favour of infant baptism provided by pre-Christian Jewish practice and confirmatory evidence

[1] Cf. *supra*, 73ff.

provided by the comparatively early appearance of infant baptism within the Christian church. The New Testament witness remains indecisive.

The way ahead lies in the recognition that the overriding appeal must always be to New Testament theology rather than New Testament practice. Practice must be the corollary of theology; the clarification of the latter must precede the revision of the former. But to attempt to delineate the structure of baptismal theology is at once to be driven back to more basic doctrines, to questions of Christology, ecclesiology and eschatology. This our initial discussion has already made plain. If the provision of an answer to the problem of the rightful recipient of baptism must always take the form of an epilogue to the theological story, then to pursue the questions we have found to lie at the heart of that story is but to recognize that theology and practice cannot be sundered, that the epilogue must be more than a detached tailpiece.

The methodology is dictated by the theme. Since baptism initiates into the fulness of redemption, into the crucified and glorified humanity of the Lord, the pattern of the Christ event must be interpretively decisive. That pattern may be viewed and explicated from different points of vantage. It is the pattern of the incarnation, of the union of the human and the divine, unconfusedly and unchangeably yet indivisibly and inseparably. It is the pattern of the cross and resurrection, of brokenness and renewal, of judgment and fulfilment, of the divine "No" and the divine "Yea", of negation and transformation. It is the pattern of the ascension and the parousia, of completeness and incompleteness, of fulfilment and unfulfilment, of real presence and advent presence, of first fruits and harvest. That is to say that, in the end, it is the pattern of the whole Christ seen in its proper eschatological perspective. It is this that is determinative for baptismal theology.

The life of the incarnate Son is the life of one who was truly God and truly Man, the divine and the human met together in union, indivisibly yet without confusion. The priority is always with God, for the incarnation is rightly to be understood not in terms of Adoptianist Christology but of the *assumptio carnis*; and this principle remains regulative for the theology of baptism. Nevertheless, the inseparability of divine action and human response must never be denied. Though we confess the miracle of Bethlehem to be sheer act of divine grace, the humanity of the Lord to have concrete subsistence only in and as a result of the hypostatic union, yet we must never forget that the incarnation itself is preceded and made possible by the obedience of the Virgin Mary—"Behold I am the handmaid of the Lord; let it be to me according to your word" (Luke 1: 38)—and followed and perfected by the filial human response of the one who "although he was a Son, he learned obedience through what he suffered" (Heb. 5: 8).

It would be tempting to argue analogically that baptism is act of grace, preceded by parental (or church) response and perfected by filial obedience, and thus to draw a straight line to the practice of infant baptism; but the temptation must be resisted, and that on three grounds. In the first instance, the miracle of Christmas is itself rooted in the rhythm of the trinitarian life, of fatherly initiation and filial response. Secondly, the incarnation belongs within the whole structure of the redemptive act of God in Christ, as one "moment" in the process of salvation; it is not to be treated in isolation from the ministry and its consummation. Baptism is not a sacrament of the incarnation[1] but of the whole Christ. Finally, the application of the Christological pattern to the theology of baptism is safeguarded from extravagance and subjectivism only if the historical basis of the rite is allowed to remain properly normative. Christian baptism is grounded in the baptism at Jordan and its fulfilment is the cross, resurrection and ascension, not in the incarnation of the divine Word.

Perhaps it is the failure to keep these fundamental facts relentlessly in view that persistently leads Paedo-Baptists astray so far as the application of the concept of regeneration to baptism is concerned. The rite is not primarily to be seen as a sacrament of creation or incarnation but of the cross and resurrection, or rather of the whole Christ in His work from Bethlehem to the ascension and beyond. Incorporation

---

[1] Cf. The Church of Scotland, *Interim Report of the Special Commission on Baptism*, Part I (May 1955), 29, 47-49. Would the Commission have arrived at a truer formulation if it had begun with a description of baptism not as a "sacrament of the incarnation" but as a "sacrament of the Word made flesh (and sin)"? In the end, the distinction is more than verbal.

is always and of necessity based on atonement. There is no simple analogical relationship between creation and new creation, "natural" birth and birth "from above". True, we are born into the world apart from any decision of our own, created by sheer act of divine grace; but the univocal predication of such categories to rebirth and recreation cannot be sustained. Baptism effects regeneration and new birth because and only because it sets us at Golgotha and the empty tomb.

We must, then, look steadily at the whole life and ministry of the incarnate Lord who was "born to die" if we are to make sound theological assertions with regard to the interdependence of the human and the divine in baptism. The primacy of the divine is clearly shown forth in the experience of the Christ at Jordan; yet the obedient response of the True Man is here made crucial and explicit. It is upon Him who freely descends into the water "to fulfil all righteousness" that the Spirit abides. Himself the truly faithful One, He makes from Jordan to Jerusalem the perfect offering of a perfect human life in faith and obedience, crowning the response of *verus homo* by the submission at Gethsemane and the agony at Calvary. It is as mediator and only as mediator, God grasping hold of His fallen creation and man rendering back full homage and free submission, that He atones.

This gives us no warrant for questioning the ability of God to act for and in men on the basis of vicarious faith[1] or of no faith at all. Considered as a statement of a general principle governing the vehicles of God's activity, a formulation such as *ex opere operato non ponentibus obicem* is unexceptionable.[2] There is nothing of superstition here. What is, however, demanded of us is a reading of baptism in terms of the redemptive work of the God-man which fits uneasily with the Paedo-Baptist position. Salvation is not to be effected outside of, apart from, over the head of man. To deny this would be to deny both the principle of incarnation and the pattern of the life and death of the incarnate Son. But just as the baptism unto death of the Lord is constituted by the conjunction of divine action and human response, so the baptism into His death of His followers demands for its

---

[1] Matt. 8: 10; Mark 2: 5; 9: 14ff.

[2] See B. Leeming, *Principles of Sacramental Theology*, 7-10.

reality their ratification of His response, in obedience to the word proclaimed to them.

Already we have been forced onwards from the incarnation to the cross-resurrection with its pattern of negation and fulfilment, and at this point a central problem imposes itself upon us. Must the new covenant in Christ be related to the past in terms primarily of continuity or of discontinuity? It is in the answers that by their baptismal practice they implicitly give to this question that the Baptist and the Paedo-Baptist will again and again reveal essential difference of understanding. The latter may argue that just as in Old Israel Jewish children were recognized as belonging to the covenant people of God, so in New Israel the children of believers take their automatic place within the sphere of the new covenant and are thus fit recipients of the initiatory rite. The solidarity of the family remains constant and determinative.

Within the New Testament itself supporting evidence is claimed. "For the unbelieving husband is consecrated through his wife, and the unbelieving wife is consecrated through her husband. Otherwise, your children would be unclean, but as it is they are holy" (1 Cor. 7: 14). So writes Paul, bringing his insight to bear upon an issue not covered by a "word of the Lord". But clearly this does not take us very far. Either we draw the conclusion that such children are, by virtue of birth, made members of the Body of Christ, and thus baptism, which effects this very thing, is redundant, or else the possession of this holiness involves something other than membership of the New Israel, and is not directly relevant to the initiatory rite of baptism. In the one case we have proved too much, in the other case too little. The most that can fairly be claimed is embodied in Cullmann's cautious statement: "From the idea of holiness represented here there is a direct line to infant baptism, but none to a baptism based on a later decision of those sons and daughters who are born in a Christian home."[1]

Certainly it is by no means as obvious as Cullmann supposes that we can draw the additional conclusion that "this text may certainly be said to presuppose an idea of collective holiness, . . . in the sense of a reception into

[1] *Baptism in the New Testament*, 44.

the body of Christ. . . ."[1] This savours too much of theological legerdemain, and imports too many answers into an already ambiguous question. Paul's concern is with the question of the marital relationship; in the exposition of this theme he introduces, as an assumption which will not be questioned, the concept of collective holiness. If he is claiming that a child is incorporated into the Body of Christ by birth to Christian parents, then, by the same token, he is asserting the incorporation of an unbeliever by virtue of marriage to a Christian partner. But it may in fact be questioned whether any of this is his present concern. The uncertainties here are too many for confident corollaries to be drawn.

A far stronger case is to be made out by reference to the circumcision analogy; especially when infant baptism is seen as the counterpart and completion not only of circumcision but also of proselyte baptism, not only of the initiatory but also of the purificatory Jewish rite. Cullmann is clearly in the better position when he argues, as against Barth, that circumcision is not bound up with natural and racial succession, but with divine salvation-history, with the Abrahamic covenant of promise, universal and supra-racial in its reference.[2] From the New Testament perspective, the Jewish people and the Israel of God could never be completely coterminous. Gentiles were circumcised and received into the covenant community. The parallel with infant baptism is complete, with faith as subsequent response rather than essential prerequisite.

But it is not without significance to remark how Cullmann can discuss baptism and circumcision with such little reference to the cross and resurrection, to the "general Baptism" which he has earlier so finely illuminated. It is hard to resist the conclusion that, at this point, continuity has got the bit between its teeth. The stream from Abraham to Paul does not run through Golgotha without a troubling of the waters. The Christological catalyst leaves Israel broken and remade. The form of the new initiatory rite stems from proselyte baptism. The rite itself replaces circumcision. But its meaning and content are to be "read off" primarily from the Christ event, which from its pivotal position transfigures the old covenant and governs the new, shedding its

---

[1] *Baptism in the New Testament*, 44.   [2] *Ibid.*, 58-59.

rays over both past and future. Whether the theme be collective holiness or circumcision, the concern is never with racial succession, always with *Heilsgeschichte*. Thus it is that the implications of baptism are never to be derived from the circumcision rite of old Israel. Rather is it in the light of Christian baptism or, to be more exact, the cross-resurrection governing baptism, that circumcision is weighed, vindicated and condemned. By the discontinuity in unity of salvation-history, the continuities of history κατὰ σάρκα are broken and judged.

Yet if the Paedo-Baptist case is exposed to grave objections and harbours serious weaknesses, the Baptist position in many ways fits even more uneasily with Biblical theology. Its preoccupation with the recipient and the mode of baptism at the expense, so often, of the meaning and purpose of the rite, has constantly exposed its supporters to the charge of tithing mint and anise and cummin whilst neglecting the weightier matters of the law. And if Paedo-Baptism is often tied too firmly to the continuities of natural history, the Baptist case persistently violates the unity of *Heilsgeschichte*, sundering old covenant and new covenant, old Israel and new Israel.

Nor is the Baptist emphasis on the necessity of faith immediately adequate to the complexities of the Biblical pattern. That faith is indissolubly connected with the New Testament rite we may not deny; but this very fact poses our question rather than providing for us our simple solution. Baptism is a sacrament of the Gospel, not of our experience of it; of God's faithfulness, not of our faithful response to Him; and any theological formulation which lends itself so readily to an interpretation of the rite primarily in terms of a public confession of faith must at once be suspect. That baptism is "unto faith" all would agree; but that initiation into the Israel of God is no longer possible without a prior individual act of faith and repentance is an assertion involving apparently sweeping distinctions between the old covenant and the new which may not hastily be accepted. Indeed, the precise nature of the covenantal differentia is not readily apparent. Any attempt to distinguish between the old and new covenants by setting a natural and racial succession determined *by birth* over against a supra-racial succession determined by human choice and divine election conspicuously fails to do justice either to the religious basis of old Israel or to the continuity of sacred history. Nor is an explanation in terms of development from primitive ideas of collectivism, which swallowed up the individual in the group, to the rich flowering of the recognition of individual personality any less misguided.[1] The truth is that any distinction drawn in terms of general concepts must break down. By the cross and resurrection the old covenant is both negated and fulfilled. It is the Christ event and that alone which governs interpretation, the measure both of continuity and discontinuity. The Christological pattern must be all-controlling.

But the Christological pattern is not only the pattern of the incarnation and of the cross and resurrection, it is also the pattern of the ascension and the parousia. Baptism belongs to the "time" of the church, to the *regnum gratiae*, to the people of God who live in the "overlap of the ages", in a perpetual season of advent. It is marked by the dual sign of fulfilment and unfulfilment which constitutes it a sacrament of inaugurated eschatology. So it is that it points beyond itself for its understanding, driving us back inexorably to the consideration of questions concerning the kingdom, the church and the nature of redemption.

For the question of the relationship between the kingdom and the church is precisely the question of eschatology. In the cross, resurrection and ascension of the Lord redemption has been actualized, concretely and finally, and the kingdom has moved into the world to reconstitute, reconcile and renew. Τετέλεσται! It is finished. There is nothing that essentially can or need be added. God in Christ has overcome the estrangement that marked His fallen creation and

[1] E. Jacob, *Théologie de l'Ancien Testament*, 125-26 (Fr. edn.): "The attempt often made to divide the history of Israel into two periods, one dominated entirely by collective punishment, the other ushered in by the great champions of religious individualism, Jeremiah and Ezekiel who would have been the first to herald the individual's advancement, fails to do justice to Israel's historical development. . . . It must never be forgotten that if the individual embodies in himself the group, he is also personally responsible and that the Old Testament never envisages the people as a neuter entity but as the assembly of individuals, each of whom enjoys a bond of personal relationship with God. . . . Even a passage like the Decalogue, which takes its stand on the level of the election and the covenant and is addressed to the people as a collective whole, expresses its commandments in such a way that their carrying out is possible only by individuals."

has established His universal lordship. Yet the "now" strains forward to the "not yet" and the kingdom actualized reaches after the kingdom acclaimed; and within and beneath the kingdom lives and grows the Body of Christ, the microcosm within the macrocosm, the representation of what is yet to be. The church works and worships, serves and suffers, after the pattern of her Lord, as the gathered people of God who *recognize* the finished work and *acknowledge* the present lordship and *understand* the truth about the world, though the world know it not. She is the bridgehead through which the kingdom advances and extends, until the divine purpose be realized and what is hidden be revealed and God be all in all. By the power of the Holy Spirit, through word and sacrament and reconciling fellowship, she makes the future in the present and summons the world to its destiny.

So it is that the story of our redemption contains three great "moments". Our redemption was accomplished at the cross and resurrection; it is accomplished at baptism; it will be accomplished at the parousia. It is the maintenance of the separateness and the unity of these "moments" that provides us with our problem and our task. The cross is the sign of the kingdom actualized and established; the parousia is the sign of the kingdom perfected and acclaimed; and between them stands the baptismal rite which is the sign of the church, the locus of the kingdom acknowledged and extended. It is not that the kingdom and the church can or may be separated, but that the relationship between them is a dynamic one wherein both unity and distinction must be observed. The mark of the cross is substitution; the mark of baptism is incorporation. The representative man died and rose again for "the many", but His death and resurrection must be enacted in "the many". Baptism is grounded in the cross, incorporation in substitution; but *Christus pro nobis* must become *Christus in nobis*, if redemption is to be realized. Once this necessary distinction is accepted, an argument such as that of Cullmann loses its force. He writes:

> Is a man who is unable as yet either to understand or to have faith capable of even the passive acceptance of this baptismal gift? . . . We could simply retort with the counter-question: How could the event of Golgotha benefit all men, when they

had no faith that they could thus be redeemed, or rather manifestly disbelieved and denied it?[1]

The answer must surely be that no simple theological fusion of kingdom and church, cross and baptism, *extra nos* and *in nobis*, can be justified. Incorporation into the *Totus Christus*, which baptism embodies, is rooted in the substitutionary work of the God-man and shares its character of divine act, but the differentia of the human response must never be denied. If the response itself be *opus dei*, yet incorporation must wait upon that Amen being spoken.

It is because the church is the priestly body of Christ, standing between ascension-pentecost and parousia, marked by the pattern of the cross and resurrection, taken up into the substitutionary sacrifice of its Head which constitutes it the representative of the Creator to His creation and the universe to its Lord, living *for* the world, charged with the mission of the kingdom, that infant baptism must be weighed and found wanting. In the Christ event the kingdom has been established, the *eschaton* has broken into history, the new creation has burst the confines of the old order, the new age has finally and irrevocably laid hold of fallen time. Henceforth the whole of the human race, from infancy to old age, is marked with the seal of redemption, and no sign is needed to declare it, save only the cross which shouts its triumphant message from a hundred thousand churches. Yet the world still awaits its redemption, living in the tension of its brokenness and its hope, whilst the judgment is held back and the powers of the age to come press forward, till the *Totus Christus* be perfected and God be all in all.

Hereby we know that the final destiny of every human soul, from infancy to old age, lies hidden in the hand of the ascended Lord until the final day, and that no rite can infallibly guarantee or declare it. But "between the times", between the Christ who has come and the Christ who will come, lives the church, the visible embodiment of the kingdom, the community of those who have heard the Word and responded to it, and by baptism have been engrafted into the Body of the Lord. Where the church, too simply related to the cross, is defined in terms of *Volkskirche* and baptism is seen as declaratory sign, the practice of infant

[1] *Op. cit.,* 41.

baptism is logical. Where the church, too simply related to the parousia, is defined in terms of "ark of redemption" and baptism is seen as effective mediator of salvation, the practice of infant baptism is inevitable. Where the church, Biblically related to the double advent, is defined as instrument of the kingdom, priestly body of Christ straining towards fulfilment and completion, and baptism is seen as means of incorporation in response to the redemptive Word, the practice of infant baptism is suspect.

Yet the questioning of the legitimacy of Paedo-Baptism carries with it no necessarily absolute condemnation. Nor is there involved therein any simple, unqualified approval of the characteristic Baptist position. The practice of believers' baptism does not automatically authenticate any theology that may lie behind it. In the light of the conclusions for baptismal theology that the Christological pattern has dictated, certain facts have become evident. On the one hand, there is demanded of us some closer examination of infant baptism. On the other hand, it is clear that the problem of the theology of childhood cannot be evaded. To such questions we must now turn.

From the earliest times infant baptism has been a practice in search of a theology; in many quarters it is still so to-day. If the custom arose in response to a deep-rooted Christian instinct and a widespread popular demand,[1] yet when the western Fathers came to provide its theological explanation it was to the doctrine of sin that, in the main, they turned. The sequence was almost inevitable. As the fulness of the New Testament exposition faded, baptism was related to sin in disproportionate measure. Upon the basis provided by Tertullian and Cyprian in their doctrine of original sin, Ambrose and Augustine superimposed a theology of original guilt. From such guilt infant baptism guaranteed deliverance.

We may reject the theory of original guilt and deprecate a view which speaks too much of sin as stain, infection, some *thing* in man, and too little of man himself as sinner, against God, estranged from his creator and redeemer; but we may not therefore assume that the instinct of the church was necessarily at fault. History has repeated itself. Among the

[1] For a summary of the factors which prompted its rise, see *supra*, 187ff.

Baptists, in recent decades, there has grown up the practice of the blessing of infants. Again it arose in response to popular Christian demand.[1] Again it has been, more or less unsuccessfully, in search of a theology ever since. The Baptist apologist may well pause in his polemic to listen for a *tu quoque*. The theologian may well find ground for reflection in such a phenomenon.

Nowhere is there greater need for clear thinking than at this point, thinking that is free both from unbiblical individualism and from unethical sentimentality. The electing purpose of God is known in His eternal Son. We cannot go behind the face of Jesus Christ to seek some decree of double predestination; we can only rejoice that in Him the whole world is chosen for salvation. Yet the full revealing of individual destiny awaits the last judgment. We cannot penetrate the hidden secrets of God and anticipate the divine verdict; we can only submit ourselves in fear and trembling, yet with boldness and confidence, to the mercies of grace. Because the world is tied to Calvary no confusion of redemption and conversion is possible. Because the world moves towards the parousia no separation of redemption and conversion is absolute.

Yet in the time between the two advents a real, though relative, double distinction must be drawn. On the one hand, we must distinguish between believers (and their children) and unbelievers (and their children).[2] The former belong to the sphere of the Body of Christ; the latter belong to the world which is marked with the seal of redemption and the humanity which, by incarnation, the Son has brought into union with Himself. On the other hand, we must distinguish between believers and their infant children.[3] The former are those to whom the Word of God can be addressed and has been addressed, from whom a response has been elicited, who have been engrafted into the *Totus Christus*. The latter are those who, by the fact of their birth, are specially related to the Body of Christ.

---

[1] The same desire obviously arose among the Paulicians, who also laid stress on believers' baptism. (Cf. *supra*, 224.)

[2] This was a distinction made by Browne in the early days of independency. (Cf. *supra*, 261.)

[3] The failure of Baptists to define the place of infants in the Gospel and in the church has already been alluded to. (Cf. *supra*, 102.)

W

That relationship is not primarily to be explicated in terms of God's covenantal dealing with lost humanity; for while we may not dispute the Christological unity of Scriptural revelation and the real continuity of sacred history that ties together the old covenant and the new, yet we have continually to hold fast to the crucial element of discontinuity which the Christ event brings with it. Rather must we see the "one flesh" *henosis*, which Christian marriage enshrines, as providing the link between the children of Christian parents and the Body of the Lord. Christian marriage is rooted in redemption; it is reality only as it is within the Body of Christ. He is the Head; the church is His body; to that body the baptized belong as members. So, within the redemptive circle of the union of member with member and body with Head, there is enacted the union of male and female whereby the two become one flesh, reflect the mystery of the *Totus Christus* (cf. Eph. 5: 31-32) and know that healing of the brokenness of their humanity which anticipates the resurrection of the body and the perfected communion of saints. From the marital union "in Christ" derives the theological relation of the infants of Christian parents to the church; and that relationship is a real, though indirect, one.[1] Empirically, it is manifested in the influences of grace which constantly press in upon such infants, as they grow amid the ceaseless commerce of church with home, and home with church.

Let us be clear at this point. There is no question here of insertion into the Body of Christ, and baptism is, therefore, not in issue. There is, however, a serious question of relationship to the Body of Christ, which is grounded in the "one flesh" union of two of its members. The instinct of the church has not been at fault in seeking for some solemn ritual expression of this fundamental reality, and the adaptation for this purpose of the practice of the blessing of infants, which the gospels record (Matt. 19: 13-15, Mark 10: 13-16, Luke 18: 15-17), is altogether fitting. Yet the rite itself will be significant only as it serves its proper function. We are not basically concerned with human vows, human acts, human promises. We are concerned with the recognition and

---

[1] Cf. the teaching of 1 Cor. 7: 14, and J. Héring, *La Première Épître de Saint Paul aux Corinthiens*, 53.

THE THEOLOGY OF BAPTISM

declaration of an act of God, by which a child has been specially related to the redeemed community, and with the claim and demand which that *opus dei* imposes upon church and parents alike. All this the rite should express. If Paedo-Baptists have sown theological confusion by the introduction of infant baptism at this point, the persistent Baptist myopia in respect to the prevenience of divine grace, so far as infant blessing is concerned, has been scarcely less disastrous. Perhaps the way forward would lie in the recognition that, whilst all have sought the expression of one reality, Paedo-Baptist practice has made use of the wrong rite, and Baptist practice has enshrined the wrong emphasis.

From that relationship to Christ in His church which infant blessing declares, the line moves forward to that insertion into the Body of the Lord which believers' baptism accomplishes. Divine action through the Holy Spirit remains the controlling, all-decisive, factor; but at baptism the question of the response of faith emerges. This faith is not a human act, some autonomous, human element in the transaction of redemption, separable from the divine gift and summons. It is the creation of the Spirit of God and, as such, it belongs not to some artificially distinguished, conscious level of human personality but to the whole man called to the wholeness of redemption. H. H. Farmer's reminder of the problem of "how to think together the idea of God meeting the human person in a genuinely personal and ethical 'I-Thou' relation and the idea of Him as immanent within the personality" is timely, and wholly relevant. He rightly asserts that we must

> do justice to the Christian encounter with, and apprehension of, God as this is exhibited in its fullness in the act of worship and is summed up in the triune name of God. When we do that we find that, whatever may be the ultimate and perhaps insoluble theoretical problems involved, the two things—the "I-Thou" relation to God and the divine indwelling—are not set in opposition to one another but are rather held together in a way that is deeply and characteristically Christian . . .[1]

To recognize this is to hold together Christology and pneumatology in baptismal interpretation, and to understand faith both as man's free act and as God's hidden creation.

[1] *Revelation and Religion*, 72.

Word calls to Spirit and Spirit responds to Word, and within the divine dialogue room is provided for man to find his freedom in a surrender which is truly his own. The Word is proclaimed to him and he is summoned to responsible decision. By the power of the Spirit he opens himself and is opened to the action of God and, through baptism, is set within the σῶμα Χριστοῦ. This is union with Christ; this is faith.

Thus it is that, in the dispensation that is the "time" of the church, Word and sacrament belong inseparably together. It is the Word and the Spirit that give to baptism its efficacy and its significance. It is the response to the Word which the Spirit empowers that makes baptism Christologically congruous and ethically meaningful. Existence in Christ is churchly existence, that is to say, baptismal and eucharistic existence. Towards the pattern of Christian initiation which most fully, richly and completely declares this we are called to move. But if we assert that such a summons directs us back to the practice of the early church, it is not because of antiquarian bias or of belief in the existence of some universal and unvaried norm. The precise practice of the past is not necessarily sacrosanct, and diversity confronts us as far back as we can trace. Nevertheless, we may claim to discern within the primitive church a general pattern of initiation which does justice to the theological understanding towards which our examination has directed us.

That pattern consists in the progression of baptism, laying on of hands and first communion. It is, of course, true that Syriac-speaking churches preserved a different order, that chrism found a place in many composite initiation rites, that there was not always any clear separation made within the wholeness of baptism between the washing with water and the laying on of hands. Nor may we create of the laying on of hands a third sacrament, parallel to baptism and eucharist. What we are concerned to assert is that the fulness of Christian initiation is to be found in the conjunction of baptism (whether or not accompanied by the laying on of hands) with first communion. This is the pattern of insertion into the priestly body of Christ.

Judged by this standard, both Baptist and Paedo-Baptist practice may be found defective. In the latter case, it may be necessary to question the adequacy of a constant practice of affusion; for the mode of administration cannot be regarded as a matter of no significance. We have no warrant for making any one mode obligatory; but to give to immersion a normative place is to recognize the importance for sacramental practice of the closest possible correspondence between sign and signification. Still deeper issues emerge at the point of the separation of infant baptism and confirmation by which many Paedo-Baptists have done violence to the wholeness and unity of Christian initiation. In many quarters it is increasingly recognized that baptism as administered to infants cannot bear the full theological weight Scripturally attaching to the rite; and there is, accordingly, a growing desire to expound infant baptism and confirmation as parts of a larger initiatory whole, temporally divided, yet theologically one. Yet while the tendency must be applauded as marking a welcome advance, we must maintain that the sundering of the rite perpetuates an intolerable theological and practical confusion.

Nevertheless, such criticism carries with it no sweeping endorsement of Baptist practice. Here also, confusion reigns. The Baptist communion bids fair to become the only major branch of the Christian church where baptism is not of universal observance—a somewhat curious basis from which to attempt to justify a separate denominational existence. First communion is received by many apart from, and prior to, baptism, and thus the whole theological and sacramental progression proper to initiation is ignored and denied. Finally, the rebaptism as believers of those who have received baptism in infancy constitutes a blow at the heart of the Christian faith.[1] As there is one Lord, and one faith, so there is but one baptism. To the very end the Christological pattern must remain decisive. Baptism stands under the *ephapax* of redemption. The whole meaning of the rite hinges on its once-for-allness, its unrepeatability. The assertion of the partial nature of infant baptism and the serious theological distortion it involves does not carry with it the unqualified dismissal of it as "no baptism"; rather does the eschatological nature of the rite forbid so negative a verdict.

---

[1] For Scriptural evidence concerning the repetition of baptism, cf., for example, *supra*, 159-63, 185.

For no baptism can lack its proleptic element, and every baptism points forward for its completion and fulfilment. So unqualified a denial of infant baptism could be theologically justified only if accompanied by a willingness to "un-church" all Paedo-Baptist communities and to uphold separation at this point in the name of the One True Church. Can we, in this day and age, follow our forefathers to so radical a conclusion?[1]

The better way lies in the remembrance of that One Great Church towards which we move, for which we pray, and in the humbling recollection that our most cherished possessions may be, in God's sight, empty vessels, waiting to be filled. In the mercy of God there are again and again given to churches treasures of faith and practice beyond their deserving. Yet a church that settles on its past and closes its mind to new truth thereby seals its own death warrant. With thought and prayer, patience and understanding, Baptists are summoned to bring the treasure of believers' baptism and expose it to the traffic of the ecumenical market place, sure that, if the talent be of God, the Lord of the Church will, in due time, receive His own again with usury. Loyal to our tradition, yet open to God's future, we are called to wait in humble obedience for the guidance of the one Spirit of truth—to Whom with the Father and the Son belong all honour and glory, world without end.

---

[1] Cf. *supra*, 224f., 226.

SELECT BIBLIOGRAPHY

For obvious reasons, it is not possible to list here every book and article referred to. Full details have therefore been given either in the text or in the notes, and those which are referred to more frequently, or which are specially related to baptismal discussions, are listed below. For the most part, the divisions of the bibliography correspond to the divisions of the book.

I. GENERAL AND THEOLOGICAL

BAILLIE, D. M., *The Theology of the Sacraments*. 1957. London.

BARTH, K., *The Teaching of the Church Regarding Baptism*. 1948. London.

BRUNNER, E., *The Divine-Human Encounter*. 1944. London.

BRYAN, F. C. (ed.), *Concerning Believers' Baptism*. 1943. London.

CLARK, N., *An Approach to the Theology of the Sacraments*. 1956. London.

CULLMANN, O., *Baptism in the New Testament*. 1950. London.

—— *Early Christian Worship*. 1953. London.

—— *The Early Church*. 1956. London.

DILLISTONE, F. W., *Christianity and Symbolism*. 1955. London.

DIX, G., *The Theology of Confirmation in Relation to Baptism*. 1946. Philadelphia.

FORSYTH, P. T., *The Church and the Sacraments*. 1949. London.

JENKINS, D., *Tradition and the Spirit*. 1951. London.

LEENHARDT, F.-J., *Le Baptême chrétien*. 1944. Neuchâtel.

—— *Pédobaptisme catholique et Pédobaptisme réformé*. 1950. Montpellier.

PAYNE, E. A., *The Doctrine of Baptism*. 1951. London.

QUICK, O. C., *The Christian Sacraments*. 1927. London.

ROBINSON, H. W., *Baptist Principles*. 1911. London.

SCOTT, E. F., *The Kingdom and the Messiah*. 1911. Edinburgh.

WHITE, R. E. O., "Theology and Logic", in *B.Q.*, xvi (1955-56), 356ff.

WILLIAMS, N. P. *The Ideas of the Fall and of Original Sin*. 1929. London.

II. BIBLICAL

ADLER, N., *Taufe und Handauflegung*. 1951. Münster.

BARRETT, C. K. *The Gospel According to St. John*. 1955. London.
—— *The Holy Spirit and the Gospel Tradition*. 1947. London.

BARTH, M., *Die Taufe—Ein Sakrament?* 1951. Zollikon-Zürich.

BEARE, F. W., *The First Epistle of Peter*. 1947. Oxford.

BERNARD, J. H., *St. John, i, ii*. (I.C.C.) 1928. Edinburgh.

BORNKAMM, G., *Das Ende des Gesetzes*. 1952. München.
—— "Die neutestamentliche Lehre von der Taufe", in *T.B.* (1938), 42ff.

BORNEMANN, W., "Der erste Petrusbriefe—ein Taufrede des Silvanus?" in *Z.N.W.*, xix (1919-20), 143ff.

BROOKE, A. E., *The Johannine Epistles*. (I.C.C.) 1912. Edinburgh.

BULTMANN, R., *Das Evangelium des Johannes*. 1953. Göttingen.
—— *Theology of the New Testament*. 1955. London.

CARSON, A., *Baptism*. 1844.

CHURCH OF SCOTLAND, THE, *Interim Report of the Special Commission on Baptism*, Part I. 1955. Edinburgh.

CRANFIELD, C. E. B., *The First Epistle of Peter*. 1950. London.

CROSS, F. L., *I Peter: a Paschal Liturgy*. 1954. London.

DAUBE, D., *The New Testament and Rabbinic Judaism*. 1956. London.

DILLISTONE, F. W. (ed.), *Scripture and Tradition*. 1955. London.

DOBSCHÜTZ, E. VON, "Sakrament und Symbol im Urchristentum", in *T.S.K.*, 78 (1905), 1ff.

DODD, C. H., *The Interpretation of the Fourth Gospel*. 1953. Cambridge.
—— *The Johannine Epistles*. (Moffatt Commentary.) 1946. London.

EVANS, P. W., *Sacraments in the New Testament*. 1947. London.

FEINE, P., "Taufe I. Schriftlehre", in *R.T.K.*, 19 (1907), 396ff.

FINDLAY, J. A., *The Fourth Gospel*. 1956. London.

FLEMINGTON, W. F., *The New Testament Doctrine of Baptism*. 1948. London.

FOHRER, G., *Die symbolischen Handlungen der Propheten*. 1953. Zürich.

GAVIN, F., *The Jewish Antecedents of the Christian Sacraments.* 1928. London.

GOGUEL, M., *L'Église Primitive.* 1947. Paris.

HOSKYNS, E. C., *The Fourth Gospel.* 1947. London.

HOWARD, W. F., *Christianity according to St. John.* 1943. London.

—— *The Fourth Gospel in Recent Criticism and Interpretation* (revised by C. K. Barrett). 1955. London.

JACKSON, F. J. FOAKES, and LAKE, K. (eds.), *The Beginnings of Christianity.* 1933. London.

KUMMEL, W. G., "Das Urchristentum", in *T.R.*, 18 (1950), 1ff.

LIGHTFOOT, R. H., *St. John's Gospel.* 1956. Oxford.

LUNDBERG, P., *La Typologie baptismale dans l'ancienne Église.* 1942. Leipzig and Uppsala.

MACGREGOR, G. H. C., *The Gospel of John.* (Moffatt Commentary.) 1928. London.

MARCEL, P. CH., *The Biblical Doctrine of Infant Baptism.* 1953. London.

MARSH, H. G., *The Origin and Significance of New Testament Baptism.* 1941. Manchester.

MENOUD, PH. H., *L'évangile de Jean d'après les recherches récentes.* 1947. Neuchâtel.

ODEBERG, H., *The Fourth Gospel interpreted in its relation to Contemporaneous Religious Currents.* 1929. Uppsala.

OESTERLEY, W. O. E., and BOX, G. H., *The Religion and Worship of the Synagogue.* 1907. London.

PERDELWITZ, R., *Die Mysterienreligionen und das Problem des I Petrusbriefes.* 1911. Giessen.

PIERCE, C. A., *Conscience in the New Testament.* 1955. London.

PREISKER, H., *Die Katholischen Briefe.* 1951. Tübingen.

RENDTORFF, F. M., *Die Taufe im Urchristentum im Lichte den neueren Forschungen.* 1905. Leipzig.

RIGG, W. H., *The Fourth Gospel and its Message for Today.* 1952. London.

ROBINSON, H. W., "Hebrew Sacrifice and Prophetic Symbolism", in *J.T.S.*, 43 (1942), 129ff.

ROWLEY, H. H., "The Origin and Meaning of Baptism", in *B.Q.*, xi (1942-45), 309ff.

—— *The Unity of the Bible.* 1953. London.

SCHNACKENBURG, R., *Das Heilsgeschehen bei der Taufe nach dem Apostel Paulus*. 1950. München.

—— "Todes- und Lebensgemeinschaft mit Christus, Neue Studien zu Rom. 6.1-11", in *M.T.Z.*, vi (1955), 32ff.

SCHNEIDER, J., *Die Taufe im Neuen Testament*. 1952. Stuttgart.

—— *Baptism and Church in the New Testament*. 1957. London.

SCHWEITZER, A., *The Mysticism of Paul the Apostle*. 1953. London.

SELWYN, E. G., *The First Epistle of St. Peter*. 1946. London.

SPICQ, C., *L'Épître aux Hébreux*. 1956. Paris.

STRACHAN, R. H., *The Fourth Gospel, its Significance and Environment*. 1941. London.

WESTCOTT, B. F., *The Epistles of St. John*. 1866. London.

WINDISCH, H., "Zum Problem der Kindertaufe im Urchristentum", in *Z.N.W.*, xxviii (1929), 129ff.

ZIMMERLI, W., and JEREMIAS, J., *The Servant of God*. 1957. London.

III. HISTORICAL

BENDER, H. S., *Conrad Grebel*. 1950. Goshen.

BENOIT, A., *Le Baptême chrétien au Second Siècle*. 1953. Paris.

BIGG, C., *The Christian Platonists of Alexandria*. 1886. Oxford.

BLANKE, F., *Brüder in Christo*. 1955. Zürich.

BROMILEY, G. W. (ed.), *Zwingli and Bullinger*. (Library of Christian Classics, xxiv.) 1950. London.

—— *Baptism and the Anglican Reformers*. 1953. London.

BURRAGE, C., *The Early English Dissenters*. 2 vols. 1912. Cambridge.

CONYBEARE, F. C. (ed.), *The Key of Truth*. 1898. Oxford.

COTE, W. N., *The Archaeology of Baptism*. 1876. London.

CREHAN, J. H., *Early Christian Baptism and the Creed*. 1950. London.

CROSS, F. L., *St. Cyril of Jerusalem's Lectures on the Christian Sacraments*. 1951. London.

FARNER, O., *Huldrych Zwingli*. 3 vols. 1943-54. Zürich.

FRIEDMANN, R., "Recent Interpretations of Anabaptism", in *Church History*, xxiv (1955), 132ff.

GOETERS, G., *Ludwig Hätzer*. 1957. Gütersloh.

GRATZ, D., *Bernese Anabaptists and their American Descendants*. 1953. Scottdale.

HARNACK, A., *History of Dogma*. 1894. London.

HEGE, C., and NEFF, D. C. (eds.), *Mennonitisches Lexicon*. 40 lieferungen (so far). 1913—. Frankfürt on Main.

HOLL, K., *Gesammelte Aufsätze*, I. Luther. 1932. Tübingen.

HORSCH, J., *Mennonites in Europe*. 1942. Scottdale.

HUGHES, P., *The Reformation in England*. 3 vols. 1952-54. London.

JENNY, B., *Das Schleitheimer Täuferbekenntnis*. 1951. Thayngen.

JEREMIAS, J., *Hat die Urkirche die Kindertaufe geübt?* 1949. Göttingen.

JONES, R. M., *Studies in Mystical Religion*. 1909. London.

JORDAN, W. K., *Development of Religious Toleration in England*. 4 vols. 1932-40. London.

KELLY, J. N. D., *Early Christian Creeds*. 1950. London.

KNAPPEN, M. M., *Tudor Puritanism*. 1938. Chicago.

KRAJEWSKI, E., *Felix Mantz*. 1957. Kassel.

LAMPE, G. W. H., *The Seal of the Spirit*. 1951. London.

LIGHTFOOT, J. B., *The Apostolic Fathers*. 1891. London.

LITTELL, F. H., *The Anabaptist View of the Church*. 1952.

MENOUD, PH. H., "Le Baptême des enfants dans l'Église ancienne", in *V.C.*, ii (1948), 15ff.

MIGNE, J. P., *Patrologia Graeca*. (P.G.) 1857-66. Paris.

—— *Patrologia Latina*. (P.L.) 1844-65. Paris.

MURALT, L. VON, and SCHMIDT, W. (eds.) *Quellen zur Geschichte der Täufer in der Schweiz*, I. 1952. Zürich.

OEPKE, A., βάπτω, in *T.W.N.T.* 1933. Stuttgart.

—— "Urchristentum und Kindertaufe", in *Z.N.W.*, xxix (1930), 81f.

PEACHEY, P., *Die soziale Herkunft der Schweizer Täufer in der Reformationszeit*. 1954. Karlsruhe.

PEEL, A., *The First Congregational Churches*. 1920. Cambridge.

PEEL, A., and CARLSON, L. H., *The Writings of Robert Harrison and Robert Browne*. (N.C.T., II.) 1953. London.

RIDEMAN, P., *Confession of Faith*. 1950. London.

ROGERS, C. F., *Baptism and Christian Archaeology*. 1903. Oxford.

SMIRIN, M. M., *Die Volksreformation des Thomas Müntzer und der grosse Bauernkreig*. 1952. Berlin.

SMITH, C. H., BENDER, H. S., et al., *The Mennonite Encyclopaedia*. 2 vols. (so far). 1955—. Scottdale.

SMITHSON, R. H., *The Anabaptists*. 1953. London.

TORRANCE, T. F., *The Doctrine of Grace in the Apostolic Fathers.* 1948. Edinburgh and London.

TROELTSCH, E., *The Social Teaching of the Christian Churches.* 2 vols. 1931. London.

UNDERWOOD, A. C., *A History of the English Baptists.* 1947. London.

WACE, H., and BUCHHEIM, C. A. (eds.), *Luther's Primary Works.* 1896. London.

WHITLEY, W. T., *A History of the British Baptists.* 1932. London.

—— *The Works of John Smyth.* 2 vols. 1915. Cambridge.

WILLIAMS, C. H., and MERGAL, A. M. (eds), *Spiritual and Anabaptist Writers.* (Library of Christian Classics, xxv.) 1957. London.

ZWINGLI, H., *Sämtliche Werke.* (Ed. by Egli, Finsler, Köhler, etc.) Corpus Reformatorum, 88. 1900. Leipzig.

INDICES

(a) SUBJECTS